Prairie Metropolis

Prairie Metropolis

New Essays on Winnipeg Social History

Edited by
Esyllt W. Jones and Gerald Friesen

University of Manitoba Press

University of Manitoba Press
Winnipeg, Manitoba
Canada R3T 2M5
www.umanitoba.ca/uofmpress

Printed in Canada.

Cover design: Jessica Koroscil
Interior design: Relish Design Studio
Maps: Weldon Hiebert
Index: Adrian Mather

Cover image: Lotus Room, Chan's Café, Winnipeg (1957), Winnipeg Tribune Photo Collection, University of Manitoba Archives and Special Collections.

Library and Archives Canada Cataloguing in Publication

Prairie metropolis : new essays on Winnipeg social history / edited by Esyllt W. Jones and Gerald Friesen.

Includes bibliographical references and index.
ISBN 978-0-88755-713-2

1. Winnipeg (Man.)—History. 2. Social institutions—Manitoba—Winnipeg—History.
3. Winnipeg (Man.)—Social conditions. I. Jones, Esyllt Wynne, 1964– II. Friesen, Gerald, 1943–

HN110.W5P73 2009   971.27′43   C2009-901769-5

The University of Manitoba Press gratefully acknowledges the financial support for its publication program provided by the Government of Canada through the Book Publishing Industry Development Program (BPIDP), the Canada Council for the Arts, the Manitoba Arts Council, and the Manitoba Department of Culture, Heritage, Tourism and Sport.

Publication of this book has been made possible with the generous support of the Winnipeg Foundation.

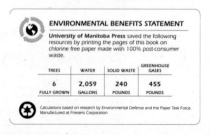

Contents

Acknowledgements

W e would like to thank the Winnipeg Foundation and its chief executive officer, Richard Frost, for the financial support that made possible the preparation of this volume. Mr. Frost is an enthusiastic supporter of research that contributes to knowledge of the city's history. His creative thinking inspired the development of a graduate student fund for the development of local historical research in the University of Manitoba and University of Winnipeg's Joint Master of Arts program in History. This book represents the culmination of that research.

History students at the University of Manitoba began writing essays on local history in a concerted fashion in 1968–69, when Professor J. Edgar Rea launched the first course dedicated to the history of Winnipeg and Manitoba. It is fitting that the late Professor Rea's last public address on the city's history, delivered to a local Rotary Club luncheon, should provide an epilogue for this volume.

We thank all the students who contributed papers. It has been a pleasure to work with them and to see the emergence of interesting essays on the history of this community. Dr. Barry Ferguson, now Associate Dean of Arts, administered the graduate program when many of the students entered, and we owe him thanks for his support as well as his editing of several of the papers. Other members of the original committee included David Burley and Tamara Myers of the University of Winnipeg and Tom Nesmith and Adele Perry of the University of Manitoba, and we thank them as well.

The University of Manitoba Press has been a stalwart supporter of local historical study for a generation. Once again, its director, David Carr, and his two associates, Cheryl Miki and Glenn Bergen, have been wonderful to work with and we thank them for their unfailing support.

List of Maps

City of Winnipeg (detail)

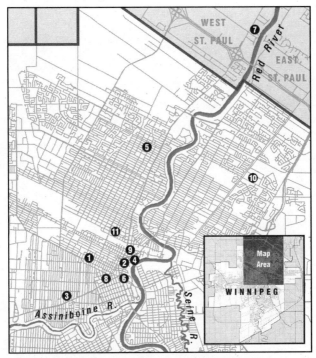

© Base map data reproduced under licence from Her Majesty the Queen in Right of Canada, with permission of Natural Resources Canada.

Locations Discussed

1. Christian Women's Union Maternity Hospital, c. 1883–1887 (see Chapter 1)

2. Police station, Rupert Ave. and Louise St., c. 1908 (see Chapter 2)

3. Juvenile Detention Home, 226 Simcoe St., c. 1908 (see Chapter 3)

4. Margaret Scott Nursing Mission, 99 George St., 1905–1943 (see Chapter 4)

5. West Kildonan dairy farms, c. 1916 (see Chapter 5)

6. Winnipeg School of Art, Winnipeg Industrial Bureau, Water Ave. and Main St. (see Chapter 6)

7. Old Folks' Home, Middlechurch, 1907–1946 (see Chapter 7)

8. Greater Winnipeg Bureau for the Voluntary Registration of Canadian Women, Portage Ave. and Hargrave St., c. 1939 (see Chapter 8)

9. Royal Alexandra Hotel, Main St. and Higgins Ave. (see Chapter 9)

10. Palliser Furniture factory, Gateway Blvd. (see Chapter 10)

11. Indian and Métis Friendship Centre, 45 Robinson St., 1959–present (see Chapter 11)

Growth of Winnipeg, 1872–1966

SOURCE: Adapted from Historical Growth Pattern, Plate 4, *Metropolitan Winnipeg Development Plan* (City of Winnipeg, Planning Division, 1966). http://www.flickr.com/photos/manitobamaps/2175798383.

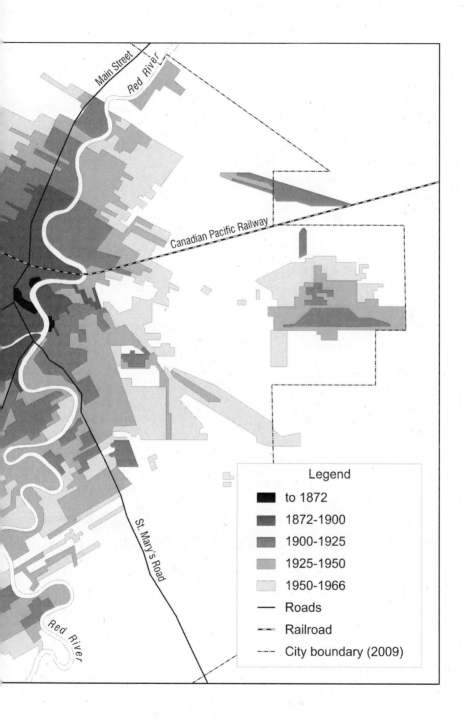

Legend

■ to 1872
■ 1872-1900
■ 1900-1925
■ 1925-1950
■ 1950-1966
— Roads
-■- Railroad
-·-·- City boundary (2009)

Greater Winnipeg Municipal Boundaries, 1870–1945

1870-1874

1. Nov. 8, 1873 City of Winnipeg incorporated

1875-1879

1. 1875 City of Winnipeg annexation
2. 1876 Municipality of Kildonan incorporated

1880-1882

1. 1880 Municipality of Assiniboia incorporated
2. 1880 Municipality of St. Boniface incorporated
3. 1882 City of Winnipeg annexation

1883-1907

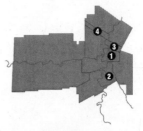

1. 1883 Town of St. Boniface incorporated
2. 1903 Municipality of St. Vital incorporated
3. 1906 City of Winnipeg annexation
4. 1907 City of Winnipeg annexation

1908-1920

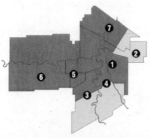

1. 1908 City of St. Boniface incorporated
2. 1912 Town of Transcona incorporated
3. 1912 Municipality of Fort Garry incorporated
4. 1912 Municipality of St. Vital annexation
5. 1913 Town of Tuxedo incorporated
6. 1913 Municipality of Charleswood incorporated
7. 1915 Municipalities of East and West Kildonan incorporated

1921-1945

1. 1921 Old Kildonan detached from West Kildonan
2. 1921 Village of Brooklands incorporated
3. 1921 Municipality of St. James incorporated
4. 1925 North Kildonan detached from East Kildonan

SOURCE: Adapted from Original Area and Municipal Development, Plate 3, in Metropolitan Planning Committee and Winnipeg Town Planning Commission, *Background for Planning Greater Winnipeg* (Winnipeg: Metropolitan Planning Committee and Winnipeg Town Planning Commission, 1946). http://www.flickr.com/photos/manitobamaps/3131023426.

Prairie Metropolis

Introduction

This collection of essays grew out of support given by the Winnipeg Foundation to nurture historical study of the city of Winnipeg. The foundation was established in 1921 by William Forbes Alloway, who fits perfectly the myth of the self-made man, a myth at the heart of the story that Winnipeg (like many other cities in the North American West) likes to tell itself about its history. Arriving with the colonizing forces of the Wolseley Expedition in 1870, Alloway went on to earn his fortune as, among other occupations, veterinarian, tobacconist, freighter, horse buyer and trainer, and private banker. His firm, Alloway and Champion, also dealt in land scrip during the period of Métis and Aboriginal dispersal from Red River and played a central role in facilitating immigrant settlement in and around Winnipeg. Like many others of his social class, Alloway engaged in charitable work and ultimately left to the Winnipeg Foundation most of his sizeable estate.

Alloway died in 1930, one of the wealthiest entrepreneurs of his generation. His lifetime corresponds with an era when Winnipeg saw itself as a contender as a North American city, although the city's boom years were long gone by his death. This period in Winnipeg's history has long received the greatest attention from historians and geographers. The seminal history of Winnipeg, Alan Artibise's *Winnipeg: A Social History of Urban Growth, 1874–1914*, begins with the incorporation of Winnipeg and ends with the beginning of the Great War. Over thirty years after its publication, it remains the standard scholarly monograph on the city's history, and its periodization has set the dominant tone ever since. Artibise was part of the "new" urban history of the 1970s and 1980s, a school that was heavily influenced by theories and concerns surrounding urban development and civic planning, what Artibise calls "the city-building process."[1] Emerging before post-war urban sprawl and inner city decay had really made their mark on Canadian cities, this body of work focussed on the early years of urban growth as the pivotal era for explaining the future of urban life in Canada. Artibise meant his work to be considered in a comparative context, to illustrate what Winnipeg residents might have had in common with other cities, not as an argument for Winnipeg as exception. He was hoping to contribute to a more rigorous analysis of urban history in Canada, and criticized the historical profession for its lack of interest in "local history."[2] His goal was to write a history that made synthesis possible.

Even as the "new" urban history was being developed, however, it was being supplanted by social history that was motivated by a desire to understand the experience of non-elite Canadians and uncover the lives of the marginalized. Out of this grew rigorous attention to categories of difference in society: class, gender, ethnicity, race, sexuality. While these themes are not entirely absent from Artibise (particularly class and ethnicity), they are articulated in the urban histories of the 1970s more as demographic categories than as living forces shaping personal experience, culture, state development, and political movements. The "new" urban history was, at times, apologetic about the "vagueness" of historical practice as compared with the technical skills of sociology and political science. Although Canadian historians might have felt a similar inadequacy in the face of critical theory in the 1990s, the authors of the essays in this collection confidently use a broad range of sources and interpretive tools. The creative way in which social history pushed the boundaries of what are considered legitimate historical source materials is clearly manifest in their use of case files, patient records, and the institutional memories of organizations such as the Margaret Scott Nursing Mission, which had scarcely been noticed by urban historians of an earlier generation.

Canadian popular culture's current trope in talking about Winnipeg, a city apparently in decay, revolves around its "specialness," the closeness and intelligence of its arts and cultural community, its unique capacity to nurture talent, from writer Miriam Toews to visual artist Marcel Dzama to songwriter John K. Samson and filmmaker Guy Maddin, despite its apparently minor metropolitan status. What explains this distinctiveness? The tension between what is "special" about a place and time and what can be integrated into a broader synthesis is actually one of the most fruitful rewards of a historical approach. It confronts anyone interested in the dynamic relationship between the individual and the society, the local and the national or transnational, the particular case and the theory. The new scholars in this collection tend to take it for granted that Winnipeg's urban past, while distinctive in certain senses, can be placed within a larger frame. Their work is engaged with questions of gender, sexuality, class, ethnicity, race, and religious identity. Several of the essays also move outside of the boundaries of the Canadian nation-state. Transnational/translocal and imperial history, which has challenged the primacy of the nation-state as the basis for historical understanding, suggests a fruitful course of future research into the development of the city.

Kurt Korneski, for example, gives new insight into the history of social reform in Winnipeg, situating the Anglo-Canadian social activist Minnie Campbell not only as a maternalist middle-class reformer, acting in response to the perceived fallout from a rapidly urbanizing industrialized society, but coincidentally as an "ardent imperialist," engaged in a settler colonialist enterprise in a frontier city. Many of Winnipeg's earliest "reform" organizations and institutions were established before extensive urban industrial growth took place, although these groups quickly adapted to confronting the evils of urban growth, immigration, and worker unrest.

Minnie Campbell and her husband Colin, who would become a prominent lawyer and Conservative politician, arrived in Winnipeg in 1882, when the city was "still a muddy frontier outpost." Campbell, like other "ladies of the city," represented civilizing forces that would mould the city to conform to the values of the Empire. They also, Korneski notes, "worked according to a logic of patriarchy," that saw elite men and women take on separate roles, considered appropriate to their gender. From within this logic, they took on positions of public authority that served to challenge patriarchal limitations. Minnie Campbell was an extraordinarily active and capable organizer and fundraiser in groups such as the Winnipeg General Hospital Auxiliary, YMCA, Christian Women's Union, YWCA, and the Imperial Order Daughters of the Empire (IODE), in which she played a key leadership role for twenty years. Through the IODE, Campbell promoted her belief in the natural superiority of the "British race" and exhorted women, men, and children to adopt institutions and practices that embodied the "British spirit."

Situating Winnipeg in the context of British imperial expansion and anxiety in various colonial spaces around the globe, Korneski notes that "for [Minnie Campbell] and her counterparts … their city was both an industrial and a colonial centre." Drawing upon Adele Perry's work on British Columbia, Korneski understands Winnipeg, too, to be a place "on the edge of empire" at the turn of the twentieth century, with distinct differences in social and cultural life from the more established urban centres of eastern Canada. Thus, his essay helps us to understand the specific features of social reform in Winnipeg. The city's place in space and time meant a coming together of forces of settler colonialism and urban "regeneration" in a uniquely compressed fashion.

An issue to which reform organizations and the developing state turned their attention was the perceived lawlessness and lack of control on the city's streets. One of the first acts in 1874 of the newly established Winnipeg town council was to appoint a police chief and police constables. When the police force was formed,

Winnipeg was a town of 2000, including many Aboriginal and Métis people. By the turn of the century, the community had increased in size tenfold, mainly through the influx of single male European immigrants, significant numbers of whom were transient workers. Police patrols targeted Aboriginal and Métis peoples. Megan Kozminski's essay looks at the emergence of a modern police force in Winnipeg, examining the daily police reports of Constable John Grady for evidence about the nature of criminality and law enforcement in this "wicked" and "wild" city. What she finds is a relatively staid community, albeit one where officers like Grady "defended … middle and upper class ideals of order and morality." Despite public anxieties about criminality, Kozminski's data show that the proportionate incidence of crime was actually declining during the first twenty-five years of the city's growth. The issues that preoccupied law enforcement were those related to maintaining public order—alcohol abuse and prostitution.

What is especially interesting about Kozminski's essay is its revelations about the identity and work culture of Winnipeg's earliest police officers. Urban policing was viewed as "a job for real men" and was, as such, framed within notions of masculinity and lower middle-class respectability. Police officers were expected to be hard-working, mature, sober, and deserving. In early policing, militaristic values of obedience and loyalty were also emphasized. Policemen needed to be physically strong and healthy. Indeed, as Kozminski argues, the hard work of policing ruined the health of some men. The physical and mental demands and relatively low pay of policing meant that many men did not last long in the job. As she points out, in their daily encounters with citizens, police officers were not only enforcing the law of bourgeois moral order, they were also called upon to help men, women, and children in distress. Policemen performed what Kozminski calls social service functions, including difficult tasks like coping with the mentally ill and the homeless, or helping to locate missing children. Life on the beat was complex, often unpredictable, and occasionally violent. It could also be incredibly mundane and boring. There was little public appreciation of their task. In a community without adequate welfare supports for the poor, the police force had to address the fate of the most desperate of residents. Kozminski concludes that the number of urban poor overwhelmed the police force in the 1880s and 1890s, and that efforts to provide temporary shelter for the homeless and needy "ultimately provided little benefit to the larger population of dispossessed members within urban society." Neither did the state, via police enforcement, intervene to prevent domestic violence or child abuse. These were considered "private matters."

The state was, however, concerned about the apparent rise in juvenile delinquency and ostensibly expanding criminality. While there has been considerable scholarly interest in juvenile delinquency and the law in recent years, very little of this literature addresses Winnipeg's experience with the juvenile justice movement. Manitoba established the new Winnipeg Juvenile Court in 1909, the first Canadian city to implement the provisions of the 1908 federal *Juvenile Delinquents Act*. The development of Winnipeg's Juvenile Court, Cassandra Woloschuk argues, was especially influenced by juvenile courts in Chicago (established in 1899) and Denver (opened in 1903). This suggests an interesting cross-border flow of ideas and practices between midwestern North American cities, rather than institutions shaped entirely within the bounds of the nation-state.

Manitoba's attorney general, Colin Campbell, believed in the value of a social welfare approach to regulating the behaviour of children and youth. Children were no longer tried and punished in adult institutions. Winnipeg legislators and social welfare advocates, in theory, emphasized guidance and rehabilitation over punishment for children in violation of legal and social norms. This did not necessarily mean the end of incarceration, however, because many youth were sentenced to the detention home. Through new programs (such as probation) and juvenile justice institutions, children and youth were put under a system of surveillance and control. As Woloschuk notes, there were important gender, class, religious, and ethnic differences in children's experiences with early juvenile justice. Winnipeg's reformers tended to see delinquent children as products of their environment and viewed working-class homes as suspect.

Her chapter makes fruitful use of government records and case files of Marymound, a Catholic reform school for girls. Like other scholars, Woloschuk argues that female sexuality was a target of the juvenile court. Even before sexual immorality was added to the *Juvenile Delinquents Act* in 1924, girls were regularly brought before the court for violations of sexual norms. Links were made between "feeble mindedness" and sexual immorality. Female delinquency was medicalized, and girls were subjected to medical examinations (mental and physical, including gynecological exams) and testing. In 1919, the court added a psychopathic department, which gathered what was considered critical information in developing the profiles of delinquent girls and boys. Such medical information formed an important basis for sentencing in the court.

Essays by Miller and McKay also reveal the centrality of medicine, nursing, and public health to the process of institution building and state development in Winnipeg.

The energy and achievement of women reformers is demonstrated in Tamara Miller's essay on the Margaret Scott Nursing Mission, which, from 1905 to 1943, provided basic health care in the home to the poorest of the city's working-class and immigrant population. As an organization founded and administered by philanthropic women, the mission was a key health care institution in Winnipeg, receiving financial support from both private donations and government sources. The role of the mission makes clear that urban public health in the early twentieth century in Canada cannot be understood only as a state project; indeed, health policy should be viewed as a hybrid private-public enterprise that women (and men) sought to influence not just through the discourse and debate of social reform movements, but also through the actual provision of services. The mission's clientele (particularly up until the 1920s, when immigrant flows to Winnipeg slowed down) was largely European immigrant families, and predominantly women, a reflection of the fact that the mission's nurses provided pre- and post-natal, and obstetric care. Its clients were those who, according to the mandate of the organization, could not afford private medical or nursing care. Mission nurses, administering care in the context of dire poverty, helped to sustain working households through the provision of household goods, such as linen and clothing. Despite what must have been significant linguistic barriers between the white, middle-class Anglo-Canadian women employed by the mission and their immigrant patients, mission nurses recorded being recognized and positively received in neighbourhoods many of their own social background would have avoided. While the organization's namesake, Margaret Scott, brought a missionary zeal and religious faith to her efforts, the mission itself was explicitly non-denominational. Nonetheless, its precepts were demonstrably those of Protestant urban reformers. As Miller shows, the mission's attitude toward its clients was typical of the broader reform project: it carried into immigrant homes a belief that their clients needed to be educated in the proper health standards and behaviour of "Canadians." Yet, nurses also exhibited sympathy and sensitivity to their cases, and praised some women for their efforts in creating a comfortable home despite their poverty.

Miller makes a valuable contribution to debates regarding medical and nursing professionalization by considering the shape of nursing practice in a context outside of the hospital domain. The mission's nurses formed an interesting link between curative health care and public health goals of prevention, especially in the maternal and child welfare services it provided to poor mothers. While they attended to illnesses and childbirth, they also ran a depot to provide pure milk for babies, attempting to prevent infant mortality. Nursing care often included feeding and cleaning their patients and their patients' homes. Nurses worked with physicians, who provided their services *gratis*, yet physicians had to conform to the rules and preferences of the mission. In such a context, the normal hierarchical superiority of physician over nurse, male over female, was subverted. Miller argues, as does Judi Coburn for the case of public health nursing in Ontario, that the mission's accountability was to the community, not to the hospital or physician. Thus, nurses and the female-run administrative board of the mission had room for autonomy and the opportunity to engage in an extended health care delivery model distinct from the mainstream, increasingly hospital-based, system.

The development of public health policy and programming in Winnipeg is explored, from a different angle, in Marion McKay's essay on attempts to purify the city's milk supply to control the spread of tuberculosis. Tuberculosis posed a major health threat to city residents and, despite its popular image as the disease of poets and aesthetes, greatly impacted those living in poverty and poor housing. Tuberculosis was a disease that was difficult to definitively diagnose in the early twentieth century, and the means of preventing it were hotly debated and poorly understood. Between 1894 and 1922, the city of Winnipeg focussed significant energy on ridding the city's milk supply of *mycobacterium bovis (m.bovis)*, known to be the causative agent for tuberculosis in cattle, and potentially transferable to humans through the milk supply. This was to be accomplished through the tuberculin testing of the city's dairy herds and, ideally, the pasteurization of the milk supply. There was little scientific consensus around the role of *m. bovis* in tuberculosis-prevention strategies, however, and in following the *m. bovis* debate, McKay reveals the shifting parameters of professional expertise and credibility in medicine, animal health, and public health.

In the 1890s, Winnipeg was attempting to prevent the spread of this deadly disease with restricted resources and limited powers of public health regulation. Its attempts to test and cull infected cattle from dairy herds raised the ire of local dairymen. In a debate reminiscent of that surrounding "mad cow" disease in our own time, milk producers complained that tuberculin testing was a flawed process and objected to their cattle being destroyed without government compensation. In an era when most health expenditures fell on the shoulders of under-resourced municipal governments, the *m. bovis* campaign did not receive sufficient funding from the provincial or federal governments. New life was given to the effort to purify the milk supply in the wake of the 1904 typhoid epidemic in Winnipeg because tainted milk was believed to be one important vector for the spread of the disease. Yet, by the early

1920s the results of the clean-milk campaign were mixed at best, with many dairy cattle still testing positive for *m. bovis.*

McKay draws our attention to the fact that the impact of the pure-milk campaign fell unevenly upon the city's residents. A disproportionate cost was laid upon dairy producers to guarantee clean milk. An element of ethnic discrimination entered into the city health department's attitude toward farmers, as many of the small dairy producers in and around Winnipeg were European immigrants, whom health officials accused of lacking knowledge and high standards for cleanliness in their herds. The consumer impact of milk supply policies was felt more keenly by immigrants and working-class people. Stringent regulation increased the price of milk, making it difficult for many to afford, and during World War I, Winnipeg experienced a severe shortage in the milk supply. Only the better-off could afford the more expensive milk that was certified as tuberculosis-free. McKay, like other scholars of North American public health, notes that the emphasis upon a bacteriological approach to preventing tuberculosis "deflected professional and public attention from the more nebulous social causes of tuberculosis such as poverty."

The relationship between cultural activity and business development is explored in the final essay in Part 1, by Angela E. Davis. Davis focuses on the role of Winnipeg's visual artists in commercial illustration and engraving between 1900 and 1940. The availability of commercial employment helped to nurture the early Winnipeg art scene. Winnipeg's artists worked for the Toronto Engraving Company (later Brigden's Limited), founded in part by British immigrant artist Frederick Brigden. Brigden's was a large commercial firm, which had been producing images for the Eaton's catalogue since the later nineteenth century. They opened a branch in Winnipeg in 1914 to produce art for Eaton's western Canadian catalogue.

Although commercial graphic arts firms resembled assembly lines and artists performed highly specialized labour (drawing only boots, jewellery, furniture, etc.) under poor conditions, Davis argues that many Winnipeg artists "credited their years spent working for the graphic arts houses as having provided them with a discipline and technical skill which they might otherwise have lacked." Brigden's also provided employment in an era when it was almost impossible to be an independent artist. Thus, the firm "played no small part in the remarkable development of art in western Canada." Winnipeg already had a strong community of visual artists, many of whom worked for commercial graphics firms and competed with Brigden's. But Brigden's brought some important changes to the Winnipeg commercial art scene. Their photo-engravers were unionized, and in a city where organized labour was strong, experience with unions benefited the firm. Arnold Brigden, the manager of the Winnipeg branch, was, according to Davis, an "inspired" manager, hiring for his art department talented and experienced art directors and some of the city's most promising artists. Artists who worked for Brigden's included Charles Comfort and Eric Bergman. Comfort, who would go on to teach at the University of Toronto and become the director of the National Gallery, was apprenticed at Brigden's while taking art classes in the evening. He worked as a commercial artist until the late 1930s. The experience of these artists, Davis points out, tends to undermine the historical argument that artists' commercial employment was "temporary and unimportant, an unfortunate means to an end."

This collection reflects the reality that research into the interwar and post-war social history of the city is still a wide-open field. Only very recently have scholars turned their attention to Winnipeg's evolution after the city's early years of spectacular growth were clearly past. Crista Bradley's essay on the Middlechurch Home melds these eras and confirms the enduring role—and the evolution—of institutions founded early in the century. The Christian Women's Union, in which Minnie Campbell was actively involved along with other Anglo-Canadian women of her class, in 1883 founded the Middlechurch Home, originally a home for single women and mothers and, after 1907, a residential care home for the elderly. Crista Bradley follows changing attitudes toward and services for the institutionalized elderly in her essay that examines the history of the home through the 1980s. Within this extended time frame, Bradley is able to demonstrate some significant improvements to the quality of life for the elderly, from more pleasurable surroundings to greater active involvement in controlling their own living environment. Over time, the institution came to be perceived as a "place for life" rather than a place where the old waited for death. Building upon the work of scholars such as Megan Davies, Bettina Bradbury, and James Snell, Bradley documents experiences with aging.

In the early years of its operation, Middlechurch Home was to fulfill the need for institutional care among the city's poor and destitute elderly. It functioned in a manner similar to a nineteenth-century poorhouse, with residents expected to contribute their labour to the operation of the home in lieu of fees. Men and women living in the home lost their personal freedom and autonomy and were subject to rules governing their behaviour. For example, they could not leave the home without permission, and visitors were strictly limited. By mid-century, however, residents were afforded greater freedom to determine their own daily activities. There was an increased emphasis in the home's annual reports on recreational and leisure activities for residents and also on a corresponding view of the elderly as interested in living active and full lives, socially and physically. Greater attention was paid to making the living environment comfortable, attractive, and less institutional-seeming: "the virtues of kindness and warmth quickly gained importance ... at the expense of the images of structure and sterility that had been favoured in the past." Residents were also able to be involved in the community outside of the institution. Many of these changes had begun to occur by the 1920s and 1930s, with an intensification of change in the post-World War II period. These were in keeping with a more positive public perception of aging.

Important in this process was the professionalization of health care, a theme that weaves through the essays on health care in this collection. Bradley views the professionalizing of staffing at Middlechurch Home as part of an overall trend toward better experiences for the institutionalized elderly. An emphasis on hiring trained staff was particularly evident from the 1950s, part of a growing post-war concern about old age and improved state support. The home hired not only nurses, but experienced social workers as well. It provided staff professional development opportunities and helped to train students in professions related to aging.

Jody Perrun evaluates volunteerism during the Second World War. Significant continuity with an earlier era can be found here in the overwhelming response of women in Winnipeg to the demand for volunteer mobilization in a myriad of activities, from recycling materials to providing care packages to soldiers overseas, to fundraising. As Perrun's research demonstrates, volunteerism was also essential to the health and well-being of injured war veterans, through fundraising efforts for the Deer Lodge Military Hospital, hospital visitation, and care packages. Prisoners of war overseas received packages containing food, clothing, and news from home. Soldiers on leave enjoyed the facilities of the United Services Centre, a transformed Eaton's annex that housed a canteen, lounges, a dance floor, a games room, and a place where soldiers could have their uniforms mended. Over a thousand visitors per day, including soldiers from all over the world, visited the centre. Perrun's detailed research demonstrates the degree to which every aspect of a soldier's wartime experience was mediated by the efforts of volunteers "at home," the vast majority of them women.

A primary concern of women's "home front" organizations was to ensure the well-being of families whose spouses and fathers were serving in the military. Groups such as the Fort Garry Horse Auxiliary provided women with opportunities for socializing and mutual support, holding summer picnics and Christmas parties for the children of the regiment. Social welfare committees gave material support to families struggling financially. Volunteer women also confronted the sad and difficult task of visiting or writing to families of men killed or injured at war. As one woman testified, "for all its sadness, it was an unforgettable experience. To meet courage and faith and character in the face of despair, as we did most undoubtedly, is to be immeasurably strengthened."

Wartime mobilization developed and provided an outlet for the organizational and leadership skills of countless Winnipeg women. Their work ultimately gained them wide public recognition in North America. At the outset of the war, 1800 Winnipeg women created the Central Volunteer Bureau (CVB). Aware that the demands of wartime might undermine volunteer support for existing social services in the city, the group decided that their organization would coordinate both existing community work and new wartime projects. It was the first North American volunteer group to do so, and its model became known as the "Winnipeg Plan." A 1941 National Film Board production, *The Call for Volunteers*, established the Winnipeg CVB as a model for wartime volunteer mobilization in Canada and the US.

Groups, including the CVB, worked together as part of a broadly based Greater Winnipeg Coordinating Board. Perrun argues that Winnipeg's experience in this regard was remarkably successful, in comparison with cities such as Edmonton and Calgary or national organizations, many of whom competed and offered overlapping services. This success is partly attributable to the openness and apparent democratic functioning of the coordinating board. Its inaugural meeting in June 1941 saw participation from 150 delegates, representing a diversity of community groups. Unlike other Canadian cities, working women, men, and children participated in volunteer work in Winnipeg: "it was not just married, upper-class housewives with little to do that took part."

Perrun's work anticipates some of the public arenas into which women moved after World War II. Dale Barbour's essay on the liberalization of liquor consumption laws in the early 1950s shows a limited inclusion of women in what was previously the male-only terrain of public drinking. In the post-war era, discourses of middle-class consumerism and the self-governing subject co-existed with ongoing debate about gender roles, sexual and moral propriety, and class. A new liquor law introduced in 1956 allowed "mixed drinking" in restaurants. The presence of women transformed the previously homosocial space of male public drinking into a heterosocial space. This new reality, however, failed to put to rest older anxieties and prohibition-type discourses that drew links between alcohol consumption and immorality, illicit sexuality, and prostitution, while at the same time expressing racialized notions of

Aboriginal moral weakness and susceptibility to alcohol addiction. Despite considerable critical attention to the working-class male drinking culture, new laws maintained the all-male beer parlours.

Manitoba was one province that, in the wake of the prohibition era, had established all-male beer parlours. Despite the provision in the *Manitoba Liquor Act* (1928) for gender-segregated beer parlours with separate spaces for women to consume alcohol, only one short-lived women's beer parlour was ever established. In Manitoba, beer parlours were male-only spaces, and women's public entertainment was confined to non-alcoholic establishments. In the post-war years, gender boundaries began to shift, a change that Barbour locates in Winnipeg's ethnically based social clubs, and veterans clubs, where members could drink in mixed company. At the same time, the general public began to resist the confines of liquor control laws, and drinking under the table at heterosocial events such as supper clubs became an open secret. Changes to the law, therefore, were rearguard actions in a society that was already transforming itself. This is not to suggest, however, a painless transition into a public leisure culture where men and women mixed freely. As the temperance tenor of the Report of the Manitoba Liquor Enquiry Commission (1955) demonstrated, alcohol consumption continued to be problematized as anti-social, particularly when it was done by the working class, European ethnic groups, and Aboriginal people. Add women to the mix, and the potential for immoral behaviour was seen as self-evident. However, some commentators approached normative heterosexuality from a different but nevertheless gendered angle when they argued that a woman's presence (especially that of wives) in a male drinking establishment might improve its civility. In the end, the commission read the public mood and recommended less restrictive laws while urging self-restraint.

Janis Thiessen's research looks at one prominent non-Anglo-Canadian Winnipeg business, and its attitudes toward work and unionism. Palliser Furniture, owned and operated by the Mennonite DeFehr family, emerged as a Winnipeg business success story in the 1970s. Post-war urban migration greatly increased the presence of Mennonites in Winnipeg and resulted in an "increased engagement with industrial capitalism." The 1970s were an era of considerable labour unrest and social democratic activism in Manitoba, and the owners of Palliser found that they had to re-evaluate ideas about employer-employee relations and unionism within their Mennonite religious tradition.

Thiessen provides a fascinating look at the intersections between ethnic, class, and religious identities during a period of societal change. Unlike immigrant groups in Winnipeg such as Jews and Ukrainians, whose participation in labour and leftist politics was critical to those social movements, Mennonites were opposed to union activity, socialism, and communism. The Mennonite Church rejected union membership in the 1930s, responding to the apostle Paul's admonition: be ye not unequally yoked together with unbelievers. Many Mennonites also objected to conflict or resistance of any kind, including class conflict, conflict on the picket line, the lockout, or the blacklist. Unions were also seen as driven by materialism. By the 1950s, this ban on union membership was softened, yet Manitoba's Plymouth Brethren were influential in the New Democratic Party's (NDP) introduction in 1974 of a religious exemption to compulsory union membership for employees covered by collective agreements. The Mennonite Central Committee (MCC) pushed the NDP government to guarantee the right of Mennonite workers to refuse to join a union, even though some Mennonite denominations no longer formally opposed union membership. In the mid-1970s, MCC organized community forums on labour relations, which had an anti-labour message. Thiessen describes Mennonite views on unions into the 1990s as ambivalent.

However, Mennonite employers did not necessarily employ only Mennonites, and here the values of their group encountered the resistance of others. Although it had introduced profit-sharing schemes to minimize worker unrest in the 1980s, Palliser Furniture, a leading Mennonite manufacturer in Winnipeg, experienced a union-organizing drive in 1996 among workers of Métis, Aboriginal, and Asian immigrant backgrounds. An important source of worker antipathy was the firm's mandatory chapel attendance policy; another concern was low wages. Unionists also argued that Palliser exploited the ignorance and limited English-language skills of immigrants by claiming that legally mandated contributions to the Canada Pension Plan, Employment Insurance, and Workers' Compensation were special company benefits. The firm successfully defeated the unionization drive, in part by threatening to close the plant and move it to North Carolina. Palliser today operates plants in Mexico, Indonesia, and Lithuania, making it a player in a global economy that rarely recognizes workers' right to organize.

Leslie Hall's piece begins to address a serious lacuna in the history of Winnipeg—the experience of Aboriginal peoples in the post-war era, when increasing numbers left their home reserve communities and migrated to the city. In the political context of Aboriginal movements for greater justice and equality in Canadian society beginning after the Second World War, one of the first Indian and Métis Friendship Centres (IMFC) in Canada opened in Winnipeg in 1959. The centre was created to offer newly urban Aboriginal people improved access to employment and housing and to provide a space for socializing and cultural activities. By the 1950s, the challenges facing urban Aboriginal peoples had been widely investigated by white society. Hall argues that Aboriginal experiences with health, education, employment, and the justice system were rendered problematic in rhetoric that attempted to make Aboriginal individuals "the problem that the rest of Canadians must 'solve.'" In the view of some commentators, Aboriginal culture and values were themselves obstacles to successful integration into urban life, and an inherent tension existed between "traditional" Aboriginal and "modern" white, urban ways of life. As Hall notes, this was not an interpretation with which Aboriginal peoples agreed. From their point of view, Aboriginal peoples coming to the city lacked access to services the rest of the community enjoyed, while being hampered by social isolation and the legacies of colonialism, such as residential schooling. In Winnipeg, Aboriginal individuals faced discrimination.

The creation of the IMFC was the result of cooperation between non-Aboriginal activists in the Welfare Planning Council (later the Social Planning Council of Winnipeg) and Aboriginal elders from the Urban Indian Association. The Welfare Planning Council organized a series of Indian and Métis conferences in the 1950s to discuss the needs of Winnipeg's Aboriginal residents. Yet, there was little Aboriginal involvement in these early conferences, which were dominated by non-Aboriginal community members, including Beatrice Brigden and W.L. Morton. Aboriginal voices were almost completely missing before 1958, despite the commitment of organizers to the principles of community development. A community-development approach sought to facilitate the efforts of Aboriginal peoples to address their own issues with the support of (non-Aboriginal) technical staff. In 1958, members of the Urban Indian Association attended the Indian and Métis Conference. Its Aboriginal membership included several individuals of talent and commitment, such as Marion Meadmore, who would go on to become the first Aboriginal woman lawyer in Canada. The Urban Indian Association had long been working, largely without financial resources, to help their community make the transition from reserve and residential school to life in Winnipeg. The association resolved to work with the planning council to open an agency to help Aboriginal people in Winnipeg find jobs, housing, health care, education, and other supports. Some Aboriginal participants were sceptical and feared that the proposed friendship centre would be "shaped in [the planning council's] own image without Aboriginal influence." In the early years, in fact, the Board of Directors of the IMFC was dominated by non-Aboriginal individuals, with an Indian Advisory Council. This arrangement is remembered by some as signalling Aboriginal inequality in the IMFC. Not all Aboriginal participants perceived it this way, however. The IMFC effectively made the transition to an all-Aboriginal board (achieved in 1968) and staff (1963).

The IMFC received financial support from the provincial and federal governments, despite the ongoing struggle between the two levels of government to pass off responsibility for urban Aboriginal residents. Neither level saw the city as a place where Aboriginal peoples could or should maintain their cultural heritage or identity; theirs was essentially an assimilationist perspective. As Hall notes, community development worked for the provincial government because it "allowed the province to channel some grant money into programming for Aboriginal people without overtly accepting responsibility for the problems encountered by Aboriginal people in urban centres." Aboriginal supporters of the IMFC never shared the funders' assimilationist goals but, rather, believed that the organization should be "a stepping stone into society for everything."

Hall's contribution suggests, as do many others in this volume, opportunities for future research in the history of Winnipeg. That there is a popular demand for a greater historical understanding of the city is quite evident: new works in Winnipeg history are generally received with a great deal of public support and attention by citizens. Thus, historians are privileged in having a fruitful relationship with an informed and interested community, supportive of archival research and new knowledge.

Our volume concludes with an epilogue written by the late Ed Rea, who taught the history of Winnipeg at the University of Manitoba for many years, and guided numerous students through their own research into the past life of the city in which they lived. Professor Rea writes, "every city has a personality." We hope he would be pleased with the personality that emerges from these new thoughts on the subject.

Notes

1   Alan Artibise, *Winnipeg: A Social History of Urban Growth, 1874-1914* (Montreal and London: McGill-Queen's University Press, 1975), 1.
2   Ibid, 2.

Minnie J.B. Campbell, Reform, and Empire

Kurt Korneski

During the late nineteenth and early twentieth centuries, a host of Winnipeg's journalists, ministers, medical doctors, businessmen, lawyers, labour leaders, politicians, club and professional women, and others called for an assault on poverty, slums, disreputable boarding houses, alcoholism, prostitution, sweatshop conditions, inadequate educational facilities, and other "social evils." Although they represented an array of political positions and advocated a range of strategies to deal with what they deemed social ills, this assortment of people and institutions has collectively been termed "reform" or the "reform movement" by historians. In the past decade and a half or so there has been a proliferation of writing about the history of reform in Canada. While in some ways these scholars have transformed our thinking about the history of reform by analyzing the men and women and institutions that were at its core through the lens of gender and race, most have assumed or explicitly argued that in Canada reform was a response to urban-industrial development.[1] That is, they have accepted that in Canada reform was a fairly straightforward middle-class response to indigence, illness, and "deviance" that increased as more men and women came to live in large, impersonal, urban-industrial centres.

This paper considers the life of prominent reformer M.J.B. Campbell in Winnipeg during the late nineteenth and early twentieth century. It is not, however, a biography in the traditional sense of that term. Rather, it is an effort to use Campbell as an entry point into the history of reform in Winnipeg. From the early 1880s to the 1930s, Campbell organized and/or worked through literally dozens of organizations to deal with everything from child poverty to unemployment, to convalescing soldiers, to juvenile delinquency. In many ways she was a typical female reformer. She was a maternal feminist who accepted to a considerable degree what Mary Poovey has called the "binary logic" of nineteenth-century gender systems.[2] Thus, she viewed it as her duty to act as a saintly, nurturing woman and as a mother to the nation, while leaving the menfolk to deal with the trials and tribulations of a capitalist economy and a liberal polity. At the same time, Campbell was also an ardent imperialist. Indeed, one of the most frequently recurring elements manifested in the articles, reports, and addresses that M.J.B. Campbell wrote and delivered are references to British or imperial "tradition." She saw herself as a member of a select group descended from British subjects, the United Empire Loyalists (UEL). To her mind, the Loyalists' devotion to the crown was so great that they unflinchingly faced the considerable suffering and privation that was the result of their decision to leave their homes in the newly born American Republic for the wilderness of British North America.[3] Campbell delighted in recounting her family history and, particularly, in relating the tales of woe surrounding her ancestors' exodus.[4] In her view, however, her genealogy was more than an interesting story. She believed that she was the proud inheritor of traditions of strength, perseverance, commitment to principle, loyalty, and devotion to the British crown that her ancestors had implanted in Canada approximately a century before her birth.[5] These traditions were, she thought, at the core of "Canadian-ness." If Canadians acted in accordance with them, they would find themselves rewarded in the future just as "the founders" had been rewarded in the past.[6] She viewed her own efforts as in accordance with, and conceived to build on, the hard-won gains that she believed were her inheritance by extending and expanding them through fostering an "imperial spirit" in Canada and, more generally speaking, a closely knit imperial federation throughout the world.[7]

Considering Campbell's role as a reformer in Winnipeg does not challenge the prevailing view that ultimately the reform movement began as a response to urban-industrial society. It does suggest, however, that there were important differences in the history of reform in the long-established centres in which it first emerged and its history elsewhere. Indeed, as a committed reformer and an ardent imperialist, Campbell in some ways embodied the social forces that were key to the city's development. She operated in a centre that developed as a strategic transfer point in a nationalist project of settler colonialism, and the form and appeal of reform for her and her counterparts reflected that their city was both an industrial and a colonial centre. Existing on the edge of the Empire, as opposed to the centre, meant that men and women went west with knowledge of the social and institutional practice in the centres and of the ideological perspectives that underlay them. In contrast to long-established centres, in Winnipeg the first reform institutions actually preceded extensive urban-industrial development, and they emerged in large part as a result of the needs of a colonial elite. Even as the city became larger and more industrial, the social ills typical of such urban centres failed to overshadow anxieties about gender imbalance and housing shortages, qualities associated with frontier outposts. The concerns of an "outpost of Empire" continued as central causes of "deviance" in Winnipeg.

I

Minnie Julia Beatrice Campbell was born in Palermo, Ontario, in 1862 to Anson Buck and Keturah Adelaide Howell.[8] Though Campbell revealed little about her mother, she rarely missed an opportunity to discuss her father, a physician and municipal politician in Ontario, who, according to Campbell, was of a "progressive mind set."[9] He strongly believed, Campbell related, that "girls could do anything boys could." However, when Campbell decided that she would like to follow in her father's footsteps by becoming a doctor, she clearly tested the bounds of his progressivism. Rather than attending medical school at the University of Toronto, as she would have liked, she "was sent ... to the Wesleyan Female College" in Hamilton.[10] She remained there for three years studying classics, science, mathematics, art, and music. On graduating in 1880 as a Mistress of English Literature, she taught in the Primary Department of the Ottawa Ladies College before marrying and moving to Winnipeg with up-and-coming lawyer Colin H. Campbell in 1884.[11]

Colin Campbell, also from Ontario, was a rising legal, business, and political figure.[12] After graduating from an Oakville, Ontario, high school, he studied law at Osgoode Hall in Toronto. On completing his degree in 1881, he worked for a short time in the office of Colonel George Taylor Denison and later entered into practice with John Billings.[13] In 1882, he travelled to Winnipeg, where he first practised in the firm of Aiken, Culver, and Hamilton. For the next twenty years or so he formed a host of partnerships. From 1903 until 1914 he was senior partner in the firm of Campbell, Pitblado, Hoskin, Grundy, Bennet, Haig, Drummond-Hay, Montague, and Gauld.[14] He entered public office in 1899 when, after his election to the provincial legislature, he served as minister without portfolio in the Conservative government of Hugh John Macdonald. During the years from 1900 to 1914, he served in the government of Rodmond Roblin as minister of education, minister of public works, and attorney general.[15]

Campbell's decision to move west was not unusual in the 1880s, though even as little as forty years earlier the site that became Winnipeg was part of a fur-trade hinterland that most outside observers viewed as uninhabitable and unappealing.[16] After that time, many Britons and Euro-Canadians began to name, to divide, and to view this colonial space very differently. What once was of marginal value became the core of an envisioned prosperous, populous, liberal-capitalist society. We shall return to this imagined future later. The shift itself, however, is worth reflecting upon, for it signalled important changes within the long-standing, mutually determining, dialectical processes of material and ideological transformation that linked colonizing centres and their peripheries. Rebellions in Jamaica, India, and New Zealand at or around the middle of the nineteenth century produced a crisis in imperial administration.[17] At the same time, an increase in the number and extent of industrial centres in the world and the opening of agricultural hinterlands flooded world markets with both agricultural and industrial products, thereby producing a global economic downturn that contemporaries referred to simply as the "Great Depression."[18] In this context, "the settlement of British peoples in colonial spaces emerged as an expedient way of securing Britain's interests abroad and of relieving pressures at 'home.'"[19]

In northern North America, the Aboriginal population was comparatively small and weakened by disease and war. Thus, the fact that the mid-century rebellions caused imperial officials to question whether Native populations could become self-governing peoples within the Empire likely had less significance in Canada than it did elsewhere. Nevertheless, the region did come to be viewed as a potential market and as a "vast empty space" that could receive settlers and act as a safety valve for mounting social pressure in Britain.[20] According to British and Canadian politicians, businessmen, and editors, moreover, staking a claim to the interior of northern North America was important not only because it would help to relieve a perceived "crisis in overproduction" in Britain, but also because it would serve as the basis for a nation above the forty-ninth parallel that they hoped would meet the challenge of American expansion.[21] It was the will to develop a Canadian nation that encompassed a vast territory, then, that made the expansionary nationalist visions of men like George Brown, Allan Macdonell, William Macdonell Dawson, William Kennedy, William McDougall, Phillip M. Vankoughnet, and Alexander Galt realistic, reasonable, and relevant.[22]

From Confederation onward, the nation builders' strategy was to ensure economic vitality for Britain and the new Canadian nation through reproducing and extending a liberal-capitalist politico-economic system among a newly settled population in the periphery. After procuring the region from the Hudson's Bay Company, extinguishing Aboriginal land rights through treaties, and negotiating the surrender of the Métis provisional government in Red River, the "Fathers of Confederation" arranged to have the region from the foothills of the Rocky Mountains to the Ontario border carved into square-mile sections and 160-acre quarter sections. To compete with the United States, which had offered "free homesteads" of 160 acres in the *Homestead Act* of 1862, the Dominion government undertook similar measures—first by orders in council, and later in the *Dominion Lands Act* of 1872. According to the Act, for a negligible fee prospective immigrants could obtain a quarter section of land. The understanding was that homesteaders would bring the land under cultivation and, after the railway connected them to the East, would exchange agricultural commodities for industrial manufactures produced in the East, thereby providing for the economic viability of the nation.[23] The nation, in turn, would be a trading partner for Britain and a "frontier of investment" for its financiers.

Even after politicians and investors were willing to press for and to underwrite the national project, it is likely that Winnipeg would have developed into little more than a modest town had its business elite not convinced the Canadian Pacific Railway (CPR) to route its mainline through their city.[24] From that point on, Winnipeg became the gateway to the interior, and virtually everything and everyone who travelled to or from the West had to pass through it. Not surprisingly, at about the time Campbell arrived in the city, a central part of the city's economy was linked directly to railway construction and maintenance. While construction was ongoing, for example, the demands of track maintenance supported local firms producing tents and construction materials fabricated from lumber and iron, and needle trades firms produced work clothing to be worn by farm workers and labourers employed on the railway.[25] After construction was complete, the CPR and, later, the Grand Trunk Pacific and Canadian Northern railways all established repair and workshops and yards in Winnipeg or in the suburb of Transcona. The number of men employed in these firms grew over the course of the late nineteenth and early twentieth centuries as the tide of grain and livestock going east and supplies going west swelled with each passing year.[26]

By 1902, Winnipeg handled more grain than Chicago, and by 1906, a local firm, Gordon, Ironside, and Fares, was the largest exporter of cattle in the British Empire.[27] The influx of goods spurred the development of firms that processed agricultural products. Thus, there were slaughterhouses, flour mills, malting facilities, breweries, and dairies. The increased number of people in the region and the need for building materials supported firms that produced construction materials, paint, lumber, bricks, finished steel, and cement.[28] As the population increased, and there developed a local demand for a wide variety of goods not related to railways and construction, firms that produced everything from printed materials to soap and candy were soon added to the list of businesses operating in the city.[29]

Moreover, as Gerry Friesen has pointed out, the city was central to industry of another sort as well. Even though farming was vital to western development, throughout the late nineteenth and early twentieth centuries, the region also contained numerous mine towns, timber camps, and construction sites.[30] The camps, towns, and sites needed workers, and from its incorporation in 1874 through to the early twentieth century, Winnipeg served as a labour bazaar for the entire region. Usually workers and employers connected with each other through one of the city's many employment agencies. Often little more than "ramshackle store fronts" located on the streets stretching from the CPR rail station into the heart of the business district, these agencies posted lists of available jobs. Workers perused the postings and, sometimes after paying a fee for the privilege of work, signed on for a stint in a camp of one kind or another.[31]

As the number of people on the prairies increased, the city also became home to a considerable number of wholesalers who supplied retail stores in newly emerging hamlets and in the city itself.[32] Indeed, during the 1880s and 1890s the board of trade successfully campaigned for freight-rate reductions, which meant that wholesalers in Winnipeg benefitted from "substantial preferences—as much as 15 to 30 per cent reductions in freight rates—over competitors in eastern Canada and in other prairie cities, as well as advantages of large inventories and ... rapid response time when orders arrived."[33] By the first years of the twentieth century, then, the wholesale sector employed thousands of Winnipeggers. The extent of this business was (and still is) evidenced by the prominence of the warehouse district in the city's urban landscape.

II

For Minnie, the move west was a turning point. She left her family and friends and a comparatively comfortable existence in Ontario for what was, in the early 1880s, still a muddy frontier outpost. Perhaps more importantly for our purposes was that her marriage to Colin Campbell also signalled the end of her paid working life and the beginning of her involvement in the reform organizations and patriotic societies that held her attention for most of the duration of her lifetime. Almost immediately after her arrival, for example, she became involved with the Winnipeg General Hospital, which had been organized more than ten years before her arrival in the city. The majority of those who raised funds to build the hospital, and who monitored its day-to-day functioning, were "the ladies of the city"—women like Mrs. George Bryce, Mrs. A.G.B. Bannatyne, and Mrs. W.G. Dennison.[34] On arriving in Winnipeg, Campbell joined these women in raising funds and collecting supplies needed to maintain the institution. Like the other women involved with the organization, she worked under a board of management comprised of men like Gilbert McMicken, W.N. Kennedy, George Bryce, A.G.B. Bannatyne, and J.H. Ashdown, who were some of the city's foremost businessmen. Often the husbands of the women who devoted themselves to the day-to-day operations of the hospital, these men also oversaw the construction of buildings, controlled finances, and were, at least for the first decades of its existence, the hospital's chief financial backers.[35]

Like other, similar institutions in the nineteenth century, the hospital served those who could not afford, or had no access to, private, home-based care.[36] Organizers viewed some of the patients they served as having fallen ill due to circumstances beyond their control. Victims of one of the city's regular outbreaks of typhoid, for example, fell into this category. Those who suffered injuries in work camps, a particularly large number of whom came from railway construction camps, also generally were not stigmatized.[37] Organizers were, however, also proud that they operated an "up-to-date facility." Drawing on the thinking of reformers in the US and Britain, they believed in a strong link between poverty and sickness and, in turn, between spiritual and moral failings and poverty. They concluded that, in addition to treating symptoms of illness, in many cases "social medicine" was necessary. Like those who worked through settlement houses and other similar institutions elsewhere, Campbell and others who were involved with the hospital sought to educate patients about the supposedly deviant or morally questionable practices that might have contributed to their impoverishment and illness in the first place.[38]

In addition to her work at the hospital, Campbell also helped out with the Winnipeg branch of the YMCA. Founded in 1879 by many of the same men and women who developed the hospital, the organization offered the large number of young, single men who frequented the city instruction on how to be good Christian husbands and fathers, as well as lodging and a social setting apart from the city's "disreputable" hotels and saloons.[39] Members of the YMCA also visited the hospital, immigrant sheds, the jail, and the more notorious boarding houses in an effort to prevent drunkenness, prostitution, and other "immoral" practices.[40] Campbell's role in this organization appears to have been primarily as a "help-mate." That is, she and other elite women in the city dealt with food preparation, cleaning, and other requisite "domestic duties."

She also played a role in the Christian Women's Union (CWU). Organized the year before she arrived in the city, this organization had as part of its mission to provide a much smaller population of single, female wage-earners, most of whom in the early 1880s went west to work as domestic servants, with an evening refuge and boarding house where they could pass the time reading or sewing.[41] Soon after its inauguration, however, CWU organizers also set up a maternity or lying-in hospital.

Initially the hospital was intended for poor married women who could otherwise get little privacy in the "comfortless shanties and over-crowded houses" that many called home.[42] Though some of the women who actually took advantage of these services were poor married women, as Campbell later explained, it soon dealt mainly with "the unmarried mother in particular."[43]

Campbell and other women who worked for the CWU were uneasy about providing shelter to such women because doing so did not sit well with some of their middle-class counterparts. As the organization's first president, C. Rowe, noted, they found "little support, financial and otherwise, for their organization largely owing to the fact that there has ... been an amount of misconception as to its motive and aim, many being under the impression that providing a home for these unfortunate ones was but to encourage the sin, and make it easy for the sinner."[44] According to C. Caitlin, matron of the Maternity Hospital, most of the women inmates were not inherently corrupt but were the victims of their circumstances. As she explained, "The majority of these patients are poor friendless girls drawn here by the prospect of higher wages. They seek, as a rule, positions which offer the greatest pecuniary advantages. These being chiefly hotels and restaurants, they are at once thrown into the midst of temptation, to which, too often, alas, they yield, and their bright dreams end in ruined prospects and a blighted life."[45] When women found themselves in this position, she further explained, "the Hospital steps in and offers its shelter and care." The aim was not to give these women an easy way out. Rather, it was to reform them. The CWU, according to Caitlin, sought to "surround her [the unwed mother] with a purer atmosphere, to restore the self-respect, too often almost gone, and by mercifully helping her to bear her burden of sorrow and of shame."[46]

Considering the name of the organization itself, it is not surprising that part of the "purer atmosphere" included regular Bible lessons.[47] It involved a great deal more. Expecting or recent mothers had to keep the home clean and tidy. They also covered some or all of the cost of their and their child's stay by working for the home, which took in laundry work, knitting, and sewing. Though at first these endeavours were a relatively modest part of the organization's income, by the late 1880s the board of management for the CWU established an Industrial Home for Women and, as of 1891 when they opened a new building, had reportedly vastly expanded their laundry operation.[48] According to the women who operated the CWU, requiring "inmates" to maintain the home and to work for their lodging and food made them "more happy by their being independent of charity." It also provided them with the habits they would need to be "respectable" women. That is, it taught them to sew, to cook, and to keep a tidy home.[49]

Throughout most of the next two decades, Campbell continued on with work of a similar nature. In the 1890s, for example, she took a leading role in Winnipeg's Christian Endeavor movement, a church-based movement aimed at fostering inter-denominational cooperation in addressing social problems.[50] In 1892 she, along with other of the city's prominent men and women, developed a Free Kindergarten to allow "faithful, kind women" to instruct "foreigners and the very poor English speaking children" who became more numerous as families moved to the city or men and women already there began to have children.[51] "In the pleasantest manner possible" these women ensured that students' "faculties were bent in the right direction." For the organizers of the kindergarten, the "right direction" meant that boys were enrolled in industrial schools and girls in sewing classes.[52] In 1907, she expanded the work she first began in the CWU by establishing a YWCA to provide a growing number of single female wage earners with reasonably priced accommodation in a "place where they would be under Christian influences."[53] Finally, in 1908 she organized the Winnipeg portion of a broader campaign to provide assistance to destitute women—or, as she termed them, "female sufferers"—and their children by collecting clothes, money, and food.[54]

Though she remained active in a host of organizations, after 1909 her main focus was the Imperial Order Daughters of the Empire (IODE).[55] A Montrealer named Mrs. Clark Murray reportedly founded the order in 1900 as a response to the outbreak of the Boer War. Murray, who was in England when the war began, related that she "met many women who were anxious to help on the home front but who were hand-icapped by a lack of channels through which to work." On returning to Canada, she "resolved to form an organization based on the foundations of patriotism, loyalty, and service."[56] These rather vague organizational precepts translated into, among other things, a program of promoting "in the Motherland and in the colonies the study of the history of the Empire and of current Imperial questions; to celebrate patriotic anniversaries; to cherish the memory of brave and heroic deeds and the last resting places of our heroes and heroines, especially such as are in distant and solitary places; to erect memorial stones on spots that have become sacred ... either through great struggles for freedom, battles against ignorance, or events of heroic and patriotic self-sacrifice."[57]

Initially there were chapters in Ontario, Quebec, and New Brunswick. Within two years of its founding, the order had established chapters in the Bahamas, Bermuda, and in the United States, where the organization was known by the exceed-ingly prolonged title, "The Daughters of the British Empire in the United States of

America."[58] The western Canadian organizing drive did not materialize until 1909.[59] Many Manitoba women apparently received the order's representatives warmly, for the organizers were able to establish five new chapters—including the Fort Garry, Prairie Gateway, Brandon, Lord Selkirk, and Earl Grey chapters.[60] Campbell served as the regent of the Fort Garry Chapter for thirteen years, as president of Manitoba's Provincial Chapter for fourteen years, and as a councillor on the National Executive from 1911 until at least the 1930s.[61]

As is implied in the quote above, a central purpose of the order was to commemorate and celebrate the Empire and the imperial connection. Campbell worked with great enthusiasm to imbue her fellow Canadians with an "imperial spirit" through flag campaigns, raising monuments, providing presentations to schoolchildren on Empire Day, essay contests, and so forth. Yet, her imperialism involved a great deal more than saluting the flag and singing "Rule Britannia" on Empire Day.

Indeed, for her reform and imperialism were fundamentally linked. The connection between Empire and reform for Campbell was tied up with a relatively complex understanding of the causes of human social development, which was more often implicit within her writings and speeches than explicitly stated. For Campbell, as for a host of other Winnipeggers, human history was teleological.[62] The movement was away from "savagery," "incivility," and "backwardness" and toward a fully human or "civilized" and "modern" society. According to her view, societies that contained within them the values, practices, and systems of governance that were most closely aligned with what was natural to human beings found success, meaning that they were more affluent and powerful than other societies. Britain was an example of such a society. With "success," however, came responsibility, and it was the duty of "advanced" peoples the world over to bring the "lesser races" up to the level of the British, thereby moving humanity as a whole toward a more happy, affluent, socially peaceful existence.[63]

It was because the Empire represented the spreading of the principles and values that accorded with humans' nature that made it worth celebrating and commemorating. Yet, the apparent confidence that Britain was destined to remain globally predominant because it somehow accorded with a broader design running through human history is deceptive. At the same time that Campbell joined her imperialist counterparts in extolling the virtues of the "Anglo-Saxon" or "British race," she could not help but notice that "progress" toward the end of a happy, socially peaceful existence was slow in coming in Britain, Canada, and other parts of the Empire. The apparent disconnect between what the Empire supposedly represented, and the reality of social life for millions of people, did not cause Campbell to abandon the imperial mission. Rather, she believed that the "British spirit" and the traditions and institutions in which it was manifested did indeed accord with the end toward which human history was ostensibly moving. The problem was that men and women often failed to live completely in accordance with that spirit. The result was that misery and poverty persisted in Canada and elsewhere. Her task was to advance humankind through ensuring that men and women adopted the attitudes and practices of "true Britishers."[64]

Rather than signalling a shift in direction for Campbell, her commitment to the IODE, then, represented a continuation of her earlier work. In addition to a truly Herculean effort to collect money and supplies for the war effort after 1914, she helped to furnish part of the children's ward of the general hospital.[65] Additionally, she worked through the order to raise funds for a host of other causes. In 1918, for example, she reported that the order had contributed some of the nearly $150,000 it collected that year for the Children's Hospital, the Children's Aid Society, Children's Khaki Club (a home for the orphan children of soldiers), the St. Dunstan's Home for the Blind, Citizens' Christmas Cheer, the Red Cross, and a host of relief organizations and other societies.[66]

Her work evolved as conditions in the city changed. For instance, especially after the turn of the century, an increasingly large number of settlers were non-Anglo-Canadians. Many of the newly arrived had little money and found that Anglo-Canadian racism barred them from higher-paying jobs. While structural inequality and racism were at the core of immigrants' plight, Campbell and other reformers tended to take the symptoms of poverty for its causes. She responded to the fact that the "foreign quarter" was an "endless grey expanse of moldering ruin" as though it were an "immigrant problem."[67] Like fellow Winnipeggers J.S. Woodsworth, George Chipman, Charles Gordon, William Ivens, and others, Campbell believed that the appropriate response was to "refine" a presumably crude mass of humanity that flowed into the country.[68]

As she noted in 1911, "the city of Winnipeg ... has doubled its population in ten years." She further observed that in the city's "public schools forty-five languages [were] spoken." To her mind, this state of affairs presented "many opportunities for the Order to do its part in making British Canadians of the cosmopolitan population of the prairie city."[69] What she deemed "other," and what she viewed as "British" and, therefore, "Canadian," however, involved not merely flags and symbolism, but also modes of behaviour and conditions of existence. To her mind, the often abhorrent conditions in which immigrants lived were contrary to the "British-Canadian" way. The means by which the immigrants' condition might be ameliorated was not through addressing social or economic matters, but through instructing immigrants on the finer points of British "civilization." These included English speech and the adoption of modes of existence like those Campbell revered. In particular, she saw women as properly suited to domestically oriented work of the "private sphere." The degree to which they accepted "civilized" habits would be reflected in whether or not they kept clean, tidy residences, the hallmark of a well-managed home and a central part of being a "British-Canadian" woman.[70]

As the number of people in need of assistance increased, Campbell also supported efforts to centralize, regulate, and coordinate "relief work." As early as 1908, Campbell later recounted, the city established the Council of Associated Charities and hired a "professional" social worker. The social worker's job was to coordinate the various charities in the city and to ensure that aid to the ill and indigent was administered "scientifically."[71] About six years later, the council was superseded by the more extensive and rigidly structured Social Welfare Association, in which Campbell played a central role. The association was operated and governed by the voluntary societies that many middle-class women in the city had been central to organizing and operating. Reform organizations in the city were represented in the association according to the size of their membership. It held monthly meetings and decisions made by association officers were binding on affiliated societies. The establishment of the Social Welfare Commission of the City of Winnipeg in 1917 signalled a reversion to a government-centred system. The major difference between the commission and the Social Welfare Association was that the commission was headed up by employees of the city rather than a board elected exclusively by participants in private reform organizations.[72] The move from private to public was a matter of changing the procedure for choosing leaders and of formalizing what had been up to 1917 a regular, if slightly varied, expenditure by city council.[73]

III

In some ways Campbell's case confirms what historians have claimed about reform and reformers for several decades. It is clear, for example, that she worked according to a logic of patriarchy that other scholars have dubbed the "doctrine of separate spheres." Those who accepted this view believed that men and women had radically different natures that made them suited to different realms or "spheres" of activity. Men were presumably more intellectually astute, physically stronger, aggressive, and suited to the "public" world of political decision making, physicality, and competition. Women, supposedly mentally and physically weaker and adept at care giving and nurturing, were suited to the private world of home, family, and emotion.[74] Historians of reform contend that such a conceptualization reflected and naturalized the idea that the "normal" and "desirable" arrangement was that of the nuclear family dependent on a male breadwinner whose earnings came from employment earnings. They also argue that reform organizations both functioned according to this logic and defined as deviant and targeted social practices that strayed from it.[75]

Campbell's acceptance of this view was implied in the way she carried out her efforts. She, for example, helped with food preparation, cleaning, and other requisite "domestic duties" in male-centred institutions like the YMCA because she believed they were part of the "female sphere." Moreover, her support of organizations like the CWU and the YMCA indicate that she was willing to put a significant amount of effort into dealing with single female wage earners who came to Winnipeg and the West. Her belief that such agencies were needed was rooted in the idea that women outside of a male-headed household represented a "problem."[76] Campbell at times explicitly voiced her approval of this patriarchal logic. In 1912, for example, a *Manitoba Free Press* reporter asked her for her views about what Mary Kinnear has termed the "single unifying aim" of nineteenth- and early twentieth-century feminism—female enfranchisement. She stated flatly that she, as a "respectable woman," was "not a suffragette."[77] She further explained that "if the laws of the land need[ed] righting, men [were] quite able to look after them," and that women would "be able to get what they want[ed] by going to men and asking them for it."[78] To her mind, women's "best and truest work" was to be done in their "own great sphere."[79]

However, while reform institutions and the state agencies that grew out of them functioned on the premise that the nuclear family dependent on a male breadwinner was the "normal" and desirable arrangement, Campbell's own practice confirms some scholars' contention that women "exploited their authority as mothers" to challenge the subordination of women entailed by that norm.[80] The CWU, YWCA, Free Kindergarten, and IODE, for example, were organized and operated entirely by women. In acting as "mothers to the nation," they took on positions of authority, positions that were usually designated male. Moreover, Campbell was also involved in the various umbrella organizations that served as the models for the city's early forays into reform. Thus, as Mariana Valverde, Nancy Christie, and others have argued, the relationship between the state and civil society is a flexible one and the programs that eventually fell under the authority of the state were often shaped by reformers who were not state officials.[81] When Campbell and other middle-class women took a leading role in voluntary societies, they shaped the institutions that "constituted an important (but often overlooked) site of public policy and, ultimately, state formation."[82] That is, they managed to exert considerable influence even though they were excluded from policy and formal political decision making.

In addition to these now familiar contours of female agency and social reform, Campbell's social activism also demonstrates the importance to the Winnipeg context of the challenges to success within the industrial capitalist order nationally and internationally. Even though some settler capitalists benefitted from protective tariffs, the success of commercial and industrial concerns in the city depended on the ability of their owners to compete with increasingly large concerns abroad.[83] In replicating forms of ownership and production that existed in those centres, they also reproduced attendant social realities—including the increased poverty, illness, and social dislocation that accompanied a growing disparity in wealth throughout the industrial world.[84] Changing social practices also contributed to new social concerns.

The increased number of single female wage earners, which middle-class men and women termed the "girl problem," was partly linked to the fact that the growth of mass production and distribution was accompanied by an increase in and feminization of tertiary and retail work.[85] It is difficult to say for certain why Campbell and others observed a substantial number of unwed mothers in the city in its early years. It is probable, however, that some of these "fallen women" sought to deal with economic hard times and restrictive labour practices by engaging in prostitution, which was widespread in the city throughout the later nineteenth and early twentieth centuries. These "deviant" outcomes, rooted in social conditions, impelled reformers to develop community institutions intended, as Campbell argued, to "make British Canadians" loyal to prescribed notions of family, nation, and empire.

That there were similarities between the organizations with which Campbell was involved and those in other parts of Canada, the United States, and Britain should not be surprising. Often they were either modelled on, or, as we have seen, were actually branches of, organizations developed in large urban centres elsewhere. Winnipeg's social ills, however, were not interchangeable with those of other centres like Toronto, London, or New York. When Campbell became involved in reform in the city, it was not yet the sprawling hub that it would become. Even though by that time Winnipeg was linked to the East by rail and the population swelled to more than 7000, visitors were not struck by the city's modern amenities. Emma Louisa Averill, for example, travelled to Winnipeg from Liverpool just before Campbell's arrival. Like many others who ventured into the city in these years, she was dismayed that Winnipeg consisted of a collection of often shabby wooden and brick, or brick-veneered, buildings that were connected by streets that appeared as rivers of thick greasy mud bordered by partially submerged plank sidewalks.[86] She also noted, however, what struck her as peculiar about the city. She thought the local men and women "rather showy" in their striving to be "in accordance with English taste." This behaviour was all the more striking since local residents often performed these theatrics alongside the large number of Aboriginal men and women who frequented the city. As she put it, it was "very curious to see the Indians walking about in their blankets amongst their stylish neighbors."[87] In fact, for Averill, the large number of Aboriginal people in the city and in the area surrounding was deeply unsettling. Many of those who lived in a camp on the edge of town were "dirty and untidy much like some of the swarthy Gypsies at home." She recorded that they inspired within her "a feeling of repugnance" and also some distress. Averill's concerns, however, had less to do with the often abysmal conditions in which these people lived than they did with the fact that she "did not like the idea of having them walk in and out of our house as I am told is their habit."[88]

Campbell herself later recalled that the Winnipeg of her arrival contrasted sharply with the city in later years.[89] While indigence no doubt existed throughout even the earliest years of the city's history, reform institutions also appealed partly because they satisfied needs among middle-class men and women themselves. At the same time that reform became increasingly pervasive and accepted in capitalist hubs in Europe and the United States, the "Canadian nation" was largely a collection of ideals. It was an imagined future—a liberal social vision that had been projected onto the interior of northern North America. The founding of "the nation," thus, did not mark the point at which a developed centre came to exist. Rather, it was the point at which prominent men and women (many of whom were, like Campbell, also at the core of the reform movement in Winnipeg), backed by the British government and eastern Canadian, British, and American investors, undertook in earnest to convince and compel those living in the territory over which they sought dominion, and those travelling to it, to order their lives in ways that made an imagined future nation an actually existing social situation. Canada was a colonial project, and Winnipeg had the characteristics of a frontier outpost.

The infatuation with showing commitment to the Empire and a connection to the "civilized world," which was expressed particularly in Campbell's capacity as a Daughter of Empire, was not exceptional. Despite the mud and the lack of a stable urban infrastructure, for example, many early Winnipeggers were adamant about pausing each day for afternoon tea, reportedly spoke in contrived English accents, kept abreast of and adorned themselves in the latest English fashions, held balls in which they sought to replicate the costumes and practices of the metropole, and spent lavishly on fireworks displays to honour important imperial events like the Queen's birthday.[90] Perhaps more important for understanding reform is to note that early Winnipeggers also saw "British institutions" as central. Before there was a railway connection, and before the permanent population exceeded 7000, Winnipeg had foreign missionary societies, shooting clubs, colleges, a university, a theatre company, numerous churches, a private men's social club, fraternal societies, and sporting organizations.[91] For Campbell and her counterparts it was also partly to demonstrate their *own* civility that they developed a host of modern reform institutions through which to deal with "morally ill" people in ways that were "up to the requirements of modern science." As one author explained, Winnipeggers had "not failed to attend to the moral and intellectual wants within [their city's] limits."[92]

We have already seen that the ideal of the nuclear family headed by a male breadwinner informed how reformers organized themselves, what they identified as a "problem," and what habits they tried to instill in those they identified as deviant. While this norm may have been typical, the reasons that Winnipeggers deviated from it were distinctive. As other scholars have shown, in long-established centres with permanent industry and a fairly equal number of men and women, declining real wages, abandonment, and women's dissatisfaction with their subordinate status stood as key obstacles to the society middle-class reformers like Campbell envisioned.[93] When Campbell arrived in Winnipeg, the city had little fixed industry and, as she later noted, "it was a young man's town." Some of these men were reportedly "excited with the fascination of a busy and money making life," and others simply intended "to make their little pile as soon as possible and to go back to the old spot where they once lived surrounded by all the comforts that Ontario or Quebec could afford them."[94] Whatever their intentions, they drifted into and out of the city as they followed the seasonal rhythm of work on the Prairies.[95] Owing to housing shortages, they not only had to crowd into hotels and boarding houses, but also often had to share accommodation with other men. As one observer noted after spending a considerable amount of time searching for accommodation in 1882, "I am not the only one who has had to hunt for quarters. Fellows are always on the hunt. It is the greatest bete noir of Winnipeg." He ended up sharing a bed and "two very good empty rooms" with a Mr. J.H. Hoore.[96] Winnipeg was a rapidly expanding centre populated by a disproportionate number of men. At least some "deviant" behaviour transpired because there simply were not enough residences, jobs within the city, and potential "female helpmates" to allow them to achieve the standards of "normal" life.

Such conditions persisted. Even as the city developed into a sizeable industrial and commercial hub, it also functioned as a centre of the labour market for the Prairies. The skewed ratio of men to women and the housing shortages ebbed as new immigrants came west. Thus, in the first decade of the twentieth century, reformers found that they were put under tremendous pressure as they sought to find homes for and deal with diseases and "vice" that increased as successive "waves of predominantly male migrants" arrived in the city.[97] As of 1912, the number of men reported to be living in the city outnumbered women by 10,000. The actual number of men in the city was probably larger as census takers sometimes ignored or missed residents of crowded tenements and seasonal workers who were in Winnipeg only during the winter months.[98]

IV

Examining Campbell and the reform initiatives with which she was connected does not fundamentally challenge conventional wisdom about the rise of reform. It does suggest, however, that we cannot presume that the patterns of social development in metropolitan centres apply to all Canadian locales. As a project of settler nationalism, Canada was a process in which the aim was to ensure economic vitality for Britain and the new Canadian nation through reproducing and extending a liberal-capitalist politico-economic system among a newly settled population in the periphery.[99] That the country developed as a part of a more general "empire of capital" means there were two distinct, but related, social dynamics at play for Campbell and her counterparts. There were settlers who sought to build a modern industrial nation and who had to deal with the social ills that inadvertently arose out of their efforts. They were located, however, on the outer "edge" of an empire, and as such the history of their city and the social movements that developed within it must also be explicitly analyzed as enmeshed within and shaped by a web of social relations that was global in scope.

Notes

1   See, for example, Alvin Finkel, *Social Policy and Practice in Canada: A History* (Waterloo: Wilfrid Laurier University Press, 2006); Nancy Christie, *Engendering the State: Family, Work, and Welfare in Canada* (Toronto: University of Toronto Press, 2000); James Struthers, *The Limits of Affluence: Welfare in Ontario, 1920–1970* (Toronto: University of Toronto Press 1994); Margaret Little, *No Car, No Radio, No Liquor Permit: The Moral Regulation of Single Mothers in Ontario, 1920–1997* (New York: Oxford University Press, 1998). These scholars' work draws on and is part of a more general rethinking of reform and the welfare state in Britain, the US and Canada. See, for example, the pioneering work of Mimi Abramovitz, *Regulating the Lives of Women: Social Welfare Policy from Colonial Times to the Present* (Boston: South End Press, 1996 [1988]) and Linda Gordon, *Women, the State and Welfare* (Madison: University of Wisconsin Press, 1990).

2   Mary Poovey, *Uneven Developments: The Ideological Work of Gender in Mid-Victorian England* (Chicago: University of Chicago Press, 1988).

3   Archives of Manitoba (hereafter AM), Campbell Papers (hereafter CP), P 2503, folder 15, "The Supremacy of the Flag," 2.

4   See, for example, AM, CP, P 2505, folder 2, "A Daughter of Empire," *Winnipeg Once A Week*, c. 1911, 3; AM, CP, P5145, folder 2, "51 Years in Winnipeg," 1935.

5   Other historians have noted that these views were widespread among elites, particularly those in Ontario, in the last years of the nineteenth and first years of the twentieth century. They also note, not surprisingly, considering that the status of "UEL" was conferred on those with a particular family history, that there was also an intense interest in genealogy. See, for example, Norman Knowles, *Inventing the Loyalists: The Ontario Loyalist Tradition and the Creation of Usable Pasts* (Toronto: University of Toronto Press, 1997). See also Carl Berger, *The Sense of Power: Studies in the Ideas of Canadian Imperialism, 1867–1914* (Toronto: University of Toronto Press, 1970), esp. 78–108.

6   AM, CP, P 2503, folder 15, "The Supremacy of the Flag," 2.

7   AM, CP, P2503, folder 15, "The Supremacy of the Flag," 2. Other scholars have noted that this was a more general late nineteenth- and early twentieth-century phenomenon. See, for example, Anna Davin, "Imperialism and Motherhood," *History Workshop* 5 (Spring 1978): 14–15; Julia Bush, *Edwardian Ladies and Imperial Power* (London: Leicester University Press, 2000), 36–70.

8   AM, CP, P 2497, folder 10, draft copy of entry for "Who's Who and Why," 994.

9   Anson Buck's life is memorialized in several articles and interviews with Campbell. See, for example, AM, CP, P 2503, folder 2, "A Daughter of Empire," *Winnipeg Once a Week*, c. 1911, 3; AM, CP, P 2503, folder 2, "Review of the Life of Anson Buck," *Oakville Star*, 25 August 1933; AM, CP, P 2503, folder 2, "Mrs. Colin H. Campbell, OBE, Wears Honors of Two Nations," *Brantford Expositor*, 23 July 1936. AM, CP, P 2503, folder 6, S.H. Corrigan, "Anson Buck, M.D., M.R.C.S. Eng. 1833–1919."

10 AM, CP, P 2497, folder 10, "Mrs. Colin H. Campbell Fifty Years in Winnipeg: Daughter of the Late Anson Buck and Former Resident of Palermo," [1934].

11 AM, CP, P 5145, folder 2, "Sixty One Years in Winnipeg: Mrs. Colin Campbell, U.E., O.B.E., Winnipeg, Manitoba, 1884–1945," [1945].

12 While most biographical accounts of Colin Campbell emphasize his legal career, he was also well entrenched in local business dealings. He was president of the Equitable Trust Company, the Winnipeg Investment Company, the Mercantile Investment Company, the Investors Limited, Columbia Coal and Coke Company, the Scottish Investment Company, the Ontario, Manitoba and Western Land Company, and the Chandler Fisher Company. He was also a director for the Alloway and Champion Banking Company, the Houghton Land Company, Lethbridge Collieries Limited, the Peoples' Investment Company, the Crown Securities Company, the Real Estate Investment Company, the Canadian Provinces Investment Company, and the Bank of Hamilton.

He belonged to such elite social clubs as the Manitoba Club, the St. Charles Country Club, the Adanac Club, the Grosvenor Club (London, England), and the Albany Club of Toronto. This information comes from Edwin McCormick, ed., *The Leading Financial, Business, and Professional Men of Winnipeg* (Winnipeg: Stark, [c. 1912]).

13   Charles G.D. Roberts and Arthur L. Tunnell, eds., *A Standard Dictionary of Canadian Biography: The Canadian Who Was Who* (Toronto: Trans-Canada Press, 1934), 85.

14   For a listing of these partnerships, see AM, CP, P 5145, folder 2, "Honourable Colin H. Campbell, K.C., F.R.C.I., 1859–1914" undated.

15   AM, CP, P 5145, folder 2, "Honourable Colin H. Campbell, K.C., F.R.C.I., 1859–1914," undated. See also, *Manitoba Pictoral and Biographical, Deluxe Supplement VI* (Winnipeg: S.J. Clarke Publishing, 1913), 75–77.

16   On changing conceptions of the region, see Doug Owram, *Promise of Eden: The Canadian Expansionist Movement and the Image of the West, 1856–1900* (Toronto: University of Toronto Press 1980), 48. See also, B. Kaye and D.W. Moodie, "Geographical Perspectives on the Canadian Prairies," in Richard Allen, ed., *A Region in the Mind: Interpreting the Western Canadian Plains* (Regina: Canadian Plains Research Center 1973), 17–46; and D.W. Moodie, "Early British Images of Rupert's Land," in Richard Allen, ed., *Man and Nature on the Prairies* (Regina: Canadian Plains Research Center 1976), 1–20.

17   Bernard Porter, *The Lion's Share: A Short History of British Imperialism, 1850–1995* (London and New York: Longman 1996), 28–118.

18   For a discussion of this period, see Alan Cairns, "Empire, Globalization, and the Fall and Rise of Diversity," in Cairns, et al., eds., *Citizenship, Diversity, and Pluralism: Canadian and Comparative Perspectives* (Montreal and Kingston: McGill-Queen's University Press, 1999). See also E.J. Hobsbawm, *The Age of Empire* (New York: Vintage 1987), 35 and 59; P.J. Cain and A.G. Hopkins, *British Imperialism, 1688–2000* (London: Longman 2001), 228–242.

19   Adele Perry, "Whose World Was British? Rethinking the 'British World' from an Edge of Empire," in Patricia Grimshaw and Stuart Macintyre, eds., *Britishness Abroad: Transnational Movements and Imperial Culture* (Melbourne: Melbourne University Press, 2007), 12.

20   Some local men and women accepted such a position. See, for example, John W. Dafoe's editorial in the *Manitoba Free Press*, 16 June 1906; and his, "Western Canada: Its Resources and Possibilities," *American Review of Reviews* 35, 6 (June 1907), 702–26. It was also a more general sentiment among British and other European policy makers. See E.J. Hobsbawm, *The Age of Empire*, 56–73.

21   On the US-British relationship, see Cain and Hopkins, *British Imperialism*, 270–283. For other corroborative discussions of Confederation, see A.A. den Otter, *Civilizing the West: The Galts and the Development of Western Canada* (Edmonton: University of Alberta Press, 1982), 41; and his, *The Philosophy of Railways: The Transcontinental Railway Idea in British North America* (Toronto: University of Toronto Press, 1997), 185–207; Peter J. Smith, "The Ideological Origins of Canadian Confederation," *Canadian Journal of Political Science* 20 (1987): 28.

22   Some of the men listed here are well known. Others are not. All were early proponents of western expansion who used their positions within the government, as newspapermen, and as businessmen to draw attention to the issue. George Brown, for example, was the editor of the *Toronto Globe*. Allan Macdonell was an early expansionist who was instrumental in the development of the North-West Transportation, Navigation and Railway Company. William Macdonell Dawson was a one-time employee of the Crown Lands Department and was involved with Macdonell in the above-mentioned company. Vankoughnet was the president of the Executive Commission and the Commissioner of Lands. Finally, William McDougall was originally the editor of the *North American*, but later merged with and worked as part of the staff of George Brown's *Globe*. See Owram, *Promise of Eden*, 38 and 57. A.A. den Otter has also provided insights into the lives and thoughts of these and other similar individuals. See his *The Philosophy of Railways*.

23 On the survey system, see Gerald Friesen, *The Canadian Prairies: A History* (Toronto: University of Toronto Press, 1987), 182–184.

24 Alan Artibise, *Winnipeg: A Social History of Urban Growth, 1874–1914* (Montreal and Kingston: McGill-Queen's University Press), 61–76

25 Ruben Bellan, *Winnipeg, First Century: An Economic History* (Winnipeg: Queenston House, 1978), 53.

26 Friesen, *The Canadian Prairies*, 275.

27 Bellan, *Winnipeg*, 61.

28 Bellan, *Winnipeg*, 60–61; Friesen, *The Canadian Prairies*, 276.

29 Bellan, *Winnipeg*, 77; David Bercuson also provides insight into the city's increasingly large and diverse industrial sector in *Confrontation at Winnipeg: Labour, Industrial Relations, and the General Strike* (Montreal and Kingston: McGill-Queen's University Press 1990 [1974]), 1–5. For useful contemporary overviews of industry in the city, see Steen and Boyce, *Winnipeg Manitoba and Her Industries* (Chicago and Winnipeg: Steen and Boyce, 1882); C.F. Roland, "Industrial Manitoba," in C.N. Bell, et al., eds., *A Handbook to Winnipeg and the Province of Manitoba* (Winnipeg: W. Sanford Evans, 1909), 57–63.

30 Richard Pomfret has noted that economic development in the West in the years before the turn of the twentieth century probably had more to do with mining, exports of which rose by more than 500 percent than with wheat production, exports of which took off only after 1901. See Pomfret, *The Economic Development of Canada* (Toronto: Methuen 1981), 157; Friesen, *The Canadian Prairies*, 274.

31 Michael Harris (his real name was Michael Hrushka) was a Ukrainian immigrant who arrived in Winnpeg in 1911 and eventually became a labour reporter for the *Winnipeg Free Press*. He later recalled the practice of buying jobs. See AM, Harris Papers, MG 9 A 43. "Excerpts from the Autobiography of Michael Harris," n.d., 49. Friesen mentions the city's role as a regional labour market in *The Canadian Prairies*, 277–278.

32 Bellan, *Winnipeg*, 11.

33 Friesen, *The Canadian Prairies*, 276.

34 Mrs. George Bryce, "Historical Sketch of the Charitable Institutions of Winnipeg," *Manitoba Historical and Scientific Society Transactions* 54 (February 1899): 4.

35 Bryce, "Historical Sketch," 1.

36 Mrs. George Bryce, "Historical Sketch," 1–4; Edith Patterson discusses the General Hospital and those to whom it catered in its early years. See *Winnipeg Free Press*, 1 February 1969 and 15 February 1969.

37 Patterson, *Winnipeg Free Press*, 15 February 1969.

38 Initially these counselling sessions seem to have been carried out by the hospital's organizers. Later organizations like the YMCA often sent their members to visit patients in the hospital and elsewhere. Annual reports of the YMCA throughout the 1880s mention that the organization sent representatives to the hospitals for these purposes. See, for example, AM, P 3797, YMCA, folder 2, *Annual Report 1880-1*, 4; *Annual Report 1882-3*, 2. Mrs. George Bryce, "Historical Sketch of the Charitable Institutions of Winnipeg," 4. Lesley Thomson also discusses the origins of the hospital in her *100 Years of Caring: The History of the Convalescent Home of Winnipeg, 1883–1983* (Winnipeg: Convalescent Home Archives Committee, 1983).

39 Minnie Campbell comments on the origins of the YMCA in AM, CP, P 2503, folder 7, "Historical Sketch of Winnipeg's First Cooking School," n.d. On the origins of the organization see also, AM, P 3797, YMCA, *Annual Report 1880-1*, 2; and, Legislative Library of Manitoba, Historical Scrapbook 8, "Winnipeg's YMCA," 129.

40 AM, P 3797, YMCA, folder 1, *Annual Report 1880-1*, 4.

41   AM, MG 10 B 13, Christian Women's Union, *21ˢᵗ Annual Report of the Christian Women's Union of Winnipeg, 1903*, 1. See also Margaret F. Taffe and Mrs. George Bryce, "Pioneer Work of C.W.U.," in Minnie J.B. Campbell, ed., *Pioneer Winnipeg Women's Work, 1883–1907* (Winnipeg: *Winnipeg Telegram*, 1908), 35–36. This book is a reissue of the *Winnipeg Women's Paper*, which Campbell edited, and the *Winnipeg Telegram* published in 1907 as a part of an effort to raise funds to build and furnish a new YWCA facility.

42   AM, P 2131 The Middlechurch Home of Winnipeg (hereafter MHW), folder 1, *Annual Report 1884*, 4. Minutes and annual reports for the Christian Women's Union are located in the papers of the Middlechurch Home of Winnipeg, in the papers of the Convalescent Home of Winnipeg, and in the papers of the Christian Women's Union. The reason that its papers are found in all of these locations is that, as we shall see, it became transformed, or branched off, into new directions as Winnipeg grew and changed.

43   AM, CP, P 2503, folder 10, "Fifty Years in Winnipeg: Some Data re. Mrs. Colin H. Campbell's Work," [1934].

44   AM, P 2131, MHW, folder 1, *Annual Report 1884*, 4.

45   AM, P 2131, MHW, folder 1, *Annual Report 1884*, 10.

46   AM, P 2131, MHW, folder 1, *Annual Report 1884*, 10.

47   Campbell's role in these classes is mentioned in AM, P2132, MHW, folder 1, *Annual Report 1889*, 4.

48   AM, P 2131, MHW, folder 1, *Annual Report 1891*, 8.

49   AM, P 2131, MHW, folder 1, *Annual Report 1889*, 3.

50   The Christian Endeavor movement was founded in Portland, Maine, in 1881 by Dr. Francis E. Clark. Clark's intent was to strengthen spiritual life and to encourage ordinary men and women to engage in Christian living. Though the movement began in Portland, Maine, two years after its beginning it spread throughout all major cities in the United States and by 1895 had branched into enough nations abroad to merit the establishment of a World Union. Campbell provides insight into this movement in general and in Winnipeg. See AM, CP, P2503, M.J.B. Campbell, "The First Social Survey of Winnipeg, 1893," 2.

51   AM, P664, Social Planning Council of Winnipeg, *Free Kindergarten Annual Report for 1892*, 2. On the Free Kindergarten Association, see also Helen B. Atkinson, "Free Kindergarten," in Campbell, ed., *Pioneer Winnipeg Women's Work*, 40–41.

52   AM, P 664, Social Planning Council of Winnipeg, folder 1, *Free Kindergarten Annual Report 1892*, 1 and 8.

53   AM, P 3854, Young Women's Christian Association, Board of Directors Minutes – Minutes for 6 September 1897.

54   The report of her efforts with "female sufferers" appeared in the *Manitoba Free Press*, 10 August 1908.

55   Campbell was involved with numerous organizations. She was a member of the Women's Art Association, a member of the Art Gallery Association, a charter member of the Aberdeen Association, a member of the Women's Christian Temperance Union, and a member of the first Board of Management of the Margaret Scott Nursing Mission. For a listing of all of her organizational affiliations, see AM, CP, P 5145, folder 2, "51 Years in Winnipeg, 1884–1935," [1935].

56   Imperial Order Daughters of the Empire, *The Imperial Order Daughters of the Empire, Golden Jubilee, 1900–1950* (Toronto: Imperial Order Daughters of the Empire 1950), 1.

57   AM, CP, P 2503, folder 5, "The Imperial Order Daughters of the Empire and Children of the Empire Founded February 13ᵗʰ, 1900, by Mrs. Clark Murray of Montréal: Provincial Chapter of Manitoba, A Brief Historical Sketch by Minnie J.B. Campbell" (hereafter IODE: Brief Historical Sketch), 1929, 2.

58   AM, CP, P2503, folder 5, "IODE: Brief Historical Sketch," 2.

59   AM, CP, P2503, folder 5, "IODE: Brief Historical Sketch," 2.

60 AM, CP, P 2503, folder 5, "IODE: Brief Historical Sketch," 3.

61 AM, CP, P 5145, folder 2, "51 Years in Winnipeg — 1884–1935." Campbell was the subject of a number of articles listing her organizational affiliations and work throughout her life in Winnipeg. Seemingly these articles were part of a more general phenomenon of commemorating the lives of Winnipeg pioneers. When this article appeared in 1935, Campbell still served as a councillor of the National Executive. She also held a variety of honorary posts, including Honorary National Vice President, Honorary Regent of the Fort Garry Chapter, and Honorary Provincial Vice President, from 1926 presumably until her death.

62 This quality of her thinking underlies most of her tracts, articles, speeches, and so forth. See, for example, AM, CP, P 2503, folder 15, "The Supremacy of the Flag," 1911. For other examples, see George Bryce, *Manitoba*, 358; and his *The Canadianization of Western Canada* (Ottawa: The Royal Society of Canada 1910). Other similar views are found in Elliot, *Winnipeg as it is in 1874 and as it was in 1860*; and in, James Elder Steen, *An Illustrated Souvenir of Winnipeg, Manitoba, the Capital of Manitoba and Trade Centre of the Canadian North-West: A Historical and Descriptive Sketch of its Wonderful Growth, Progress, and Prosperity* (Winnipeg: Telegram Printing Company, 1903). Other scholars have mentioned the pervasiveness of these grand visions among late nineteenth- and early twentieth-century Winnipeggers. See, for example, Owram, *Promise of Eden*, 125–167.

63 For Campbell's view, see AM, CP, P 2503, folder 15, "The Supremacy of the Flag," 1911, 2. Thomas Dickens, "Winnipeg, Imperialism, and the Queen Victoria Diamond Jubilee Celebration, 1897" (MA thesis, University of Manitoba, 1982). Robert Wardhaugh has provided an excellent account of imperial sentiment in Winnipeg. See his "'Gateway to Empire': Imperial Sentiment in Winnipeg, 1867–1917," in *Imperial Canada, 1867–1917*, ed. Colin Coates (Edinburgh: University of Edinburgh, 1997), 206–219.

64 AM, CP, P 2503, folder 15, "The Supremacy of the Flag," 1911, 2.

65 Campbell and her sister Daughters of Empire collected and/or produced an enormous quantity of goods for the war effort. In the span of a few months in the fall of 1915, for example, IODE women in Manitoba collected or produced, among other things, 8588 pairs of socks, 122 scarfs, 506 dozen handkerchiefs, 2252 packages of cigarettes, 17 pounds of other tobacco products, 4474 wash cloths, 48,067 surgical wipes, and 593 surgical dressings. Over the course of the entire war, the order in Manitoba raised an astounding $5 million and collected goods estimated to be of a similar value. This information comes from a report that Campbell delivered to the Manitoba Provincial Chapter of the IODE in 1915. See AM, CP, P 2499, folder 6, "Oct. 23rd Meeting of the Prov. Chapter I.O.D.E.," [1915], 3-5; AM, CP, P 2498, folder 2, "Notebook Re. IODE Fort Garry Chapter," 109-116; AM, CP, P 2502, "Prospect and Retrospect I.O.D.E.," 10 August 1920, 3.

66 AM, CP, P2501, folder 1, "Account of Seventh Annual Meeting of the Provincial Chapter of Manitoba Imperial Order Daughters of the Empire," 1919, 13.

67 This description of the North End of Winnipeg comes from John Marlyn's *Under the Ribs of Death* (Toronto: McClelland and Stewart, 1957), 11. Maryln was a Hungarian immigrant who grew up in this area of the city.

68 For insight into Woodsworth's perspective, see his *Strangers Within Our Gates* (Toronto: University of Toronto Press, 1972 [1909]) and *My Neighbour* (Toronto: University of Toronto Press, 1972 [1911]); see also Charles Gordon (a.k.a. Ralph Connor), *The Foreigner: A Tale of Saskatchewan* (Toronto: Westminister Company, 1909); University of Manitoba Archives and Special Collections, MSS 56, Gordon Papers," box 30, folder 9, "The Eastern European Immigrant," 1912; William Ivens, "Canadian Immigration" (MA thesis, University of Manitoba, 1909); G.F. Chipman, "Winnipeg: The Melting Pot," *Canadian Magazine* 5 (September 1909): 413–414; and his "Winnipeg: The Refining Process," *Canadian Magazine* 33 (October 1909): 548–554.

69 *Manitoba Free Press*, 11 April 1911.

70 These attitudes underlay much of Campbell's efforts. See, for example, AM, CP, P 2501, folder 6, "Toronto Convention," 1921.

71 AM, P2503, CP, folder 9, M.J.B. Campbell, "The First Social Survey of Winnipeg – 1893," [1930?], 2.

72 For a discussion of this succession of institutions, see City of Winnipeg Archives, City Clerk, *City of Winnipeg Municipal Manual 1921*, 1921, 40. See also AM, P2503, CP, folder 9, M.J.B. Campbell, "The First Social Survey of Winnipeg – 1893," [1930?], 3–4.

73 A survey of city council minutes reveals that up through the first decade of the twentieth century funding from the city for reform organizations was sporadic. After that time, however, city council approved grants of between $2000 and $3000 per month to the Social Welfare Association.

74 There are a host of works directed toward understanding the origins of this conception of gender. See, for example, Allison Jagger, *Feminist Politics and Human Nature* (Sussex: Rowman and Allanheld, 1983), 27–50. Leonore Davidoff and Catherine Hall have argued that the increasing tendency to organize social life according to this conceptualization was central to middle-class formation. See their *Family Fortunes: Men and Women of the English Middle Class, 1780–1850* (Chicago: University of Chicago Press, 1987). In Canada, historians have been less concerned with understanding the origins of this conceptualization of masculinity and femininity, though they have been aware of its existence in Canada's past. See, for example, Ramsay Cook and Wendy Mitchinson, eds., *The Proper Sphere: Women's Place in Canadian Society* (Toronto: Oxford University Press 1976); Linda Kealey, ed., *A Not Unreasonable Claim: Women and Reform in Canada, 1880s–1920s* (Toronto: Women's Press, 1979); and Janet Guilford and Suzanne Morton, eds., *Separate Spheres: Women's Worlds in the 19th Century Maritimes* (Fredericton: Acadiensis Press, 1994).

75 Alvin Finkel, Nancy Christie, Mimi Abramovitz, and others suggest that these were important qualities of reform and welfare states. See, for example, Finkel, *Social Policy and Practice in Canada*; Christie, *Engendering the State*; Struthers, *The Limits of Affluence*; Little, *No Car, No Radio, No Liquor Permit*; Abramovitz, *Regulating the Lives of Women*; Gordon, *Women, the State and Welfare*; Jane Ursel, *Private Lives, Public Policy: 100 Years of Intervention in the Family* (Toronto: Women's Press, 1992); Jane Lewis, *The Voluntary Sector, the State, and Social Work in Britain* (Brookfield: Elgar, 1995).

76 Carolyn Strange has mentioned that contemporaries believed that single, wage-earning women were both endangered and endangering. See her *Toronto's Girl Problem: The Perils and Pleasures of the City, 1880–1930* (Toronto: University of Toronto Press, 1995).

77 Mary Kinnear has provided a study of a woman similar to Minnie Campbell named Margaret MacWilliams. This quote comes from her *Margaret MacWilliams: An Interwar Feminist* (Toronto: University of Toronto Press, 1996), 9. Campbell discussed her views about women's "proper" place with an interviewer in 1912. See *The Winnipeg Telegram*, 14 September 1912. It is worth noting that, in comparing Campbell to Dafoe and Gordon, it is evident that, ironically, both men were more willing to part company with these liberal precepts than was Campbell.

78 *Winnipeg Telegram*, 14 September 1912. There is also evidence to suggest that Campbell did not significantly alter her position in the ensuing years. In the last months of World War I, even after Manitoba women had obtained the right to vote, she persisted in imploring her counterparts in the order to remain committed to distancing themselves from the political realm. For her views, see AM, CP, P 2500, folder 4, "Impressions of the Eighteenth Annual Meeting of the Canadian National Chapter of the Imperial Order Daughters of the Empire and Children of the Empire, May 27–31st, 1918," 2.

79 *Winnipeg Telegram*, 14 September 1912.

80 This quote comes from Seth Koven and Sonya Michel, "Womanly Duties: Maternalist Politics and the Origins of Welfare States in France, Germany, Great Britain, and the United States, 1880–1920," *American Historical Review* 95 (October 1990): 1079.

81 Mariana Valverde, *The Age of Light, Soap and Water* (Toronto: University of Toronto Press, 2008), 166–7. This line of thinking is apparent in Nancy Christie and Michael Gauvreau, *A Full-Orbed Christianity: The Protestant Churches and Social Welfare in Canada, 1900–1940* (Montreal and Kingston: McGill-Queen's University Press, 1996), 117; for similar findings in other contexts, see Seth Koven and Sonya Michel, "Womanly Duties," 1076–1108. See also Koven and Michel, *Mothers of a New World: Maternalist Politics and the Origins of Welfare States* (New York: Routledge, 1993); Theda Skocpol, *Protecting Soldiers and Mothers: The Political Origins of Social Policy in the United States* (Cambridge: Harvard University Press, 1992); Gisela Bock and Pat Thane, eds., *Maternity and Gender Policies: Women and the Rise of European Welfare States, 1880s–1950s* (New York: Routledge, 1991), esp. 1–20.

82 Koven and Michel, "Womanly Duties, 1079.

83 David Burley, "The Social Organization of Self-Employment in Winnipeg, Manitoba, 1881–1901," *Histoire Sociale/Social History* 31 (May 1998): 35–69.

84 On these broad developments, see E.J. Hobsbawm, *The Age of Empire* (New York: Vintage, 1987), 34–55.

85 On the feminization of retail and office work, see Graham S. Lowe, "Mechanization, Feminization, and Managerial Control in the Early Twentieth-Century Canadian Office," in *On the Job: Confronting the Labour Process in Canada*, eds. Craig Heron and Robert Storey (Montreal and Kingston: McGill-Queen's University Press, 1986), 177–209; David Monod, *Store Wars: Shop Keeping and the Culture of Mass Marketing, 1890–1939* (Toronto: University of Toronto Press, 1996), 47–49, 88–90, and 114–115. On women wage workers in the city, see Linda Kealey, "'No Special Protection—No Sympathy': Women's Activism in the Canadian Labour Revolt of 1919," in *Class, Community and the Labour Movement: Wales and Canada, 1850–1930*, eds. Deian Hopkin and Gregory Kealey (St. John's: CCLH, 1989), 134–159, and her *Enlisting Women for the Cause: Women, Labour, and the Left in Canada, 1890–1920* (Toronto: University of Toronto Press, 1998).

86 AM, MG 14 B2, George William Baker Papers, "Diary of G.W. Baker in Winnipeg, 1881–1882," 6-8; AM, P5386, Brown – Journal, 15–30 May 1883. There are a few surviving entries of what appears to have been a much lengthier journal. The information about conditions in Winnipeg appear in an undated entry. It is clear, however, that the surviving entries all were written between 15 and 30 May 1883. George Bryce, "Early Days in Winnipeg," *Transactions of the Historical and Scientific Society of Manitoba*, Series 1, 46 (1894), 1–8; United Church Archives, PP4 f, folder c, George Bryce, "The Gospel in Western Canada," 1911; George H. Ham, *Reminiscences of a Raconteur* (Toronto: Musson, 1921), 29.

87 AM, P267, Emma Louisa Averill, "A Journey From Liverpool to the Far West of Manitoba, 1880," 1881, 16. George Elliot also mentioned the prevalence of Aboriginal people in the city at its incorporation. See his *Winnipeg as it is in 1874 and as it was in 1860* (Winnipeg: *Manitoba Free Press*, 1874), 44–45.

88 Averill, "A Journey From Liverpool," 18.

89 See, for example, M.J.B. Campbell's description in AM, P2503, folder 9, CP, "The First Social Survey of Winnipeg," 1930; see also AM, P 2503, folder 9, "My First Legislative Opening, March 19, 1885," 1934.

90 The number of rituals, commemorations, and celebrations that were carried out to celebrate the empire in Winnipeg in the late nineteenth and early twentieth century is too vast to mention here. Thomas Dickens mentions some of them in his "Winnipeg, Imperialism, and the Queen Victoria Diamond Jubilee Celebration, 1897" (MA thesis, University of Manitoba, 1982), esp. 146–183. See also AM, P5386, Brown – Journal, 15–30 May 1883. There are a few surviving entries of what appears to have been a much lengthier journal. The information about the Queen's birthday in Winnipeg appears in an undated entry. It is clear, however, that the surviving entries all were written between 15 and 30 May 1883. Bryce mentions the emphasis on English fashions in his *Manitoba*, 358. George Elliot also made note of these tendencies in his *Winnipeg*, 40–42. Phillip Buckner mentions festivities in Winnipeg in his "Casting Daylight Upon Magic: Deconstructing the Royal Tour of 1901 to Canada," in *The British World*, eds. Bridge and Fedorowich, 158–189.

91   Steen and Boyce, *Winnipeg, Manitoba and Her Industries* (Chicago and Winnipeg: Steen and Boyce, 1882), 130. See, for example, Bryce, *Manitoba: Its Infancy, Growth, and Present Condition* (London: Gilbert and Rivington, 1882). Especially revealing are his discussions of these institutions in the last two chapters of the book (entitled "Ten Years of Progress, 1871–1881" and "The Attractions of Manitoba" respectively). Manitoba Club, *The Act and Incorporation, Constitution, Rules and Regulations and List of Members of the Manitoba Club, Established 1874* (Winnipeg: Stovel Printers, 1897). Contemporary newspaper reports also emphasized these organizations. See, for example, *Manitoba Free Press*, 20 July 1874, for a discussion of the Manitoba Rifle Association; *Manitoba Free Press*, 22 August 1874, for a similarly oriented account of Manitoba College. Approximately a decade later the tone of many articles was unchanged. See *Manitoba Free Press*, 3 January 1885, for a discussion of the Commercial Travelers Association; *Manitoba Free Press*, 12 February 1885, for an extended discussion of the city's Masonic Lodge. The lodge's "spacious dimensions and elegant appearances" were said to rival those of lodges in Britain. See *Manitoba Free Press*, 11 February 1885, for an account of the Literary Society; and *Manitoba Free Press*, 18 March 1885, for a discussion of Manitoba's "up-to-date" asylum.

92   Steen and Boyce, *Winnipeg*, 130.

93   See, for example, Peter Flora and Arnold J. Heidenheimer, *The Development of Welfare States in Europe and America* (New York, NY: Transaction Books, 1981); Douglas E. Alfred, *The Emergence of Welfare States* (Oxford: Basil Blackwell, 1986); Abram de Swaan, *In Care of the State: Healthcare, Education and Welfare in Europe and the USA in the Modern Era* (New York: Oxford University Press, 1988); John Charlton, "Class Struggle and the Origins of State Welfare Reform," in *Class Struggle and Social Welfare*, eds. Michael Lavalette and Gerry Mooney (New York: Routledge, 2000), 52–70; Bernard Harris, *The Origin of the British Welfare State: Social Welfare in England and Wales, 1800–1945* (New York: Palgrave, 2004).

94   Minnie Campbell mentioned this quality of the city in AM, CP, P 2503, "My First Legislative Opening, March 19, 1885," 1934. These quotations come from George Baker. See AM, MG 14 B2, George William Baker Papers, "Diary of G.W. Baker in Winnipeg, 1881–1882," 1–10.

95   Artibise mentions this in Artibise, *Winnipeg*, 247. See also Friesen, *The Canadian Prairies*, 277–278.

96   AM, MG14 B2, George William Baker papers, "Diary of G.W. Baker in Winnipeg, 1881–1882," 9.

97   Lesley Thomson, *100 Years of Caring*, 9.

98   Blanchard, *Winnipeg 1912* (Winnipeg: University of Manitoba Press, 2005), 9 and 13–14. The problem of determining how many people actually were in the city at a given time was constant throughout the city's early history. In 1872, for example, before there were 300 permanent residents, the *Manitoba Free Press* undertook an enumeration of who was in the as yet unincorporated "city" in early November. The enumerators found that there were 1467 people, of whom 1019 were male and 448 were female. The bulk of these people were transient workers. Nevertheless, all reports indicate that the gender imbalance was constant throughout the late nineteenth and early twentieth centuries. See *Manitoba Free Press*, 9 November 1872.

99   Gregory Kealey and Tom Mitchell have shown for the national and Winnipeg contexts respec-
      tively, that the state functioned toward this end. See Gregory S. Kealey, "The Early Years of State
      Surveillance of Labour and the Left in Canada: The Institutional Framework of the Royal Cana-
      dian Mounted Police Security and Intelligence Apparatus, 1918–26," *Intelligence and National
      Security* 8 (July 1993): 129–148; "State Repression of Labour and the Left in Canada in 1914: The
      Impact of the First World War," *Canadian Historical Review* 3 (1992): 283–314; "The Empire
      Strikes Back: The Nineteenth-Century Origins of the Canadian Secret Service," *Journal of the
      Canadian Historical Association* 10 (1999): 2–18. Tom Mitchell has focussed on the late and
      immediately post-World War I years. He nevertheless sees 1919 efforts to sustain a particular
      moral order as the reimposition of the sort of order mentioned above. See his "'To Reach the
      Leadership of this Revolutionary Movement': A.J. Andrews, the Canadian State and the Suppres-
      sion of the Winnipeg General Strike," *Prairie Forum* 18 (Fall 1993): 229–255; and his "'The
      Manufacture of Souls of Good Quality': Winnipeg's 1919 National Conference on Canadian
      Citizenship, English-Canadian Nationalism, and the New Order After the Great War," *Journal
      of Canadian Studies* 31 (Winter 1996–97): 5–28. Other scholars and observers have noted that
      the Royal Canadian Mounted Police in particular was the earliest representative of the state in
      western Canada, and one of their key roles was ensuring respect for private property. See R.C.
      Macleod, "Canadianizing the West: The North-West Mounted Police as Agents of the National
      Policy, 1873–1905," in *Essays on Western History*, ed. Lewis H. Thomas (Edmonton: University of
      Alberta Press, 1976), 103; Sam Steele, *Forty Years in Canada* (Toronto McClelland and Stewart,
      1915), 196–200. Carolyn Strange and Tina Loo have mentioned the force's role as moral regulator
      in their *Making Good: Law and Moral Regulation in Canada, 1867–1939* (Toronto: University of
      Toronto Press, 1997), 3–36.

Empty-handed Constables and Notorious Offenders: Policing an Early Prairie City "According to Order"

Megan Kozminski

One balmy fall evening in Winnipeg, Constable John H. Grady, a dedicated Methodist Irishman of the Winnipeg police force, visited Point Douglas Common "in search of Drunk Indians"[1] to lock up for the evening. After answering a domestic abuse call and returning a lost child home to its family, Grady set back towards the station, somewhat disappointed to be returning "empty-handed" from his night on the beat. A few blocks from the station house he stumbled over the "notorious" Charlotte Spence lying drunk on the sidewalk. Unable, or unwilling, to remove Spence from the street on his own, Grady employed a dray to transport the prisoner back to the station. In the meantime, he made a final visit to hotel row to ensure that all the licensed saloons and barrooms were appropriately shut down for the evening. A tipsy but reputable local merchant requested that Grady escort him home, as he felt unsafe on the dark streets of the city on his own. Constable Grady eventually returned to the police station around 3:00 a.m. to compose and record his official occurrence report. Reflecting upon the duties he had performed that evening in 1879, he began: "Patrolled the streets according to order and found…"

Sensational descriptions of Canadian frontier towns and cities often emphasize the lawless nature of the "wild west" and depict law enforcement officers as the "brave defenders" of peace, order, and good government.[2] Though it was the most prominent urban centre in the Canadian West during the late nineteenth century, the city of Winnipeg also had a reputation for being "wild" and "wicked."[3] Yet there is little evidence to support clichés of Winnipeg as an uncontrollable or notably uninhibited city in its early days. For the most part, what the municipal police "bravely defended" within the urban centre were middle- and upper-class ideals of order and morality.

The role of the Winnipeg force during the late nineteenth century was not limited to coercive activities; local constables were also called on to perform social service functions, addressing the basic needs of a limited assortment of destitute or mentally ill persons. The identity, work, and culture of Winnipeg's earliest police officers was, therefore, somewhat conflicted. Police were expected to uphold the moral order of the city according to political and elitist interests, yet encouraged to serve the needs of the diverse and expanding urban community; the reality of life on the beat was multi-faceted: unpredictable, mundane, challenging, physically arduous, hazardous, discretionary, and sometimes exciting. Faced with less than ideal working conditions and the limited independence associated with the status and title of "policeman," local officers shared a common identity within society and worked together to overcome the obstacles associated with their work and social position.

The daily records of Constable John Grady expose the fascinating character of policing "on the job" in early Winnipeg. Grady's activities on the beat are well documented and candidly reported throughout the Occurrence report log books of the Winnipeg police. His perception and policing of disorder are particularly revealing; Grady frequently reported on a variety of offences, characters, events, or personalities he encountered on the beat and described his response to such in an articulate and personal manner. Furthermore, his descriptions of daily life as a member of the Winnipeg police force reflect the social boundaries that the Winnipeg force patrolled "according to order" during the period.

The Origins of Policing in Winnipeg

The nineteenth-century development of the Red River Settlement and the village of Fort Garry proceeded rather modestly. The first regular police force in the colony was a volunteer corps modelled after the British Army. This military force was replaced after ten years by a small force of constables and volunteer watchmen.[4] With the town of Winnipeg firmly established by 1870, the founding of a municipal police force in 1874 was one of city council's earliest orders of business: by-laws no. 4 and no. 10 relate to the appointment of the first chief of police and police constables in the city.[5] The chief of police was in command of the constables, and management of the force originally lay in the hands of the Licence and Police Committee of city council. In 1883, the Winnipeg Board of Police Commissioners (comprised of the mayor, the judge of the county court, a police magistrate, and a recording secretary) was founded and empowered with administration of the force.[6]

Within a year of its founding, the Winnipeg police force increased in size to five constables (in addition to the chief), and the officers were uniformed and armed with badges, batons, whistles, "wrist-snappers," and revolvers.[7] The police force developed alongside the flourishing city during the late nineteenth century, swelling to a size of forty-five in 1884 and later levelling off at around thirty full-time constables by the turn of the century. Though the force remained small in size throughout much of the late nineteenth century, it served as an important branch of civic administration.

The need to maintain order in the city of Winnipeg was influenced by the extent and nature of population growth during the period. At the time of its incorporation, Winnipeg consisted of approximately 2000 people, who were predominantly French, English, Aboriginal, and Métis. By 1880, the population had approximately tripled, and by 1886, it had grown to over 20,000. The city's inhabitants numbered approximately 40,000 by the turn of the century.[8] The nature of the city's growth was also significant; immigration was the major determinant of expansion, and natural population increase was largely limited by a shortage of women. The character of the city was further influenced by the large floating population, which predominantly consisted of single men in search of work.[9]

The combination of immigrants, labourers, transients, and strangers that descended on the city contributed to its profile as a "wild west" frontier town and to local elites' anxious desire to order and control the diverse population; however, little evidence of escalating crime exists to justify the concern of the elites. There was a five-fold increase in the population of the city between 1879 and 1889, yet the incidence of crime increased by only one-third (see Table 1). Winnipeg's reputation as a "wild" city, and the social anxieties of elites, reformers, and middle classes that emerged during the period, were relatively unfounded.

Table 1: Population Growth and the Crime Rate in Winnipeg, 1879–1899

	1879	1889	1899
Population of the city[10]	4113	21,328	40,112
No. of arrests per year[11]	656	938	1137

SOURCES: Alan Artibise, *Winnipeg: A Social History of Urban Growth, 1874–1914* (Montreal: McGill-Queen's University Press, 1975); Annual report of the chief of police for 1879 (CWAR, Council Communications, no. 1796.5 [8 January 1880]); Winnipeg police arrest reports (Winnipeg Police Museum, Arrest reports [1889, 1899]).

Facilitating the policing and regulation of the expanding urban community were a series of by-laws passed by city council. The early force was responsible for the day-to-day enforcement of licensing by-laws, by-laws pertaining to the obstruction of sidewalks, dangerous building practices or materials near streets and sidewalks, and "furious" driving of bicycles or drays. The police records reveal that officers were also actively involved in detecting and reporting public nuisances.[12]

From its very inception, however, the predominant activity of the Winnipeg police force was the monitoring of public order and morality. Morality offences were not formally defined by a municipal by-law until the turn of the century. The

"By-law of the City of Winnipeg relating to Public Morals," pertaining to begging, drunkenness, vagrancy, insulting language, gambling, prostitution, and "indecency," was passed on 8 May 1899.[13] It vaguely identified a wide variety of indecent, immoral, and disorderly activities and empowered the police and courts to penalize offenders. By-law No. 1599 formally decreed the moral policies that the police had been actively enforcing throughout the preceding quarter century.

Police Work and Culture

The policemen of the late nineteenth century were appointed not only to impose moral order on the Winnipeg population, but also to promote the ideal of a powerful yet respectable working man through the "exaggerated masculinity" of their appearance.[14] Notions of respectable masculinity determined who was appointed to municipal police forces across the country. Policing was considered to be a "job for real men,"[15] who had the strength, health, and authority to maintain order, yet who were also deserving, sober, and steady in their character and manner.[16] In their search, urban forces often looked to men with military experience. Many qualities possessed by soldiers, such as obedience and loyalty, were thought to be desirable—as well as applicable—to a career in policing.[17] While the physical endurance or strength of younger men was often desired, the maturity and experience that older men brought to the forces was also indispensable. Most Canadian municipal policemen came from the working or lower middle classes, and their ages generally ranged from twenty to fifty years.[18]

Becoming a police officer in late nineteenth-century Winnipeg shared commonalities with other towns and cities in Canada. Men appointed to the Winnipeg police force were tall, brawny, and imposing in stature.[19] They ranged in age from twenty-three to fifty years, with the largest percentage of men aged between thirty and thirty-nine years. The western migration of men from Ontario and Nova Scotia significantly affected the composition of the force. An overwhelming number of early Winnipeg policemen were Canadian-born, Anglo-Saxon, and Anglo-Celtic Protestants.[20] Many of the men touted some past military or policing experience, and the majority had married prior to their move west.[21] Several historians suggest that the late-nineteenth-century Winnipeg police exhibited a specific fondness for Scots; however, there were a significant number of Irish and British men who also worked as police officers.[22] In the Canadian census records of both 1881 and 1891, less than one-half of the officers registered were of Scottish ancestry.

The Winnipeg police force experienced a high turnover rate of constables throughout much of the late nineteenth century.[23] One of the first two men appointed a police constable in 1874 resigned after only two weeks of service.[24] As the force increased to over thirty men during the "boom years" between 1880 and 1882, there were at least twelve resignations. While a handful of officers served four, five, or as many as twelve years on the Winnipeg force, significantly more men served between two months and two years.

Constable John Grady was of Methodist and Irish ancestry, and his name first appears in the record books of the Winnipeg police force in late 1878.[25] Grady was born in New Brunswick and joined the force when he was thirty-two years old, at a time when the force was in its infancy and consisted of only a handful of men. Little information is available about his professional background, such as whether or not he had any prior experience in policing or in the military. Grady eventually discovered that the life of a policeman was a challenging and exhausting one; he resigned his position on the force in December 1881 after approximately three years of service. Following his resignation, Grady became the proprietor of the British Lion Hotel on Main Street.[26]

A variety of factors contributed to the high turnover rate of the Winnipeg police and the constant shortage of men on the force. Drill exercises, which were implemented in the attempt to strengthen the resolve of constables who worked the beat, combined with long shifts of ten to twelve hours to physically exhaust many officers.[27] Concerns about the weather, working conditions, and illness dominated resignation letters. The relatively low salaries of policemen and the high cost of living in the city also contributed to a constant shortage of men on the force. Inflation made it increasingly difficult for policemen to live off their wages, especially those with families to support. Upon resigning from the force, one constable apologetically explained that he could not make enough income to pay rent, buy fuel, and support his family in the city, and that he had "accordingly accepted an offer of a more remunerative situation in Emerson."[28]

Beginning in 1875, there were often more constables on night patrol than during the day, due to the chief's concern that there was "more danger to be feared in the still hour of the night to life and property than in broad day."[29] Walking the beat at night, and often alone, was wearing on the physical energy and mental determination of police officers. Finding the demands of night patrol overwhelming, one constable resigned his position on the force after only two months of service, stating that "I have found the night work very wearing and trying to my constitution."[30]

During the coldest periods of the year, constables often had little to report other than the challenges of extreme weather: "the coldest of the night was the greatest obstacle I had to encounter."[31] The challenges of policing were also little improved by the "comforts" of the police station house. The original station house was well known for its poor condition; Chief Murray petitioned the city council throughout the late 1870s and early 80s for improvements to the officers' sleeping quarters, prison cells, and the ventilation and insulation of the station building.[32] Though the chief stated his concern about the health of the men and prisoners who were confined to the decrepit structure on several occasions, city council was slow to respond. The state of the station house, described by one officer as "primitive,"[33] remained so abysmal that it served as a deterrent to offenders. During the summer of 1881, the *Winnipeg Daily Times* warned its readers: "Every cell in the provincial jail is let. This should be a solemn warning to offenders of the law, as they will have to rusticate in the cells at the police station until a vacancy occurs."[34] After the new police station was built in 1883, conditions of station duty were relatively improved. The significant amount of time that officers were expected to work, sleep, and be on call in the station, however, remained a challenging aspect of life on the force.

Despite the hazards associated with police work in the late nineteenth century, many policemen reflected positively on their experiences with the Winnipeg force, wrote fondly of fellow officers, or tendered their resignation with feelings of regret. One constable's regretful resignation in 1883 included substantial praise and appreciation of the Winnipeg force: "The kindness and courtesy of the officers ... is all that can be desired ... *the harmony amongst the men* is a matter of remark as it is seldom that men are found to be working in as much unison as the constables of the Winnipeg Police Force."[35]

The shared experiences of maintaining order in the city seemed to quickly cement the bonds between members of the Winnipeg police. Constables often came to rely upon each other for assistance with difficult or dangerous situations or suspects during their policing careers. The challenges of beat patrol, the small size of the force (especially in the early years), and the cramped police quarters further contributed to close and lasting connections between officers. The policemen were also governed by a code of conduct that collectively regulated their behaviour. Reports of Winnipeg constables suggest that the values of order, sobriety, and morality that the force represented and enforced on the streets of the city were mirrored by officers' own belief systems.

Many early Winnipeg policemen seemed to take pleasure in, and appreciate, aspects of their work. A sense of pride is communicated in officers' reports in response to arrests of "notorious" criminals, drunks, or disreputable characters. Constable

Grady openly expressed disappointment when he returned "empty-handed" to the station after a night on the beat.[36] Many officers also made noticeable efforts to record the variety of social services they provided to the community, from kindly rescuing homeless or transient strangers during the winter to personally walking children home who were wandering alone around the streets of city.

Further contributing to the "harmony amongst the men" were the shared social positions and aspirations of the officers with respect to class and status. As "working-class aspirants to middle-class independence,"[37] Winnipeg policemen of the late nineteenth century collectively situated themselves safely within the lower middle class, which had both its advantages and disadvantages. The liminal identity of the class position, betwixt the labouring classes and the more secure middle classes, helped to perpetuate the culture and identity of policemen as a professional group. Yet their position between social classes also served to socially isolate the officers from broader society: a policeman was never really able to dissociate himself from his role as a "police officer" because his personal identity and character were inherently defined by his membership in the force. Several factors testify to at least some degree of social isolation from the urban populace: the police force was relatively small and shared no obvious associations with religious, cultural, or fraternal societies or associations; and the population of the city (especially the working class) was ethnically diverse, and strong class polarizations quickly evolved during the period.

Evidence suggests that the duties performed by police officers went largely unappreciated by the urban community at large. In one of his annual reports, Chief Murray recognized the demanding and unrewarding nature of life on the force: "Few people unless they have taken the pains to study and examine the life and duties of a patrolman have the remotest idea of what is expected of him, of the hardships and dangers he has to undergo.... he is expected to patrol the streets ... whether in rain, storm or sunshine. Not only is he expected to care for and protect the lives and property of the citizens while they sleep, but he must be present at all times and on all occasions."[38] The constables and chiefs of the Winnipeg force, however, made significant efforts to gain appropriate recognition and compensation for their efforts; they petitioned city council to raise their wages on more than one occasion during the period. The *Winnipeg Daily Times* supported the appeal made by the policemen in late 1881: "The police have signed a petition to the council asking for an increase of pay. They say the commonest labourer can earn $2.50 a day, while they have to work day and night for $1.66. Their position is certainly a responsible and also a dangerous one, and it is nothing but fair that they should be paid in accordance with the times."[39] In a letter submitted to city council in 1882, seven constables repeated the effort, specifically requesting that their monthly stipend be increased from sixty to eighty dollars. They pointed to the fact that the police of Minneapolis and St. Paul made over eighty dollars per month, and that the cost of living was comparatively lower over the border.

The efforts of the members of the Winnipeg force were rewarded with an increase in pay by the end of 1882. The city council also implemented a new resolution to encourage men to become career policemen. The resolution stipulated that after each period of one-half year, patrolmen would receive a bonus of ten dollars per month for the preceding six months of service, so long as they continued to serve on the force.

Maintaining Social and Moral Order

The Winnipeg police imposed its view of moral order upon the civic population primarily through the regulation of activities related to alcohol, prostitution, and public behaviour.[40] While on duty, a constable visited a routine set of locations, many of which were within the boundaries of his designated beat. The urban sites that Constable Grady and his fellow officers most commonly visited included the train station, "the flats," the immigrant sheds, Point Douglas commons, the river bank, disorderly houses, "half breed" ranches and shanties, and "out west" where the houses of prostitution were located. Grady described frequenting these locations in response to the orders of the chief, the requests of citizens, or at his own discretion. Members of the force arrested intoxicated individuals on the streets, and many individuals were also removed from hotels, saloons, or private residences. Records available for selected years during the late nineteenth century reveal that drunk and disorderly offences prompted the majority of arrests made by the Winnipeg police.

The police also made consistent efforts to regulate prostitution within the city throughout the period. Arrests made for inhabiting, frequenting, visiting, or keeping houses of ill fame (or disorderly houses) were second in frequency to alcohol-related offences. Rather than arresting individual offenders, however, the police often conducted raids on houses of ill fame and "pulled" all of the inhabitants at one time. In November of 1880, for example, one constable reported that he "went in company with Chief Murray and other members of the police force at 8:30 to assist in pulling the Houses out west."[41]

Unlike alcohol- and prostitution-related arrests, other types of offences were less predictable and common. Though they rose between 1876 and 1879, the arrest statistics for assault and vagrancy remained relatively steady for most of the period.

Property crime exhibited a rather consistent increase and surpassed prostitution-related arrests in 1889 to become the second-largest category of offence.

While maintaining the moral order of the urban populace was the main responsibility of Winnipeg constables, an array of other unpredictable, exciting, and even bizarre events also kept policemen occupied. While on beat patrol, Constable Grady often encountered runaway teams of horses, furious drivers, and other disorderly behaviour which made the streets of the frontier city dangerous for community members. It was not uncommon for Grady to chase down these anxious culprits on foot.

Grady and his fellow officers also had to track and capture prisoners who escaped from the station house. Two days subsequent to one prisoner's original arrest for "wearing women's clothes" on 26 September 1879, Grady reported: "Francis made his escape between 8 and 9 p.m. we could find no trace of him."[42] Grady continued his search for the missing prisoner out west, and the prisoner was eventually re-arrested and subjected to an investigation into his sexual identity. On 11 October 1879, Grady's occurrence report reads: "Frances the Mafridite was examined this afternoon by the Mayor and a doctor from Toronto in company with John McTavish of the HBC they pronounce him or her a woman."[43]

Opportunities to conduct unusual chases, searches, and raids were occasionally dangerous. On one such occasion, Constable Grady reported that he was assaulted while trying to make an arrest: "I arrested one Indian for drunk and fighting when a Squaw and two other Indians got me down and tore my pants and otherwise abused me I finally captured two and brought them to the station."[44] Determined to make an arrest, Grady managed to capture his two assailants despite his injured condition and without the help of any other officers. Grady was more suspicious of danger on one particular evening in November 1880, when he was called to arrest a drunk man who had drawn his revolver in the St. Nicholas Hotel. After calling for backup from a fellow constable, Grady was able to apprehend and arrest the offender. It took the strength of both constables Huston and Grady to transport the prisoner, who "resisted the whole way down to the station."[45]

Beat patrol, however, was not always a very exciting or adventurous undertaking. The mundane details of urban life often consumed officers, whose beats proved less than disorderly on any given date. On many evenings, Grady filed occurrence reports on events such as the arrival time of the trains, people out walking on the streets, or rooms and houses with their lights on late into the night. The daily reports of Constable Grady and other policemen also contain numerous descriptions of the social service activities that occupied a significant portion of officers' time on duty.

Like other early Canadian police forces, the Winnipeg force functioned in an era preceding the rise of social service agencies, and as a result, policing was forced to encompass various social service roles. The service most commonly provided by the Winnipeg police force was the recovery of missing or lost children. Parents and concerned family members approached the police and provided them with details concerning missing children with surprising regularity. In 1886 the police were involved in the search for or recovery of up to ten children per month. In one report, the complainant Norman Mathew reported a neighbourhood child named Gertie Hooper lost from 14 Ellen Street: "Gertie is tastefully dressed and gets lost frequently and is four years of age."[46] Children registered as missing or lost generally ranged in age from sixteen months to thirteen years, and almost all were located and safely returned home.[47]

The Winnipeg force was also called upon to assist missing or lost adults; reports of missing husbands, wives, or grown children were often brought to the attention of the police. Mrs. Flett of St. Andrew's reported losing her twenty-one-year-old daughter to the city in November of 1886: "Caroline Flett came to town about 2 months ago with the intention of returning home soon after but has not yet returned."[48]

The early Winnipeg police force provided general services related to the health and welfare of the urban community as well. Many officers on the beat dealt with requests for directions or an escort to the residences or offices of local doctors. Seriously ill or incapacitated community members often relied on the police to gain admittance to the local hospital. In January 1887, a phone call from the Rossin House alerted the police to a very sick man residing in the hotel. In response, the police sergeant received permission to admit the man to the hospital and helped to arrange a ride for him. The reports indicate that the sick man desperately required the help of the police as "he had no funds or any friends in the city."[49] In June 1880, a constable described going to the hospital by order of the sergeant to retrieve a mentally ill patient by the name of Davis. Upon returning to the police station with Davis, the constable charged him with "Being Luney."[50] The majority of persons suffering from "insanity" during the period were charged by the police and locked up in the provincial jail.

Occasionally, constables were also responsible for delivering provisions to institutions and families in need. In March of 1879, Constable Lawler describes distributing bread to the Winnipeg General Hospital (sixty loaves), St. Boniface Hospital (forty loaves), and eight families (ten loaves each).[51] In the annual police report of 1876, the chief of police notes that the charitable and delivery responsibilities of the police force consumed a significant portion of their time: "as sometimes they have to go from one extreme end of the city to the other to perform the work."[52]

The police station house itself served as a community resource during the late nineteenth century. The occurrence reports of the police reveal that the station occasionally served as a shelter or layover destination for transients, travellers, and tramps, as well as the poor and homeless. For example, in 1879 one constable reported that "there was two Half Bread Wimen came to the station at 9pm and told me that they were strangers in the place and had know money to pay for there lodging and there was two men chasing them they appeared frightened so I put them in for the Knight."[53] Despite some of their efforts, the presence, condition, and large number of urban poor eventually overwhelmed the police force and the city during the period.[54] Though the police occasionally hosted the destitute or needy in the station house over an evening, such efforts ultimately provided little benefit to the larger population of dispossessed members within urban society.

Petitions to city council reveal that the benevolent labours of the Winnipeg police were not sufficient in the eyes of the broader community. The Knights of Labour made several complaints to council during the late 1880s regarding the large number of immigrants who were refused entry to the immigrant sheds and were "turned away from the police station without aid."[55] Appealing to city council and the police force's sense of fairness, the Knights of Labour insisted that "in a civilized community, boasting itself as belonging to the Christian religion ... it is a positive disgrace and shame to the City that persons should be compelled to wander the streets."[56]

Evidence suggests that the majority of policemen held a narrow view of their social responsibilities, particularly when it came to domestic violence and family matters considered to be inherently "private." In response to calls to settle domestic disputes made by wives, neighbours, mothers, and children, constables reported that they repeatedly arrived too late to be effective. In December 1879, Constable Grady reported that there was a domestic row reported in the flats, "but as usual we were late."[57] Police responses to domestic issues rarely resulted in any arrests or police action, especially when the dispute was non-alcohol-related: "Mrs McKenzie sent for the police about 10 am when we got there all was quiet she complained of her husband ill using her she wanted us to arrest him but he was sober."[58] Generally police officers exhibited an aversion to "interfering" in domestic life, regardless of the potential hazard posed by the parties involved: "he was abusing his wife braking furniture and raising a general disturbance but ... I thought it best not to interfere."[59]

Reports of child and family abuse were also registered at the police station. A report pertaining to a boy who was temporarily in the care of the police at the station house reads: "He wont go home he says his mother beats him."[60] In cases of family abuse, even those in which officers witnessed disturbances first hand and where children were involved, the police offered guidance more often than they took action. In December 1879, the daughter of Mr. H. Patton turned to the police for help with a family dispute. In response, the officers involved passed on some friendly advice: "H. Pattons daughter at 1230 reported that her father was drunk and abusing her mother and the rest of the family. John and I went to the house and all was quiet but when we went in, things took a fresh start and they all joined in the chorus calling each other liars we gave them a few words of advice and retired from the scene."[61] Members of the community also looked to the police force to discipline their violent, disorderly, or uncontrollable family members. On 9 April 1886, Mr. Alexander McRae asked the police to lock up his son because he "stays out at night."[62] Ten days later, Mr. McRae brought his son down to the station to be locked up as he was "refusing to go to school and acting smart."[63] The police maintained a general practice of non-involvement towards the majority of community members who looked to them to discipline their unruly family members.

Though the Winnipeg police participated in a variety of social service activities, they were barely effective in "serving" the needs of the diverse urban population. Ultimately, the only social services successfully performed by the police during the period were those that served to maintain a larger "web of police legitimation" within the city.[64] Maintaining, in the least, a reputation for caring, compassion, and assistance offered some justification for the authoritative role of the police within the urban community.

Policing Boundaries in Late Nineteenth-Century Winnipeg

Constables who were responsible for patrolling late nineteenth-century Winnipeg "according to order" relied upon their powers of observation, as well as notions of reputation, class, ethnicity, and gender. The annual police reports and daily patrol records of Constable Grady suggest that police work was extremely vulnerable to the discretion, practices, and prejudices of the members of the force.

Evidence presented in the arrest and occurrence reports of the police suggest that class was a significant factor in policing initiatives. Approximately one-half of all persons arrested each year in Winnipeg were labourers and prostitutes. Tradespeople and farmers combined to account for approximately one-fifth of the total yearly arrests made by the police, and less than one-tenth of all persons arrested were identified as vagrants, unemployed, bookkeepers, clerks, boarding house and hotel keepers, and professionals.[65] The *Winnipeg Daily Times* suggested that disorderly behaviour was the common result of a week's worth of work: "The fun-loving mechanic, and other artisans, with a week's pay in their pockets are apt to regard the end of the week as a fitting time for a spree."[66]

While unruly workers and women in the sex trade comprised the majority of arrests (and were the targets of the local press), the middle class and elite were predominantly involved in by-law infractions. Local businesspeople consistently received warnings from the police or the city engineer's office for obstructing streets and sidewalks with goods, building materials, or waste. Prominent men and community leaders, such as J.H. Ashdown, were consistently identified in police reports for by-law infractions, though charges were rarely laid against such offenders.[67] A communication from May of 1884 notes that bad examples were set by several "wealthy and influential" parties in the city, representing Canada Pacific Railway Company, Rutherford and Company, and Minning and Gillespie, and that the police were in the habit of overlooking such behaviour: "in nearly all cases where the parties are wealthy or influential, they have either neglected or refused to pay attention to the matter."[68]

The ethnicity or race of residents seems to have also had an effect on the activities of the police. During the earliest years of the city's history, the police perceived the activities and behaviour of the local Métis population as most offensive and threatening to urban order. The annual reports of the chief of police for 1879 and 1880 reveal that "half breed" was the most common nationality of persons arrested, despite the growing diversity of the city's population.[69]

A significant portion of Constable Grady's patrolling activities were directed at Aboriginal and Métis peoples. Grady monitored the tents and ranches of those he referred to as "half-breeds" more consistently than any other location within the city. In his reports, he described going to such sites to "fish" for offenders and visiting certain locations "in search of drunk Indians."[70] Grady regularly visited the poorer neighbourhoods on his "fishing trips" for drunks, but when the "usual quantity of drunks" partied at an annual summer ball very early into the morning, he showed little concern.[71] Similarly, upon discovering established, respectable male community members drunk on the street outside of a saloon late into the evening, Grady took no regulatory action. Rather the opposite: Constable Grady escorted such men of privilege safely home or to a hotel room and put them to bed for the evening. Grady's occurrence report of one such occasion reads: "Met John Lauder at 4 am he was Drunk he gave me over $300 to keep for him I put him to bed in the International Hotel."[72]

Constable Grady conducted many policing operations based upon his impression of the reputation or notoriety of local community members. He often described disreputable characters in his occurrence reports as "notorious." In June 1879, he noted that he "met the notorious AnnaBella Sutherland she is back to town"; in February 1880, he reported that he "arrested the Notorious Charlotte Spence at 2pm drunk lying on the sidewalk of the Post Office Street"; and he also describes having "met the notorious Mary Trouchie" in July 1880.[73] Grady's "notorious" category may have arisen out of the police force's privileged knowledge of certain individuals as active offenders or recidivists. Yet other Winnipeg constables did not refer to suspects or offenders in the same manner, suggesting that the labelling was predominantly the endeavour of Constable Grady. Grady, however, was not entirely alone in his stigmatization of certain offenders as "notorious"; the local press also participated in the practice. In December 1881, the *Winnipeg Daily Times* reported that a prisoner brought into the station "first thought to be a boy ... was the notorious Mary Trochu."[74] It is likely that the newspaper announcement was based on a direct account provided by the chief or by one of the members of the Winnipeg force responsible for providing the local press with police reports.

Regardless of its origins, the regular attachment of notoriety to suspects and offenders is significant because it testifies to the biases and prejudices of the police that negatively impacted upon the urban community. Not only were women the only individuals labelled "notorious" by Grady, the occurrence reports reveal that he consistently arrested as many, if not more, females as males.[75] Furthermore, Grady exhibited a greater tolerance towards drunk men and "boys" than towards women in a similar condition. For example, on 28 February 1879, Grady was requested to detain Mr. Henry, who was "crazy with whiskey."[76] Grady visited the Henry residence but did not arrest the man, despite his inebriated and potentially dangerous condition. Similarly, in September 1880, Grady reported that "there was quite a number of boys ... on the beer" on his beat, yet he did not report any attempt to arrest or reprimand the men.[77] Virtually every occasion of women drinking, making noise, staying out late at night, or acting disorderly on Grady's beat, however, resulted in an arrest. Grady arrested two women for "using Profane and Indecent language on Main Street" at 10:30 p.m. one evening, yet the "loud talking & swearing done by some Frenchmen" on another occasion went unregulated.[78]

From Grady's perspective on the beat, the most disruptive characters to the moral order of the city were women and, more specifically, prostitutes. Grady consistently monitored the actions and whereabouts of prostitutes and "street walkers." He often included details in his reports regarding the prostitutes he had seen in the city, the hotels they were seen going into, the amount of time they spent in any one location, and the people with whom they were seen associating. Grady failed to police any offences, such as drunkenness, vagrancy, loitering, or disorderliness, as strictly as he did when such offences related to or involved the presence of women in urban spaces. On behalf of the Winnipeg police force and the municipal government, Grady upheld unequal, gendered standards of order on the city streets.

Despite the degree to which Grady allowed notions of reputation, class, race, ethnicity, and gender to influence his work as a policeman, many community members continued to look to him for assistance. Revealing their trust in uniformed officers, some community members handed over cash or valuables to policemen for "safe-keeping." Constables also responded to numerous requests from wives and mothers to protect them from their drunken husbands. Grady responded to many domestic calls, and though he very rarely arrested any of the men for drunkenness or assault, he was often called upon by the same women for assistance.

While Winnipeg officers were no strangers to heavy-handed policing, they were also not without compassion or empathy for their fellow community members. On several occasions, Grady displayed such consideration, giving "a chance" to those characters he would usually lock up. According to one of his reports, Grady and the chief exhibited leniency towards two young Métis girls who were loitering in the private home of a respected community member. The officers' sympathy that evening seems to have been driven by the fact that the girls were young, sober, and put up little fight: "Capt Flanigan sent for the police at 8:30 p.m. to remove some half breeds out of his house I went in company with the chief and found two girls in his room they were sober and quiet and we let them go."[79] Grady also exhibited some compassion for lost children he escorted home, transients and tramps he provided shelter to, or agitated husbands and wives involved in domestic disturbances.

Grady's unequal and somewhat irregular policing of the city yielded similarly uneven appreciation and treatment from the community. Upon his resignation in 1882, city council decided to give Grady one hundred dollars in recognition of his service on the force. A total of four policemen resigned within the same month, yet he was the only man to receive such consideration. In January 1882, the *Winnipeg Daily Times* reported: "Ex-constable Grady desires us to thank the members of the city corporation for the gratuity of $100 voted him at their meeting last evening, on the occasion of his retirement from the Police force."[80] Not long after Grady communicated his gratitude to the city, a concerned citizen sent a letter to council stating that it was unacceptable and illegal to award Grady one hundred dollars of the "peoples money."

Conclusion

Late nineteenth-century Winnipeg police officers were responsible for upholding the reputation, power, and morality of the city centre. Winnipeg constables such as John Grady bore witness to powerful forces of modernization at work during the period; what was once a morally coherent and self-contained community gave way to a modern urban metropolis serving as the gateway to the West. Members of the early Winnipeg police force struggled with the crises of representation and identification that accompanied social change, and as the shifting character of the city initiated specific policing operations by the state and local government, constables' powers of observation and regulation rose to the forefront of policing activities.

As policemen performed their duty to maintain social and moral order and fulfilled various social service responsibilities around the city, their identity, profession, and status became entrenched within local society. A significant portion of the diverse population found them accessible; community members increasingly looked to the force for assistance with their personal and family problems, even though officers rarely felt comfortable "interfering." Grady's activities suggest that the early Winnipeg force was primarily concerned with (and specifically prejudiced towards) "notorious" suspects, women, Aboriginal and Métis peoples, and the lower classes.

The strong police culture and shared identity of local policemen cemented personal and professional bonds amongst members of the early Winnipeg police. Yet patrolling the streets "according to order" remained a solitary and subjective experience, for which the local police received little preparation or training. In the end, though it was a demanding undertaking, a policeman's life on the beat was largely absent of "wild" and "wicked" sources of corruption in the city. Outside of the "notorious" set of suspects and offenders, and likely to the great disappointment of local elites and reformers, constables regularly returned empty-handed to the Winnipeg station house.

Notes

1   Winnipeg Police Museum [hereafter referred to as WPM], Occurrence reports (16 September 1880).

2   Lawrence H. Larsen, *The Urban West at the End of the Frontier* (Lawrence: Regents Press of Kansas, 1978), 81–84; W.L. Morton, *Manitoba: A History,* 2nd ed. (Toronto: University of Toronto Press, 1967), 171.

3   Alan Artibise discusses Winnipeg's "wicked" reputation during the late nineteenth and early twentieth centuries in Chapters 9 and 14 of *Winnipeg: A Social History of Urban Growth, 1874–1914* (Montreal: McGill-Queen's University Press, 1975). W.L. Morton describes Winnipeg's "wild" reputation in *Manitoba: A History,* 141.

4   Greg Marquis has suggested that colonial forces shared core elements with the Royal Irish Constabulary rather than with British models. See "The 'Irish Model' and Nineteenth-century Canadian Policing," *Journal of Imperial and Commonwealth History* 25, 2 (1997): 194.

5   City of Winnipeg Archives and Records Centre [hereafter referred to as CWAR], City Clerk, Minutes of Council (26 February 1874; 9 March 1874).

6   Robert Hutchison, *A Century of Service: A History of the Winnipeg Police Force, 1874–1974* (Winnipeg: Winnipeg Police Force, 1974), 15.

7   Jack Templeman, *From Force to Service: A Pictorial History of the Winnipeg Police Department, 125th Anniversary* (Calgary: Bunker to Bunker, 1998), 11–13.

8   Based on Winnipeg population statistics as provided by Alan Artibise in *Winnipeg: An Illustrated History* (Toronto: James Lorimer and Co., 1977), 40.

9   Discussion of the nature of Winnipeg's population growth is based on Alan Artibise's exploration of "Population Growth and Ethnic Relationships" in *Winnipeg: An Illustrated History*, 38–42.

10   Population statistics based on "City Assessment Office figures" identified by Alan Artibise in *Winnipeg: A Social History*, 130.

11   Number of arrests based on annual report of chief of police for 1879 (CWAR, Council Communications, no. 1796.5 [8 January 1880]) and Arrests reports of Winnipeg police (WPM, Arrest reports [1889, 1899]).

12   CWAR, Council Communications register, Series I: 1874–1881; WPM, Occurrence reports (1879 and 1880).

13   *By-laws of the City of Winnipeg, 1874–1899* (Winnipeg: Stovel Company, 1900).

14   Greg Marquis, "Working Men in Uniform: The Early Twentieth-century Toronto Police" *Histoire Sociale/Social History* 20 (November 1987): 270.

15   John C. Weaver, *Crimes, Constables and Courts: Order and Transgression in a Canadian City, 1816–1870* (Montreal: McGill-Queen's University Press, 1995), 97.

16   Nicholas Rogers, "Serving Toronto the Good: The Development of the City Police Force, 1834–1884," in *Forging a Consensus: Historical Essays on Toronto*, ed. Victor L. Russell (Toronto: University of Toronto, 1984), 126.

17   Ibid.

18   Greg Marquis, "Power from the Street: The Canadian Municipal Police" in R.C. Macleod and David Schneiderman, eds., *Police Powers in Canada: The Evolution and Practice of Authority* (Toronto: University of Toronto Press, 1994), 37; Marquis, "Working Men in Uniform," 261.

19   Based on information provided by letters of application and visual images of members of the force from the period.

20   Census of Canada, 1881; Census of Canada, 1891.

21   While little information is available regarding policemen's previous occupations, many applications to the force mention military or policing experience, suggesting that it was a preferred qualification.

22   See James H. Gray, *Boomtime: Peopling the Canadian Prairies* (Saskatoon: Western Producer Prairie Books, 1979) and Greg Marquis, "Power from the Street."

23   The records predominantly pertain to the careers of policemen during the 1870s and early 1880s. While little information is available regarding the careers of policemen during the late 1880s and 1890s, it seems that the turnover rate of officers was a problem that continued to plague the Winnipeg force. The names of officers appear and disappear from the police record books with surprising regularity throughout the period of this study.

24   Templeman, *From Force to Service*, 10.

25   While it is unclear when Grady first arrived in the city, there is a record of a "John Grady" living in Winnipeg as early as 1876, according to *Henderson's Directory of the City of Winnipeg and Incorporated Towns of Manitoba* (Winnipeg: 1876).

26   *Henderson's Directory of the City of Winnipeg and Incorporated Towns of Manitoba* (Winnipeg: 1882).

27 The fatigue of men is revealed in their resignation letters, and in letters of the chief asking city council to appoint more men to the force.

28 CWAR, Council Communications, no. 3146 (5 March 1883).

29 CWAR, Council Communications, no. 330 (June 1875).

30 CWAR, Council Communications, no. 2699 (26 May 1882).

31 WPM, Occurrence reports (15 March 1879).

32 CWAR, Council Communications, no. 145 (25 October 1874), no. 415.5 (1 July 1875), no. 1568 (7 April 1879), no. 1643 (16 June 1879), no. 1739 (13 October 1879), no. 1796.5 (8 January 1880), no. 2216 (18 April 1881).

33 J.C. McRae, "I Remember," Manitoba Legislative Library (hereafter referred to as MLL), Manitoba Biography Scrapbook, B5: 58.

34 MLL, *Winnipeg Daily Times*, 29 August 1881.

35 CWAR, Council Communications, no. 3146 (5 March 1883). Emphasis added.

36 WPM, Occurrence reports (1 March 1879; 16 September 1880).

37 Marquis, "Working Men in Uniform," 260.

38 Annual report of the chief of police for 1880 (CWAR, Council Communications, no. 2120b [27 January 1881]).

39 MLL, *Winnipeg Daily Times*, 12 December 1881.

40 Tina Loo and Carolyn Strange note that municipal police forces across the nation actively "imposed morality" by focussing on public order violations in *Making Good: Law and Moral Regulation in Canada, 1867–1939* (Toronto: University of Toronto Press, 1997), 28.

41 WPM, Occurrence reports (25 November 1880).

42 WPM, Occurrence reports (26 September 1879; 28 September 1879).

43 WPM, Occurrence reports (11 October 1879).

44 WPM, Occurrence reports (23 June 1881).

45 WPM, Occurrence reports (23 November 1880).

46 WPM, Occurrence report (5 April 1886).

47 WPM, Occurrence reports (1886 and 1887). On 25 July 1886, Robert Bourne reported that his young boy of sixteen months was lost. The police report indicates that the child was located after three hours of having gone missing. On 26 July 1887, the occurrence report reads that Joseph Poole, a "Coloured boy about 13 years old Came to station saying that he could not find his way home." Police reports reveal that several children were reported found by their parents before they could be found by the police.

48 WPM, Occurrence reports (4 November 1886).

49 WPM, Occurrence reports (28 January 1887).

50 WPM, Occurrence reports (17 June 1880).

51 WPM, Occurrence reports (28 March 1879).

52 CWAR, Council Communications, no. 1013.5 (24 January 1877).

53 WPM, Occurrence reports (8 October 1879).

54 Randolph Rostecki notes that the significant population of urban poor in Winnipeg became apparent by the early 1880s. Randolph Rostecki, "The Growth of Winnipeg, 1870–1886" (MA thesis, University of Manitoba, 1980), 5.

55 CWAR, Council Communications, no. 1019 (1889).

56 CWAR, Council Communications, no. 1019 (1889).

57 WPM, Occurrence reports (5 December 1879).

58 WPM, Occurrence reports (9 March 1879).

59 WPM, Occurrence reports (30 November 1880).

60   WPM, Occurrence reports (6 October 1879).

61   WPM, Occurrence reports (19 December 1879).

62   WPM, Occurrence reports (9 April 1886).

63   WPM, Occurrence reports (19 April 1886).

64   Marquis, "The Police as a Social Service," 357.

65   Annual reports of the chief of police for 1879 (CWAR, Council Communications, no. 1796.5 [8 January 1880]); Annual report of the chief of police for 1880 (CWAR, Council Communications, no. 2120b [27 January 1881]). The records identifying occupation relate to two consecutive years; additional information on the occupation of persons arrested during the period remains unavailable.

66   MLL, *Winnipeg Daily Times*, 15 April 1879.

67   WPM, Occurrence reports (1879).

68   CWAR, Council Communications, no. 4084 (May 1884).

69   CWAR, Council Communications, no. 1796.5 (8 January 1880), no. 2120b (27 January 1881).

70   WPM, Occurrence reports (23 August 1879; 16 September 1880).

71   WPM, Occurrence reports (17 April 1879).

72   WPM, Occurrence reports (6 December 1880).

73   WPM, Occurrence reports (29 June 1879; 18 February 1880; 15 July 1880).

74   MLL, *Winnipeg Daily Times*, 26 December 1881.

75   Grady's habit of arresting more women than men is especially significant considering that the population of the city during the period included more men than women. See Alan Artibise, *Winnipeg: A Social History*, 146–147.

76   WPM, Occurrence reports (28 February 1879).

77   WPM, Occurrence reports (9 September 1880).

78   WPM, Occurrence reports (23 September 1879; 27 April 1879).

79   WPM, Occurrence reports (6 May 1880).

80   MLL, *Winnipeg Daily Times*, 11 January 1882.

Protecting and Policing Children: The Origins and Nature of Juvenile Justice in Winnipeg

Cassandra Woloschuk

In February 1909, four girls under the age of sixteen ran away from home. Detained by police and brought before the Winnipeg Juvenile Court, they became the first to be processed under the 1908 federal *Juvenile Delinquents Act*.[1] Before the establishment of this youth-oriented judicial institution, cases involving young people had been heard in city police court and offenders were incarcerated in adult jails, prisons, and penitentiaries. This new approach was designed to offer such youths guidance and rehabilitation rather than punishment. The establishment of the Winnipeg Juvenile Court reflected significant changes in the way the city treated its children. It also allowed for earlier provincial child protection laws, such as the *Children's Protection Act* of 1898, to be better enforced. The close association of the juvenile court with separate but parallel institutions in the city such as the Office of Neglected Children and school truant officers provided a new level of regulation of these young people. Private trial and separate confinement of youth also enabled officers in the system to better define, analyze, and treat delinquent behaviour. This essay considers the purpose and nature of the regulatory institutions, the ideology and character of their officials, and a rough outline of the "regulated" children in the prairie city.[2] It focuses on the roles of juvenile court and school officials, as well as children and youth who appeared before the court. It illustrates deeply ingrained patterns of discrimination based on class, ethnicity, and religious affiliation and suggests that young females were targeted by these institutions.[3] And it contends that, despite its progressive veneer, the apparently progressive, child-centred legislation actually represented close surveillance of working-class youth, especially young women.

The Establishment of the Winnipeg Juvenile Court[4]

In early 1908, in anticipation of federal legislation regarding juvenile delinquents, Felix J. Billiarde was appointed provincial Superintendent of Neglected Children under the *Children's Protection Act* and probation officer for juvenile delinquents.[5] When the federal *Juvenile Delinquents Act* was enacted on 20 July 1908, the Manitoba Department of the Attorney General took steps to establish a detention home and appoint the necessary officers to bring the Act into force in Winnipeg. In October 1908, a detention home was opened at 226 Simcoe Street. The building, originally an institution for neglected children operated by the Salvation Army, became an incarceration facility used to segregate children from adult criminals.

Winnipeg brought the *Juvenile Delinquents Act* into force on 22 January 1909 by order-in-council, making it the first Canadian city to comply with the new law.[6] The juvenile court was established within the detention home. Colin H. Campbell, the Conservative attorney general of Manitoba from 1900 until 1911, was instrumental in the appointment of Thomas Mayne Daly as its first judge. Daly, a former Conservative member of Parliament and the presiding police court magistrate, was said to be kind, fair, and just in his dealings with young offenders. His perception of youth crime was based on a belief that a poor environment contributed to criminal behaviour. He advocated social change and probation as the most effective means of preventing delinquent behaviour.[7] Campbell and Daly therefore shared a similar philosophy regarding child welfare. Daly was followed on the bench by David M. Walker, also a former Conservative politician, and F.J. Billiarde, a Conservative Party supporter. They presided jointly over the juvenile court between 1911 and 1915. D. W. McKerchar, a Liberal, took over as both police court magistrate and juvenile court judge in 1915.

Colin Campbell was a central figure in the establishment of the juvenile court. He felt it was wrong for children to be treated as common criminals for youthful indiscretions. In a letter to his son, Campbell wrote that he "had long thought that we were very unwise in dealing with little boys and girls for errors of judgment and harmless escapades, forgetting all the time that they were guided a great deal by their instincts, and that they were not fully capable of exercising a mature judgment. Many a little boy has been injured for life by being dragged to a Police Court for doing something which in a more fortunate boy would go unnoticed."[8] He noted the implication of social class and felt that children who were forced to undergo the ordeal of police court proceedings would be permanently scarred by the experience. He realized that even though a child might commit a crime, it was the "act of a child that deserved treatment in a more kindly way." Such children may have committed legal offences, but their "hearts were in reality full of goodness if properly directed."[9] Campbell explained that by having a separate juvenile justice system "hundreds of children are made better, and their homes are made better, and child life is made an inspiration for better things."[10]

In 1910, Campbell directed F. J. Billiarde, the Superintendent of Neglected Children, to compile a pamphlet entitled *Laws for the Protection of Children* in order to educate the general population in the laws devised especially for youth. In this pamphlet (and in his subsequent 1917 publication, *Canada's Greatest Asset: Are We Safeguarding It?*), Billiarde outlined the various ways to keep children from falling prey to degradation and immorality.[11] While this message was directed at all classes, the implication was clear that more had to be done to protect working-class children from their own environment. Both men believed that delinquent children were products of their environment and required guidance and rehabilitation rather than punishment. Their commitment to child welfare helped to establish the juvenile court in Winnipeg.

The first session of the juvenile court occurred on the afternoon of 5 February 1909 in the dining room of the detention home. Present with Daly were Billiarde, Inspector Newton of the Winnipeg Police Department, Polish interpreter Jacob Kwiatowsky, Salvation Army Staff Captain McAmmond and his wife, the matron of the detention home. The four immigrant girls mentioned at the opening of this chapter were the first to be tried under the *Juvenile Delinquents Act* for running away from home. They were given a suspended sentence and placed in the care of Billiarde.[12]

When the juvenile court first began operation, it was held whenever juvenile cases arose. It took until 1911 to establish regular sessions of the court on Mondays and Thursdays.[13] In these early years, delinquent boys made up the majority of cases. Of the 335 cases Daly heard between 7 February 1910 and 28 December 1910, 81.5 percent (273) were boys and 18.5 percent (62) were girls. He described the twenty-eight boys he sent to training school as "smart, clever little chaps" and predicted that many of them would "turn out bright and capable citizens."[14] Excerpts from Daly's annual report reveal that 44 percent (30 of 68) of the girls who appeared before him in 1909 were described as "immoral." In 1910, 24.2 percent (15 of 62) of the girls were charged with "immoral delinquencies."[15] Of the nine girls he sent to training school in 1910, he commented, "Words fail to express my gratitude to the Government for undertaking the training of these girls; it relieves all concerned of a great responsibility and means the saving of these children and their being turned from sin and trouble to usefulness and goodness. From the reports so far received, their training is working wonders."[16] Daly commented further on "immoral" girls when he gave evidence to the Royal Commission in 1911 regarding prostitution in the city: "I was constantly face to face with the fact that numbers of young girls were being brought before me, the juvenile court, and these girls were taken from immoral surroundings in houses and blocks and other places through the city, and on investigation everyone of these girls were found to be immoral. Their ages ran from 13 years of age to 15, some of them were diseased."[17]

Since there was no Canadian precedent for administering a court for juvenile delinquents, the Winnipeg Juvenile Court borrowed ideas and practices from the juvenile court established in Chicago in 1899 and, to a lesser degree, the juvenile court established in Denver in 1903, both of which emphasized informal procedure and correction rather than punishment.[18] Campbell and Billiarde followed the progress of prominent American juvenile courts, regularly commented on their successes, and sporadically utilized statistics from these courts in their own reports. Billiarde also corresponded with Benjamin Lindsey, judge of the Denver Juvenile Court, sending him updates on the work of the Winnipeg Juvenile Court.[19]

Like American juvenile court judges, Daly embraced the *parens patriae* [father of the people] legal principle and attempted to establish a non-threatening courtroom environment. Hearings were confidential and informal and did not rely on a dock, raised platform, or bench. Daly acted in the role of a firm yet caring parent, looked for individualized ways to correct a child's misbehaviour, and disregarded generalized approaches to justice. He presented himself as a friend and a father-like figure, assuming the appropriate role as the circumstances dictated. Staff Captain McAmmond offered this description of Daly's interaction with the boys who came before his court: "It was the greatest thing in the world to se [sic] him handle a headstrong boy who had got into trouble. He never used two of them alike. He seemed to be able to tell at a glance just how to take every one of them. Some he was severe with, others he joked with, but he was kind to every one of them and every one of them loved him. ... they all confessed everything to Mr. Daly, just like telling it to one of their chums."[20]

The character of the early juvenile court in Winnipeg was paternalistic in nature and, like other juvenile courts, was heavily influenced by its officials.[21] As in the Denver model, it relied on probation officers. And, as in Chicago, it also utilized systematic investigations of a child's history. Probation officers prepared profiles on each child for the Winnipeg court by working closely with a variety of different agencies. The profiles contained information on the child's background, including age, ethnicity, religion, detailed parental information, physical and mental exam reports and, where applicable, any previous juvenile court documentation and probation officer and social worker reports.

In the spirit of *parens patriae*, the juvenile court required special facilities to carry out its mandate. A detention home served as a short-term jail in which youths were isolated from adult criminals. And, from 1911, a truant school enabled delinquent youth to obtain an academic education while in detention so they would be able to re-enter the appropriate grade once they were released into the regular school system. This feature distinguished Winnipeg from juvenile courts established subsequently in other jurisdictions.[22]

The jurisdiction of the early juvenile court was limited to Winnipeg children under the age of sixteen, except in cases where the child was determined to be a "juvenile delinquent" and made a ward of the court. Cases against non-ward adolescents between the ages of sixteen and twenty-one in police court help illustrate the latitude of the definition of delinquency. Adolescents whose cases were heard by Daly in police court were frequently sentenced to the detention home. When Emma and Billy were brought to the police court on vagrancy charges, Billy was given a suspended sentence but Emma was handed over to the detention home.[23] Alfred was convicted of theft and sentenced to six months in the detention home.[24] And Grace was sentenced to the detention home after she was found guilty of being an inmate of a bawdy house.[25]

Adolescent cases that were heard in police court offer some insight into the thinking of the sitting judge. Though neither Daly nor Walker left written statements regarding adolescent cases in the police court, McKerchar did comment on the adolescents who appeared before him in his capacity as police court magistrate: "It frequently happens that youths and maidens who have passed their sixteenth birthday fall into the hands of the police as first offenders. In order to save these young people from the stigma of a police record, the police bring them to the Juvenile Court to be dealt with by me in my capacity of a Police Court magistrate."[26] In his 1916–17 report, McKerchar noted that he had arranged for the juvenile court and the Crown prosecutor for Winnipeg to cooperate when dealing with adolescents between the ages sixteen and twenty-one. The cooperation was believed necessary to prevent a gradual decline from delinquency into criminal activity and was generally regarded as successful.[27]

Less than a year into its operation, the juvenile court moved to a large, three-storey building that had its own courtroom, a schoolroom, and living accommodations, with girls residing on the second floor and boys on the third floor. The general atmosphere was conceived to be a homey one, bearing no resemblance to a prison. In his report on the first year of the juvenile court's operation, Daly discussed how youth were treated during their initial processing: "Instead of children being taken to the Police Station and locked up in cells, they are taken to the Detention

Home, where everything is so homelike and unprison-like, that the child is not terrorized and frightened half to death. Instead of being locked up in cells or ward-rooms, they are put into comfortable bedrooms, first being scrubbed and cleansed."[28] Daly concluded that, "the influence for the betterment of the child must surely be with our present mode of treatment."[29] Billiarde repeatedly expressed his view that the Winnipeg Juvenile Court was less a court of justice than "an aid to the home, the school and the church in the moral training of the child. If the latter fail, the court, through probation methods, does the best it can to supply the deficiency."[30] In his report, he said that "in nearly every case where a child has been detained for any length of time ... a marked improvement has taken place in its physical appear-ance; no doubt this is due to regular hours of sleep, good plain food and absolute cleanliness, together with the absence of exciting causes of injurious and deleterious nature."[31] However, in 1920, McKerchar argued that the juvenile court was only a last resort in ensuring the proper upbringing of the child and added, "The court has no jurisdiction to deal with the moral, ethical or religious standards of any child who has not transgressed some man-made law, or who has not been neglected or ill treated by its parents or guardians."[32]

The charge of delinquency proved to be an extremely wide net that could be applied to any number of behaviours. Young girls were consistently brought before the court to answer charges of sexual immorality, even before the charge of sexual immorality was officially added to the *Juvenile Delinquents Act* in 1924.[33] In 1914, as the number of juvenile cases continued to increase rapidly, Billiarde explained that in his experience with girls "of an immoral tendency," many were "of a feeble mind or of a mentally defective type."[34] He requested an additional room at the detention home be equipped for use by a doctor "with the necessary instruments for testing and examining such children."[35] He remarked further, "children whose delinquency appears to be of an obstinate and persistent character which does not yield to ordinary methods of supervision and probation should be examined by a competent medical specialist."[36] Some children, he held, could only be dealt with through institutionalization, including delinquent children for whom probationary care had failed, "defective" or "sub-normal" children, destitute children, and those with physical disabilities.[37] Buried in his request is a description of delinquent girls that reflects the popular eugenic belief at the time that mental defectiveness was a significant cause of crime and delinquency.

Prior to 1919 mental examinations were ordered by the juvenile court, but it often fell to Winnipeg's social welfare agencies or reformatories to make the necessary arrangements. In March 1919, Dr. Alvin T. Mathers opened the Psychopathic Department of the Court and began to examine and report on children referred by the juvenile court.[38] His department's profiles of individual delinquents became an increasingly important factor in the conduct of juvenile cases. Psychiatrists and psychologists utilized a range of intelligence tests that measured supposed mental deficiency and provided classifications for children according to their mental age. Medical examinations included dental and eye exams, and girls were subjected to invasive gynecological examinations as well.[39] The juvenile court relied on the results of physical and medical exams when determining the appropriate treatment and length of sentences.

Education and the Office of Neglected Children

The Manitoba Schools Question of 1890–96 had been a bitter fight over who controlled education and who had the right to define what it entailed. The debate had not been resolved with the Laurier-Greenway Compromise of 1896 or subsequent legislation in 1897 and continued to cast a shadow over the relationship between politics and religion in the province. Drafted in this context, the *Juvenile Delinquents Act* considered the religion of children important to their proper treatment and training and stated that the religion of the child had to be respected. Probation officers and social agencies made special efforts to identify delinquents' religious backgrounds. The juvenile court, through its Protestant officials, subscribed to non-sectarian ideals of education but could not always place children in the appropriate institution.[40] Detention homes and reform institutions filled quickly and overcrowding became a problem.

Protestant institutions, which accommodated significantly fewer children and youth than their Catholic counterparts, struggled to meet the demands, but many of them closed after brief periods of operation. Reform institutions were dominated by Catholic orders since the Catholic community chose to establish convent-style homes supported by the labour of nuns. The success of the Catholic institutions meant that Protestant and Jewish adolescents often served their sentences in them, illustrating the contemporary belief among justice officials that the value of rehabilitation and reform outweighed the risks of religious mixing. The court and juvenile justice system, however, continued to be run predominantly by Protestants.

There were only two institutions for delinquent girls in the province: the Salvation Army Industrial Home for Protestant girls and Marymound for Catholic girls. Within Marymound, the Soeurs du Bon Pasteur's objective was to reform bad girls through incarceration and religious training.[41] Marymound opened in April

1911 when five French-speaking nuns of the Soeurs du Bon Pasteur order came to Winnipeg from Montreal at the request of Thomas Mayne Daly. Daly was Anglican and an opponent of separate schools, but he defended the remedial legislation that would have restored separate schools to the Catholics.[42] Daly's request to the Soeurs du Bon Pasteur illustrated the widespread view that educational and religious training were necessary if a child was to be rescued from delinquency. By 1920, however, McKerchar noted, "Whilst the sectarian classification of delinquents is not indicative of the superiority of one religious teaching over another, it does tend to show that, so far as delinquents who have appeared before the Juvenile Court at Winnipeg during the past year ... are concerned each religious denomination or sect has been about equal in its failure to reach all the children of parents claiming adherence to such denomination or sect."[43]

The early juvenile court targeted delinquency, especially truancy, which was defined as a "pre-delinquency."[44] This preoccupation with truancy reflected changing attitudes toward education and directly corresponded to the compulsory schooling laws established by the provinces. The Manitoba legislature amended the *Children's Protection Act* in 1913 to include compulsory school attendance for children between the ages of seven and fourteen. Probation officers supervised the enrolment and school attendance of children between those ages by patrolling streets during the day and regularly asking school administrators and teachers about truancy.[45] Though school principals commended the work of the probation officers in reducing the numbers of truants, they recognized that the compulsory school legislation was unrealistic given the circumstances faced by working-class families in Winnipeg who relied on children's wages to supplement the family income. The legislation forced these families to limit their expectations of wage contributions to the work of adults and children over the age of fourteen.[46]

Truancy was also one of the primary concerns of the Office of Neglected Children. Its methods of enforcing regular school attendance included a patrol of the city streets, established in 1910. The Office of Neglected Children, separate but parallel to the juvenile court, was responsible for the administration of the 1898 *Children's Protection Act* throughout the province. It dealt with students who were skipping school. In his campaign to limit truancy, Billiarde divided the city into districts and assigned a probation officer to each of these districts during regular school hours. The majority of probation officers patrolled working-class neighbourhoods in the city's North End, particularly the streets near schools.[47] Children observed on the streets were questioned regarding their absence from school, their current activities, the school they attended, their grade, and how long they had been absent. Parents were also questioned to corroborate the children's statements.[48] While many cases of truancy were the result of errands, illness, insufficient clothing, or parental unemployment, others were simply children playing hookey. Probation officers were under strict instructions to cooperate with the parents and the school authorities to ensure the child's regular attendance at school.[49]

Probation officers frequently inquired about irregular attendance and school principals referred cases to the Department of Neglected Children. Once a child was found to be truant, the probation officer would visit his or her home to ascertain the reason for the absence. If no reasonable explanation was provided and the officer determined the parents had failed in their responsibility, they would first be warned and subsequently issued a summons to appear before the court. Parents were held accountable for their child's irregular attendance at school in the same way that they were accountable for their child's delinquent behaviour. Billiarde noted that warnings were often sufficient in ensuring regular school attendance, and despite cases where fines were imposed to "impress upon them a sense of their responsibility in the matter," the officers found parents "most anxious to cooperate with them."[50]

The attendance of children who were under the supervision of probation officers was monitored closely with the help of the school. Probation officers assigned to these cases reported on the child weekly, calling both the school and home regularly to compile a complete history of the case. Children who persisted in being absent from school were confined to the detention home and attended the truant school all year round without summer holidays. The length of stay was based on the reports received from the teacher. Billiarde reported that the threat of year-round schooling proved to be a valuable deterrent to those under constant supervision, though absences were dealt with more severely during the regular academic term than during the last two or three weeks as the summer holiday approached. Probation officers entered department stores, "cheap picture" shows, bowling alleys, saloons, and pool rooms during their patrols to ensure adolescents did not frequent those places, and also attempted to deter adolescents from reading dime novels.[51] Nightly patrols of the city streets during the summer months occurred between nine p.m. and midnight, and focussed on loitering or idle children who kept "undesirable company."[52] Billiarde also noted that patrolling the streets had "played a very important part in reducing the number of girls charged with immoral conduct."[53] He advocated the inauguration of a playground system to help reduce the level of delinquency among youth. While attendance at school would help ensure that children were protected from criminality, playgrounds offered children a healthy alternative to the temptation of the streets. Taken together, schools and playgrounds would help ensure the proper character development in children and reduce the factor of idleness that was believed to be a primary cause of delinquency.[54]

Beyond the Usual Suspects: Class, Gender, Ethnicity, and Religion

Annual reports by the Superintendent of Neglected Children provide an impression of the type of offences and backgrounds of children labelled delinquent in the early years of the juvenile court's operation. In 1911, for example, 538 children were brought to the juvenile court on delinquency charges. Of this number, 83.8 percent (451) were male and 16.2 percent (87) were female. Truancy, theft, and incorrigibility were the most common charges listed. A gender breakdown of these offences shows the gender bias of the system: 14.4 percent (65) of boys and 5.7 percent (5) of girls were charged with truancy; 32.4 percent (146) of boys and 10.3 percent (9) of girls were charged with theft; and 4.7 percent (21) of boys and 14.9 percent (13) of girls were charged with incorrigibility. The average length of probation was 2.9 months and probation officers visited with each child an average of twice per week. The probation officers noted that the character of the parents was generally good, the home conditions were usually recorded as fair or good, and physical and mental conditions were overwhelmingly recorded as being normal. Girls were more likely to face reform school than boys. Those sentenced to reform school, as a percentage of those charged, resulted in an incarceration rate of 26.4 percent for girls and 8 percent for boys.[55] It should be noted that, between 1908 and mid-1914, the Office of Neglected Children dealt with over 3100 cases. Boys accounted for four out of five cases.

In its first decade, the juvenile court treated truancy as a minor delinquency. Children and youth who appeared before the juvenile court for chronic truancy could be detained in the detention home for months or years to ensure their regular school attendance, but they were not sentenced to reform or industrial schools. The court moved away from policing truancy as other delinquencies increased. Thus, truancy cases rose rapidly following the introduction of Manitoba's compulsory schooling laws in 1913, peaking at 997 in 1915, but then dropped significantly and remained quite low.[56] In 1923 and 1924 the juvenile court heard no truancy cases. Cases for delinquencies other than truancy or neglect and destitution, however, which had numbered only a few hundred annually, almost tripled from 325 in 1917 to 948 in 1918, after which the volume of cases rose steadily through the 1920s.

Ethnic tensions between Winnipeg's Anglo-Canadian elite and the immigrant population were reflected in the juvenile justice system, where discrimination varied according to ethnicity and religion. The probation officers who regulated the behaviour of children during the court's first decade, like the education system officials, were middle-class, Anglo-Canadian Protestants. Their enforcement of the rules ensured that class, gender, ethnicity, and religion were important factors in the definition of delinquency. Based on evidence about their home neighbourhoods and their fathers' occupations, the overwhelming majority of children and youth who entered the juvenile justice system were working-class. These young people lived in poverty with single parents or parents who were required to work long hours to support the family. They became targets because neglect was regarded by the court as leading to delinquency. Economic instability, as evidenced through transience, foster care, or neglect, was a common characteristic among the girls sentenced by the juvenile court to reformatories.

In terms of perceived susceptibility to delinquency, white, working-class children, whether Protestant or Catholic, Canadian or English-born, ranked the lowest. Other European and Eastern European immigrants (or children of immigrants), despite their age, were subjected to greater scrutiny. When the Eastern European immigrant population in the city rose, so too did concerns about delinquency, which resulted in differences in the degree of regulation. Probationary patrols focussed heavily on Winnipeg's North End, a working-class area with a significant Eastern European immigrant population. Youth residing in more affluent neighbourhoods, such as the Crescentwood area of Winnipeg, were less likely to be strictly regulated since those areas received little attention.

As Gloria Geller argues, the contemporary classic image of the delinquent was an immigrant child from a broken home who lived in a slum, resisted parental control, and acted aggressively.[57] The perception of delinquent youth held by probation officers in Winnipeg corresponds to this image. Children of European background did figure disproportionately in the justice system. In 1911, for example, the Slavic population in the city was only 9.8 percent, but Slavic children represented 20.8 percent of the total number of juvenile court cases.[58] Catholic youth were also overrepresented among those sentenced to reform institutions. While they comprised approximately half of those youth brought before the court at any time, they were sentenced to reformatories much more frequently than their Protestant counterparts.[59] As early as 1917, the juvenile court had begun to rely on the voluntary assistance of Reverend Harry Atkinson, a Methodist minister, in supervising delinquent boys and securing them employment on farms,[60] but he had no Catholic colleague until 1 February 1919 when the court acquired its first Catholic priest as a voluntary worker. Reverend

Father Heffron began to regularly attend the sessions of the juvenile court, and juvenile court judge McKerchar stated that "the court ha[d] been favored during the year in having [Heffron] as a voluntary worker."[61] Heffron had spent seven years dealing with institutionalized juvenile delinquents in New York City.

In the post-war years, boys continued to appear before the juvenile court more frequently than did girls. Between 1917 and 1919 the court heard 2319 cases. Girls made up less than 10 percent and boys accounted for just under 88 percent.[62] From 1920 to 1924, the court formally dealt with about 1500 cases each year. Boys under sixteen made up 84 percent of these cases while boys between sixteen and nineteen made up a little over 2 percent.[63] Girls under sixteen comprised 10.7 percent of these while girls between sixteen and twenty-one made up 0.69 percent.

The cases initiated against girls provided court officials with a means to regulate femininity and morality. In his capacity as Superintendent of Neglected Children, Billiarde labelled youth between the ages of twelve and fifteen as "dangerous" but his successor, D.S. Hamilton, indicated that "amongst the delinquents requiring the most attentive supervision are girls from 15 to 17 years of age."[64] Girls were more likely to be brought before the juvenile court for status offences such as running away, incorrigibility, and sexual immorality. Feminist scholars have devoted much attention to how gender conditioned juvenile court responses to delinquency, and the statistics from the Winnipeg Juvenile Court confirm what these scholars have found.[65] There is a noticeable lack of attention devoted to girls in official court reports, while delinquent boys generated considerable interest on the part of court officials. Only one regular woman probation officer was attached to the juvenile court to investigate and report on girls, while two regular male probation officers assisted by an entire staff of male volunteer workers dealt with boys' cases.[66]

It is possible to gain a clearer picture of the delinquent girls because the records of one important institution, the Marymound School, have survived. This Roman Catholic institution was created for the confinement of Catholic youth in the province. Its population was therefore largely Catholic, though the institution did accept Protestant, Jewish, and other "non-Catholic" girls as well. These files suggest that girls from European immigrant backgrounds were disproportionately subjected to incarceration. In 1911, Slavic girls represented 23.7 percent of the population at Marymound.[67] They represented the highest percentage of admittances between 1911 and 1948, peaking at 62.6 percent between 1931 and 1935. Between 1926 and 1935 the number of Slavic girls was more than three times higher than girls of other ethnic groups.[68] One might surmise that the overrepresentation of immigrant girls at Marymound was a consequence of ethnic tensions in the city and the fact that working-class immigrants were targeted by the juvenile justice system.

Much more significant than the girls' ethnicities, places of birth, or religion, however, was their overwhelming poverty. By the most modest estimate, more than 75 percent of the girls incarcerated at Marymound had fathers who, if they held employment at all, worked in semi-skilled or unskilled occupations. Most of the families relied heavily on social assistance, with those mothers who did work often performing menial tasks such as domestic labour. Many mothers were widowed or had been deserted by their husbands. Many girls also came from families suffering other crises than economic difficulties. More than half of the girls at Marymound came from broken families. Almost two-thirds of the girls had at least one deceased parent; in most cases it was the mother. And almost one quarter of the girls were without parents at all due to death or desertion. The absence of a natural parent, especially a mother, through death or abandonment was a common factor precipitating a girl's entrance into reform institutions.[69] Marymound's program of reform focussed on academic and domestic training, which prepared the girls for their future lives as domestic servants, and reflected the class, religious, and ethnic divisions in the city. It was an incarceration facility characterized by convent boarding-school discipline, and its religious atmosphere was a powerful reinforcement of religious and moral values.

Conclusion

Ethnicity and religion played important roles in selecting the children and youth who received the court's attention. There was a greater likelihood that Slavs and French Canadians, as well as Catholics, would be incarcerated. Boys in the juvenile court overwhelmingly and consistently outnumbered girls, yet girls were overrepresented in reform institutions. A higher percentage of status offence convictions for girls than boys demonstrated that the juvenile court's response to delinquent behaviour was gendered. While boys' offences were often against property, girls were more likely to be brought before the court for offences of character or morality. Female sexual immorality was defined in terms of social norms and would, it was believed, eventually lead to crime and, ultimately, social instability. Those girls sentenced to Marymound were most likely to fare well in the institution's program of reform. Beyond gender, class inequality was also evident in the system. Children of low-income or working-class families were disproportionately represented in the dock. When all other methods of treatment were deemed to have failed, delinquent youth were sentenced to reform institutions.

Surveillance and control of children remained a constant in early Winnipeg. The *Juvenile Delinquents Act* of 1908 provided the framework for the establishment of the Winnipeg Juvenile Court. The school, the probation officer, the school attendance officer, and the court all took part in these operations. Once children entered the system, their lives were subjected to regular scrutiny by probation officers, schools, and the court itself. Surveillance was believed to be necessary to prevent delinquency and did not abate after the child's behaviour was "reformed." The juvenile court and the Office of Neglected Children shared similar regulatory motivations that facilitated their good relations and established extensive child and family surveillance commencing with school attendance. Indeed, formal education was regarded by the authorities as the crucial alternative to delinquency. When education and probationary care failed, the next step of the authorities was to confine the children in reform schools.

Notes

1   "First Session of the Juvenile Court," *Manitoba Free Press*, 6 February 1909, 9; D.W. McKerchar, "Juvenile Court," in Department of Education, *Annual Reports*, 1919–1920, 120; *Manitoba Free Press*, 1 February 1919; see also Roy St. George Stubbs, "The First Juvenile Court Judge: The Honourable Thomas Mayne Daly KC," *MHS Transactions* 3, 34 (1977–1978 Season), http://www.mhs.mb.ca/docs/transactions/3/daly_tm.shtml. The Department of Education annual reports contain a plethora of information authored by judges regarding the status and efficiency of the juvenile court. They also contain detailed reports by the Superintendent of Neglected Children. The provincial Office of Neglected Children was responsible for the administration of the *Children's Protection Act* throughout the province as well as for the administration of the *Juvenile Delinquents Act* in Winnipeg. The Superintendent of Neglected Children regularly commented on delinquency and provided detailed statistics. I have used these statistics to determine the breakdown of delinquency by type, ethnicity, class, gender, and religion. The Department of Education records provide significant insights into the earliest period of the surveillance and control of youth wielded by the juvenile justice system in Winnipeg.

2   Bruno Théorêt, "Espace social et régulation juridique des jeunes: le fonctionnement du tribunal des jeunes de Winnipeg" (Thèse du doctorat, Université du Québec à Montréal, 1993); Bruno Théorêt, "Psychiatry, Juvenile Justice, and Delinquent Identity: A Case Study at the Juvenile Court of Winnipeg, 1930–1959," *Journal of Human Justice* 6, 1 (Autumn 1994): 64–77; Lorna Hurl, "An Analysis of Social Welfare Policy: A Case Study of the Development of Child Welfare Policies and Programmes in Manitoba, 1870–1924" (MSW thesis, University of Manitoba, 1981); and Lorna Hurl, "The Politics of Child Welfare in Manitoba, 1922–1924," *Manitoba History* 7 (Spring 1984), http://www.mhs.mb.ca/docs/mb_history/07/childwelfare.shtml.

3   See Angus McLaren, *Our Own Master Race: Eugenics in Canada, 1885–1945* (Toronto: McClelland and Stewart, 1990), 91–92; Mona Gleason, *Normalizing the Ideal: Psychology, Schooling, and the Family in Postwar Canada* (Toronto: University of Toronto Press, 1999), 22; and Tamara Myers, "Criminal Women and Bad Girls: Regulation and Punishment in Montreal, 1890–1930" (PhD diss., McGill University, 1996), 183–188.

4   W.L. Scott, "The Juvenile Delinquent Act," *Canadian Law Times and Review* 28, 11 (November 1908): 892–894. In November 1908, W.L. Scott, head of the Ottawa Children's Aid Society and a key author of the federal *Juvenile Delinquents Act* (*JDA*), provided both a commentary on and

an analysis of the newly established legislation. He held that children were products of their environment, thus reflecting the belief that flawed surroundings contributed to the making of criminals. It was widely accepted, most notably by social reformers and legal authorities, that delinquent youth often developed into hardened adult criminals.

5   Colin H. Campbell, "Report of the Department of the Attorney-General for the Year Ending 31st of December 1908," *Sessional Papers*, 1909, 745–746.

6   *Canada Gazette* 42, 39 (27 March 1909): 2693–2694. A proclamation dated 22 January 1909 and published in the 6 February 1909 *Canada Gazette* intending to bring the *JDA* into force in Winnipeg inadvertently omitted the words "in the said City of Winnipeg," thereby making it ineffective. This clerical error was corrected in the proclamation issued in the 27 March 1909 *Canada Gazette* and related back to the 22 January 1909 date.

7   See especially Thomas Mayne Daly, *A Treatise on the Winnipeg Juvenile Detention Home* (Toronto: Salvation Army Printing House, 1909).

8   Colin H. Campbell, "Letter to His Son," 2 December 1913, as quoted in Stubbs, "The First Juvenile Court Judge."

9   Ibid.

10   Ibid.

11   Felix J. Billiarde, *Laws for the Protection of Children. From the Dominion and Manitoba Statutes* (Attorney-General, Manitoba, 1910); Felix J. Billiarde, *Canada's Greatest Asset: Are We Safeguarding It? A Vital Question for all Canadians!* (Winnipeg: s.n., 1917).

12   See "First Session of the Juvenile Court"; McKerchar, "Juvenile Court," in Department of Education, *Annual Reports*, 1919–1920, 120; *Manitoba Free Press*, 1 February 1919; Stubbs, "The First Juvenile Court Judge."

13   Felix J. Billiarde, *Annual Report of the Superintendent of Neglected Children for the Province of Manitoba, 1912* (Winnipeg: Attorney General's Department, 1912), 55.

14   Colin H. Campbell, "Report of the Department of Attorney-General for the year ending 31st of December 1910," *Sessional Papers*, 1911, 609.

15   Ibid.

16   Ibid.

17   "Proceedings of the Royal Commission on Vice in Winnipeg, 1911," as quoted in Stubbs, "The First Juvenile Court Judge."

18   In his analysis of child welfare and the implementation of the *Juvenile Delinquents Act* in Canada, Neil Sutherland argues that Canadians looked to Philadelphia, which established its juvenile court in 1901, rather than Chicago or Denver for the model for their juvenile courts. Neil Sutherland, *Children in English-Canadian Society: Framing the Twentieth-Century Consensus* (Toronto: University of Toronto Press, 1976), 119. The evidence in Winnipeg suggests otherwise, at least in the case of the juvenile courts. Philadelphia modelled its *Juvenile Court Act* on the Illinois legislation, but a constitutional challenge forced an amendment in 1903. Its jurisdiction was restricted to minor crimes until 1933 when it was extended to include all crimes except murder committed by children under age sixteen. In 1939 it was amended to include all children under eighteen.

19   Pennsylvania Juvenile Court Judges' Commission. *Pennsylvania Juvenile Delinquency Benchbook* (Harrisburg, PA: Pennsylvania Juvenile Court Judges' Commission, 2006). The early administration of the Winnipeg Juvenile Court was influenced by and corresponds more closely to the juvenile courts in Chicago and Denver than Philadelphia. Reference is frequently made to the Chicago and Denver juvenile courts in the Manitoba Department of Attorney General and Department of Education reports.

20   "Children's Confessor," *Manitoba Free Press*, 26 June 1911, 16.

21 In Winnipeg, the concerns of male reformers dominated efforts to find new ways of dealing with wayward children while female reformers played minor and supplementary roles. Increasing feminine influence in the Winnipeg juvenile justice system began to surface upon the appointment of a regular female probation officer in 1920 and another in 1923. See D.S. Hamilton, "Department of Neglected Children and Juvenile Court," in Department of Education, *Annual Report*, 1920–1921, 128; and D.B. Harkness, "Juvenile Court for the Eastern Judicial District of Manitoba," in Department of Education, *Annual Report*, 1923–1924, 69–70.

22 D.W. McKerchar, "Juvenile Court," in Department of Education, *Annual Report*, 1917–1918, 139. See also "Report of J.F. Greenway, Supervisor of School Attendance," in Department of Education, *Sessional Papers*, 1915–1916, 391. Campbell, "Report of the Department of Attorney-General for the year ending 31ˢᵗ of December 1910," 607; and Report of the Department of Attorney-General for the year ending 31ˢᵗ of December 1911, Sessional Papers, 1912, 403 and 405–406. See also Lorna Hurl and Bruce Tucker, "The Michigan County Agents and the Development of Juvenile Probation, 1873–1900," *Journal of Social History* 30, 4 (Summer 1997): 905–935; and David Wolcott, *Cops and Kids: Policing Juvenile Delinquency in Urban America 1890–1940* (Columbus: Ohio State University Press 2005).

23 Winnipeg Police Court [hereafter WPC], no. 24125 (15 February 1909).

24 WPC, no. 26911 (15 August 1910).

25 WPC, nos. 40522 and 40523 (both 15 December 1910).

26 McKerchar, "Juvenile Court," in Department of Education, *Annual Report*, 1919–1920, 122–123; Hamilton, "Department of Neglected Children and Juvenile Court," in Department of Education, *Annual Report*, 1920–1921, 128.

27 D.W. McKerchar, "Juvenile Court," in Department of Education, *Annual Report*, 1916–1917, 264.

28 Daly, *Treatise*, 10.

29 Ibid.

30 See especially Felix J. Billiarde, "Superintendent Billiarde's Report, 1914–1915," in Department of Education, *Annual Report*, 1914-1915, 170.

31 Felix J. Billiarde, "Superintendent Billiarde's Report" in the *Report of the Department of Education for the Year Ending June 30ᵗʰ 1914* (Winnipeg: James Hooper, 1914), 162.

32 D.W. McKerchar, "Juvenile Court," in Department of Education, *Annual Report*, 1920–1921, 132.

33 On the 1924 amendment adding sexual immorality to the *JDA*, see Bruno Théorêt, "Régulation juridique pénale des mineures et discrimination à l'égard des filles: la clause de 1924 amendment la Loi sur les jeunes délinquents," *Canadian Journal of Women and the Law* 4 (1990–91): 539–555.

34 Felix J. Billiarde, "Superintendent Billiarde's Report, 1913–1914," in Department of Education, *Annual Report*, 1913–1914, 163.

35 Ibid.

36 Felix J. Billiarde, "Report of Superintendent Billiarde – Juvenile Court," in Department of Education, *Sessional Papers*, 1915–1916, 386.

37 Felix J. Billiarde, "Juvenile Court," in Department of Education, *Annual Report*, 1915–1916, 266. McKerchar also mentioned that the lack of a properly equipped psychopathic clinic hindered the work of the juvenile court. McKerchar, "Juvenile Court," 1917–1918, 140.

38 D.W. McKerchar, "Juvenile Court," in Department of Education, *Sessional Papers*, 1919–1920, 123–124 and 128.

39 Gynecological examinations were not regularly administered by the juvenile court until the late 1930s. Prior to this, reform institutions arranged for these exams and made special provisions for girls with venereal disease and those who were pregnant.

40 In Winnipeg, the reform institutions were Protestant or Catholic.There were no Jewish reform institutions in the city, suggesting that Jewish girls were admitted to Marymound or the Salvation Army Industrial Home. It is also possible that Jewish orphanages absorbed delinquent Jewish children. A Jewish orphanage opened in 1912 and another in 1913 but merged in 1917 to form the Jewish Orphanage and Children's Aid Society of Western Canada. See Tamara Myers, "On Probation: The Rise and Fall of Jewish Women's Antidelinquency Work in Interwar Montreal," in *Negotiating Identities in Nineteenth and Twentieth Century Montreal*, eds. Bettina Bradbury and Tamara Myers (Vancouver: University of British Columbia Press, 2005), 175–201.

41 For the processing of delinquent girls within Marymound, see Tanya Woloschuk, "Preserving the 'Moral Formation of the Child': The Regulation of Catholic Girls in Winnipeg, 1908-1948" (MA thesis, University of Manitoba, 2005), Chapter 3.

42 Stubbs, "The First Juvenile Court Judge."

43 McKerchar, "Juvenile Court," in Department of Education, *Sessional Papers*, 1919–1920, 125.

44 Dorothy Chunn notes that truancy was often the major preoccupation of juvenile courts in Canada during the 1910s and 20s; Dorothy Chunn, "Boys Will Be Men, Girls Will Be Mothers: The Legal Regulation of Childhood in Toronto and Vancouver," *Sociological Studies in Child Development* 3 (1990): 97. Tamara Myers and Mary Anne Poutanen note this was not the case in Quebec because compulsory schooling did not exist until 1943. See their "Cadets, Curfews, and Compulsory Schooling: Mobilizing Anglophone Children in WWII Quebec," *Histoire sociale/ Social History* 37, 76 (November 2005): 367–398.

45 See Billiarde, "Neglected and Delinquent Children," in "Report of the Department of Attorney-General for the Year Ending 31st of December 1911," 402–403.

46 As Théorêt points out, this meant the legislation focussed more on educating children than ensuring families had survival wages. Théorêt, "Espace social et régulation juridique des jeunes," 157.

47 See Billiarde, "Neglected and Delinquent Children," in "Report of the Department of Attorney-General for the Year Ending 31st of December 1911," 402-403. The 1898 Act had established the position of superintendent but it remained unfilled until 1908. Both the Office of Neglected Children and the Juvenile Court resided within the Department of Education until September 1924 when the Juvenile Court was transferred to the Department of the Attorney General. The Juvenile Court significantly assisted in the enforcement of the *Children's Protection Act*. The court's jurisdiction was limited to the city of Winnipeg until the *Juvenile Delinquents Act* was extended to include the Eastern Judicial District in March 1917. The *Children's Protection Act*, however, covered all of Manitoba.

48 Felix J. Billiarde, "Truancy Report of Mr. Billiarde, Superintendent of Neglected Children," Department of Education, *Annual Report*, 1912–1913, 147–148.

49 Ibid., 147.

50 Ibid., 147-148.

51 Billiarde, "Truancy Report of Mr. Billiarde, Superintendent of Neglected Children," 147–148; Billiarde, "Superintendent Billiarde's Report, 1913–1914," in Department of Education, *Annual Report*, 1913–1914, 162; Billiarde, "Superintendent Billiarde's Report, 1914–1915," in Department of Education, *Annual Report*, 1914–1915, 168.

52 Billiarde, "Superintendent Billiarde's Report, 1913–1914," in Department of Education, *Annual Report*, 165–166.

53 Felix J. Billiarde, "Neglected and Delinquent Children," in Department of the Attorney-General, *Sessional Papers*, 1912, 403.

54   Campbell, Daly, and a variety of other prominent citizens also supported the idea of public play-grounds. Daly noted that playgrounds would "uplift, elevate or engage their [children's] minds after school hours." Thomas Mayne Daly, "Letter to R.H. Smith, Esq., Secretary of the School Board, Winnipeg," 15 December 1908, as quoted in Billiarde, *Public Playgrounds for Winnipeg Children: A Series of Articles* (Winnipeg: n.p., 1909?), 25–26.

55   Billiarde, *Annual Report of the Superintendent of Neglected Children for the Province of Manitoba, 1912*, appendix i–xi.

56   Only five cases were dealt with in 1917 and only six in 1922.

57   Gloria Geller, "The Streaming of Males and Females in the Juvenile Justice System" (PhD diss., University of Toronto, 1981), 63.

58   Statistics for Winnipeg in 1911 taken from Alan Artibise, *Winnipeg: An Illustrated History* (Toronto: J. Lorimer, 1977), 204–205.

59   Manitoba, Department of Education, *Sessional Papers*, 1912–1920; Manitoba, Department of Education, *Annual Reports*, 1911–1924; Manitoba, Department of Attorney-General, *Sessional Papers*, 1911–1913, 1916; Billiarde, *Annual Report of the Superintendent of Neglected Children for the Province of Manitoba, 1912*.

60   McKerchar, "Juvenile Court," in Department of Education, *Annual Report*, 1917–1918, 142; McKerchar, "Juvenile Court," in Department of Education, *Annual Report*, 1920–1921, 131.

61   D.W. McKerchar, "Juvenile Court," in Department of Education, *Annual Report*, 1918–1919, 122.

62   The remaining 2 percent of cases heard in the juvenile court concerned adults who had contributed to the delinquency of children and youth.

63   Manitoba, Department of Education, *Sessional Papers*, 1917–1921, 1923–1924.

64   Hamilton, "Department of Neglected Children and Juvenile Court," in Department of Education, Annual Report, 1920–1921, 128. Girls sentenced to reform institutions consistently fell between the ages of sixteen and eighteen. Their numbers increased noticeably after the province increased the maximum age limit of the *Juvenile Delinquents Act* from sixteen to eighteen in 1930.

65   Myers, "Criminal Women and Bad Girls," 173–176; Joan Sangster, *Regulating Girls and Women: Sexuality, Family, and the Law in Ontario, 1920–1960* (Oxford: Oxford University Press, 2001), 131–167; Joan Sangster, *Girl Trouble: Female Delinquency in English Canada* (Toronto: Between the Lines, 2002), 31–39; Franca Iacovetta, "Parents, Daughters, and Family Court Intrusions into Working-Class Life," in *On the Case: Explorations in Social History*, eds. Franca Iacovetta and Wendy Mitchinson (Toronto: University of Toronto Press, 1998), 312–337; Bryan Hogeveen, "'Impossible Cases Can Be Cured When All the Factors Are Known': Gender, Psychiatry and Toronto's Juvenile Court, 1912–1930," *Canadian Bulletin of Medical History* 20, 1 (2003): 57.

66   McKerchar, "Juvenile Court," in Department of Education, *Annual Report*, 1918–1919, 122; Hamilton, "Department of Neglected Children and Juvenile Court," in Department of Education, *Annual Report*, 1920–1921, 128; Harkness, "Juvenile Court for the Eastern Judicial District of Manitoba," in Department of Education, *Annual Report*, 1923–1924, 69–70.

67   Statistics compiled from Marymound Logbook, 1911; Billiarde, *Annual Report of the Superintendent of Neglected Children for the Province of Manitoba 1912*, 135.

68   Marymound Logbook, 1911–1948. The numbers of Protestants remained consistently low, never reaching higher than 22 percent of the total number of incoming girls. In fact, Protestant girls were not sent to Marymound until 1918, and girls of other religions were only admitted in three years: 1925, 1936, and 1948. Given the lack of reformatories in the city, girls not sentenced to Marymound were likely sent to the Salvation Army Industrial Home. Only a minority of youth who appeared before the juvenile court were sent to reform institutions. Girls for whom probationary care had failed were more likely to be incarcerated. Marymound is one of the earliest institutions for girls in early twentieth-century Winnipeg with surviving records. Marymound created records on every girl it admitted, and boxes of case files sit uncategorized in the attic.

Every file in the three boxes of case files (numbering from 1 to 1227) between the early 1920s and 1948 was reviewed. Since case files dated primarily from the 1920s, 1930s, and 1940s, information about girls in the 1910s was taken from Marymound's logbook. Though the information contained in the logbook is limited, an analysis of the statistics gleaned from it does reveal important trends in the type of girl being incarcerated, the age at which girls were incarcerated, and their ethnic and religious backgrounds.

69 Myers, "Criminal Women and Bad Girls," 264; Sangster, *Girl Trouble*, 112–113; Barbara Brenzel, *Daughters of the State: A Social Portrait of the First Reform School for Girls in North America, 1856–1905* (Cambridge, Massachusetts: MIT Press, 1983), 77.

"All our friends and patients know us": The Margaret Scott Nursing Mission

Tamara Miller

In 1909, Mrs. M, an Italian immigrant who had been living in Winnipeg for three years, filled in an application for confinement attendance with the Margaret Scott Nursing Mission.[1] Her husband, a labourer, had been out of work for months, and with three other children to feed, the family was unable to pay anything for midwifery care. So they turned to the mission, a well-known local benevolent nursing organization, serving the city's poor.

This paper focuses on the role of the Margaret Scott Nursing Mission in turn-of-the-century Winnipeg as a means of examining the fledgling social and health care services taking root in early twentieth-century Canada. Canada's much-loved "social safety net" was many years away, and the management of services for the poor and indigent was just beginning to migrate from the church to the state. An examination of the mission—a fixture in Winnipeg's working-class and immigrant quarter—and its clientele provides a snapshot of germinating social welfare and health care systems.

Mrs. M and her family were, in fact, fairly representative of the immigrant population resident in Winnipeg in the early twentieth century. The cultural make-up of the Margaret Scott Mission patients was reflective of the diverse population concentrated in Winnipeg's "North End." While those of British heritage represented 73 percent of the city's overall population in 1916, only 39 percent of the North End population identified as British.[2]

Like Mrs. M and her family, many North End immigrants were among the city's poor, living, at times, in deplorable conditions. J.S. Woodsworth, a Methodist clergyman, wrote of Winnipeg in 1911: "It is difficult to find an actual working man's family budget which maintains a normal standard."[3] The social aid system in Winnipeg was woefully inadequate, and the charity system in place rested on the principle of "worthy recipients." Thus, candidates for assistance needed to conform to the appropriate model and conduct, not always an easy task for an immigrant family with cultural traditions that may have differed from that of the dominant British class.

It was in this arena that the female-dominated Margaret Scott Mission was able to carve a place for itself in turn-of-the-century Winnipeg society. Coping with exploding demographics, a large and poor immigrant population and immature health care structures, Winnipeg provided an opportunity for the mission to establish itself without threatening the male-dominated medical profession seeking to lay claim to similar ground.

The recognized founder of the mission, Margaret Ruttan Boucher (1856–1931), was born on 28 July 1855, into a wealthy family in the town of Colborne, Ontario. At the age of twenty-two, she met and married William Hepburn Scott, a lawyer and member of the Ontario legislature, and settled into a predictable and respectable life as a middle-class wife. However, at the untimely death of her husband in 1881, her life would adopt a radically different course, earning her the moniker "the angel of poverty row." Widowed and in need of employment to support herself, Scott obtained a clerical position with Midland Railways in Peterborough, Ontario. Five years later, in 1886, she took up employment with the Dominion Land Office in Winnipeg, where she met the Rev. C.C. Owen of Holy Trinity Anglican Church.

Arriving only sixteen years after the incorporation of Manitoba as a province, Scott was struck by the plight of the immigrant poor in Winnipeg's North End and volunteered her services for the Reverend's relief work. By 1898, she had given up her position in the Land Commissioner's Office to devote all her time to the work of the Winnipeg Lodging and Coffee House, a hostel for the destitute and transient. She lived with Rev. and Mrs. Owen and offered her services by visiting and counselling female prisoners and helping them find employment and residence. Eventually, she moved into the coffee house. Despite her lack of nursing training, she began making "rounds" among the poor, offering care to the sick. Scott's work was financed by donations from wealthy patrons. Mr. E.H. Taylor, a local businessman and long-time supporter of the coffee house, became her strongest benefactor when he offered to pay the salary of a trained nurse to assist Scott through the winter months. Upon Taylor's death, the city agreed to assume the cost of a full-time nurse, while Rev. C.W. Gordon offered the funds for a second nurse.[4]

From simple beginnings, the mission became part of Winnipeg urban folklore. At the closing of the mission in 1943, a newspaper eulogy revealed the community's familiarity with the mission and its namesake: "The clop clop of a shaganappi pony's hoofs have died away from George street. The Margaret Scott Mission home at No. 99 is sold. The picture of the white haired lady who started the Mission in 1905 and made her nursing rounds with pony and trap has been taken down from the mantel and stored away in a trunk."[5] The organization that bore her name was closely associated with the legend of Margaret Scott. The history of the organization, however, was equally steeped in the traditions of social welfare prominent in Canadian society at the turn of the century. While Scott was the centrepiece of the legend, the evolution of the Mission involved a community of social reformers, led by women, whose class and cultural beliefs fuelled their benevolent work.

Margaret Scott, in fact, was not instrumental in securing funding for the founding of a formal mission. Rather, a group of middle-class women, chaired by a close friend of Scott's, Mrs. A.M. Fraser, organized a meeting with prominent citizens and representatives from several of the city's churches on 26 May 1904. The attendees of the meeting carried social assumptions about the city's immigrant poor, noting that they were: "responding to an undercurrent movement towards a closer relation between churches and the homes of the *ignorant* poor in congested and unhealthy districts of the city."[6] The objective, as outlined by the chairman of the meeting, John S. Ewart, a prominent lawyer and political commentator, was to "secure a house that will answer as a central home for nurses to which application can be made, clothing and subscriptions sent, where benefits of consultation and cooperation may be had, and where women who have time and ability to devote to such work, can get first hand experience, thus forming a band of nurses to supplement the work of the regular district nurse."[7] On 12 November 1904, a second meeting was held for the purpose of selecting an advisory board, a board of directors, and a board of management. At that meeting, it was resolved that membership to the mission would be "open to all upon payment of an annual subscription fee of one dollar."[8] This fee, while relatively minor, would have immediately limited the membership of the mission and, therefore, restricted the pool of eligible candidates to sit on the management boards. Only those with some form of disposable income would have been able to pay in order to embark on charity work. Consequently, it was likely that only middle- and upper-class citizens were involved in the administration positions.

The administration of the mission was composed of a "Board of Directors, such Board to be composed of an Advisory Board of ten gentlemen … and a Board of Management of twenty-five ladies."[9] The gender division between the two boards was demonstrative of the gendered split in reform work.[10] While both the Advisory Board (all male) and the Board of Managers (all female) were involved in the organization of the mission, including the structuring of by-laws and purchasing of land, the day-to-day operation of the mission was left solely to non-medically trained middle-class women on the Board of Management and the nurses who served on staff.[11] In the *Annual Report* for 1905, the officers and board of the mission listed were all women. The staff was listed as Miss Beveridge, the nursing superintendent, three other trained nurses, two final-year nurses from the Winnipeg General Hospital, a housekeeper, and Mrs. Scott.[12]

A consequence of the prevalence of middle-class women in the day-to-day operations of the mission was that the cultural and class biases of the organizers rooted themselves into the treatment of poor and working-class patients. Historian Mariana Valverde has argued that the "language of Missions and of purity work reflected pre-existing power relations," and relied on beliefs about class, gender, and race to establish structural authority.[13] In the case of the mission, the nurse's role within the patient's home was not just as a caregiver but also as a *purifier*, elevating the poor through missionary care. A description of a typical home visit by a mission nurse was laced with assumptions about working-class families:

Here is a little shack in the North End; you might almost pass it by without noticing it, as it stands modestly back from the road, as if it was almost ashamed to be seen. We knock on the door and go in. The room is full of men and children and steam. The little girl has been washing and the damp clothes hang all around. The men (father and sons) are out of work, they say, as it is about 40 below and too cold for outdoor work. The indoor work devolves on two little girls who cannot afford to be idle. The washing and cooking has to be done, the bread made (such as it is!) and the baby cared for. We pass into the inner room where we find one of our nurses busy bathing and dressing the baby and making the mother comfortable for the day. The poor woman's eyes are sparkling as she gazes at a bright colored quilt on her bed sent by the Mission. She is Polish and cannot speak English, except to say "Tank you, tank you," but her eyes show her pleasure. The baby, which had only been wrapped in dirty cotton rags before, is now washed and dressed in pretty little baby clothes which nurse has brought with her. The mother and children look on admiringly.[14]

While not overtly critical of the living conditions of the family, the language used to describe the situation is laden with meaning. Words such as "ashamed," used to describe the shack, were reflective of the writer's assessment of the family. The sceptical tone with reference to the men hinted at the overall impression the writer had of the immigrant family, discreetly imposing a value judgement. However, it was the language referring to the nurse that stands out in the above passage. In comparison to the language used to describe the family, the nurse, and the items she brought into the home, were "bright," "washed," and "pretty." The Margaret Scott nurse stood in contradiction to the squalor that bathed immigrant communities and families. Their role as reformers was "a discourse as much about class as about gender."[15]

The authority of scientific theory bolstered the work of the mission as a nursing organization. Nurses, therefore, often assumed a superior and instructive role in the homes of their patients. The language used by the nurses betrayed class attitudes predicated on their belief system. As a pupil nurse, J.G. Morrison condemned the conditions of home nursing service: "How can a case be conducted with such a state of affairs existing? It seems to be a desecration of the term technique."[16] Like her medical brethren, the nurse ascribed to a strict "technique," whose replication was seen as difficult in the homes of patients.

The nurse's gender allowed her admittance to the home as a nurturer and caregiver, but the nurse's training and class offered her a position of authority. Because of her expertise and education, she was allowed to manage even the husband, a role not typical for women in turn-of-the-century society: "First of all, friend husband's hitherto useless and often frantic energies are turned into a useful channel. He is made a hewer of wood and carrier of water, also making himself indispensable in giving general information re: the hiding place of different articles."[17] Admittedly, the man in question was not a professional of similar social class to that of the nurse. Nonetheless, in the home nursing scenario, a man acted as an assistant to a female professional, turning the tables on many preconceived notions of gender roles.

The involvement of nurses in home childbirth attendance represented a particularly special bridge between traditional practices and the movement towards physician-attended, and ultimately hospitalized, birth experiences. The care accorded by nurses, while true to the premises of scientific theory, nonetheless represented the unique characteristics of women as primary caregivers in the family and community. Historian Karen Buhler-Wilkinson described the blend of domesticity and scientific training in nursing care: "Good nursing care was thought to include keeping the air in the room fresh and wholesome, the patient, the patient's bed and sick room clear and quiet, establishing regularity in the giving of nourishment and medicines, skilled observation of the patient's condition, carefully recorded or communicated to the doctor, and the taking of appropriate measures to prevent the spread of contagious diseases."[18] The containment of contagion spoke to a nurse's scientific training, while the care of the room and feeding of the patient were similar to the role of any woman in the home. Historian Susan Reverby in her study of American nursing has referred to this dual nature of nursing work as the "dilemma of professionalism."[19]

A visit from a Margaret Scott nurse exemplified the dual nature of nursing work. Many of the nurses, upon entering the homes of patients, assumed some of the domestic chores that the incapacitated mother would be unable to perform effectively: "When the neatly uniformed nurse arrives all is quickly changed. A bright fire is soon blazing; the mother is made comfortable, and the wee baby is washed and dressed; warm food is prepared; the house is made tidy; tactful suggestions are given as to better modes of management, while many bright and encouraging words are spoken, elevating to higher things.... Wherever the nurses go they give out their best energies, attending to the sick, chopping wood, drawing water, lighting fires, cooking food, bathing patients, dressing wounds."[20] While the nurse was present because of her training, her position was also firmly rooted in her identity as a woman. Historian Kathryn McPherson has argued, "nursing relied on an image of feminine respectability to legitimate nurses' presence in the health-care system and their knowledge of the body."[21] Consequently, the duties the nurse assumed were reflective of her domestic role in society.

It is interesting to note that, by the end of 1905, the board of directors at the mission had arranged for assistants to perform household chores while the nurses attended the sick and provided instruction. In the *Annual Report* for 1905, it was noted that the "assistants to the nurses shall do the chores in the homes of the sick ... so that the trained nurse's more valuable time may not be dissipated. These helpers are, as a rule, foreigners, thus being very useful among our cosmopolitan population."[22] This change may have been reflective of the increased movement of nursing towards professionalization. Although writing about a later period in nursing history, McPherson did note that the "introduction of subsidiary patient-care attendants ... substantially enhanced the professional standing of graduate nurses."[23]

Throughout its history, the role of the Margaret Scott Nursing Mission exemplified the feminine side of urban missionary work. Despite its best intentions to provide uniquely nursing services, the mission expanded its role because the socio-economic conditions of the area it serviced rendered the provision of nursing services impractical without social service work. "We still supply extra nourishment in cases of illness," noted one mission member in 1929, "also clothing, when we have supplies on hand. We have a loan cupboard with sheets, night-dresses, etc. The Auxiliary keep up our supplies of these articles, also making pneumonia jackets, infants and children's clothing, etc. as required."[24]

While the links to the social welfare work were ever-present, mission nurses, increasingly trained in the institutional environment of the hospital, often brought the rigid hierarchical structure of the hospital environment into their patients' homes, including subservience to physicians. Upon its inception, the mission recognized the notion that the hospital was a central institution in health care delivery. "It will, of course," noted the *Annual Report* in 1905, "be borne in mind that this is auxiliary to established hospitals."[25] While the mission operated independently of any health care organization, many of the city's physicians attended mission cases free of charge. Almost all patients, therefore, were accorded a visit from a physician, many of whom held attending positions at the Winnipeg General Hospital. The mission's association with the hospital structure was further reinforced in June 1905 when District Nursing was added to the curriculum of the Winnipeg General Hospital School of Nursing. Arrangements were made for student nurses to receive practical training for two-month periods through the mission.[26] This association indicated that the mission and the hospital shared similar views on nursing roles and expectations.

Nurses managed cases daily, but their role was always deferential to that of the physician. The 1938 nursing care standing orders, for example, drawn up by the Medical Advisory Committee, were "to be used only when there is no physician in attendance or when previous orders have not been left by the attending physician, in which case they should be used only until it has been possible to communicate with the physician."[27] Nursing practitioners understood the hierarchical structure of the medical system.

Public health nurses, nonetheless, often operated outside the rigid hierarchy of the hospital system. While they continued to ascribe to the social and class mores they had been taught in training schools, their involvement with the family and community garnered public health nurses a more autonomous working environment. In a study of women at work in Ontario, Judi Coburn noted of public health nurses: "their responsibility was often to a community rather than a hierarchic institution."[28] The board of directors, for example, was not always amenable to the requests of the hospital. In August 1907, the board received a letter from Dr. McCalman in the Department of Obstetrics at the Manitoba Medical College (affiliated with the Winnipeg General) requesting that "arrangements be made providing that [medical] students of the final year be called to cases of confinement conducted by the Nurses of their Mission."[29] While the board did not dismiss the request, they put the matter off for several months, and the request had not been decided upon as late as December 1907. Ultimately, the board accepted the hospital's request, but not without insisting that a committee representing the mission "meet the Doctors and consult with them on the subject, the committee to act at once with the power to accept or reject."[30]

The Board of Management never expressly voiced its concerns, but in a letter to the board following his original request, McCalman promised that "students should not personally attend or conduct any case presenting any difficulty whatsoever.... In all instrumental and complicated cases one [a doctor] of experience should be called upon to do the work."[31] Whether the mission administration, or its nurses, were concerned about the skills of students, and the potential danger, is not certain. However, McCalman's letter, addressing solely this issue, indicated that it was of some importance to the mission board.

The minutes of the mission board meeting also point to a deviation from the traditional subservient relationship between doctors and nurses characteristic of a hospital setting. Expecting full cooperation from the mission, Dr. McCalman outlined procedure for calling students to cases in a letter written in October. The board at that time, however, had still not made a pronouncement on the issue, nor were they intending to until such time as a meeting could be arranged.[32] As historian Kathryn McPherson noted: "The women who occupied administrative and nursing positions within private religious institutions and organizations wielded administrative and medical authority which often surpassed that of their peers in public, secular hospitals."[33] Within the confines of the day-to-day activities of the mission, the board and nurses maintained a degree of authority not necessarily customary in the doctor-nurse dynamic.

While Margaret Scott and her nurses were the figurehead and faces of the organization, the overall character of the mission can also be seen in its funding foundations. Funding for the Mission was derived from a combination of public and private sources. Consequently, the work of the mission was necessarily directed by the needs of the medical advisors or community. In addition to private donations, the mission received $2000 from the City of Winnipeg as contribution to a building fund, and $500 from the Province of Manitoba as start-up money. The total budget for the first year of operation was $6753.27.[34] The city and province continued to provide significant funds to the mission for its entire history. While the majority of funds were collected through patient fees or private donations, the mission, like public hospitals of the period, relied heavily on public funding. As a result, some of the money was earmarked specifically for public health work identified by the city. From July 1910 until September 1914, the city provided a grant to the mission uniquely to pay the salary of a nurse to carry out child welfare work. When the city began providing district nurses for child welfare work, it continued the grant to the mission to carry on work as a milk depot.[35] This is evidence that the work of the mission was influenced by the requests of its largest contributor.

The Dominion Government also provided some funds through the Department of Immigration. Health service organizations could collect one dollar for each immigrant treated, if they could prove that the applicant was indeed a recent immigrant. In 1906, federal monies totalled $291.89 but diminished to $178.49 by 1907. Because the burden of proof was placed on the mission, the Department of Immigration often rejected applicants based on the fact that the names did not appear on ship manifests.[36]

In the summer of 1905, the mission moved from a temporary location on Pearl Street to its permanent home on George Street. While they wore the uniform, mission nurses were treated with respect and admiration. When offered a police escort travelling through the more crime-ridden parts of the city, a nurse responded: "I am not afraid to go anywhere at any time in my uniform as all our friends and patients know us."[37]

In its first year of operation, 1905, the mission recorded 6937 visits. The mission cases were described as "the infinite number of cases that must otherwise go to hospitals, or else be neglected—cases where a mother must remain, even in her anguish, to take care of her home, or chronics where a daily call will tide the sufferer over the day, or where the home or even the patient supplied some measure of self-help, when guided by the District Nurse."[38] More complete statistics available for 1912 also reveal that a greater proportion of Mission patients were more often women and children. Out of a total of 1330 patients, 686 were female, 600 were children, and only 44 were male.[39] Obstetrical cases, therefore, invariably occupied a great deal of the mission's time and attention. Until the 1930s, more than 20 percent of nursing visits were related to obstetrical cases.

At a time when national attention was turned towards the maternal mortality rate, the conditions faced by the working-class mothers were a consistent topic in the mission's *Annual Reports*. The nurses echoed the fears and concerns of working-class mothers and spoke to the socio-economic conditions faced by the immigrant population of Winnipeg's North End. Writing in 1908, one of the mission nurses remarked of the plight of the poor mothers under her care: "Among dirt and squalor, one finds mothers giving up their lives for their children, and what should be an occasion for joy, too often is looked on as a calamity, another mouth to be filled, another little piece of humanity to be clothed, when there is already scanty enough measure for the family."[40] Nurses, perhaps because of shared gendered experiences with the women they cared for, acknowledged the financial strain that childbirth had on the family. They sympathized with the mother whose responsibility was to provide for the new arrival. District and public health nurses seemed to display a better understanding of the living conditions in working-class communities. Their jobs were predicated on their ability to circumvent, or accommodate, the surroundings in order to care for the patient.

Whenever possible, nurses upheld the principles of their training. But, they also recognized the limitations imposed by poverty. As one nurse noted: "The provision made by the mother in view of coming need is often of the most inadequate description, and here the Mission steps in and does good service, lending linen, and otherwise providing for those who would be practically destitute of comfort at a time when they should have all consideration that can be given. In other cases, however, where the utmost thrift had been practiced, nothing was lacking in the preparation made and the little stranger who came, found warm hearts ready to receive him, and ample care for his comfort."[41] This points to further evidence that the mission acted as a social welfare organization, providing many of the necessities for a safe and comfortable birth.

The typical maternity case attended by a Margaret Scott nurse was significantly different from the routine she would have learned in her training. Nurses were forced to adapt to the surrounding conditions. Unlike their medical brethren, home nurses had to be more flexible and autonomous in their approach to individual cases.[42] A student nurse described the sight of her first obstetrical case:

> Nurse arrives, not preceded by the doctor, as is the case in the hospital. Probably the only light in the tiny room is furnished by a small coal-oil lamp, which burns waveringly and spasmodically, the patient lying on the low, wide, sagging bed in the corner; the nearest telephone two blocks away; absolutely no sterile dressings other than the few carried in the bag; dear me!

> Household articles are found to make admitable substitutes in the absence of the proper utensils; if mother has positively only one nightie and it is essential to make a change, why, husband's best shirt is just the thing.... What a lesson in bedside nursing is learned! Such a contrast to hospital routine.[43]

The tone of the nurse was perhaps related to the fact that, as a woman, she felt a higher degree of comfort in the home. The domestic role would have been part of her job, and therefore, the duties associated with this would not have jeopardized her role as a professional. In describing a similar situation in 1924, the *Annual Report* exclaimed: "Did you say, What a miserable place? How unhappy they must be! Oh no, they are not unhappy. They have each other and the baby.... Mere things cannot make you happy or unhappy. Contentment is needed, and they are content yet full of ambition, and for their wonderful child they will struggle, and will 'make good,' and in this 'making good' will become good Canadian citizens."[44]

The language focussed more on the ambitions of a missionary service—the mission's second role. Not surprisingly, the use of moral reform rhetoric infiltrated the annual reports. The Board of Managers, who wrote the report for potential donors, would have used the language familiar to their community. The issue of "Canadianizing" foreigners was common political rhetoric among members of the middle-class who addressed social problems.[45]

Margaret Scott nurses were also involved in prenatal and postpartum visits. In 1928, for example, 23.4 percent of all visits were obstetrical, 2.5 percent were related to prenatal or follow-up, and 23.9 percent were to maternity infants. "On calling," noted the 1928 annual report, "the nurse examines the infant and thus learns if the child be properly bathed, clothed and nourished, and when necessary gives instructions and returns to see if they have been properly carried out."[46] Overall, the nurse's role in the postnatal period focussed on teaching a new mother how to "mother"—how to clothe, feed, and bathe her baby.

Starting in 1905, arrangements were made with the Winnipeg General Hospital to have two student nurses from the School of Nursing serve a public health training period with the mission.[47] Student nurses, therefore, became a steady supply of labour for the mission. By 1935, the mission had five graduate nurses and eight student nurses attending to the needs of its patient population. The graduate to student ratio, however, would become a problem. In 1937, the Board of Managers appointed a committee to review the work of the mission, with specific emphasis on the staffing situation:

> Early in the year the Board became conscious of having outgrown its dress. Changed social conditions in the city and a new consciousness of the require-ments of a Public Health Nursing Service made the members realize that some reorganization was necessary... It was deemed advisable to call in the Super-intendent of Nurses (acting) for the Winnipeg General Hospital, the Superin-tendent of Nurses for the Children's Hospital, as from these two hospitals came our student nurses, and the Executive Secretary for the Manitoba Association of Registered Nurses, they to form a small committee to go carefully into the nursing situation and give the Board the benefit of their experience.[48]

The structural reorganization was likely a response to criticisms that the mission had more student nurses than experienced graduates working among patients. The long-time practice of using student nurses would likely have undercut the cost of salaries for graduate nurses, especially for a benevolent organization operating in a working-class community in the 1930s. Kathryn McPherson has identified just such economic issues as being a primary contributor to a professional crisis in the interwar years.[49] Doubt was raised as to the ability of student nurses to adequately perform without supervision. Further, with nursing struggling to establish its legitimacy, the use of student nurses may have undercut nurses' professional positions.

After the committee was struck, the mission replaced the entire nursing staff, revised the organization, and implemented a new system of record keeping.[50] Ultimately, the committee recommended that the permanent staff be increased by one to a total of six and that the number of pupil nurses be decreased to one.[51] The nurses were also reminded of their role in medical care. The Obstetrical Standing Orders for nurses drawn up by the Medical Advisory Committee in 1938 effectively omitted all reference to the actual delivery, focussing only on the pre- and postnatal care duties.[52]

Whether the mission actually heeded the advice of the committee is difficult to determine. A report on the services of the mission, written around 1941, outlined the use of student nurses as a fundamental flaw in the Margaret Scott Mission:

> One of the present practices of the Margaret Scott Nursing Mission is to be frankly condemned and that is its program of accepting for training five or six student nurses ... let us not forget that the primary objective of this training or exposure should always be to provide an experience of true educational value to the student nurse and not to obtain cheap service. While doubtless not by intent, the result of the student nurse training program at the Mission has been largely to obtain cheap service. That this is true is fairly well substantiated by the figures for the nursing service. The Victorian Order report for 1940 gives a total number of nursing visits of 17,356. The Margaret Scott Nursing Mission reports 17,554 nursing visits. The Victorian Order has eight field nurses, the Margaret Scott five.[53]

Within a year, the mission would be incorporated into the Victorian Order of Nurses (VON).

The targets of the mission's services during its tenure of operation, one nurse stated, were "the poorer immigrants and the foreign element."[54] In 1914, arrangements had been made with the VON to ensure that the two organizations did not duplicate services. The mission took on only those patients who were unable to pay, while the VON took those who were able to pay their fee of twenty-five cents.[55] In order to receive nursing attendance, prospective patients filled out an application for service. The information received allowed the mission to compile a statistical portrait of its patient population. This information was published in the annual reports beginning in 1909.[56] That year 9984 visits were made to 1192 patients. Of these, there were 181 Canadians (15 percent), 289 English (24 percent), 48 Irish (4 percent), 86 Scottish (7 percent), 17 Americans (1 percent), and 571 other (48 percent). Further, 622 were classified as Protestant (52 percent), 418 Roman Catholic (35 percent), 115 Jewish (10 percent), and 37 unknown (3 percent). Female patients represented 71 percent of recorded cases, while attendance of infants and sick kids represented 29 percent of overall visits.[57]

How representative was the patient population of the mission of the overall Winnipeg population? In order to make a preliminary comparison, data have been drawn from the 1921, 1931, and 1941 Census of Canada and the annual reports from the mission for those same years. First, an examination of the gender breakdowns demonstrates that women used the mission more often than men, even though census data reveal a more or less even split between men and women.[58] The higher proportion of female patients may perhaps be explained by the high proportion of visits accorded to maternity cases.

According to the census material, Winnipeg citizens listing Canada as their place of birth totalled 93,854 in 1921. This represented over half of the city's population. Statistics available through the mission's annual report, however, were much more reflective of the ethnic diversity of the North End. More than 53 percent of the patients attended by mission nurses were from countries other than the designated English-speaking nations of Canada, England, Scotland, and Ireland. This discrepancy can be attributed partially to the location of the mission, teetering on the edge of the North End. However, the mission patient portfolio also demonstrates a socioeconomic division based on cultural and ethnic divisions in Winnipeg. Those in need of mission care were the poorest inhabitants of the city, and the high number of non-British patients testified to the social composition of the city. The middle-class and better-off working-class people—those who could afford to pay something for nursing care—were predominantly British-Canadian, while the working poor were principally foreign immigrants. The statistical data demonstrate that the patient population at the Margaret Scott Nursing Mission would have been predominantly immigrant women.

The mission continued to draw a high proportion of immigrant patients in 1931. However, the changing character of the city was influencing the ethnicity of the North End community. The mission treated a higher proportion of Canadian-born patients, reflecting the fact that immigration had slowed in the interwar period.

During the interwar period, as demographers Roderic Beaujot and Kevin McQuillan have demonstrated, "immigration did not make a striking impact on the country. The settlement pattern of the Prairies, involving high proportions with origins other than British or French, was established by 1914 and the immigration of the two following decades had little impact on settlement patterns in the country."[59] As a result, Winnipeg experienced a rise in the numbers of native-born citizens, as first- and second-generation immigrant communities established families. The influences of the changing demographics were felt among the North End population serviced by mission nurses.

By 1941, the ethnic character of the mission patient population closely resembled that of the overall Winnipeg population. In fact, the mission population had a slightly higher proportion of Canadian-born patients than in the overall Winnipeg population. The phenomenon of slowing immigration, already influencing the city in 1931, continued to shape the cultural characteristics of Winnipeg.

However, the shift in treatment focus of the mission also likely contributed to the shifting cultural character of the patient portfolio. The 1937 reorganization, which had eliminated obstetrical cases, had also reoriented the primary focus of mission activities. That year, chronic and long-term care patients represented the highest proportion of nursing visits. Of a total 14,787 visits, chronic care consumed 4012 (27 percent), while postpartum and newborn care accounted for 4254 (29 percent) visits.[60] Previously, as has been shown, the work of the mission was steeped in maternity and infant care, incorporating a number of young, more mobile, families into their patient load. The increasing number of chronic care cases may have resulted in a higher proportion of elderly patients. The character of the nursing service had undergone a fundamental change, and that had a bearing on the patient base.

By the late 1930s, increased hospitalization and the decline of immigration into Winnipeg had begun to alter the patient population of the mission. The Great Depression had brought the reluctant federal government into the realm of health care. As historian David Naylor has shown, to federal politicians and bureaucrats, hospitals and physicians were seen as the most efficient front line in health care delivery.[61] As a result, the mission adopted more chronic care cases, while most acute patients sought attendance in hospital. Home births decreased and nurses were no longer required to provide prenatal care, a task assumed by obstetricians as technologies advanced and promised safer deliveries. The 1942 incorporation of the mission into the VON demonstrated the transformation in health care delivery. The VON offered subsidized home nursing care in collaboration with local governments and medical insurance providers.

The Margaret Scott Nursing Mission represented a clear example of a medical care delivery organization filling a void in social and health care services in early twentieth-century Winnipeg. The statistics available for the mission show that a large portion of the nurses' caseload consisted of obstetrical care in the early years, including childbirth attendance in addition to pre- and postnatal home care.[62] In keeping with the traditions of female reformers prominent in turn-of-the-century Canada, the mission represented a clear alternative to physician care for those who could not afford a doctor or simply eschewed the necessity.[63] As a social service organization, the mission was typical of the Victorian health reform movement. It was administered by a group of middle-class women, with support from male professionals, and the values espoused by the organization reflected the values of British-Canadian culture.

The patient experience at the mission was similar across Canada for those individuals who sought out benevolent attendance. While the discourse that surrounded the mission certainly had religious overtones, the mission did not have direct affiliation with any specific denominational church. The mission statement firmly noted that the nursing organization would not be specifically connected with any denomination in order to offer care to the many immigrants of various religious backgrounds. The mission was interdenominational and, as expressed in one of its resolutions, cooperated "in its work with all Churches and Clergy of the City and Benevolent Associations prosecuting like or similar charitable objects."[64]

The objectives of the mission also often paralleled those of settlement houses such as the one pioneered by Jane Addams in the United States.[65] The nurses boarded at the mission house in the heart of Winnipeg's central core, and they were encouraged to make use of visits for instruction and education in addition to providing the necessary care. The nurses' presence in the community set them apart from health care providers associated with medical institutions. They brought their institutional training into the community, acting as a bridge between care giving and scientific medicine.[66] They also brought with them their middle-class mores and assumptions, which they often imposed on their patients, despite the obvious economic and cultural gaps. The nurses were young, single, middle-class and white; in dealing with the immigrant poor, they often demonstrated class and cultural biases.[67]

While the mission had connections with the medical community, it nonetheless operated fairly autonomously. Until 1937, most decisions were left up to the staff and the Board of Managers, all of whom were women.[68] In other words, all administrative and medical decisions were left in the hands of women and were readily accepted by the larger medical community.

A large proportion of the cases attended by mission nurses were, in the early years, women in need of childbirth attendance. Through their services, the nurses became an extension of the traditional community of women who surrounded birthing mothers. The home nursing program responded to the needs of poor women by directly addressing the fears of their patients, including the expense of medical attendance and those associated with a new baby.[69] Margaret Scott nurses not only provided medical care, but also assisted with household chores and often brought food or clothing for the children.

Operating for nearly forty years as a legitimate and respected health care alternative to hospitalization in Winnipeg, the Margaret Scott Mission was perceived as part of the recognized health care network. The mission's associations with local physicians and its teaching collaboration with the Winnipeg General Hospital demonstrate its acceptance in the Winnipeg medical community. Influenced by the greater social reform movement prevalent in Canada at the time, the mission also conformed to the standards of "purity" orchestrated by middle-class reformers who sought to inject their values into poor, often immigrant, communities. The mission was an active, and desired, participant in health care delivery in one of Canada's largest metropolitan centres. In addition, it represented a public health component of the broader social reform movement prevalent throughout much of North America at the time.[70]

Still, the mission maintained its local Winnipeg characteristics due primarily to its large immigrant patient population and its locally based administrative body. The organization had a perspective on health that differed from the mainstream medical community of the day. The gendered administrative board, staff, and patient population created an environment that was predisposed to the needs of working-class, immigrant patients, and women, in particular. The organization was a manifestation of the gendered side of social reform, a distinctively female-led movement that aligned itself with the broader moral reform agenda, rather than the distinctly feminist agenda, which was more focussed on suffrage and a political voice for women.

The historical importance of the mission, therefore, is twofold: it provides insight into the scientific developments of health care delivery, while furnishing a record of the experiences and demographics of the city's immigrant, working-class populations. For most of their patients, Margaret Scott nurses would clean house, provide child care or cook meals in addition to medical nursing duties. In the home of patients, these nurses had an extended role beyond that of health care delivery—an approach that coloured health care policy in early twentieth-century Canada.

Notes

1   The Archives of Manitoba has granted access to the files of the Margaret Scott Nursing Mission on the condition that patients not be identified. Biographical details drawn from an *Application for Nursing Attendance and Relief*, Margaret Scott Nursing Mission collection [hereinafter MSNM], Archives of Manitoba [hereafter AM], MG 10 B9, Box 7.

2   Alan Artibise, *Winnipeg: A Social History of Urban Growth, 1874–1914* (Montreal: McGill-Queen's University Press, 1975), 158–165.

3   Cited in Artibise, *Winnipeg*, Appendix 4, 312.

4   Biographical information compiled from article clippings held in the MSNM, AM MG10 B9, Box 2; and, Helena Macvicar, "Margaret Scott: A Tribute," c. 1939, MSNM, AM MG 10 B9, Box 2.

5   Lillian Gibbons, "The Shaganappi Pony That Went Along George Street," *Winnipeg Tribune*, 15 May 1943. Found in MSNM, AM MG 10 B9, Box 1.

6   *Board of Management, Minutes of Proceedings*, 12 May 1904. MSNM, AM MG 10 B9, Box 4. Emphasis added.

7   Cited in Macvicar, "Margaret Scott," 18.

8   Cited in Macvicar, "Margaret Scott," 19.

9   Cited in Macvicar, "Margaret Scott," 19. For a list of individuals, see Appendix 2.

10 Veronica Strong-Boag, *The Parliament of Women: The National Council of Women of Canada, 1893–1929* (Ottawa: National Museums of Canada, 1976), 2.

11 Macvicar, "Margaret Scott," 19.

12 *Annual Report for 1905 of the Margaret Scott Nursing Mission*, 5–6. MSNM, AM MG10 B9, Box 6.

13 Mariana Valverde, *The Age of Light, Soap, and Water: Moral Reform in English Canada, 1885–1925* (Toronto: McClelland and Stewart, 1991), 42 and 43.

14 *Annual Report for 1907 of the Margaret Scott Nursing Mission*, 9. MSNM, AM MG10 B9, Box 6.

15 Valverde, *The Age of Light, Soap, and Water*, 32.

16 *Annual Report for 1926 of the Winnipeg General Hospital*, 24. MSNM, AM MG10 B9, Box 6.

17 *Annual Report for 1926 of the Winnipeg General Hospital*, 24. MSNM, AM MG10 B9, Box 6.

18 Karen Buhler-Wilkinson, *False Dawn: The Rise and Decline of Public Health Nursing, 1900–1930* (New York: Garland Publishing, 1989), 28.

19 Susan Reverby, *Ordered to Care: The Dilemma of American Nursing, 1850–1945* (Cambridge: Cambridge University Press, 1987), 1.

20 *Annual Report*, 1905, 4–5. MSNM, AM MG 10 B9, Box 6.

21 Kathryn McPherson, *Bedside Matters: The Transformation of Canadian Nursing, 1900–1990* (Toronto: University of Toronto Press, 2003), 16.

22 *Annual Report*, 1905, 5. MSNM, AM MG10 B9, Box 6.

23 McPherson, *Bedside Matters*, 226.

24 Document 1213, author unknown, MSNMC, AM MG 10 B9, Box 2.

25 *Annual Report*, 1905, 5. MSNM, AM MG10 B9, Box 6.

26 Board of Management, "Minutes of Monthly Meeting, June 10, 1905," MSNM, AM MG 10 B9, Box 4.

27 "Standing Orders," Document 686. MSNM, AM MG10 B9, Box 1.

28 Judi Coburn, "'I See and Am Silent': A Short History of Nursing in Ontario, 1850–1930," in *Health and Canadian Society*, ed. David Coburn, Carl D'Arcy, George Torrance, and Peter New, 2nd ed. (Markham: Fitzhenry and Whiteside, 1987), 150.

29 D.H. McCalman to the Board of Directors, MSNM, 9 August 1907, MSNMC, AM MG10 B9, Box 1.

30 Board of Management, "Minutes of Monthly and Annual Meetings," 11 November 1907. MSNM, AM MG10 B9, Box 4.

31 Letters, 9 Aug. 1907, 12 Sept. 1907, 10 Oct. 1907. MSNM, AM MG10 B9, Box 1.

32 D.H. McCalman to the Board of Directors, MSNM, 10 Oct. 1907, MSNMC, AM MG10 B9, Box 1.

33 Kathryn McPherson, "Skilled Service and Women's Work: Canadian Nursing, 1920–1939" (PhD diss., Simon Fraser University, 1990), 20.

34 *Annual Report*, 1906. MSNM, AM MG 10 B9, Box 6.

35 Board of Management, "Monthly Meetings," 10 Dec. 1923. MSNM, AM MG 10 B9, Box 4.

36 "Memorandum for the Superintendent of Immigration, 1906," MSNM, AM MG 10 B9, Box 1.

37 Cited in McPherson, *Bedside Matters*, 181.

38 *Annual Report*, 1905, 5. MSNM, AM MG 10 B9, Box 6.

39 *Annual Report*, 1912. MSNM, AM MG 10 B9, Box 6.

40 *Annual Report for 1908 of the Margaret Scott Nursing Mission*, 10. MSNM, AM MG 10 B9, Box 6.

41 *Annual Report for 1908 of the Margaret Scott Nursing Mission*, 10. MSNM, AM MG 10 B9, Box 6.

42 McPherson, *Bedside Matters*, 59.

43 *Annual Report for 1926 of the Margaret Scott Nursing Mission*, 24. MSNM, AM MG 10 B9, Box 6.

44 *Annual Report for 1924 of the Margaret Scott Nursing Mission*, 20-21. MSNM, AM MG 10 B9, Box 6.

45 For a discussion, see Robert Craig Brown, and Ramsay Cook, *Canada, 1896–1921: A Nation Transformed* (Toronto: McClelland and Stewart, 1974), 73; see also Donald H. Avery, *Reluctant Host: Canada's Response to Immigrant Workers, 1896–1994* (Toronto: McClelland and Stewart, 1995).

46 *Annual Report for 1913 of the Margaret Scott Nursing Mission*, 4. MSNM, AM MG 10 B9, Box 6.

47 The number of student nurses was augmented to five in 1925, when the Children's Hospital provided three additional students in training. Dr. Ross Mitchell to Miss Beveridge, MSNM, 30 July 1925, MSNM, AM MG10 B9, Box 1.

48 *Annual Report for 1937 of the Margaret Scott Nursing Mission*, 7. MSNM, AM MG 10 B9, Box 6.

49 McPherson, *Bedside Matters*, 115–163.

50 *Annual Report for 1937 of the Margaret Scott Nursing Mission*, 7. MSNM, AM MG 10 B9, Box 6.

51 *Annual Report for 1937 of the Margaret Scott Nursing Mission*, 7. MSNM, AM MG 10 B9, Box 6.

52 Medical Advisory Committee, "Standing Orders," MSNM, AM MG 10 B9, Box 1.

53 "Report of the Margaret Scott Nursing Mission made in Dr. Buck's Survey," c. 1941. MSNM, AM MG 10 B9, Box 2.

54 "The Margaret Scott Nursing Mission from the standpoint of a nurse of the Winnipeg General Hospital," handwritten manuscript. MSNM, AM MG 10 B9, Box 2.

55 Document 1213, "Margaret Scott Nursing Mission." MSNM, AM MG10 B9, Box 2.

56 Applications are only available for the years 1908 to 1912.

57 Of a total of 9984 visits, 2643 were classified as infants and sick kids. *Annual Report*, 1919. MSNMC, AM MG 10 B9, Box 6.

58 These years were chosen because of the coinciding of census years with comparable data available in the reports.

59 Roderic Beaujot and Kevin McQuillan, *Growth and Dualism: The Demographic Development of Canadian Society* (Toronto: Gage Publishing, 1982), 94.

60 *Annual Report for 1937*. MSNM, AM MG10 B9, Box 6.

61 For a discussion of the involvement of the federal government in health care delivery, see David Naylor, *Private Practice, Public Payment: Canadian Medicine and the Politics of Health Insurance, 1911–1966* (Montreal: McGill-Queen's University Press, 1986).

62 The earliest statistics available are for 1905 that show a total of 1731 obstetrical visits out of a total of 7000 visits for that year, representing 25 percent of the overall workload.

63 For a discussion of the association between the first wave of feminism and health reform, see Valverde, *Age of Light, Soap and Water*.

64 *Annual Report*, 1905, 3. MSNMC, AM MG 10 B9, Box 6.

65 For a discussion of the settlement movement and moral /health reform see Allen Davis, *Spearheads for Reform: The Social Settlements and the Progressive Movement, 1890–1914* (New York: Oxford University Press, 1967).

66 See Charlotte G. Borst, *Catching Babies: The Professionalization of Childbirth, 1870–1920* (Cambridge, MA: Harvard University Press, 1995), 118–126.

67 For a discussion of the class conflict of middle-class reform organizations, see Christine Stansell, *City of Women* (Champaign, IL: University of Illinois Press, 1986), especially Ch. 2, and Wendy Mitchinson, *Giving Birth in Canada, 1900–1950* (Toronto: University of Toronto Press, 2002), 168–169.

68 *Annual Report*, 1937, 11. MSNMC, AM MG 10 B9, Box 6. It should be noted, however, that the mission often consulted physicians and was subject to the same hierarchy present in hospitals as described by McPherson, "Skilled Service," 260–62.

69 For a more complete discussion of fears associated with childbirth for working-class women, see Ellen Ross, *Love and Toil: Motherhood in Outcast London, 1870–1918* (New York: Oxford University Press, 1993), Ch. 4.

70 For a discussion of the relationship between health care and the social reform movement, see Ch. 1 in Tamara Miller, "Never Forget Her Sex: Medicalizing Childbirth in Manitoba, 1880s to 1920s" (PhD diss., University of Manitoba, 2002).

"The Tubercular Cow Must Go": Business, Politics, and Winnipeg's Milk Supply, 1894–1922

Marion McKay

Tuberculosis was a major threat to public health in late nineteenth and early twentieth century Canada. The disease was linked to a variety of causes, including the inherited constitutional weakness of its victims, overcrowded living conditions, poverty, and the consumption of contaminated milk and meat. The earliest publicly funded programs to control the spread of this dreaded disease were organized by civic health departments to regulate dairy producers supplying milk to urban consumers. Using Winnipeg as a case study, this article examines the complexity of creating an effective and publicly acceptable policy to eliminate tuberculosis from the milk supply at a time when there was no consensus about the scientific evidence linking *Mycobacterium bovis* [*M. bovis*] to the etiology of human tuberculosis. Policy development was further complicated by scientific and public debates about the effectiveness of the tuberculin test in detecting tuberculosis in cattle, and the use of pasteurization as an alternative solution to the bacterial contamination of milk. Because of the lack of consensus about the most effective way to create a clean milk supply, Winnipeg's health officials were forced to negotiate the competing economic interests and/or scientific knowledge of veterinarians, physicians, dairy producers, and consumers in the development of the city's dairy policy.

Between 1894 and 1922, Winnipeg's public health department used three strategies to safeguard the city's milk supply. These were the elimination of tuberculosis in dairy herds, producer and consumer education programs, and the enactment of increasingly strict regulations requiring that certain segments of the milk supply be pasteurized. This article focuses primarily on the city's efforts to eliminate tuberculosis from the milk supply through tuberculin testing and the elimination of tuberculous cattle from dairy herds. It argues that there were three direct consequences of Winnipeg's dairy policy as it was operationalized between 1894 and 1922. First, the contentious public and scientific debates regarding the regulation of Winnipeg's milk supply enabled both veterinarians and physicians to shape public health policy in ways that created opportunities to enlarge their respective spheres of professional practice. Second, the benefits and costs of the dairy policy were unequally distributed among both Winnipeg's citizens and the province's dairy producers. Third, the dairy policy, which in large part emphasized the elimination of tuberculosis in dairy cattle rather than the elimination of all human pathogens in milk, was vulnerable to failure by both intentional and unintentional means.

Tuberculosis Control and the Pure Milk Movement

Winnipeg's early efforts to control the spread of tuberculosis coincided with one of the most turbulent social and political periods in its history. Between 1891 and 1921, according to federal census data, Winnipeg's population grew from 25,639 to 179,000 people.[1] This unprecedented and never again repeated rate of urban growth was fuelled by the arrival of eastern Canadians seeking new opportunities in Canada's fastest growing city, and immigration from the United States, the British Isles, and Eastern Europe.[2] Winnipeg's population soon segmented along economic and ethnic lines. By the beginning of the First World War, its Anglo-Canadian middle-class population was concentrated in newly developed suburbs south of the Assiniboine River. A significant portion of its working-class population, composed primarily of recently arrived non-English-speaking immigrants, was crowded in the city's famous North End. By 1916, only 38.9 percent of the population in Winnipeg's "foreign quarter" was of British origin.[3]

Winnipeg's immigrant and working-class population was viewed with considerable trepidation by the city's middle-class citizens. The overcrowded and unsanitary conditions of the working-class districts were perceived as fertile ground for disease outbreaks and political unrest that threatened the city's social stability and the peace of mind of its more prosperous citizens. The city's infant mortality rates soared early in the twentieth century, reaching the unprecedented high of 199.5 deaths/1000 births in 1912. The highest death rates were recorded among the infants of immigrants from non-English-speaking countries.[4] Sporadic outbreaks of typhoid fever, smallpox, and other communicable diseases also exacted a higher death rate amongst the city's poorest residents. But rather than recognizing that these public health issues were the consequence of the poverty and crowded conditions under which they lived, people often blamed the disease and death experienced by "the foreigners" on their own ignorance and lack of initiative. In an era when health care was the responsibility of the individual, Winnipeg's immigrant population endured disease, suffering, and death with only limited assistance from charitable organizations and the city's recently organized public health and welfare system.

In terms of tuberculosis control, Winnipeg followed a pattern already established in older Canadian, American, and British cities. Spurred by the bacteriological revolution of the late nineteenth century, civic health departments focussed their early efforts in tuberculosis control on the bovine to human transmission of *M. bovis* by enacting increasingly stringent programs to inspect civic milk and meat supplies.[5] By 1900, many North American and British civic health departments had enacted at least cursory attempts to clean up civic milk supplies and identify dairy cattle with tuberculosis.

Government-funded public health programs to monitor and control the human-to-human transmission of *Mycobacterium tuberculosis* [*M. tuberculosis*], the infectious agent associated with the highest number of cases of tuberculosis, came later. Much of the difficulty associated with controlling the spread of *M. tuberculosis* was related to the fact that tuberculosis in humans did not become a reportable disease in most Canadian jurisdictions until the second decade of the twentieth century.[6] Thus, the prevalence of tuberculosis in humans was not known or reported in the early twentieth century, and even tuberculosis mortality rates likely underestimated the death toll exacted by this disease. In the early years of the anti-tuberculosis campaign, voluntary organizations undertook a major role in the prevention of tuberculosis in humans, providing direct patient care to those in the greatest financial need and health education programs to increase public awareness of this major health problem.[7]

In Winnipeg, regulation of tuberculosis in the dairy industry began in 1894. A voluntary anti-tuberculosis society was founded in 1909. It soon employed a nurse, Miss A. Rathbone, to provide home nursing care to the city's poorest tuberculosis victims and to educate family members about how to avoid contracting the disease while living in the same household with an infected person.[8] In 1914, the city health department took over responsibility for tuberculosis nursing, employing two nurses who were "given the standing of inspectors," and incorporated within the department's Communicable Diseases Division.[9]

Winnipeg's efforts to create a safe civic milk supply can only be understood within the context of the vigorous scientific debate during the late nineteenth and early twentieth century about whether or not *M. bovis*, the causative organism for tuberculosis in cattle, could be transmitted to humans through infected milk. Robert Koch, who in 1882 identified *M. tuberculosis*, the pathogen more frequently associated with human tuberculosis, initially believed that the human and bovine forms of the disease were virtually identical.[10] Indeed, there was general agreement in the medical and scientific communities that *M. bovis* could produce non-pulmonary tuberculosis in humans. Estimates of the contribution that *M. bovis* made to the overall burden of tuberculosis in the community varied anywhere from 10 to 15 percent of all cases.[11] Children were more likely to suffer from this form of the disease. For example, in 1908, Dr. Charles Hastings, Toronto's medical health officer, estimated that upwards of 25 percent of all childhood cases of tuberculosis could be attributed to contaminated milk.[12]

In 1901, Koch reversed his position and argued that humans were only rarely infected with M. bovis.[13] He also refused to endorse the universal pasteurization of milk to prevent the transmission of tuberculosis from cattle to humans. Koch's announcement had profound implications for those interested in tuberculosis prevention. Public health officials believed that Koch was wrong.[14] They had already mounted expensive and controversial campaigns to eradicate bovine tuberculosis in dairy herds and to require the pasteurization of at least a portion of civic milk supplies. These were important strategies for medical health officers, who sought to consolidate their authority over the emerging discipline of public health and to attain influential positions within local health departments. Creating and enforcing regulations built upon bacteriological principles, as set out in dairy by-laws, placed them front and centre in efforts to control the spread of tuberculosis in their communities.

Veterinarians also believed that bovine tuberculosis could be transmitted to humans and orchestrated vigorous campaigns for the use of the tuberculin test to eliminate tuberculosis in dairy herds.[15] The anti-tuberculosis campaign was an opportunity for these men to carve out a sphere of influence in the emerging fields of animal health and public health.[16] Success in this professional project enabled veterinarians to attain positions in federal and provincial health departments as experts in animal health and, by extension, the protection of human health.

Unlike veterinarians and medical health officers, private physicians were divided in their opinion about the role that M. bovis played in the etiology of human tuberculosis, particularly in children.[17] They were also less certain that tuberculin testing and the pasteurization of milk were scientifically sound solutions to the problem. Some opposed the use of the tuberculin test in dairy cattle. Its efficacy in this application was overshadowed, in their minds, by its abysmal failure in the treatment of human tuberculosis.[18]

Many other physicians, particularly pediatricians, believed that pasteurized milk was unsuitable for infants and children because the process altered its chemical composition.[19] They also feared that pasteurization would lead to complacency and unsanitary milk production on the dairy farm.[20] These physicians believed that the best way to ensure a pure milk supply was to maintain the highest possible hygienic conditions in dairies. Physician-led milk commissions were established throughout

Canada and the United States to encourage the production of certified milk by stringently supervised dairies.[21] Milk from certified herds was believed to be tuberculosis free and, if not contaminated while being handled on the farm or while being delivered to the consumer, was also believed to be free of other pathogens. By establishing milk commissions, the medical profession vested itself with the authority to oversee the production of a safe milk supply and assume a leading role in protecting the health of the nation's children.

Because of lay and medical opposition to pasteurization, public health officials were reluctant to insist on the universal pasteurization of the milk supply. Most civic dairy regulations allowed raw milk from certified herds to be marketed within city limits. However, certified milk alone could not solve the problem of infant mortality. It was much more expensive, and most health officials freely admitted that "the high cost of production will prevent its ever being extensively used in any municipality."[22] As well, in an era when a significant proportion of dairy cattle was infected with tuberculosis, there was no guarantee that certified herds would remain disease free.[23] Finally, certified milk was still raw milk. Low bacterial counts alone could not preclude the presence of human pathogens, including typhoid fever, diphtheria, scarlet fever, septic sore throat, and cholera infantum (summer diarrhea).[24]

Regulating "Those Dirty Dairies": M.S. Inglis and the Dairy By-Laws, 1894–1900

On 3 January 1894, two months after his appointment as medical health officer, Dr. Maxwell S. Inglis initiated Winnipeg's first organized effort to regulate its milk supply.[25] Empowered by enabling provincial legislation, the city's Health Committee drafted a by-law that allowed Inglis to inspect dairies and dairy cattle supplying milk to the city. However, it was silent on the issue of what powers the city might have to eliminate diseased cows from dairy herds.[26] The by-law's passage apparently met little resistance from milk producers and vendors. Unfortunately for Inglis, this situation soon changed.

Later that year, as part of an initiative to control the incidence of bovine tuberculosis in Canada, the federal government announced that it would supply tuberculin at the users' cost to those interested in having their cattle tested.[27] Tuberculin testing had been fraught with controversy in every jurisdiction in which it had been introduced. Dairy producers believed that it was unreliable, created a health risk for their dairy herds, and resulted in the unnecessary destruction of valuable animals.[28] Since most compensation programs paid farmers only 40 to 60 percent of the value of animals destroyed, producers bore a significant portion of the cost of tuberculosis eradication programs. On the other hand, local governments and citizens feared that compensation programs could be exploited by unscrupulous dairy operators who, it was alleged, would even introduce a diseased animal into their herd to secure an easy source of revenue when the disease spread to other animals.[29] Other unintended consequences of a non-universal tuberculin testing program also existed. A writer to the *Manitoba Free Press* observed that some local dairymen traded tuberculin-positive animals to more distant farmers for "hay or anything else convenient." The danger of this practice, observed the writer, was that "one such beast, no matter how well it looks, may become a centre of fresh infection, and the test meant to protect us be made a means to spreading the evil."[30] To avoid these problems, the federal government refused to compensate owners for the destruction of tuberculin-positive cattle.[31] This policy created significant problems for local and provincial governments interested in establishing effective bovine tuberculosis-control programs within their own jurisdictions.

Despite these problems, Inglis decided to determine the prevalence of tuberculosis in cattle kept within Winnipeg's city limits. He secured enough tuberculin to test 1400 head of cattle. In a letter to the Health Committee, Inglis carefully outlined his approach to this initiative: "In making the general test it will be necessary to also take steps to eliminate the disease from cows owned by private citizens as well as dairy cows as they are all pastured together during the summer and as the disease is contagious it would not be fair to dairymen to test their cows without seeing that the others also were free from tuberculosis."[32] Inglis also raised the thorny issue of compensation for condemned animals, but made no recommendation as to what the city health department should do.

By late February, discouraging test results were already available. Of 200 animals tested, approximately 30 percent had a positive reaction. Extirpation of the disease within the city limits would require a slaughter of such magnitude that the issue of compensating owners could not be avoided. The provincial government was requested to give the city the power to control tuberculosis in dairy cattle and to offer compensation to 50 percent of the value of animals destroyed under this program.[33] Legislation allowing the city to use the tuberculin test was obtained, but the provincial government did not respond to the issue of compensation.[34] Its refusal to deal with this problem was doubtless a tactic to put pressure on the federal government to foot the bill.

A contentious debate about whether to continue tuberculin testing in Winnipeg ensued. After an impasse at the Health Committee's 6 March 1895 meeting, where a motion by alderman McCreary to discontinue tuberculin testing until the provincial government undertook responsibility for the eradication of tuberculous animals was defeated, the committee agreed to call a general meeting of "the medical men, veterinary surgeons and all the aldermen of the Council to discuss the question with a view of considering the whole question and of obtaining further information on the subject."[35] The meeting was also attended by "quite a large delegation of dairymen and milkmen."[36] While the committee certainly obtained further information, its task remained difficult. The discussion "revealed a direct difference of opinion [between veterinarians and private physicians] ... as to the serious nature of the disease and its effect on the human system."[37] The former argued, as did the two medical health officers present, that bovine tuberculosis was a significant factor in the etiology of human tuberculosis. Private physicians expressed reservations about controlling human tuberculosis by regulating the dairy industry, stating that the tuberculin test was not reliable, and that the risk of tuberculosis transmission from cattle to humans was exaggerated. The meeting adjourned at 11:15 p.m., no consensus having been achieved.[38]

Notwithstanding the general lack of consensus on the issue, Inglis embarked on a five-year campaign to toughen Winnipeg's dairy by-laws. A new by-law was drafted that empowered the city's veterinary inspector to use the "tuberculine test or any other expedient test" during dairy inspections.[39] A storm of protest erupted. On 13 May 1895, city council received a letter from the Winnipeg Dairy Association asking "that the use of Tuberculine be abolished as a test of the fitness of cows for Dairy purposes, in this city."[40] A second letter, bearing the signatures of sixty-nine local dairymen, was read in council 27 May 1897.[41]

In the meantime, the Health Committee shelved the draft by-law and commenced work on a new one that contained additional clauses to regulate the milk supply.[42] On the evening that this by-law was debated by council, the Dairymen's Association's lawyer appeared "and objected to features in almost every clause."[43] Despite his efforts, the by-law passed with only minor changes. Clearly disappointed by this outcome, Mr. Taylor, a Winnipeg dairy producer, asked that a clause providing compensation for animals destroyed because of positive tuberculin tests be inserted into the by-law. He also, according to the *Manitoba Free Press*, "accused council of taking dairymen's living out of their hands."[44]

On 30 April 1896, another dairy producer, Mr. Elliott, applied to Court of Queen's Bench to overturn the new by-law.[45] Elliott questioned the city's right to inspect rural dairies. He also argued that the health officer could not both inspect dairies and issue dairy licences because this procedure would eliminate an appeal process should the application for a dairy licence be denied. Although these were the official points of law contested in court, at the heart of the legal dispute was the dairy operators' resistance to tuberculin testing. Elliott's lawyer, in his submission to the court, stated that "numerous dairymen do not approve of the tuberculine tests and consider that they are not reliable."[46] The court ruled in favour of the plaintiff, finding that, under the 1894 *Municipal Act*, the city could not inspect or license rural dairies that sold milk to others to sell in the city. It also ruled that council could not delegate licensing authority to the city's health officer.[47]

The heated debates and legal wrangling continued. Between 1896 and 1897, city council introduced three more dairy by-laws.[48] Two were successfully contested by dairy producers.[49] In response to these legal judgements, Inglis and the city solicitors fine-tuned the regulations. Despite these efforts, the two most contentious issues, tuberculin testing and compensation for condemned animals, were not resolved.[50] Certainly, no help was forthcoming from the federal government. In 1897, it allocated $20,000 for the prevention of bovine tuberculosis and undertook the cost of tuberculin testing. However, free testing was done only at the farmer's request, and the policy of not compensating owners for the loss of tuberculin positive cattle was continued.

Winnipeg's dairy producers continued to exert pressure on council by applying for the refund of dairy licence fees collected under the disallowed by-laws. In at least two instances, legal action was threatened if the fees were not refunded with interest.[51] Public pressure was also brought to bear on council when a large public meeting was convened on 11 March 1899. After the usual debates about the efficacy of tuberculin testing and the need to compensate dairy farmers for slaughtered cattle, the meeting "almost unanimously" passed a motion urging council "to take all necessary steps to secure the purity of milk and meat & that the principle of compensation be introduced into this matter."[52]

In response to this public outcry, yet another dairy by-law was passed. However, it did little more than confirm the existing powers of city health authorities and the rights of dairy producers. Tuberculin testing was, in fact, almost a dead letter because veterinarians would only conduct the test at the request of the dairy operator. While the city's pre-1900 dairy by-laws did go some distance towards improving the hygienic standards of "those dirty dairies," the control of tuberculosis and other milk-borne diseases continued to elude health officials. Early efforts to clean up Winnipeg's milk supply had ended in a stalemate.

New Initiatives to Clean up the Milk Supply, 1900–1913

Between 1900 and 1913, Winnipeg's new health officer, Alexander J. Douglas, redoubled his predecessor's efforts to clean up the civic milk supply.[53] Regulatory strategies continued to hold centre stage during this era, and new regulations were introduced to refine and extend those already enacted. The 1904 typhoid epidemic gave Douglas the public and political support necessary to expand the dairy inspection program inherited from Inglis. The suspicion that at least some of the typhoid cases had contracted the disease from milk delivered along specific delivery routes enabled health officials to extend their regulatory strategies from milk producers to milk vendors, particularly those who delivered raw milk directly to the consumer.[54]

The department's dairy reports in the years prior to and immediately after the 1904 typhoid outbreak reveal that the dairy inspectors had retreated from the aggressive approach adopted by Dr. Dunbar, the city veterinarian, in the late 1890s. Dunbar had used the tuberculin test regularly, and often ordered dairy operators to remove diseased animals from their herds.[55] In contrast, monthly dairy reports from J.A. Roberts, the city's first dairy inspector, do not reveal much evidence of sanitary problems at Winnipeg's dairies. No tuberculin testing was documented, dairy premises were routinely reported as satisfactory, and the majority of cattle inspected were apparently clean and healthy.[56] Roberts's assessment of the city's dairies was contradicted both by members of the public and by subsequent members of the city's Dairy Department. A letter written by A. Harvey to city council in 1900 complained about "one of the worst (dairy) yards I have seen yet." Harvey characterized the dairy as a "muck hole" capable of spreading typhoid fever to nearby hotels. "The health inspector," he wrote, "was aware of all this, but there is too much favoritism [sic] shown."[57] Eight years later, L.A. Gibson, the chief dairy inspector and J.A. Roberts's immediate supervisor, confirmed that Winnipeg's dairies still fell far short of ideal sanitary conditions: "We find a few very good dairies. But the most of them are only in fair condition. We must keep continually after them to keep stables and milk houses clean."[58] The following month, Gibson reported that four dairies had been closed "on account of their being in a bad condition."[59]

Between 1908 and 1913, the health department introduced five new initiatives to refine their existing regulations. The introduction of dairy score cards, the compulsory reporting and follow-up of sickness at dairies, the clean-up of milk wagons, the establishment of a Milk Commission, and the enforcement of provincial regulations controlling the adulteration of milk enlarged the department's capacity to standardize dairy inspection and to contain or prevent outbreaks of milk-borne diseases.[60] These efforts were greatly enhanced by the appointment, in 1910, of Percy B. Tustin as head of the newly reorganized Food and Dairy Division.[61] Tustin brought to this position a level of energy, expertise, and passion that had been notably absent during the tenures of earlier dairy inspectors. Tustin was a particularly enthusiastic proponent of programs to eradicate bovine tuberculosis. "The great ravages this disease makes in the human race," he wrote in 1911, "and the enormous amount of educational matter published is beginning to awaken the public to the fact that the tubercular cow must go."[62]

The health department's dairy inspectors preferred to work with large commercial dairy producers who had the necessary capital to invest in barns, milk houses, wells, and livestock that readily met the standards established in the city's dairy regulations. Small milk producers and those who entered the commercial milk market on an intermittent basis were perceived by the health department as far more problematic. These milk producers typically entered the retail market only when the few head of cattle they owned were producing more milk than their own family could consume, or when the price of milk was sufficiently high to make the effort of milk production worthwhile. Because revenues from the sale of milk only supplemented their other sources of income, small producers were perceived by health officials as being less inclined to adhere to the sanitary standards of the health department. To ensure that they did, the dairy inspectors allocated a disproportionate amount of time to the inspection of their premises. Small dairy farms located in West Kildonan, just north of the city limits, were singled out as a major problem:

> North of the city ... a large number of dairies are congregated so close together that in about a square mile of territory we find 37 licensed dairy barns, 23 barns occupied by milk shippers and several smaller stables utilized as cow sheds, piggeries, slaughter houses, etc.... The proprietors of these dairies in many cases own very little land, perhaps merely a couple of 25-foot lots ... The manure from these stables is generally deposited on the adjacent lot ... and to such a degree has this practice developed that the dairies have become a source of nuisance to the residents, to each other, and to themselves.[63]

This situation, Tustin had observed in an earlier annual report, "would not last 24 hours within the city limits, but we have no jurisdiction outside, and can only regulate the actual premises of each dairyman."[64]

The small dairy operator was sometimes portrayed by health officials as an outsider who exploited the consumer for his own economic gain. Only unceasing vigilance on the part of the department's employees, it was asserted in the health department's *Annual Reports*, stood between the public and the careless attitudes of these uneducated milk producers. "Owing to the numbers of foreigners supplying milk to the City, our work is rendered more difficult as many of them do not understand the fundamental principles of cleanliness."[65] Jewish dairy operators experienced the most intense scrutiny, both because of their concentration in West Kildonan and because of their alleged lack of adherence to sanitary regulations when delivering milk in the city.[66]

The legal battles during Inglis's tenure had apparently convinced both civic politicians and health officials that a pure milk supply could not be attained through regulatory strategies alone. Therefore, between 1900 and 1913, the health department introduced producer education programs to supplement and improve the effectiveness of its dairy by-laws. For all that the health department decried the ignorance of some dairy producers, it preferred to help them improve their practices rather than put them out of business. "With these factors before us [the lack of knowledge of some dairy producers] we have endeavored to educate the dairymen, and have only entered into prosecutions where we found he would not live up to the instructions given him and his knowledge to do what is right."[67] Improved sanitary conditions on the farm, which depended upon both educational and regulatory strategies, was also prioritized because health authorities believed that this approach was fundamental to the elimination of bovine tuberculosis. As Tustin explained, it was counterproductive to house tuberculosis-free cattle in unsanitary barns where they would almost inevitably contract the disease.[68]

In the health department's 1913 *Annual Report*, both Douglas and Tustin expressed confidence that their interventions had borne fruit. A more rigorous approach to inspection and enforcement had convinced most dairy operators that the city was serious about creating a pure milk supply. There were more large dairy producers, and the "small dairy man and milk peddler" had become rare.[69] In the opinion of health officials, this development signalled that more producers were committed to the industry over the long term and were willing to invest the time, money, and energy necessary to sustain their operations.

Tuberculin testing was still voluntary, and no compensation was yet available for slaughtered tuberculin-positive cattle. However, health officials noted that many dairy producers believed that the higher consumer price obtained for certified milk more than compensated for the short-term economic loss incurred by eliminating tuberculous animals. Between 1911 and 1912, the number of dairy herds believed to be tuberculosis free rose from three to twelve, and an increasing number of dairy operators asked to have their herds tested.[70]

Optimism about the effectiveness of Winnipeg's dairy policies was also derived from a general decrease in the tuberculosis mortality rates and the incidence of other milk-borne infections, particularly between 1910 and 1913. Only three outbreaks of typhoid fever had been linked to the milk supply. This included two outbreaks in 1908 involving a total of thirty-eight cases and one outbreak in 1912 involving ninety-two cases.[71] Despite continuing controversies about the nutritional value of pasteurized milk, this portion of the milk supply had increased from 12 percent of the total milk consumed in the city in 1908 to 67 percent in 1913. "It looks," reported Douglas in 1913, "as though the supply of raw milk from untested herds will gradually eliminate itself without the aid of special legislation to that effect."[72]

Despite these positive developments, two major challenges to the maintenance of a pure milk supply remained unresolved. The first was the compensation of dairy farmers for animals slaughtered to eradicate *M. bovis* from their herds. City council had neither the jurisdictional authority nor the fiscal resources to compensate dairy producers, particularly those who operated outside of the city limits.

The second unresolved problem was the city's failure to obtain the legal authority to regulate the pasteurization of Winnipeg's milk supply. By-laws requiring that all milk sold within the city limits be either pasteurized or obtained from tuberculosis-free herds were developed in 1911 and 1913. However, both were shelved because the provincial government did not pass the necessary enabling legislation.[73] These deficiencies in the city's dairy regulations, the economic crisis during the First World War, and ten winters of severe milk shortages all contributed to a general decline in the quality of the milk supply between 1914 and 1922.

Crisis and Compromise: Dairy Policies Between 1914 and 1922

Between 1914 and 1922, sweeping economic and political changes had a profound impact on the health department's dairy policies. While a supply of safe milk had been the primary preoccupation during the previous era, the most pressing issues during and immediately after the First World War were the price of milk and its availability. During the economic crisis of the First World War, milk prices rose to unprecedented levels. At times it could not be obtained at any price. The city's dairy policies became the subject of considerable criticism from a variety of sources. Working-class citizens, who could barely afford to purchase milk for their children, opposed any measure that threatened to put the price of this basic commodity further beyond their reach. Suburban housewives who followed medical advice not to feed infants and children pasteurized milk opposed the universal pasteurization of the city's milk supply. Finally, rural dairy producers opposed federal price controls, which held the price of milk below the cost of production, and health officials, whose policies threatened to put them out of business.

In 1914, the health department experienced two major reversals in its campaign to clean up the city's milk supply. The first was the federal government's decision that Winnipeg was not eligible to participate in its new *M. bovis* eradication program, which, for the first time, offered dairy producers partial compensation for animals destroyed or culled from their herds.[74] Douglas had been eager to have Winnipeg participate in this program. In a letter to the Health Committee, he stated: "This is a very important act. . . . I should like to see the City of Winnipeg enter into the necessary agreement to put these regulations in force as I feel that they are sound in principle and should not be very difficult to apply."[75]

Unfortunately, the federal program required participating local governments to license all dairies selling milk or cream within their city limits.[76] Winnipeg did not license rural dairies that shipped directly to the city's pasteurizing plants, and many of the dairies that they did license could not meet these new and "rather drastic" federal regulations.[77] "To do this," stated Douglas, "would necessitate a greatly increased staff of inspectors and a vast amount of work would have to be done to the premises of farmers and others supplying milk to the creameries . . . to comply with the requirements expected from licensed dairymen."[78] Douglas realized that most Manitoba dairy producers would be unable or unwilling to embark on the necessary capital expenditures during a significant downturn in the prairie agricultural economy.[79] Although Douglas appealed the federal decision, he failed in his bid for a more lenient interpretation of the guidelines.[80] Winnipeg continued its campaign to combat tuberculosis through its certified milk program and a voluntary non-compensatory tuberculin testing program.

Just prior to the federal decision, a disturbing local development cast doubt upon the effectiveness of Winnipeg's certified milk program. Dr. Bowman, the city veterinarian, had conducted his annual tuberculin test on Joseph Carter's thirty-four-head dairy herd in June 1914. Twenty-four animals, comprising 71 percent of the herd, reacted to the test.[81] Based on these alarming findings, P.B. Tustin, the chief dairy inspector, notified the company marketing Carter's milk that it could no longer be certified as tuberculosis free.[82] Knowing that this could spell the end of his certified milk business, Carter hired two private veterinarians to verify that either contaminated tuberculin or the technique Bowman had employed in tuberculin testing of his cattle was responsible for the large swellings on his animals. The two veterinarians conducted their own tests and, while agreeing that Carter's explanation might plausibly explain swellings ranging in size from an orange to a grapefruit, they also reported that at least 50 percent of the animals tested by them were tuberculin positive.[83]

In his report to the subcommittee struck to investigate this situation, Tustin stated that Carter's dairy had conformed to the city's dairy regulations until he was given a contract to provide the Carson Dairy with certified milk. After that, standards at the dairy fell and the premises were often dirty. "I went out with the Milk Commission and inspected the dairy at 11 a.m. one morning. The stable had not been cleaned, the cattle were dirty, and the [Winnipeg Milk] Commission refused to have anything to do with them."[84] However, the case against Carter was much more serious than simply the unhygienic state of his dairy. Health officials also had evidence that Carter was keeping tuberculin-positive animals in his herd by removing their ear tags and replacing them with tags that signified that the animal was healthy.[85] In their report to the Health Committee, the subcommittee stated: "We have reason to believe that earmarks [indicating a positive tuberculin test] were obliterated from diseased animals by clipping away a portion of the ear. Tags which are numbered and indicate a healthy animal were found in the ears of animals which did not tally with the description of animals in which they had originally been placed by the veterinary inspector."[86] The Carter scandal provided conclusive evidence that the city's voluntary, non-compensatory tuberculosis eradication program was vulnerable to exploitation by any unscrupulous dairy producer willing to put profit ahead of public safety.

These events, however, were simply the prelude to several very difficult and frustrating years in the health department's campaign to create a pure civic milk supply. Three other complex and interrelated developments contributed to the decline in the quality of the city's milk supply: a decade of severe winter milk shortages (1912–22), the inflation of milk prices immediately prior to and during the First World War, and the economic crisis in the dairy industry during the same period.

The years immediately prior to and during the First World War were exceedingly difficult for Manitoba's dairy producers. The economic boom that had accompanied the expansion of agricultural production on the Prairies ended in 1912.[87] The crisis in the dairy industry emerged when wheat prices rose during the First World War. The high price commanded by wheat encouraged many prairie farmers to focus almost exclusively on its production.[88] However, large dairy operators who had invested significant capital constructing dairy barns and milk houses and establishing high quality dairy herds were not in a position to make a similar decision. During the last two years of the war, the price of oats, bran, hay, and replacement cattle nearly doubled, as did the cost of producing milk.[89] However, income from the sale of milk had not kept pace. Each cow, reported Charles Tully, a milk producer from Raeburn, generated $150 of income per year and cost $225 to maintain.[90]

The acute wartime shortage of farm workers made the difficult economic situation in the dairy industry even more serious.[91] It was almost impossible to find experienced milkers, and even when their services could be secured, they demanded much higher wages than those paid prior to 1914.[92] All of these factors created significant economic and personal hardship for farmers involved in the dairy industry. As Tustin observed in 1916, "the prospect for the ensuing year does not look good under the present conditions; a number of dairymen are contemplating reducing or disposing of their herds, on account of experiencing so much difficulty since the new year in regard to the labour question. There is no doubt that the dairyman's usually hard life has, in many cases, become almost intolerable."[93] When the Wilson Milk Commission held public hearings into the price of milk in early 1918, many dairy producers testified that they were on the verge of bankruptcy. Others had already dispersed their herds and gone out of the business.[94]

The rural economic crisis also hindered the health department's campaign to persuade all raw milk producers to voluntarily tuberculin test their dairy herds. In more prosperous times, the argument that higher priced milk from tested herds could compensate dairy producers for the loss of tuberculin reactors appeared to have provided the necessary incentive. However, during the war, this was not the case. A decline in the number of tuberculin-tested herds was observed. Even dairy producers who had previously participated in this program refused to have their herds retested "on economic grounds."[95] It was more expensive to produce milk from tested herds, and the public was now indifferent to the benefits of purer milk, or at least unwilling to pay a higher price for it.[96]

Winter "milk famines," which occurred regularly between 1912 and 1922, also had a negative impact on the health department's efforts to regulate the city's milk supply.[97] At times, shortages were so severe that the citizens of Winnipeg experienced "milkless days" where no milk was available for sale in the city.[98] In 1918, a milk famine was avoided only by producing "milk" reconstituted from milk powder, butter, and water.[99]

An inevitable outcome of the milk shortages and the higher cost of milk production was a sharp increase in the consumer price of milk. This was an extremely contentious issue in Winnipeg, and particularly so among members of the city's working class. In the years leading up to the First World War, milk prices averaged approximately ten cents per quart.[100] By 1920, the price had risen to between fifteen and sixteen cents a quart.[101] Certified milk was even more expensive. In 1917, it sold in Winnipeg for twenty cents a quart.[102]

The net effect of these developments was that Winnipeg's health officials could not enact more stringent dairy regulations because these measures would both increase the price and reduce the supply of milk. Pasteurization and tuberculin testing were perceived by many as unnecessary measures that forced small dairy producers out of business and increased the monopoly of the large milk producers and processors. In the opinion of E.C. Brown, the health department's new chief dairy inspector, it would be "economic suicide" to put any further pressure on dairy producers or the public by enacting new dairy regulations or strictly enforcing those currently in place.[103]

Unfortunately, the wartime crisis did not merely create an interval where the milk supply's quality remained static. Major problems with the purity of milk occurred during this period. Less milk was pasteurized, and there were more prosecutions for adulterating milk. Milk-borne outbreaks of typhoid and scarlet fever were also more frequently reported.[104] The health department's more lenient approach to the regulation of the city's milk supply had created a significant risk to the health of the city's hard-pressed citizens.

In the immediate post-war period, Douglas abandoned the producer education focus that had characterized the department's pre-war dairy policy, stating that unrepentant repeat violators "would have interpreted such action as a sign of weakness on our part and an indication that we were desperately anxious to keep them in business."[105] Pledging to eliminate "undesirables ... without any question of sympathy or sentiment," Douglas turned his attention to the stricter enforcement of existing regulations.[106] A new by-law, passed in March 1918, enabled city officials to cancel the licences of dairy operators and milk vendors found guilty of three infractions of the city's dairy regulations. Previously, repeat offenders had merely paid fines and continued in the business.[107]

In 1920, city health officials embarked on a campaign to eliminate the sale of raw milk from non-tuberculin-tested cattle. The minimum score in the dairy score card system was increased from 350 to 375 out of possible 500 points. Producers scoring below the minimum were denied a dairy licence.[108] The health department had also planned to increase the minimum score to 400 in 1921, but this measure proved impossible to implement. Only tuberculin testing of the dairy herd would have enabled the majority of milk producers scoring between 375 and 399 to achieve a score of 400. As the department noted in its *Annual Report*:

While the intention of the 1920 [Health] Committee was to raise the score to 400, yet it will be noted that 55 of the 80 dairies scored under 400.... This means that fully one-half of the dairies would have to make a gain of 25 to 30 points this year in order to reach 400, and practically the only method by which this could be done would be by means of the tuberculin test, application of which would be voluntary. The difficulty of having one dairyman do something which might not be required of another can be imagined; and no legal enactment could be framed to enforce such a condition.[109]

Knowing that no amount of vigilance could ensure that raw milk from untested herds was safe for human consumption, Winnipeg's health officials again pressed for a by-law requiring that all milk from untested cows be pasteurized prior to its sale within the city limits.[110] The time for this measure, they argued, was right. Only 2000 cattle required testing, and the tests could be scheduled during the summer when there would be less risk of creating a milk shortage.[111] Only the inability to compensate dairy producers stood in the way of this initiative.[112]

The solution to this problem lay in the hands of the federal government. Under revised regulations passed in 1917, the federal government provided free tuberculin testing and partial compensation for cattle destroyed under its program. Participating cities were required to enact by-laws prohibiting the sale of raw milk from untested cows.[113] Another new dairy by-law, passed by council in 1922, created the appropriate legal mechanism for Winnipeg's participation in the federal program.

The magnitude of the tuberculosis problem in dairy cattle became apparent once widespread testing was initiated in the wake of this by-law. General estimates of the prevalence of tuberculosis in dairy cattle supplying milk to Winnipeg had, as far back as the late nineteenth century, ranged from 30 to 35 percent.[114] However, the problem was far worse. Sixty-two percent of the dairy cattle initially tested under the new by-law were tuberculin positive. Only two of the one hundred herds tested were tuberculin negative. Both were new herds that had been recently established from tuberculin-negative stock.[115] The emergence of the commercial dairy producer so much favoured by the city's dairy officials may have contributed to the increased prevalence of tuberculin reactors observed in 1922. Their large dairy herds could favour the spread of bovine tuberculosis. All that was necessary to infect an entire herd was the presence of one tuberculous animal that, when housed in a barn with the rest of the animals during the winter months, would certainly spread the infection to the others.

Conclusion

Between 1894 and 1922, the campaign to clean up Winnipeg's milk supply focussed heavily on the eradication of *M. bovis* in dairy cattle. Significant human and fiscal resources were expended to pursue a regulatory strategy that required continuous inspections by city dairy officials, the drafting of fourteen dairy by-laws, several court appearances, and countless debates in city council. These efforts were not entirely successful. Although the dairy industry was both better managed and better regulated by 1922, the safety of Winnipeg's milk supply was never firmly established, and milk-borne diseases such as typhoid fever and scarlet fever continued to occur.

Even in the realm of tuberculosis control, the contribution of the health department's clean milk campaign remains uncertain. Winnipeg's tuberculosis mortality rate did decline from 114/100,000 in 1910 to 73/100,000 population in 1920. The mortality rates for children aged 0 to 4 years also apparently fell during this time period.[116] However, the extent to which the health department's tuberculosis control measures, including its dairy policies, contributed to this achievement is uncertain. What is certain is that the Winnipeg's clean milk campaign did not eliminate the tuberculous cow. The reported prevalence of *M. bovis* in dairy cattle supplying milk to Winnipeg actually doubled between 1895 and 1922.

The formulation and enforcement of the city's dairy policies enabled both medical health officers and veterinarians to make significant professional gains between 1894 and 1922. By the end of this period, almost without exception, civic health departments were headed by physicians. Their focus on bacteriology to control the transmission of tuberculosis in the urban environment highlighted the contributions this emerging science could make to public health and their professional competence in translating this knowledge into action. For veterinarians, a similar opportunity arose. The bovine tuberculosis problem provided veterinarians with an opportunity to link their professional expertise in bacteriology and animal health to growing concerns about the transmission of animal diseases to humans.[117] However, there were both professional and social costs to the bacteriological approach to tuberculosis control. Public health physicians and veterinarians endured considerable criticism from milk producers, consumers, and even their employers, particularly when dairy policies threatened to create economic hardship. And, as Barbara Rosenkrantz has observed, focussing on bacteriology also deflected professional and public attention from the more nebulous social causes of tuberculosis such as poverty.[118]

Winnipeg's experience with the regulation of its milk supply also highlights the extent to which the costs of policies directed to the protection of citizens' health are unequally distributed. Prior to the provision of partial compensation for condemned animals, dairy producers shouldered a significant portion of the direct costs of creating a safe milk supply. There was also a differential impact on milk consumers. Stringent dairy regulations created higher milk prices. Many middle-class customers may have been able to afford certified milk to protect their families from *M. bovis*. However, for most working-class families, certified milk was beyond their financial reach. It is likely that many of these families continued to purchase raw milk from uninspected milk producers whose product could not be assumed to be safe.

Finally, as the 1914 Carter scandal and the 1922 tuberculosis testing program revealed, Winnipeg's dairy policies between 1894 and 1922 were not fully effective in protecting the public against bovine to human transmission of tuberculosis. Although an increasingly rigorous dairy inspection program was conducted by Winnipeg health department, the city's milk supply continued to include the product of animals actively infected with *M. bovis*.

Notes

This article is reprinted, with kind permission, from the *Canadian Bulletin of Medical History/ Bulletin canadien d'histoire de la medicine* 23, 2 (2006): 355–380.

1   Alan F. J. Artibise, *Winnipeg: A Social History of Urban Growth 1874–1914* (Montreal: McGill-Queen's University Press, 1975), 132, Table 7.

2   Gerald Friesen, *The Canadian Prairies: A History* (Toronto: University of Toronto Press, 1987), 185–186 and 245.

3   Artibise, *Winnipeg*, 148–173.

4   Ibid., 237–238.

5   Susan D. Jones, *Valuing Animals: Veterinarians and Their Patients in Modern America* (Baltimore: Johns Hopkins University Press, 2003), 63–90; Heather MacDougall, *Activists and Advocates: Toronto's Health Department 1883–1983* (Toronto: Dundurn Press, 1990), 97–106.

6   Tuberculosis became a reportable disease in both Ontario and Manitoba in 1911. By the beginning of the First World War, many other Canadian provinces had followed suit. Even after that time, many cases were not reported because patients suffered severe social and economic consequences when their diagnosis became known. MacDougall, *Activists and Advocates*, 127–128; Katherine McCuaig, *The Weariness, the Fever, and the Fret: The Campaign Against Tuberculosis in Canada, 1900–1950* (Montreal: McGill-Queen's University Press, 1999), 25–26 and 33–34; *Statutes of Manitoba*, "The Public Health Act," 1 Geo 5, c. 44, s. 1, sections 364 and 365.

7   McCuaig, *The Weariness*, 8–10.

8   City of Winnipeg Archives [CWA], Health Department, *Annual Report* (1909): 6; *Annual Report* (1911): 11.

9   CWA, Health Department, *Annual Report* (1914): 15.

10 Thomas D. Brock, *Robert Koch, A Life in Medicine and Bacteriology* (Madison: Science Tech Publishers, 1988), 254.

11   Thomas Dormanday, *The White Death: A History of Tuberculosis* (London: The Hambledon Press, 1999), 329; Barbara Rosenkrantz, "The Trouble With Bovine Tuberculosis," *Bulletin of the History of Medicine* 59 (1985): 160. Mortality from bovine tuberculosis was estimated to constitute 5 to 6 percent of deaths from all forms of tuberculosis. See Keir Waddington, "'To Stamp Out 'So Terrible a Malady': Bovine Tuberculosis and Tuberculin Testing in Britain, 1890–1939," *Medical History* 48 (2004): 29.

12   Charles J.C.O. Hastings, "The National Importance of Pure Milk," *Canadian Practitioner and Review,* c. 1908, Canadian Institute for Historical Micro-reproductions no. 86969.

13   Brock, *Robert Koch,* 254–55; McCuaig, *The Weariness,* 158.

14   This belief was reinforced by the reports of two British Royal Commissions, the 1895 Commission on the Effect of Food derived from Tuberculous Animals upon Human Health and the 1898 Commission on Controlling the Danger to Man Through the Use as Food of the Meat and Drink of Tuberculous Animals. Both unanimously concluded that a large proportion of human tuberculosis was caused by drinking contaminated milk. See John Spargo, *The Common Sense of the Milk Question* (New York: Macmillan, 1910), 124–129.

15   Jones, *Valuing Animals,* 63–74.

16   Rosenkrantz, "The Trouble With Bovine Tuberculosis," 155–175.

17   Jennifer Koslow, "Putting It To A Vote: The Provision of Pure Milk in Progressive Era Los Angeles," *Journal of the Gilded Age and Progressive Era* 3, 2 (2004); Rosenkrantz, "The Trouble With Bovine Tuberculosis," 155–175.

18   Michael Worboys, *Spreading Germs: Disease Theories and Medical Practice in Britain, 1865–1900* (Cambridge: University of Cambridge Press, 1977), 225.

19   Richard Meckel, *Save the Babies: American Public Health Reform and the Prevention of Infant Mortality 1850–1929* (Baltimore: Johns Hopkins University Press, 1990), 81–82.

20   Spargo, *The Common Sense of the Milk Question,* 250–253.

21   Ibid. Spargo was an advocate of certified milk and supported pasteurization only as a stop-gap measure until more hygienic milk production could be assured.

22   Charles J.C.O. Hastings, "Report of the Medical Officer of Health on the Safeguarding of Toronto's Milk Supply With Special Reference to Pasteurization," 1915, 14, Canadian Institute for Historical Micro-reproductions, no. 83553.

23   Hastings, "Report of the Medical Officer of Health," 15. Hastings cites several instances where certified tuberculosis-free dairy herds were subsequently found to have high infection rates.

24   Spargo, *The Common Sense of the Milk Question,* 120–150; Hastings, "The National Importance of Pure Milk"; Hastings, "Report of the Medical Officer of Health." Septic sore throat is caused by Group A (Beta Hemolytic) Streptococcus. If not properly treated with penicillin, which was not available until after the Second World War, a case of strep throat could progress to scarlet fever and the development of rheumatic heart disease. See James Chin, *Control of Communicable Diseases Manual,* 17th ed. (Washington: American Public Health Association, 2000), 470–476.

25   Although it was not necessarily the case in every civic health department, Winnipeg's health officers were always physicians. The city's first efforts to regulate its milk supply were on pace with similar efforts in other Canadian and American cities. Milwaukee passed its first ordinance in 1887, and Toronto began to regulate its milk supply in 1893. Los Angeles had an ordinance prohibiting the adulteration of milk as early as 1874, but did not employ city officials to enforce it until 1889. See Jennifer Koslow, "Eden's Underbelly: Female Reformers and Public Health in Los Angeles" (PhD thesis, University of California), 23; Judith Walzer Leavitt, *The Healthiest City: Milwaukee and the Politics of Health Reform* (Madison: University of Wisconsin Press, 1996), 169; Heather MacDougall, *Activists and Advocates: Toronto's Health Department 1883–1983* (Toronto: Dundurn Press, 1990), 97.

26 The by-law only specified that the milk from diseased animals was not to be mixed with other milk, or sold as human food. See CWA, *City of Winnipeg By-Laws*, By-Law 721, Clause 8.

27 The current spelling of this word is "tuberculin." In the late nineteenth and early twentieth century, it was more commonly spelled "tuberculine." For purposes of consistency, unless the word is used in a direct quotation, it will be spelled tuberculin.

28 Gordon Church, *An Unfailing Faith: A History of the Saskatchewan Dairy Industry* (Regina: Canadian Plains Research Center, 1985), 17 and 272 n. 80.

29 "The Tuberculosis Scare," *Manitoba Free Press*, 6 March 1895, 3.

30 "Tuberculosis in Cows," *Manitoba Free Press*, 14 March 1895, 4.

31 Church, *An Unfailing Faith*, 16–17; "The Tuberculosis Scare" *Manitoba Free Press*, 6 March 1895, 3.

32 CWA, Market, License and Health Committee Reports. Letter from M.S. Inglis to the Committee, 29 January 1895.

33 CWA, Market, License and Health Committee Minutes, 27 February 1895, Item 642.

34 CWA, Market, License and Health Committee Reports, 13 March and 25 April 1895; Manitoba, "An Act to Amend 'The Municipal Act.'" c. 20, s. 599(m), 1894.

35 CWA, Market, License and Health Committee Minutes, 6 March 1895, Item 643; "Tuberculosis Agitation: A General Meeting of Physicians and Veterinarians to be Called," *Manitoba Free Press*, 7 March 1895.

36 "The Doctors Differ: A Conference on the Question of Tuberculosis Among Cattle," *Manitoba Free Press*, 12 March 1895, 5.

37 "The Doctors Differ," 5.

38 CWA, Market, License and Health Committee Minutes, 11 March 1895, Item 644; "The Doctors Differ," 5.

39 CWA, By-Law 1003, introduced to City Council 27 May 1895. Clauses 2 and 3 contained these proposed changes.

40 CWA, Communications to Council #3006. Letter from the Winnipeg Dairy Association, signed by Peter Arnot, Secretary Treasurer, dated 11 May 1905.

41 CWA, Communications to Council #3020.

42 By-Law 1004 was passed by city council 17 June 1895. However, By-Law 1003 was not formally withdrawn until 10 July 1895.

43 "To Secure Pure Milk: The Dairy By-Law Passed by the City Council—Objections Raised by the Dairymen—Synopsis of the Provisions," *Manitoba Free Press*, 18 June 1895, 4.

44 "To Secure Pure Milk," 4.

45 CWA, Communications to Council # 3161. The letter, from the law firm of Martin, Mathers, and Anderson, was read in council 10 December 1895. The letter is not in the existing file; Market, License and Health Committee Minutes, 14 January 1895; "Dairy Inspection By-Law: Mr. Martin Makes Application to Quash By-Law 1004," *Manitoba Free Press*, 1 May 1896, 6.

46 "Dairy Inspection By-Law," 6.

47 George Patterson and William A. Taylor, "Re: Elliot. In the Matter of By-Law 1004 of the City of Winnipeg," *Manitoba Reports*, 11 (Winnipeg: Stovel Co., 1896), 358–362; "The Dairy By-Law: Sections One and Three Quashed with Costs," *Manitoba Free Press*, 21 May 1896, 6.

48 These were By-Law 1176, passed 10 July 1896, By-Law 1313, passed 25 May 1897, and By-Law 1352, which was introduced to Council in late 1897, but not enacted.

49 "The City Dairies: Second By-Law to Regulate them is Quashed," *Manitoba Free Press*, 1 January 1897, 6. By-Law 1313 was initially sustained, but when appealed to the full court, Sections 17 and 22 were quashed. "The Dairy By-Law: Application to Quash Made Before Mr. Justice Dubuc," *Manitoba Free Press*, 13 July 1897, 6; "The Full Court," *Manitoba Free Press*, 1 December 1897; "The Dairy By-Law: Judgements Delivered by the Full Court," *Manitoba Free Press*, 13 December 1897.

50 Court of Queen's Bench did not, in any of its three judgements, comment directly on the use of the tuberculin test or on the issue of compensation. Power to use the tuberculin test was no doubt accepted under the provisions of the 1894 *Municipal Act*. In the absence of any clear indication of what level of government was responsible for compensating farmers for the destruction of tuberculous cattle, the court gave no direction to the city on this issue. For examples of the debates in council about these issues, see *Manitoba Free Press*, 9 June 1896, 5; "The City Dairy By-Law," *Manitoba Free Press*, 11 July 1896, 8; "A Long Session," *Manitoba Free Press*, 26 May 1897.

51 CWA, Communications to Council, #3392. Letter from Martin, Mathers and Anderson on behalf of several dairymen, dated 15 August 1896; #3508, Letter from Lendrum McMeans, Barrister on behalf of Mr. S. W. Mawson dated 22 February 1897; letter from Elliot and McCreary on behalf of Mr. Elliot, dated 27 March 1897. The issue of whether or not to refund dairy license fees was discussed frequently by the Market, License and Health Committee during 1897. See, for example, the minutes of 12 January, 25 February, 6 April, 4 May, and 18 May 1897.

52 "Questions of Milk Supply: Citizens Discuss the Matter in the City Hall on Saturday," *Manitoba Free Press*, 13 March 1899, 3; CWA, Communications to Council, #4049 from G.A. Greathed, secretary of public meeting dated 13 March 1899.

53 Alexander J. Douglas (1874–1940) was a graduate of the Manitoba Medical College who went on to do postgraduate training in Europe. He was appointed to the position of Winnipeg's first full-time medical health officer in 1900. He retired in 1939 as Winnipeg's longest serving civic employee. See J.M. Bumsted, *Dictionary of Manitoba Biography* (Winnipeg: University of Manitoba Press, 1999), 70; Legislative Library, Province of Manitoba, Biographical File B9.

54 CWA, Communications to the Health Committee, 7 March 1905, Item 116; Jordan, "Report on Typhoid Fever in Winnipeg," 184–186. Professor Jordan stated that contaminated milk along at least two milk routes could not be ruled out as a source of infection for twenty cases of typhoid, and that six more cases, scattered amongst three other milk routes were highly suspicious. In his recommendations, Jordan stated that "Inspection of the sources and routes of milk supply cannot be too vigilant at times when typhoid fever is known to prevail." This was the first time, at least in Winnipeg, where milk delivery rather than its production was implicated as the source of a typhoid outbreak. In response to the Jordan Report, and Mayor Thomas Sharpe's report on his tour of the sanitation systems in eastern Canada, council instructed Douglas to conduct more stringent inspections of the city's dairies, and to hire more help, if necessary.

55 CWA, Health and Relief Reports, 1874–1891. In the back of this box are a number of applications for a dairy licence dated 1894 and 1895. They are so fragile that it was not possible to conduct a thorough examination of each application. In 1898, it appears that all cattle examined by Dunbar were tuberculin tested.

56 CWA, Health Committee Communications, Box 711, 1905–1907; Box 712, 1909–1910, Items 231/2, 234–241, 303. Roberts filed monthly dairy reports during this time. On 10 June 1910, Roberts, now holding the position of assistant dairy inspector, was deemed physically incapable of continuing to do his work and placed on a pension of fifty dollars per month.

57 CWA, Communications to Council #6210. Letter from A. Harvey dated 6 October 1900.

58 CWA, Health Committee Communications, Item 1094. Letter from L. A. Gibson to A.J. Douglas dated September 1908.

59 CWA, Health Committee Communications, Item 1131. Letter from L.A. Gibson to A.J. Douglas dated 29 October 1908.

60 For Douglas's report of the use of dairy score cards in the United States, see CWA, Communications to the Market, License and Health Committee #867, dated 30 October 1907. The introduction of the cards by Winnipeg's dairy inspectors is discussed in the Health Department *Annual Report* (1908), 28. Discussions regarding the mandatory reporting of sickness on dairies can be found in the Health Department, *Annual Report* (1908), 26, and *Annual Report* (1911), 138. The clean-up of milk wagons is discussed in the Health Committee Communications, Item #82, Dairy Inspection Report for April 1909, submitted by L.A. Gibson to A.J. Douglas. Initial reports of the founding of the Winnipeg Milk Commission are found in the *Annual Report* (1909), 23, and *Annual Report* (1910), 27. Discussion of the health department's decision to enforce Section 89 of the provincial *Health Act* is found in the Health Committee Minutes of 11 December 1911, Item 578.

61 CWA, Health Committee Communications. Letter to J.F. Pearson, Chief Inspector, from P.B. Tustin. The letter is referred to in Item 638 of the Health Committee Minutes; Health Department, *Annual Report* (1919), 26–27. Tustin was first hired by the city health department in 1907 as a meat inspector. Although he did not identify any specific qualifications for the position, his letter of application, dated 14 February 1907, gave evidence of considerable experience with livestock as a cattle foreman, inspector, and veterinary assistant in Britain, South Africa, Argentina, and the United States. He resigned from the health department in 1919 to accept a position in England. Tustin's resignation was described as "a severe loss" to the health department, and A.J. Douglas described him as "one of the outstanding men in Canada ... and a recognized authority in matters pertaining to food and dairying throughout the country."

62 CWA, Health Department, *Annual Report* (1911), 131.

63 CWA, Health Department, *Annual Report* (1916), 90.

64 CWA, Health Department, *Annual Report* (1913), 129.

65 CWA, Health Department, *Annual Report* (1909), 68.

66 CWA, Health Committee Communications, Item #82, Dairy Inspection Report for April 1909.

67 CWA, Health Department, *Annual Report* (1909), 68.

68 CWA, Health Department, *Annual Report* (1910), 105.

69 CWA, Health Department, *Annual Report* (1913), 20.

70 CWA, Health Department, *Annual Report* (1911), 28; *Annual Report* (1912), 8 and 117.

71 CWA, Health Department, *Annual Report* (1908), 4; *Annual Report* (1912), 9.

72 CWA, Health Department, *Annual Report* (1913), 127. A.J. Douglas offered no specific explanation as to why these remarkable gains in the volume of pasteurized milk marketed in the city had been achieved.

73 The research for this paper did not specifically address the question of why the provincial government did not support the city health department's request for legislation. However, it is entirely possible that the Roblin and Norris governments in power during that era were very reluctant to antagonize farmers, especially in the face of a growing political movement in the farming community.

74 Church, *An Unfailing Faith,* 47.

75 CWA, Health Committee Communications #1086/1100/1115/1197. Douglas to the Health Committee, 22 July 1914.

76 Church, *An Unfailing Faith,* 53.

77 CWA, Health Department, *Annual Report* (1916), 18; Health Committee Minutes of 17 September 1914, Item 1115.

78 CWA, Health Committee Communications #1086/1100/1115/1197. Letter from Douglas to the Committee dated 16 September 1914.

79 Church, *An Unfailing Faith,* 47. For a discussion of the impact of the First World War on the western agricultural economy, see John Herd Thompson, *The Harvests of War* (Toronto: McClelland and Stewart, 1985).

80 CWA, Health Committee Communications, #1086/1100/1115/1197. Letter from F. Torrance, Veterinary Director General to A.J. Douglas, dated 17 December 1914.

81 CWA, Health Committee Communications #1154/1184/1201. Since Carter was a producer of certified milk, his herd should have been tuberculin tested at least twice a year, and individual animals could be tested whenever it was deemed necessary. See Rules and Regulations of the Winnipeg Milk Commission as Adopted October 1910, 6. This document was included with other papers related to the Board of Control Investigation of Carter's complaint.

82 CWA, Health Committee Communications #1154/1184/1201. Report of the Sub/Committee appointed to investigate the charges made by Edward Carter in respect to test of Cows for Tuberculosis, dated December 1914.

83 Drs. Rombough and McGillivray tested twenty-three animals and found eight healthy, three doubtful, and eleven tuberculin positive. They submitted a detailed report of their findings, including temperature charts on all tested animals, to the investigation committee. CWA, Health Committee Communications #1154/1184/1201. Report of the Sub/Committee appointed to investigate the charges made by Edward Carter in respect to test of Cows for Tuberculosis, 23 December 1914.

84 CWA, Health Committee Communications #1154/1184/1201. Report of the Sub/Committee appointed to investigate the charges made by Edward Carter in respect to test of Cows for Tuberculosis, 23 December 1914. See also, in this file, a letter from Tustin providing essentially the same information dated 30 November 1914.

85 The usual procedure in a tuberculin testing program was to place a tag with the letter "T" in the left ears of all animals that reacted to the tuberculin test. Animals that had not reacted to the test had a numbered and dated tag placed in their right ears. The number assigned to each animal was unique and was matched with a physical description entered in a log book kept by the veterinarian.

86 CWA, Health Committee Communications #1154/1184/1201. Report of the Sub/Committee appointed to investigate the charges made by Edward Carter in respect to test of Cows for Tuberculosis, dated 23 December 1914. See also, in this file, a letter from Tustin providing essentially the same information dated 30 November 1914.

87 Ruben Bellan, "The Development of Winnipeg as a Metropolitan Centre" (PhD thesis, Columbia University, 1958), 178–251; William L. Morton, *Manitoba: A History,* 2nd ed. (Toronto: University of Toronto Press, 1967), 329–330; Thompson, *Harvests of War,* 12 and 45–46.

88 Thompson, *Harvests of War,* 46.

89 Archives of Manitoba (AM), Animal Industry Branch, RG1 E3 1917–1965. The collection consists of a series of scrapbooks kept by the Manitoba Dairy Branch. Newspaper clippings related to the Wilson Milk Commission are found in the scrapbook dated 1917–1920. Unfortunately, the specific newspaper and date are not documented. The headline for this clipping is: "Ideal Delivery Conditions Would Reduce Cost of Milk," c. January 1918.

90 In his testimony to the Wilson Milk Commission, one dairy producer, Mr. St. John, estimated that it cost him thirty-seven cents a gallon to produce winter milk. Two years previously, it had cost eighteen cents per gallon. See AM, Animal Industry Branch, Manitoba Dairy Branch Scrapbook dated 1917–1920. The headline for this clipping is "Solution for High Milk Prices," c. January 1918. The Commission, consisting of W.A. Wilson, General Manager of the Saskatchewan Co-operative Creameries Co., Gertrude Code, representing consumers, and W.J. Cummings, a dairy producer, was appointed by J. D. McGregor, the Western Representative of the Food Controller in late 1917 to investigate "conditions appertaining to the supply, distributing and price of milk to the citizens of Winnipeg." It held several days of hearings in January

1918, during which it heard testimony from representatives of the city's two creameries, dairy producers, and consumers. The committee's report was submitted to city council by McGregor on 26 January 1918. Based on this report, McGregor set the consumer price for milk at thirteen cents per quart or seven cents per pint for the period between 1 February 1918 and 15 May 1919, and recommended that another committee representing the same three sectors be appointed immediately. One of its duties would be to set the price of milk for the period beginning 16 May 1919. CWA, Health Committee Files, Pre-1920 Health Special Committees, file #1671 re: milk supply. This file contains all of the correspondence related to the Wilson report as well as the report itself.

91 Thompson, *The Harvests of War*, 62–63 and 86–87.

92 CWA, Health Committee Communications, 16 October 1916. In his September report to the Health Committee, Tustin noted that dairy farmers were having problems finding trained milkers to work for them. See also AM, Animal Industry Branch, Manitoba Dairy Branch Scrapbook dated 1917–1920. The headline for this clipping is "Ideal Delivery Conditions Would Reduce Cost of Milk," c. January 1918. The monthly wages for a male farm worker had increased from thirty to forty dollars per month to fifty dollars per month between 1916 and 1918.

93 CWA, Health Department, *Annual Report* (1916), 98.

94 AM, Animal Industry Branch, Manitoba Dairy Branch Scrapbook dated 1917–1920. See newspaper clippings: "Solution for High Milk Prices," "Ideal Delivery Conditions Would Reduce Cost of Milk," "Evidence Shows Creamery Receives Profit on Milk Above Spread Fixed by Law." All clippings are c. January 1918.

95 CWA, Health Department, *Annual Report* (1914), 112; *Annual Report* (1916), 18.

96 CWA, Health Department, *Annual Report* (1915), 96.

97 An article reporting the retirement of Provincial Dairy Commissioner L.A. Gibson in 1945 stated: "Two or three years before Mr. Gibson entered the government service [1915] the milk industry had men scurrying all over Minnesota and Dakota to get enough milk for the fluid milk market in Winnipeg. In the winter months an average of a carload a day used to come from Minnesota." See AM, Animal Industry Branch, Manitoba Dairy Branch Scrapbook, 1921–1943. Clipping from *Winnipeg Tribune*, undated article entitled "Personality Parade," c. 1945.

98 CWA, Health Department, *Annual Report* (1920), 95.

99 CWA, Health Department *Annual Report* (1922), 57.

100 Joseph Harry Sutcliffe, "Economic Background of the Winnipeg General Strike: Wages and Working Conditions" (MA thesis, University of Manitoba, 1972), 139.

101 AM, Animal Industry Branch, Manitoba Dairy Branch Scrapbook dated 1917–1920. Address delivered by L.A. Gibson, Dairy Commissioner at the Saskatchewan Dairy Convention, January 1920.

102 CWA, Health Department, *Annual Report* (1917), 83.

103 CWA, Health Department, *Annual Report* (1919), 84.

104 CWA. Regarding tuberculosis mortality rates, see CWA, Health Department, *Annual Report* (1916), 17. Regarding decline in proportion of pasteurized milk, see *Annual Report* (1916), 18 and 95; Health Committee Communications, File #1607, Report of the Milk Committee appointed by the Western Representative of the Food Controller for Canada, 26 January 1918, 1; regarding prosecutions for adulterated milk, see *Annual Report* (1915), 94–95; *Annual Report* (1922), 57. Re: increase in milk-borne infections, see *Annual Report* (1916), 11; *Annual Report* (1917), 8–9; *Annual Report* (1918), 7–8; *Annual Report* (1919), 85–86.

105 CWA, Health Department, *Annual Report* (1920), 97.

106 Ibid.

107 CWA, Health Department, *Annual Report* (1916), 83–85; *Annual Report* (1918), 19.

108 CWA, Health Department, *Annual Report* (1920), 96.

109 Ibid.

110 CWA, Health Department, *Annual Report* (1920), 104–105; *Annual Report* (1921), 54.

111 CWA, Health Department, *Annual Report* (1920),113.

112 CWA, Health Department, *Annual Report* (1921), 54.

113 Dominion of Canada, "Regulations Relating to Tuberculosis"; CWA, Health Department *Annual Report* (1921), 54; Church, *An Unfailing Faith,* 125–126.

114 E.C. Brown, Winnipeg's Chief Dairy Inspector, reported that tuberculin testing in Saskatoon, which had commenced in 1915, resulted in a reported 8 to 10 percent reaction rate. Tuberculin testing in Winnipeg as early as 1895 had revealed a bovine tuberculosis prevalence of approximately 30 percent. Calculations of prevalence from data on tuberculin testing between 1909 and 1911 indicates a prevalence of bovine tuberculosis in dairy herds supplying milk to Winnipeg of between 35 and 38 percent. See CWA, Health Department, *Annual Report* (1909), 5; *Annual Report* (1910), 107; *Annual Report* (1911), 131; *Annual Report* (1920), 113.

115 CWA, Health Department, *Annual Report* (1922), 64–67.

116 Accurate calculation of the mortality rate in 0- to 4-year-old children is not possible because the size of the city's population aged 0 to 4 years of age is not known. Thus, the rate can only be calculated using the entire population of Winnipeg as the denominator. This calculation is accurate only if it can be assumed that the proportion of Winnipeg's population aged 0 to 4 remained constant between 1910 and 1922. Given that this time period includes the war years of 1914 to 1918, when the birth rate likely declined, this assumption may well not hold. When calculated using the total population as the denominator, mortality in 0- to 4-year olds from pulmonary tuberculosis decreased from 6.01 to 1.55/100,000 population between 1910 and 1922, and mortality from non-pulmonary tuberculosis decreased from 13.56 to 5.19/100,000 population.

117 Jones, *Valuing Animals*, 64–74.

118 Barbara Rosenkrantz, *Public Health and the State: Changing Views in Massachusetts 1842–1936* (Cambridge, MA: Harvard University Press, 1972), 170–179.

Brigden's and the Eaton's Catalogue: Business and Art in Winnipeg, 1914–1940

Angela E. Davis

The historical link between art and business is not often recognized as an important factor in the development of Canadian art. Artists' connections with commerce have been treated either as unfortunate necessities undertaken prior to moving on to the supposed higher levels of a career in the "fine" arts, or as denoting activity within a lesser form of art. These interpretations have led to the neglect of many artists working in Canada in the late nineteenth and early twentieth centuries, and to the false assumption that Canadian artistic activity was minimal until either the foundation of formalized institutions, the creation of a Canadian national art by the members of the Group of Seven in the 1920s, or the development of universal modern art after the Second World War.

It is possible to suggest, however, by examining the interrelationship between artists and commerce, that a much more active Canadian art scene existed than might be supposed from the general historical surveys. This is a view especially pertinent to western Canadian art during the first four decades of the twentieth century. It is also a view that allows artists to be considered within the context of social history rather than traditional art history. The following discussion of the connections between the graphic arts firm of Brigden's Limited, the Eaton's catalogue, and Winnipeg artists is not, therefore, concerned with aesthetic evaluations or developments in style, but with a situation that permitted artists to gain employment and use their skills at a time when to be an independent artist was rarely a practical proposition.

The association of art with commerce in the modern sense began in the nineteenth century in England as the result of the industrialization of the craft of printing.[1] This permitted mechanized reproduction of visual images and led to the introduction of illustrations into publications previously devoted solely to the printed word. Prior to this, artists who wished to have their work reproduced approached the undertaking in one of two ways. They either, like Turner, etched or engraved their work themselves or they employed other artists, whose specialty was etching or engraving, to do it for them.[2] Whichever choice they made, the whole process was manual, from copying the original onto the etching plate or the woodblock to operating the printing press. In the 1780s, however, the engraver Thomas Bewick developed a form of fine white-line engraving that was extremely suitable for repetitive reproduction,[3] and in 1814 the German inventor Friedrich König introduced the first steam-driven printing press into the printing workshop of the *Times* newspaper in London.[4]

This combination of factors completely changed the concept of the reproduction of visual images. It led by the mid-nineteenth century to what became known as commercial, or "mechanical," wood engraving and to the employment of hundreds of engravers, illustrators, and artists in an increasing number of engraving houses and graphic arts studios.[5] The work produced by these so-called "commercial" engravers fuelled the rise of the popular press that, in turn, increased pressure on the engravers for more work. Not only did the engravers reproduce the watercolour or black-and-white sketches of artist-reporters covering events at home or abroad, but they also provided portraits, local landscapes, reproductions of famous works of art and, of course, advertisements. Such journals as the *Illustrated London News* and the *Graphic* owed their success to the work of these generally anonymous engravers and illustrators.[6]

The problem with increased productivity, necessitated by public enthusiasm for the illustrated press, was that speed became a major consideration. Engravers who were, after a lengthy apprenticeship, as skilled in drawing and painting as they were in engraving, found themselves working virtually in an assembly-line situation.[7] They were frequently responsible for engraving only a small part of a much larger illustration and were, as a result, quite detached from the finished product.[8] They were ill paid, overworked and underappreciated. It is not surprising, therefore, that many of them chose to emigrate. Among those who made this decision was Frederick Brigden, an artist-craftsman, who would found a major commercial engraving house in Canada and would be of considerable importance in the development of Canadian art.

Brigden had undertaken his apprenticeship at the most important engraving studio in England, that of W.J. Linton, had studied drawing under John Ruskin at the London Working Men's College, and had worked as an engraver and illustrator for the *Illustrated London News*.[9] But in 1872, with a young family to support and with, as he felt, no prospects for advancement in his chosen profession, he left England for Toronto. After much initial hardship, he was able, in 1876, in partnership with two other immigrant engravers, to found the Toronto Engraving Company and thus begin his long association with Canadian art and Canadian business.

Canadian art developed parallel to the process of the mechanization of printing and the reproduction of visual images. With a few notable exceptions,[10] the first artists to paint the Canadian scene had been travellers or recorders, people who were passing through,[11] but by the middle years of the nineteenth century there were many who had taken up residence in the cities of eastern Canada.[12] And for these artists, some of whom would later be included among the founding members of the National Gallery and the Royal Canadian Academy, association with the world of commercial reproduction was accepted as a matter of course. In the 1860s and the 1870s, they worked for commercial photography studios and, from the mid-1880s, for commercial engraving firms. Homer Watson, George Reid, and Lucius O'Brien are among those who painted backgrounds, tinted portraits, and coloured photographs for the firm of Notman's in Montreal and Toronto in the late nineteenth century,[13] while in the early years of the twentieth century J.E.H. MacDonald, Tom Thomson, and other future members of the Group of Seven worked for the Toronto engraving firm of Grip.[14]

In 1876, the fledgling Toronto Engraving Company relied on the skills of its founders to conduct both the artistic and commercial aspects of its business. These skills were, fortunately, considerable, with the result that by the 1880s, and in spite of the fact that it was one firm among many competing for the custom of newspaper and magazine publishers, the Toronto Engraving Company was well established, with a clientele which included the publishers of the *Globe*, the *Farmer's Advocate*, and the *Telegram*.[15] By the end of the decade Frederick Brigden was sole owner of the business, and it had grown to a size where, as well as employing his sons George and Fred H. Brigden as business manager and art director respectively, Frederick Brigden was required to employ a number of other artists and engravers. In the early 1890s he further extended his resources to include the new processes of photography and photo-engraving, and in 1893, with the provision of illustrations for the mail-order catalogue, he started what was to be a long association with the T. Eaton Company.[16]

One of the more interesting aspects of the Brigden relationship with Eaton's is that it is not mentioned in any of the literature on the Eaton company. According to the Eaton sources, the catalogue, which had started as a small book of thirty-two pages in 1884,[17] was, by 1901, being produced entirely in Eaton's own Toronto printing department, with its own art department and its own artists.[18] Eaton's eventually had the facilities to provide its own art work and certainly, in 1901, had started its own printing department.[19] Prior to this it used the printing presses of the Methodist Book House and the illustrative services of the Toronto Engraving Company.[20]

In a letter written to a grandson of Timothy Eaton many years later, Fred H. Brigden described the first work done for Eaton's: "In the early 1890s our firm was called on to do some of the first illustrations for the catalogue. These were engraved on boxwood, the method mostly used at that time." He went on to explain that "photo-engraving was rapidly being developed … the first fashion illustrations … were drawn in pen and ink and reproduced by line engraving … [and] the early catalogues … were rapidly improved as the half-tone process began shortly after to be used." Mr. Eaton, he said, "encouraged us to develop a specialized art department for mail order illustration."[21] It is obvious that the commitment on the part of the Brigden firm to the established Eaton retail business[22] was considerable. Contracts were carried out for other firms, but Eaton's seems to have been the major client and the one that had the most influence on Brigden decision making. Certainly, the production of the twice yearly catalogue eventually became the focal point around which Brigden's adjusted all its other work.

Not only was the Toronto Engraving Company involved with the provision of illustrations for the early catalogues, but it was also involved in the failure of the printers' strike against Eaton's in 1901. In that year, Eaton's started to operate its own printing department. It purported to abide by union rules but, in fact, was not a union shop. The Toronto Typographical Union called a strike that, in spite of a highly successful boycott of the retail store, was settled once it became apparent that Eaton's could produce its mail-order catalogue without the skills of union workers.[23] Eaton's was able to do this because it purchased an electro-typing plant, asked a clothing department manager (one Lowry) to train his salesman in its use, and then arranged with the Brigden firm to make two sets of illustrations in case of failure in their printing.[24] The production of the catalogue would not have been possible, of course, if the Brigden photo-engravers had been unionized, something which did not take place for another three years.

In 1904, following a short strike, the Toronto Engraving Company was the first graphic arts firm in Canada to accept the International Photo-Engravers Union, a fact which Frederick Brigden described as unavoidable due to the size of his firm.[25] When he had started to provide illustrations for Eaton's in 1893, he had "from fifteen to seventeen artists and engravers" working for him,[26] mostly on the production of wood engravings, but photographers and photo-engravers were already also part of the workforce. The staff was further extended with the introduction of colour into the reproduction process; as Eaton's placed greater emphasis on coloured illustration of clothing in the catalogue, so there was a new requirement for artists trained in the area of "fashion design." The amount of work was such that in 1912 the Toronto Engraving Company moved to premises capable of accommodating all aspects of its business, including printing. In the same year the firm changed its name to Brigden's Limited, remaining under that title until it merged with Rouse and Mann in 1979.[27]

By 1913, then, the year in which Eaton's decided to produce a western mail-order catalogue, Brigden's was a leading graphic arts house in eastern Canada. It had a large workforce, with unionized photo-engravers and an art department consisting, at catalogue time, of up to seventy or eighty artists. The latter were, however, like the "commercial" engravers earlier, obliged to work under difficult circumstances. They were subject, in spite of the fact that many of them were highly skilled, to specialization or a division of labour when working on the catalogues: some drew only "boots and shoes," some specialized in jewellery, silverware, or furniture, while others devoted their skills to page decoration. A further specialist was responsible for the overall layout of the advertising material on the page, and even the fashion artists, who were described as the "aristocrats of the mail order catalogue," and were highly trained individuals, were forced to specialize. Some of them were required to paint only faces or hands and feet, while others sketched in the garment over the figure, washed in the light and shade, or drew the final details of stitching and ornamentation on the garment being advertised.[28]

It might be thought, in view of the assembly-line aspect of the work, that artistic creativity would be ruined in such a climate, but, in fact, many important Canadian artists worked for Brigden's and other similar firms. And many of them have since credited their years spent working for the graphic arts houses as having provided them with a discipline and technical skill they might otherwise have lacked. This was especially the case for Winnipeg artists who, following the opening of Brigden's Winnipeg branch in 1914, found employment as well as creative encouragement.

According to the Brigden records, the decision to open a branch in Winnipeg was the result of a direct request on the part of Eaton's. Finding the running of the western mail-order business from Winnipeg with a catalogue produced in Toronto too complicated, Eaton's put the Winnipeg shipping manager, Charles Band, in charge of organizing a western-produced catalogue. He, in turn, contacted the Brigden firm which, by this time, was being run by George and Fred H. Brigden. Fred Brigden had some doubts about the venture, but his father encouraged the move west. His theory was that "if a major customer offered you an opportunity you should grasp it no matter what the difficulties."[29] In Fred Brigden's words, his father "handed out a substantial sum to enable us to purchase an engraving plant and open a studio in Winnipeg," and, as he noted, "so began an enterprise which had some part in the remarkable development of mail order business in western Canada."[30] He might have added that it was also an enterprise that played no small part in the remarkable development of art in western Canada. Fred Brigden organized the establishment of the firm in the top three floors of the *Farmer's Advocate* building, persuaded his cousin, Arnold, to take over as manager, and opened for business in 1914. Eaton's was, therefore, responsible for bringing to the West a firm which would, in J. Russell Harper's words, parallel "the roles of Notman in Montreal and Toronto during the Victorian years and of Grip in Toronto early in the present century."[31]

In spite of the general historical assessment that no art was produced in Winnipeg prior to 1914, and that it was not until the founding of the Winnipeg Art Gallery in 1912 and the School of Art in 1913 that art began to be taken seriously by the community,[32] there were many artists already in Winnipeg at the time of the arrival of the Brigden firm and the production of the western catalogue. They were, of course, working commercially: as teachers, as cartoonists for the newspapers, or as artists and engravers for those engraving companies already established.[33] Among them, Victor Long, who had arrived in 1887, was working for the firm of Buckbee Meers; Frank Armington had opened a teaching studio in 1900; Hay Stead was drawing cartoons for the *Manitoba Free Press*, and E.J. Ransom, an engraver of considerable talent, had founded his own company early in the century.[34] Moreover, prior to the founding of the formal art institutions, a Manitoba Society of Artists had been formed in 1903, art exhibitions had been held at industrial and agricultural fairs or in private homes, and a number of large and important graphic arts firms were present in the city. Besides Buckbee Meers and Ransom's, there were such firms as Campbell's, Commercial Engravers, Stovel's, and Bulman's. Of these, Stovel's and Bulman's were the largest and the longest established and could, presumably, have taken on the Eaton's contract or, at least, offered Brigden's considerable competition.

Stovel's, founded in 1889 by the printer John Stovel, had, as early as 1905, mechanized and enlarged to the point that the firm included engraving and lithography as well as printing.[35] Similarly, Bulman's, which was established in 1892 by John Bulman, a lithographer, as a photo-engraving and lithography company, was also a thriving concern.[36] In 1916, following a fire, Bulman's reorganized itself as a lithography and printing firm, but in 1914 both firms were providing all the services required for the reproduction of art work. And working in all the various graphic arts firms were photo-engravers, wood engravers, lithographers, stereotypers, electrotypers, bookbinders, printing pressmen, and many, as it says in the Stovel record, "black and white and full colour artists."[37] There were, in fact, so many firms active in the printing and engraving field that one could assume that an extra company was unnecessary or was bound to fail. But Stovel's, which had been approached by Eaton's in the first place, had declined the work, thus leaving the Eaton's catalogue contract to Brigden's.[38] The Brigden firm was, of course, in a position to benefit from Stovel's decision. It was already practised in catalogue production and had the added advantage of experience with organized labour. Its acceptance of the International Photo-Engravers Union has been credited with being one of the reasons for the firm's stability and success,[39] while the employment of Arnold O. Brigden as manager can only, in retrospect, be described as inspired. It was Arnold Brigden who proceeded to hire highly trained art directors, to employ gifted apprentices who would later be among some of Canada's most respected artists, and to become personally involved in all aspects of Winnipeg's artistic community.

Arnold Brigden was the nephew of Frederick Brigden. He had been trained as a wood engraver and a photo-engraver but, by 1912, was working on the managerial side of a large New York graphic arts firm.[40] He was, therefore, well qualified to take over the running of the Winnipeg business. There were the usual teething problems, of course. He complained at first that the other firms were producing better art work[41] and worried that at catalogue time the photo-engraving department would not be sufficiently well organized to cope.[42] Also, in the first year, there was concern expressed about the effect of war on the local economic situation. By 1915, however, all major problems appear to have been solved and the firm had become a fixture.

Not least among the factors that allowed Brigden's to prosper under Arnold Brigden's guidance, was the succession of talented and experienced art directors. Tom MacLean, for example, who had worked at Grip in Toronto with MacDonald and other future Group of Seven members since 1896, left Toronto in 1914 to become the first head of Winnipeg Brigden's art department.[43] He was followed by such men as Jack Schaflein, an American artist who was in charge of the commercial art department in the 1920s and 1930s,[44] and Percy Edgar, who left Toronto's Brigden's in 1915 and became head of the fashion department in 1920.[45] These men were all accomplished artists, remembered by their subordinates as their first art teachers and major influences on their own careers.[46]

Apprentices entered Brigden's employment in the early years without any previous training. Their talent may have been recognized by a schoolteacher or a parent, but, generally speaking, they were trained by the art director on the job. They entered one of two specialties: commercial art or fashion art. The former included the making of illustrations for machinery, appliances, furniture, and other hard goods advertising, while the latter centred on art work for clothing, linen, and soft goods. Photo-engravers, wood engravers, and photographers worked on the top floor of the building, fashion artists on the middle, commercial artists on the lower, and the whole firm was advertised as being equipped to "supply illustrations and designs for books, catalogues, magazines and general advertising of all kinds."[47]

Customers were advertising agencies or, more commonly in the beginning, retail and wholesale firms. These included Hudson's Bay House, the Army and Navy Store in Regina, the Great West Garment Company in Edmonton, and Gaults, Birks, and the Christie Company in Winnipeg. But it was the Eaton's mail-order catalogue that provided the largest amount of work for the Brigden engravers and artists. In fact, the whole organization of the firm, in Winnipeg as in Toronto, centred on the production of two annual catalogues: from February to May and from September to December specialists were brought in from the United States, extra staff was hired for the "busy" season, and low pay was supplemented by overtime.[48]

Among the reasons given for John Stovel's refusal of the Eaton's contract was his inability to pay artists the high salary of seventy-five dollars per week they were thought to earn. This figure was obviously exaggerated, although the American artists are recorded as having earned "good money." The average starting wage for Brigden artists was closer to nine dollars per week for an eight-hour day, with overtime payments of twenty-five cents an hour extra.[49] However, at catalogue time, employees worked, as one has said, "from morning until night, each day much like the other,"[50] with the result that they considered the two periods of catalogue production as their major source of income. The photo-engravers earned union wages and, according to oral sources, had their own pension scheme, but the wood engravers and artists, whether apprentices or fully trained professionals, relied for the major portion of their income on the vagaries of the catalogue seasons. Ex-employees all talk of the low pay, the poor lighting, the lack of paid holidays, pension schemes, or sick-leave pay. The artists were somewhat envious of the photo-engravers' security, but at the same time did not consider unionizing themselves. They seem to have been grateful for any type of work connected with art and refer instead to the camaraderie they experienced: "It was fun at Brigden's," one of them recalled, "in spite of the heavy work schedule."[51]

The staff was large, from 100 to 125 employees. It included up to sixty-five artists, twenty-five engravers and five photo-engravers as well as office and sales staff. In the early years there were as many as seventeen wood-engraving apprentices, but as photo-engraving and photography took over, the numbers declined. Some were always needed for the commercial side of the catalogue, but others transferred to marketing or to photo-engraving.[52] Whichever area they worked in, ex-employees talk of the number of "characters" who worked for Brigden's—people like Harold Foster, who illustrated the first *Tarzan* books and created the comic book character *Prince Valiant*; Emile Laliberté and Jim Petrie, who painted covers for Harlequin Books; Charles Thorson, who was considered to be the creator of Bugs Bunny; and Angus Shortt, who went on to become a noted painter of Canadian wildlife.[53] There were also highly talented artists who have not been given their due, individuals appreciated locally but not nationally, such as Cyril Ashmore and Alison Newton[54] (who came from England), Newton Brett (who had trained in New York and Chicago before joining the firm in 1914), and Pauline and Christine LeGoff, who worked for Brigden's from 1918 to 1940. The former, under her married name of Boutal, became famous for her theatrical sets and costumes and her own paintings, while the latter has been described by all who knew her as "the best fashion artist in Canada."[55] At times the artists who worked for Brigden's resembled a "Who's Who" of Canadian art. Charles Comfort and Eric Bergman were with the firm from the start, while Victor Friesen, Nicholas Grandmaison, Caven Atkins, Fritz Brandtner, Philip Surrey, William Maltman, Gordon Smith, and William Winter were among those working there for various periods during the 1920s and 1930s. The work they did for the catalogue never changed, but as William Winter has said, "all of us, talented or not, had to go into commercial art, there was no chance of earning a living at anything else."[56]

By the time of the economic crisis of the 1930s, Arnold Brigden was accepted as a noteworthy, if somewhat eccentric, personality in Winnipeg. His business opinions were quoted in the *Free Press*, he was a member of the Art Committee of the Industrial Bureau, which supported the art gallery and the art school, and his camping trips and "alpine" hobbies, which included an Alpine Club in his backyard,[57] were well known. He may not have been a member of the local "elite," but among artists, art teachers, and collectors he was an important figure. Not only did he purchase the private work of many of his employees,[58] at a time when few Canadians supported their own artists, but during the Depression he also assisted them to take classes at the Winnipeg School of Art. Many of the artists had attended the school in the evenings or during the slack periods between the twice-yearly catalogue rush, but in the 1930s the situation was somewhat different. Although the firm survived the Depression years, ex-employees describe the period as one when they would be arbitrarily "laid off," have their fees paid to attend the school, and then be rehired as the situation improved: as one artist has said, "it was a sort of retainer."[59]

In spite of the fact that Brigden artists were obviously working under difficult conditions, were poorly paid, and were still obliged to fulfill the monotonous assembly-line production of the catalogue, they nevertheless recall their years with the firm as rewarding. They were at least semi-employed and were able to work in an atmosphere that was congenial to their special interests. Winter says, "it was stimulating to acquire the skills, the materials of painting, the brushes, the colours, and the enthusiasm of others." He has described what he calls "a tradition of water colour painting at the commercial houses," when he and Philip Surrey and other young artists would spend their lunch breaks sketching and painting in the cold Winnipeg winters, "mixing glycerine with our paints to keep them from freezing."[60] Caven Atkins has also mentioned the stimulation of contact with other artists while at Winnipeg Brigden's: he has recorded, for example, how Fritz Brandtner introduced him to the ideas of the German Expressionists and the Bauhaus movement.[61] And Brandtner himself, already an accomplished artist when he came to Winnipeg from Danzig in 1926, was able, because of the livelihood provided by his work with Brigden's, to experiment with his version of "Canadian modernism" in his spare hours.[62] For these artists, then, Brigden's was a place where they were able to work and exchange ideas and could, at the same time, hone their skills in the hope of a different future. But for some, like Eric Bergman and Charles Comfort, it was the major impetus in their careers. They owed their start to Fred and Arnold Brigden.

Eric Bergman was to become an internationally known graphic artist who remained with Brigden's all his life, but Comfort followed a different path. It began when Fred Brigden, by this time a respected watercolour artist as well as art director of the Toronto firm, was in Winnipeg in 1913 establishing the new branch. He was asked to judge a watercolour competition at the Winnipeg YMCA and awarded first prize to the thirteen-year-old Charles Comfort. He subsequently offered him an apprenticeship at the firm for three dollars per week.[63] After some difficulty with his parents who had "something more respectable in mind," Comfort joined the Winnipeg firm in November of 1914. He carried out the usual mundane chores of drawing furniture, kitchenware, and machinery for the catalogue during the day and, in the evenings, attended the classes given by Alex Musgrave at the Winnipeg School of Art. In 1918 and 1919 he won the Eaton's catalogue cover competition and was able to go to Toronto on the proceeds. There he started working at the Toronto Brigden's, becoming, as he said, "a kind of mobile employee, moving back and forth between Toronto and Winnipeg as required."[64] He settled in Toronto permanently in 1926, becoming, as Paul Duval has said, "the star commercial designer of the country."[65] He continued working for Brigden's and other graphic arts firms, including his own, until 1938, when he began teaching at the University of Toronto. He was president of the Royal Canadian Academy from 1957 to 1960 and was then appointed Director of the National Gallery, a post he held for the next five years.[66] He became, in fact, an important figure in the history of Canadian art but one who never forgot the debt he owed to the world of commerce. Although he said that he could separate his commercial from what he called his "expressive" work, he is also recorded as saying that the blend between the two had "been a great advantage." It kept him, he said, in touch "with life and men and matters," thus avoiding the isolation from "the facts of life," which can be "one of the greatest weaknesses of painters."[67] Like Winter, he respected the discipline and skills the commercial work had given him.

Also like William Winter, Comfort emphasized the stimulation that association with other artists in Winnipeg, including those not associated with Brigden's, gave him. Among those who endeavoured to earn a living either commercially or by teaching were Lionel LeMoine Fitzgerald and Walter J. Phillips, artists who would eventually become well known both in Canada and abroad. And it is with these two that the name of Eric Bergman is most closely associated: the "Manitoba Three," they were called.[68] Fitzgerald, who was Winnipeg born, had already had a painting accepted by the Royal Canadian Academy in 1913,[69] and Phillips had arrived in the city from England in the same year.[70] Both concentrated their skills on watercolour painting and wood engraving and both spent most of their lives teaching in order to have an income.[71] When Eric Bergman arrived in Winnipeg in 1914, he found artists with compatible interests. Originally from Dresden, he was already trained as a wood engraver and photo-engraver and was employed by Brigden's straightaway. Initially, like everyone else at the firm, he was caught up in the routine of commercial work, but in the 1920s he was encouraged by Fred Brigden and Walter Phillips to extend his creative talents outside his working hours. The result was the creation of watercolours and engravings that led to international renown.[72] Unlike Comfort, however, he chose to remain in Winnipeg, working at Brigden's and going on painting trips with his friends. Both Bergman and Comfort benefited from the support and encouragement of the Brigdens. Without them their art and their careers might not have developed in the way they did in the years between the two world wars. Fred Brigden bought their work and promoted its further exposure.[73]

For Winnipeg artists in the years prior to the Second World War, connections with commerce were obviously essential. Without them, they would have been unable to work. While the School of Art and the Art Gallery gave a formal recognition to the arts,[74] it was in the commercial art houses that artists were able to earn a living and thus keep their skills alive. And in the case of Brigden's, which ended up providing work for so many artists of importance, the firm owed its existence in Winnipeg to Eaton's decision in 1913 to produce a western-based catalogue. But Eaton's gave no recognition to Brigden's and, indeed, from 1914 began withdrawing some of its work from the Toronto branch. There are comments in the Brigden correspondence that lead one to assume that the Eaton contract was not always reliable, in spite of Fred Brigden's public pronouncements on the privilege of working for Eaton's. There is no record showing that the Brigdens were conscious of the unfair practices carried on by Eaton's during the 1930s,[75] but ex-Brigden employees mention how, with the gradual development of its own advertising and art departments, Eaton's tried to lure artists away from the Brigden firm.[76] In the 1940s, Winnipeg Brigden's was producing more work for Eaton's than the Toronto branch, but in 1948 the whole catalogue production was returned to Toronto. The impression given in the Eaton's literature would lead one to suppose that all work was subsequently carried out in Eaton's own departments. As one ex-employee has said, "large companies play down buying from others."[77] In fact, according to the *Globe and Mail*, Toronto Brigden's was still doing art work for Eaton's in 1970.[78]

The Brigden connection with Eaton's and the catalogue raises a number of interesting issues concerning the interrelationship between artists and business in general, and between western Canadian artists and commercial work in particular. Because it was essential that the seasonal catalogues appear on time, speed was a pivotal factor in their preparation. This meant that the mode of work required of artists working on the catalogue was similar to that of an industrialized workforce committed to assembly-line production in a mechanized situation. Moreover, in spite of the necessary interaction between all members of a graphic arts firm, there were perceived differences between artists, photo-engravers, and other labour-related employees. And further, as Canadian art itself became more self-conscious, a division was implied between artists working in a commercial environment and artists working independently. It is this latter implication that has led to an historical interpretation of artists' commercial involvement as being temporary and unimportant, an unfortunate means to an end. In fact, as has been frequently pointed out, this was not the case.[79]

The establishment of catalogue production in western Canada affected Winnipeg artists in that it introduced a new form of visual communication. Although created specifically for western rural needs, the catalogue used techniques already practised in Toronto and thus required the same artistic skills from its local employees. For this reason, apprentices were trained by art directors brought in from Toronto. What is of more significance, however, is the fact that the Winnipeg School of Art stressed the importance of training students in commercial as well as "fine" art from its inception.[80] Certainly, all the artists who were at Brigden's worked in both fields. It is interesting to speculate on whether this had any aesthetic effect on their interpretation of the prairie environment in their private work. Watercolour painting has, indeed, remained an important element of western Canadian art.[81] But as Winter and Surrey and most of the other artists employed by Brigden's before the Second World War subsequently left Winnipeg, their influence has obviously been felt elsewhere.

Finally, in terms of business, it is apparent that the impact of a major client such as Eaton's, while instrumental in persuading Brigden's to open in Winnipeg in the first place, did not, in the end, affect the smaller firm's survival. Winnipeg Brigden's continued after the catalogue production was returned to Toronto. Following Arnold Brigden's retirement in 1956, the firm was run from Toronto by third-generation members of the Brigden family until 1963, when it was purchased by Frank Ferguson, a long-time member of the Winnipeg managerial staff. Ultimately, although it cannot be denied that it was Eaton's and the catalogue that prompted the establishment of the Brigden graphic arts firm in Winnipeg, it was the Brigden family that succeeded in providing the conditions within which art and business, and indeed labour, could work to mutual advantage.

Notes

1   See Susan E. Meyer, *America's Great Illustrators* (New York: Harry N. Abrams, 1978) for an analysis of the change from "patronage" to "employment." She says, "In the nineteenth-century … the publishing industry—replacing all traditional patrons—emerged as the chief employer of artists. The publications succeeded both Church and Court as the great showcase for artists." See also Angela E. Davis, *Art and Work: A Social History of Labour in the Canadian Graphic Arts Industry to the 1940s* (Montreal: McGill-Queen's University Press, 1995).

2   David Bland, *A History of Book Illustration: The Illuminated Manuscript and the Printed Book* (Berkeley and Los Angeles: University of California Press, 1969), 249. See also Jack Lindsay, *Turner: His Life and Work* (St. Albans: Granada Publishing, 1966), 356–362.

3   Ian Bain, ed., "Introduction," *Thomas Bewick, A Memoir of Thomas Bewick written by himself* (London: Oxford University Press, 1975), xxix and xxx. See also Kenneth Lindley, *The Woodblock Engravers* (Newton Abbot. Herts: David and Charles. 1970), 29, and Michael Twyman, *Printing 1770–1970: An Illustrated History of its Development and Uses in England* (London: Eyre and Spottiswoode, 1970), 87.

4   S.H. Steinberg, *Five Hundred Years of Printing* (Harmondsworth: Penguin Books, 1977), 277–280.

5   Davis S. Sander, *Wood Engraving: An Adventure in Printmaking* (New York: Viking Press, 1978), 17.

6   Twyman, *Printing*, 95. See also Paul Hogarth, *The Artist as Reporter* (London: Studio Vista, 1967), 23–24.

7   See F.B. Smith, *Radical Artisan: William James Linton: 1812–97* (Manchester: Manchester University Press, 1973), 7 and 145–6.

8   Lindley, *Woodblock*, 53; Sander, *Wood Engraving*, 18; Twyman, *Printing*, 97.

9   Edward J. Nicholson, *The First One Hundred Years* (Toronto: University of Toronto Press, 1971).

10 See, for example, J. Russell Harper, *Paul Kane's Frontier* (Toronto: University of Toronto Press, 1971).

11 Michael Bell, *Painters in a New Land* (Toronto: McClelland and Stewart, 1973), 9–15.

12 J. Russell Harper, *Painting in Canada: A History* (Toronto: University of Toronto Press, 1978), 179–192.

13 Ann Thomas, *Canadian Painting and Photography: 1860–1900* (Montreal: McCord Museum, 1979), 26.

14 Peter Mellen, *The Group of Seven* (Toronto and Montreal: McClelland and Stewart, 1970), 18–19; Harper, *Painting in Canada*, 183.

15 Nicholson, *The First One Hundred Years*, 19. See also J.E. Middleton, *Canadian Landscape: As Pictured by F.H. Brigden* (Toronto: Ryerson Press, 1944), 28.

16 Nicholson, *The First One Hundred Years*, 29.

17 George G. Naismith, *Timothy Eaton* (Toronto: McClelland and Stewart, 1923), 183.

18 *A Shopper's View of Canada's Past: Pages from Eaton's Catalogues: 1886–1930*, eds. G. de T. Glazebrook, Katharine B. Brett, and Judith McErval (Toronto: University of Toronto Press, 1969), vi; *Golden Jubilee 1869–1919: A book to commemorate the Fiftieth Anniversary of the T. Eaton Co., Ltd.* (Toronto and Winnipeg: T. Eaton Co., Ltd., 1919), 154 and 209.

19 Sally F. Zerker, *The Rise and Fall of the Toronto Typographical Union 1832–1922: A Case Study of Foreign Domination* (Toronto: University of Toronto Press, 1982), 147.

20 Fred H. Brigden to a grandson of Timothy Eaton, c. 1955 (no name given). Brigden papers, Metropolitan Toronto Library (MTL).

21 Ibid.

22 See Naismith, *Timothy Eaton*, and William G. Stephenson, *The Store that Timothy Built* (Toronto: McClelland and Stewart, 1969).

23 Zerker, *Rise and Fall*, 147.

24 Fred H. Brigden to Eaton grandson, c. 1955.

25 Frederick Brigden, Diary, April 1904, Brigden papers, MTL.

26 Nicholson, *The First One Hundred Years*, 22.

27 Elizabeth Hulse, *A Dictionary of Toronto Printers, Publishers, Booksellers and the Allied Trades: 1798–1900* (Toronto: Anson-Cartwright Editions, 1982), 260–261.

28 Fred H. Brigden, "Art in Relation to Business," unpublished manuscript, 9–10, Brigden papers, MTL.

29 Nicholson, *The First One Hundred Years*, 52.

30 Fred H. Brigden to Eaton grandson, c. 1955.

31 Harper, *Painting in Canada*, 315.

32 Angela E. Davis, "Laying the Ground: the establishment of an artistic milieu in Winnipeg: 1890–1913," *Manitoba History* 4 (Autumn, 1982): 10–15. See Ferdinand Eckhardt, *150 Years of Art in Manitoba: Struggle for a Visual Civilization* (Winnipeg: Winnipeg Art Gallery, 1970), 14; and Marilyn Baker, *The Winnipeg School of Art: The Early Years* (Winnipeg: University of Manitoba Press, 1984), 24–25.

33 Davis, "Laying the Ground," 14.

34 Colin S. MacDonald, *A Dictionary of Canadian Artists*, 3rd ed. (Ottawa: Canadian Paperbacks Publishing, 1979) and Davis, "Laying the Ground," 13–14.

35 Ruben Bellan, *Winnipeg: The Development of a Metropolitan Centre* (Ann Arbor: University Microfilms International, 1976), 153; Thomas Spence, *Historical Outline of the House of Stovel* (Winnipeg: Stovel Company, 1931), 9–11.

36 F.C. Pickwell, "Craftsmen for Fifty Years," *Manitoba Industrial Topics*, February 1942, reprint, 2. See also F.H. Schofield, *The Story of Manitoba*, vol. 3 (Winnipeg: S.J. Clarke Publishing, 1913), 15.

37 Spence, *Historical Outline of the House of Stovel*, 19–25.

38 Nicholson, *The First One Hundred Years*, 52. Also Fred H. Brigden to Eaton grandson, c. 1955.

39 Personal correspondence with R.C. Stovel, November 1982.

40 Nicholson, *The First One Hundred Years*, 52. Also Fred H. Brigden to Eaton grandson, c. 1955.

41 Arnold Brigden to Fred H. Brigden, 25 September 1914, University of Manitoba Archives and Special Collections (UM).

42 Arnold Brigden to Fred H. Brigden, 13 July 1915 (UM).

43 MacDonald, *Dictionary*, 1062. Also see Nancy E. Dillow, *The Transformation of Vision: The Works of H. Eric Bergman* (Winnipeg: Winnipeg Art Gallery, 1983), 7.

44 Baker, *Winnipeg School of Art*, 109.

45 Ibid., 94.

46 Interviews with Agnes Riehl, Frank Ferguson, Sid Vale, Kevin Best, and other ex-employees of Winnipeg Brigden's, December 1982.

47 Advertisement in the *Farmer's Advocate and Home Journal*, Winnipeg, December 1915, 1487.

48 Interview with Frank Ferguson, December 1982.

49 Interviews with ex-employees. Starting wages for apprentices varied from $9 to $12, although some were as low as $3. Once trained, weekly wages for skilled artists were quoted as being from $25 to $60 per week.

50 Quoted in Dillow, *Transformation*, 6.

51 Dorothy Garbutt, "Old House Stirs Old Memories," *Seniors Today*, 18 May 1983.

52 Interviews with Frank Ferguson and Sid Vale, December 1982.

53 Interviews with ex-employees. Also for Charles Thorson see Gene Walz, "Animation Central: The History of Animation in Winnipeg," *Arts Manitoba* 4,4 (Fall 1985): 18; Gene Walz, *Cartoon Charlie: The Life and Art of Animation Pioneer Charles Thorson* (Winnipeg: Great Plains Publications, 1998).

54 Baker, *Winnipeg School of Art*, 86–87 and 106.

55 Interviews with ex-employees.

56 Personal correspondence with William Winter, November 1984.

57 Patricia E. Bovey, "Introduction," *The Brigden Collection* (Winnipeg: Winnipeg Art Gallery, 1974), no pagination. See also Davis, "Brigden's and the Brigden Family," in Baker, *Winnipeg School of Art*, 92.

58 Bovey, "Introduction."

59 Interviews with Kevin Best and John Phillips, January 1983.

60 Personal correspondence with William Winter.

61 Joan Murray, "Caven Atkins: Fifty Years," *Artsmagazine*, May/June 1980, 41.

62 Helen Duffy, "The Brave New World of Fritz Brandtner," *Art Magazine*, Spring 1983, 19.

63 Charles Comfort, "Frederick Henry Brigden (1871–1956): Tribute to a distinguished Canadian Painter," unpublished manuscript, Art Gallery of Toronto, 1957, 19.

64 Margaret Gray, Margaret Rand, and Lois Steen, *Charles Comfort* (Toronto: Gage Publishing, 1976), 6.

65 Paul Duval, *Four Decades: The Canadian Group of Painters and Their Contemporaries—1930–1970* (Toronto: Clarke, Irwin, 1972), 58.

66 Gray et al., *Charles Comfort*, 40; Baker, *Winnipeg School of Art*, 93–94.

67 H.M. Jackson, "Charles Comfort: the man and the artist" (Toronto: self-published, 1935), 4.

68 See Dillow, "The Manitoba Three," *WAG magazine*, May 1981, 16–17.

69 Patricia E. Bovey and Ann Davis, *Lionel LeMoine FitzgGerald (1890–1956): The Development of an Artist* (Winnipeg: Winnipeg Art Gallery, 1978), 28.

70 Carlyle Allison, "W.J. Phillips: Artist and Teacher," *The Beaver*, Winter 1969, 6.

71 Bovey and Ann Davis, *Fitzgerald*, 16. Maria Tippett and Douglas Cole, *Phillips in Print: The Selected Writings of Walter J. Phillips on Canadian Nature and Art* (Winnipeg: Manitoba Records Society, 1982), xv-xix.

72 Dillow, *Transformation of Vision*, 24 n. 20.

73 Bovey, *Brigden Collection*.

74 Baker, *Winnipeg School of Art*, 84.

75 See, for example, Michiel Horn, ed., *The Dirty Thirties: Canadians in the Great Depression* (Toronto: Copp Clark, 1972), 122–135, and Gregory S. Kealey, "Hogtown: Working Class Toronto at the Turn of the Century," *Readings in Canadian History: Post Confederation*, eds. R. Douglas Francis and Donald B. Smith (Toronto: Holt, Rinehart, 1982), 183.

76 Interviews with Kevin Best and Sid Vale.

77 Interview with Kevin Best.

78 *Globe and Mail*, 28 January 1970, B5.

79 See, for example, James Montgomery Flagg, quoted in Meyer, *America's Great Illustrators*: "The only difference between a fine artist and an illustrator is that the latter can draw, eats three square meals a day and can afford to pay for them." For a Canadian example, see *Thoreau MacDonald: Illustrator: Designer: Observer of Nature*, ed. L. Bruce Pierce (Toronto: Norflex, 1971).

80 Baker, *Winnipeg School of Art*, 26–28.

81 See Ronald Rees, *Land of Earth and Sky: Landscape Painting of Western Canada.* (Saskatoon: Western Producer Prairie Books, 1984).

"Gloaming" to Growing: The Experience of the Institutionalized Elderly at Winnipeg's Middlechurch Home, 1907–1984

Crista Bradley

Just as aging cuts across all segments of society, issues associated with the process have breadth and depth that are relevant for many fields of inquiry. Counted among those who have a vested interest in the aged are sociologists, psychologists, educators, doctors, lawyers, pharmacists, social workers, clergy and ... historians? In fact, those engaged in historical research have much to learn from the study of the process, experience, and perceptions of aging in different societies over time. Since growing older is such an integral part of the human life cycle, further research on the matter has the potential to help society develop a better understanding of the aging process while, at the same time, bringing balance and added depth to current scholarship in the fields of economic, social, and political history.[1]

This essay focuses on the experience of Winnipeg's Middlechurch Home and its residents from 1907 to 1984.[2] The home was founded by the Christian Women's Union in 1883 as a safe place for single women and mothers. The focus of the Christian Women's Union shifted in 1907, and the home became the Old Folks' Home, Middlechurch. Even though the name changed in 1946 to the Middlechurch Home, the objective of the home (and infirmary) to provide quality care to elderly people has remained unaltered. Initially conceived as a place for impoverished elderly people who had nowhere else to turn, the home gradually became a more broad-based operation. The demand for the services of the home grew over the years. The Middlechurch Home celebrated the centenary of its service to the elderly of Manitoba in 2007.

The Middlechurch facility provides an excellent case study of institutional life on the prairies because of its inclusive nature. While the majority of the residents at the home were from Winnipeg, individuals from other locations were also admitted. It also serves as a helpful example because both women and men were accepted as residents.[3] Further, although the Christian influence on the home was evident throughout the years, it did not favour one denomination over another.[4]

The research conducted for this study points to three trends suggesting that the quality of life for residents in this Manitoba institution improved dramatically between 1907 and 1984. The first trend relates to the changing nature of seniors' homes during these years. These institutions came to be seen as places to live rather than as places to die. They placed increasing emphasis on the notion of "home" rather than "institution" and on the professionalization of their staff. Second, perceptions of the residents seemed to change markedly over the course of the century. The institutionalized elderly benefited from a more positive image, an increased degree of respect, and a greater level of independence during this period. Third, residents became increasingly involved in physical, social, and intellectual pursuits and community initiatives.

The Changing Nature of Seniors' Residential Facilities

The nature of residential care homes for seniors evolved throughout the twentieth century. From the early central Canadian institutions modelled on the British Poor Law system of earlier centuries to the multiple kinds of care facilities that are available to the elderly today, much progress has been made. This section explores the changing nature of life in the Middlechurch Home during the twentieth century.

One of the most significant changes to occur at Middlechurch was that staff in the home started to place an increased emphasis on the institution as a place for life rather than perpetuating its earlier fixation on death.[5] In the early years, the provision of care to the residents was closely associated with the gloomy motivation of "try[ing] to give [the residents] as much pleasure as possible in their last years."[6] The annual reports of the Middlechurch Home reveal that up until the 1950s, the home was viewed as a place where the elderly spent their "remaining days"[7] before death. In fact, the perceived proximity of the residents to the end of their lives permeates the records from this period. The board attempted to spare those in their "sunset days"[8] from "dread of the morrow."[9] One of the first matters of business in the 1911 annual report was a death count: "Death has been busy, eight having gone home during the year, but, of course, with increasing age we must expect this."[10]

As time went on, the dismal prospect for those who had "reached the lonely years of inactivity and helplessness"[11] was replaced with a much more upbeat and positive vision for their future. While resident deaths were included in annual reports later in the period, they do not figure as prominently in the discussion. Fewer references suggested that the home was simply a transitory place where the elderly waited for death. In fact, in 1968 the executive director's report read:

> We felt ... [at the time of construction of a Personal Care Home at Middlechurch in 1967] that people with a high degree of infirmity and incapacitation were not necessary [sic] total invalids and should not be treated as such. We felt that there

was too much of a tendency to concentrate on incapacitations and not enough thought had been given to develop and nourish the faculties that are left—no matter how limited these might be. We had seen too many people confined day after day to bed and thought that in many cases this was lazy nursing habits. Too often we had observed elderly people lose all pride of appearance because there were not the encouragement or facilities for them to be otherwise.[12]

The language used in the annual reports in later years conveys a much more optimistic and cheerful environment, where elderly people embraced life. The 1954 open house was reportedly "a big day for the old folk too, who, dressed in their best, proudly escort[ed] their relatives and friends around the grounds and to see their rooms."[13] Also, more attention was directed to ensuring the happiness of the residents. In 1958, the annual report mentioned a ninety-seven-year-old woman who was considering music lessons, prompting the secretary of the board to note that "the frailty we mention certainly has nothing to do with spirit."[14]

Other evidence also suggests that there was a shift in the tone of seniors' homes during this period. In the early days, many long-term care institutions for the elderly were given sombre and depressing names that hinted at the inevitable fate awaiting those who resided in the institution. As historian Megan Davies has suggested: "Institutional titles discarded throughout the 1940s included the Provincial Home for Incurables, the Home for Aged and Infirm Ladies, the Old Peoples' Home (Vancouver), and the Old Men's Home (Victoria).... New names shift the focus from the resident to the curative purpose of the institution, to the gardens that surround it, or to the politician who founded it."[15] It appears that a similar shift occurred at the Middlechurch Home. The Secretary's 1946 report explains:

> In the early days, when Winnipeg was known as the Gateway to the West, and the eager young settlers came to make their homes here, old people were very rare and were treated with the greatest respect. It was at that time that our Home was named "Old Folks' Home, Middlechurch." But now our city has past [sic] the days of its youth.... Our institution is proud to be able to give these dear old people a home. A number of these are of British origin and to them especially the name "Old Folks' Home" is an unfortunate one. Then, too, in this modern age, no one admits old age. So the Board decided after very careful consideration, to delete the words "Old Folks" from the name of our Home. Much to the joy of all our old people we wish to announce our new name "Middlechurch Home."[16]

These ideas may have had an influence as late as 1980–1981 when the "Hostel, Personal Care and Staff buildings" were rechristened as the "East, West and South" buildings (although the changes were purportedly motivated by a desire to provide easier access).[17] Surely the residents appreciated the efforts over the years to reduce the number of reminders of their own mortality.

A consequence of this revitalized focus at Middlechurch is apparent in the opinions voiced by elderly residents about their home.[18] The early annual reports contain little mention of any positive feelings of the residents about their environment. While the absence of this information could be attributed to the record-keeping practices and objectives of the secretary, positive impressions about the home are included in later reports. In the later years, some (although undoubtedly not all) seniors enjoyed their time at Middlechurch and were grateful for the care they received there. The 1935 report reads: "with the church services, concerts and radio their lives are not the dreary waste that old age is so often pictured to be but is, as one of the inmates expressed it, 'a very comfortable family hotel life.'"[19] Another resident expressed similar sentiments in 1950 when she said, "This is certainly one grand place to be—not only at Christmas time but all the year, and *I* know what I am talking about."[20] Obviously, then, not all residents grudgingly regarded Middlechurch as the last possible option available to them to live out their final days. Instead, some came to embrace all of the opportunities that the home offered.

Closely related to this shift in the perception of seniors' residential facilities was a growing concern about the way in which these institutions depicted themselves to their own staff. As was the case in other parts of Canada, the Middlechurch facility was increasingly promoted as a "home" rather than an "institution" during these years.[21] However, contrary to Megan Davies's and James Snell's conclusions that a true home-like environment did not necessarily result from this shift, Winnipeg's Middlechurch facility appears to have had some success in this regard. The annual reports of the home boasted about this atmosphere countless times, beginning in 1914.[22] It was clearly very important to the staff and board members that the home was viewed in this light.[23] In 1940, the secretary of the board wrote, "we feel that our Home is a haven of security and peace. The word institution is rarely used—and indeed we feel that it does not apply—rather we have a Home where each one may retain his or her own individuality yet be relieved of worry and responsibility and where they may rest assured that they will have every comfort and care."[24] The virtues of kindness and warmth quickly gained importance in the early twentieth century at the expense of the images of structure and sterility that had been favoured in the past.

In addition to the specific references to the creation of a "home" environment in the records of institutions, Megan Davies points out that seniors' residential facilities in British Columbia took active measures to reconstruct their surroundings to correspond to this image. She chronicles the attention given to the interior design of homes on the West Coast to make them more comfortable and familiar in the 1930s to 1950s.[25] While the board at Middlechurch noted that they were "very proud of [the Home's] comfortable sitting rooms" as early as 1910,[26] the impetus to redecorate intensified in the 1930s (and beyond). Structural repairs were obviously a priority, but increased mention was also made of efforts to refurnish the seniors' rooms and common spaces to make them more inviting and cheerful. In the face of hard times at the beginning of the Depression,[27] careful consideration was given to decorating Middlechurch's new building: "[it] has been a great deal of work—to get practical things, that are artistic and at the same time not to exceed the money allotted to each ward. The results, I am sure, are very satisfactory as everyone visiting the rooms can testify. They do not look like rooms in an institution. The inmates can take as much pride in them as in their own rooms at home."[28] In 1946, one of the residents expressed her delight with the redecoration initiatives. She said, "I have always wished for a pretty blue room with frilly white curtains. Now, at last, I have my wish. Isn't it wonderful!"[29] Special attention was also given to the maintenance of the gardens at the home.[30] While it might be too much to suggest that these projects would have single-handedly increased the residents' quality of life, it is fair to suggest that the redecoration of the home and beautification of the yard would have increased the appeal of these spaces for visitors and residents.

Another development that changed the nature of the Middlechurch Home and undoubtedly improved the quality of its residents' lives during these years was an increase in the number of professional staff employed by this institution. The 1907 annual report of the Christian Women's Union simply states that the organization "secured the services of a married couple as steward and matron" for the home but provides no details about the qualifications of these individuals.[31] In 1910, the home filled these positions with a couple who had some related experience,[32] and by 1912 there was a "trained nurse" on staff.[33] From the 1950s on, Middlechurch seemed to place even more emphasis on the hiring of trained staff.[34] William Smith, who had "seventeen to eighteen years experience in Social Work.... [and an] interest in old people," was hired as the home's superintendent in 1953.[35] Also during these years, increased mention is made of the workshops and conferences attended by Middlechurch staff[36] and employee completion of training relevant to their work.[37] Middlechurch also played a role in educating students in professions related to aging.[38]

This professionalization of staff was not unique to the Middlechurch Home.[39] People and professionals in all parts of Canada became increasingly concerned about the needs of the elderly population after the Second World War.[40] Seniors became the targets of heightened levels of research, study, and programming. The field of gerontology emerged and has since grown into a complex and multi-faceted discipline that draws on expertise from a wide variety of disciplines.

Changing Attitudes Towards the Institutionalized Elderly

The perception of the institutionalized elderly changed dramatically over the course of the twentieth century. During the years when death was the defining feature of homes, residents were often depicted as feeble and weak. Over time, many came to see the inhabitants of institutions in a more positive and active light. During these years, the institutionalized elderly started to receive more recognition for their skills, abilities, and contributions to society. Moreover, the regulations that governed the lives of the institutionalized elderly were reduced sharply in number and intrusiveness. With time, these seniors came to be regarded as capable individuals who deserved as much independence as they could manage.

In the early part of the twentieth century, residents of seniors' homes were often portrayed as lonely and tired people who were forced by ill health to seek refuge at institutions for care "in the gloaming of their days."[41] Although there are some early references to happy elements in the seniors' lives, the records of the Middlechurch Home frequently described the residents as though they had reached death's door where they were simply waiting for the "Great Reaper"[42] to spare them from their "weakness."[43] The 1911 annual report states that, "our two very old men are not able for much now. It is sad to see such big men growing so feeble, but they are far beyond the four-score."[44] Other references suggest that, "it is the personal interest and sympathy that is most needed" by the residents,[45] who are later referred to as "those who are unable to provide little pleasures for themselves."[46]

In concert with the evolution of the overall tone at the home, these perceptions of the institutionalized elderly gradually changed over the years. The annual reports from the later part of the period present a revised image of the elderly at Middlechurch. Rather than simply being viewed as weak patients with a multitude of medical problems in need of attention, the residents came to be seen as individuals with potential and energy. The derogatory terminology all but disappears by the later years, and individuals were encouraged to continue to live full and productive lives.

It is interesting to consider the terminology that staff and others used to refer to the patients. Although there are some affectionate references to "Daddy Bell" and

"Auntie White"[47] and the "aged brothers and sisters,"[48] residents at Middlechurch were commonly called "inmates" and "old people" until the 1940s (and even longer in the case of the latter term).[49] In later years, these labels were abandoned in favour of terms that are still in use today such as resident, patient, and senior citizen. The shift to these more positive labels would have helped to increase the self-esteem and self-image of many of the elderly people.

As the image of the institutionalized elderly improved, they came to enjoy an increase in respect and recognition. Middlechurch residents came to be seen as people with the potential to learn, grow, and serve as productive members of their home and community. In addition to the recognition that they required the specialized care of trained professionals, there are additional indications that others started to take note of the needs and interests of this group. One trend that was present at Middlechurch as early as 1913 was the board's desire to increase the privacy afforded to the residents in the home. As the institution went through several different phases of renovations over the years, more private rooms were requested on the grounds that they would add to the comfort of the residents.[50] In 1927, the president of the board stated: "We badly need several more single rooms. Nearly all the old people would be so much happier if we could give each one a room for his or her exclusive use."[51] No longer seeing them as a monolithic group whose individual needs dissolved upon admission to the home, the board members increasingly recognized the need for people with differing personalities and preferences to have private space. In 1952, "a small laundry [was] installed in a room in the basement of the main building, for the convenience of the ladies in the Home who prefer[red] to wash their own dainty articles."[52] The administration's heightened sensitivity to these issues would have undoubtedly helped to ease the minds and spirits of some of the residents.

Another sign of the increase in the respect afforded to the Middlechurch seniors during these years is that they were given more opportunities to express their opinions about the circumstances at the home. In the early years, the voices and abilities of the residents were grossly underestimated. An annual report dating from the mid-1920s closes with the following lines: "We would give thanks to our Heavenly Father for the privilege of serving these our dear old people. They are so like children in many of their ways, always anxious to tell us of their little trials and vexations, and so many of them living in bygone days. No one can imagine just how they appeal to our hearts unless you are in close contact with them—and if in any way we have helped to bring joy and gladness to them we humbly give thanks to our Heavenly Father."[53] With time, the Middlechurch seniors were given a much greater voice in the affairs of the Home. They had a residents' council,[54] published a newspaper, and raised funds for their institution. No longer passive and helpless "inmates," the residents increasingly assumed a more prominent role in the operations of the home.

In the nineteenth and early twentieth centuries, strict and specific rules governed the lives of many older Canadians in institutions. James Snell notes: "The institutionalized elderly were the most disadvantaged element among the turn-of-the-century elderly in Canada. They were largely the objects of charity and were subjected to an environment emphasizing control and loss of independence."[55] Older people were often required to work in exchange for their keep, and in some ways the situation in the early years of Middlechurch was no different. The 1907 annual report included the clause that "inmates who are able shall be required to render all possible service for the benefit of the Home and the comfort of those who are more helpless than themselves."[56] While the situation appears to have softened somewhat just four years later,[57] mention is made of the assistance provided by residents during a domestic labour shortage in 1948.[58]

It is clear that residents forfeited many freedoms when they entered the home. In the first year of operations at Middlechurch, residents' rules included "implicit obedience to the Matron," polite behaviour, the need to receive permission to leave the premises, and mandatory participation in religious activities.[59] Residents were also forced to comply with strict regulations when receiving guests. The rules relating to this matter stated: "The inmates may be visited by their friends on Tuesdays and Saturdays, between the hours of two and five o'clock. No visitors to the inmates shall be allowed to stay to meals, or over night."[60] One can only imagine the effect that these strict regulations would have had on seniors who had lived according to their own schedules and rules for their whole lives.

As time passed, the notion of "home" became a reality, and residents were afforded more freedom to manage their daily activities. While certain schedules would have still been necessary to maintain a level of order in a group setting, the seniors were not forced to abide by so many restrictions. They were given more choices about the activities they wanted to participate in and do not seem to have had such strict limitations on the hours in which they were able to receive visitors. By 1964, residents were able to ask their friends to join them for dinner on occasion.[61]

Changing Activities of the Institutionalized Elderly

Another change that served to improve the lives of Middlechurch residents during this period was the rise in the number and nature of activities available to them.[62] While special functions and events were a part of the community at the home from its earliest days, there was a marked increase in the volume and variety of activities as the years passed.[63] The 1921 annual report notes that a record number of activities were held that year.[64] In 1957, the comment was made that "our old folks are older in years than they used to be—but they seem to be younger in heart. They are certainly not sitting with folded hands while life passes them by—they are interested, busy and cheerful."[65] A special committee was established in 1959 to manage recreation programming,[66] and just two years later, a staff person was hired to focus on this work.[67] In 1981, a special facility was opened especially for the purpose of hosting activities.[68] Although it is possible that some residents were not interested in increasing their activity levels, the point is that there were more options available to those who did want to become more involved.

Over the course of this period, senior citizens at the Middlechurch Home were given more opportunities to become physically active. The home's earliest annual reports make little mention of the physical activity available to the residents. It is plausible to suggest a correlation between this presumed low level of physical activity and the perception that prevailed during these years of seniors as being feeble and weak. ("Mr. White, aged 91 years, who insist[ed] on sawing and splitting wood all day long"[69] serves as one of the exceptions to this trend.) As the years passed, more residents became increasingly involved in the physical activities that were made available to them. Horseshoes,[70] lawn bowling,[71] croquet,[72] and "a six-hole putting green"[73] proved to be sources of much enjoyment for the seniors.

The Middlechurch records reveal that there was also a rise in the number of social activities offered at the home over the course of the twentieth century. It should be noted that even in the early years there were often several events planned for the enjoyment of the residents.[74] Church services, concerts by local groups, visits from board members, annual open houses, Eaton's Christmas parties and dinners for special events were all mainstays of life at the home. The 1918 annual report notes that these activities were a highlight at Middlechurch: "If the friends who go down and entertain them with music, etc., only knew how these treats form the topic of conversation for days afterwards, they would feel amply repaid for their trouble and time."[75] Residents were pleased to receive a gramophone at Christmas in 1910,[76] and over thirty "entertainments" were staged at Middlechurch during 1923.[77]

The frequency and variety of these events increased as the years passed. Playing pool, card games, and listening to the radio became favourite pastimes of the residents.[78] Although the increase in the number of social events was interrupted during the Second World War ("owing to the difficulties of transportation"),[79] rates of socialization soared to new heights in the late 1950s and throughout the 1960s. During these years, it was noted that high levels of participation were good for the overall health of seniors.[80] Television programs and movies had a great impact on the lives of the residents, and many became quite attached to these modern methods of communication. The 1957 annual report confirms this idea: "the large television set in the concert hall is in use most evenings, and if you were to drop in on a Saturday night about 11 p.m., you could join a 95-year-old gentleman and an 87-year-old lady watching the wrestling. The interest in the World Series and the Grey Cup was so intense this year that the loud speaker system was extended to the main dining room to prevent the men bolting their lunch and rushing back to the game."[81] Clearly the increased opportunities for social activities brought much pleasure to the lives of some residents.

From the 1940s onwards, the social program at the home started to include ever more trips outside the home.[82] Outings included attendance at plays on the Rainbow Stage, tea at the homes of board members, and visits to the Museum, Art Gallery, Conservatory, Planetarium, Winnipeg Beach and Kenora. Residents also enjoyed trips to Blue Bomber games, symphony concerts, the ballet, the circus, and local shops.[83] Middlechurch's history book notes: "In 1977, the Beaver Bus began arriving at the Home twice a month to pick up residents wishing to spend the day downtown. One week it was a trip to Eatons and the next trip, to the Bay. The process was discontinued at a later date when the residents' own wheelchair-accessible bus was purchased."[84] The power of these outings to lift the spirits of the residents is illustrated by the account of the seniors' excursion to see the King and Queen during their 1939 visit to Winnipeg. The annual report tells the story:

> In a year over-shadowed throughout by the oncoming clouds of war, the visit of our King and Queen came as a radiant interlude—a rainbow across a darkened sky. It was a day of days for our old people—the subject of conversation for weeks before and weeks after. All their aches and pains were forgotten and the world seemed filled with kindliness and goodwill. Twenty two of the old ladies enjoyed a long happy day … on the line of the march. An earnest look from the King in his Navy uniform, a flash of blue and a radiant smile from the Queen and they were gone but their images were indelibly impressed upon all our hearts…. It was a day that will live long in all their memories for what it symbolizes in a world which seems to be crashing about us.[85]

Excursions such as this were sure to give the residents a greater sense of purpose than they would have felt if they had been restricted to the routine happenings of the home for weeks on end.

The number of intellectually stimulating activities available to the residents also increased at the Middlechurch Home over the years. In the early part of the period studied, references to the donation of magazines to the home offer the only real suggestion that any efforts were made to enliven the minds of residents. Indeed, there are subtle hints in the annual reports that supervisors regarded their wards as children.[86] One of the annual reports suggests that the elderly often lacked a sense of perspective: "The daily troubles (real or imaginary), what pleases and displeases, and the little incidents that mean so much in the life of our old people, are brought to [the board] through our visitors."[87] The visiting board members did note that the residents enjoyed relaying details of their past experiences, but the therapeutic effects of this activity were not explored any further.[88]

Corresponding to the increase in physical and social activities offered at the home, more was done to nurture and challenge the minds of the residents as time went on. In 1952, some entrepreneurial female residents started making handicrafts to sell at the annual open house to raise money for their flower fund for sick residents.[89] This activity soon blossomed into a "Handicraft Class" led by a university student[90] and enjoyed by both women and men at the home. The residents were keen to learn new crafts and were very pleased to exhibit and profit from the fruits of their labour in the years that followed. Sales totalled over $3000 at the open house in 1972.[91]

Another major initiative that demonstrates a marked increase in the intellectual offerings at the home was the resident-produced newspaper that Middlechurch men began to publish in 1955.[92] Writing, editing, and reading *The Middlechurch Home News* soon became a popular pastime and source of great pride for both men and women at the home.[93] By 1957, 500 copies of *The Middlechurch Home News* were printed each month.[94]

Other initiatives that served to stimulate the minds of the residents included the maintenance of a library[95] and the screening of travelogues on movie nights.[96] Discussion of current events also had a place at the home in later years. The annual reports contain several references to the intense interest in politics that existed in certain corners of the facility. While the men (referred to as the "senators") were the ones who were most often linked to this activity,[97] it is clear that women also voiced their opinions on political matters. The 1936 annual report recounts a tale worth quoting at length: "If you think sometimes that the world passes by unheeded within these walls, you should come to visit us at an election time. Political allegiance evidently dies hard as I realized when one very deaf old lady who had steadfastly refused to attend the liberal candidate's meeting, told me with enthusiasm what a fine speech the conservative candidate had made. I had watched her going through the motions of listening but I knew that she could not hear a single word."[98] It seems that many of the residents at Middlechurch Home embraced the opportunity to challenge their minds and derived a great deal of satisfaction from doing so.

The quality of life of the seniors at the Middlechurch Home also improved between 1907 and 1984 because of their increased involvement in the community outside the home. Besides making excursions beyond the Middlechurch grounds, several residents became actively engaged in charitable work. During both the First and Second World Wars, Middlechurch residents spent countless hours making clothes for the soldiers overseas.[99] In later years, the spirit of volunteerism intensified as the older people at the home raised money for charity, hosted fundraising events for other organizations, and supported children facing difficult circumstances.[100]

It is worth noting that the rise in the residents' charitable work was reciprocated by the citizens of Winnipeg, who provided entertainment at the home in increasing numbers. The annual reports make special mention of some of the relationships that developed between the residents and local school children. This increased integration in the community was surely beneficial to the Middlechurch seniors.

It is important to note that the rising participation of Middlechurch residents in activities in the home and community probably did not occur in isolation. Although some visitors reported that "the participation at Middlechurch is greater than at other Senior Citizen Residences,"[101] one only needs to consider the high level of participation by older Canadians in society today to recognize that, at some point, all regions must have experienced this shift. The increased involvement of residents at the home (which began in earnest in the 1950s and 1960s) corresponds to the time that activity (substitution) theory was being promoted. This theory asserted that in order for elderly people to be happy and healthy, they needed to keep busy with a variety of different activities. Barry McPherson, a Canadian expert on aging, explains: "This theory argued that individual adaptation involved continuing an active lifestyle of social interaction in order to maintain the self-concept and hence a sense of well-being or life satisfaction. The maintenance of this active lifestyle involved replacing lost roles, by either re-engaging in earlier roles or engaging in new roles."[102] Although the theory does not seem to be stated by name in the Middlechurch records, the increasingly well-trained staff at the home and Middlechurch's positive reputation[103] suggest that the theory may have had (at the very least) an indirect impact on its operations.[104] The authors of *Our Heritage: The Middlechurch Home of Winnipeg* note: "Mrs. James Richardson, Board Program Committee chairperson, showed some concern in her 1966 Report. 'Something must be found to interest and occupy each resident because it keeps them young. We must reach out to each resident as an individual and make him or her feel capable of participating, able to contribute and a needed part of society.'"[105] It is likely that other homes in Canada would have been influenced by the same forces.[106]

Conclusion

By the time of its one hundredth annual report in 1984, the Middlechurch Home had changed significantly from its early beginnings as a home for single women. Board members, staff, and residents were now associated with a first-class seniors' residential facility that could accommodate over 200 elderly people. The "Long Range Planning Report" included in the 1984 publication indicates a determination to continue to provide excellent and innovative care for the elderly.[107]

While the care and compassion shown to Middlechurch residents in the early years should not be underestimated, it is fair to say that in the eighty years that followed, the quality of life for those in the home steadily improved. The lives of the aged at Middlechurch (and at other homes in Manitoba) were not without problems by the 1980s, but a significant number of positive developments made their lives more attractive and interesting. Similar in some ways to the progress at institutions for older people in other parts of Canada, changes in the nature of the Middlechurch Home and the attitudes towards the residents, as well as the increased involvement of those in the institution, were central to the transformation of this facility. A dynamic shift occurred, which gave the residents at the home, who were once perceived to be in "the gloaming of their days,"[108] the opportunity to enjoy a phase of life marked by continued growth and stimulation.

Notes

I would like to thank Dr. Gerry Friesen, Brian McLean, and Cara Bradley for their helpful comments at various stages of the research and writing process. I am also grateful to the University of Manitoba's Faculty of Graduate Studies for the financial support that I received while completing this course.

1   Articles by Bettina Bradbury, Sharon Cook, and Stormie Stewart provide valuable information about the experience of aging in central Canada. See Bettina Bradbury, "Elderly Inmates and Caregiving Sisters: Catholic Institutions for the Elderly in Nineteenth-Century Montreal," in *On the Case: Explorations in Social History*, eds. Franca Iacovetta and Wendy Mitchinson (Toronto: University of Toronto Press, 1998), 129–155; Sharon Anne Cook, "'A Quiet Place...to Die': Ottawa's First Protestant Old Age Homes for Women and Men," *Ontario History* 81, 1 (March 1989): 25–40; Stormie Stewart, "The Elderly Poor in Rural Ontario: Inmates of the Wellington County House of Industry, 1877–1907," *Journal of the Canadian Historical Association* (1992): 217–33. Megan Davies's publications relating to the elderly in British Columbia and James Snell's book, *The Citizen's Wage: The State and the Elderly in Canada, 1900–1951*, also make valuable contributions to this field. See Megan J. Davies, "Old Age in British Columbia: The Case of the 'Lonesome

Prospector,'" *BC Studies* 118 (Summer 1998): 41–66; Megan J. Davies, "Renovating the Canadian Old Age Home: The Evolution of Residential Care Facilities in B.C., 1930–1960," *Journal of the Canadian Historical Association*, New Series, 12 (2001): 155–175; James G. Snell, *The Citizen's Wage: The State and the Elderly in Canada, 1900–1951* (Toronto: University of Toronto Press, 1996). All of these studies open the door for further research on this topic, highlighting especially the significant need for more investigation into the experience of aging in Canada's Maritime and Prairie regions.

2   The records of the Middlechurch Home at the Archives of Manitoba (AM) provide a rich source of continuous information on a seniors' residential institution over a period long enough to observe changing patterns and trends. The annual reports of the home, which date from 1907 to 1984, form the basis of the research presented here. Every attempt has been made to use a consistent method to cite the records of the Middlechurch Home. Due to the fact that some of the reports were originally assigned a year and an (inconsistent) number, some variation occurs in the format of the endnotes in this essay. All of the records used are contained in boxes P2132 and P2133 at the Archives of Manitoba. *Our Heritage: The Middlechurch Home of Winnipeg* was consulted as a supplementary source. See Middlechurch Home of Winnipeg Historical Society Book Committee, *Our Heritage: The Middlechurch Home of Winnipeg, 1883–1995* (West St. Paul: Middlechurch Home of Winnipeg Historical Society, 1996).

3   It interesting to note that in the early years, male residents outnumbered their female counterparts. By the 1960s, the situation had changed, and there was a preponderance of women on the waiting list.

4   Early records indicate that the population at the Home was primarily Protestant.

5   Institutions for the elderly in nineteenth-century Montreal, Ottawa, and rural Ontario also fixated on death rather than life. Bradbury, "Elderly Inmates and Caregiving Sisters," 132 and 140; Cook, "'A Quiet Place…to Die,'" 25 and 38; Stewart, "The Elderly Poor in Rural Ontario," 217.

6   AM, 29th Annual Report of the Christian Women's Union of Winnipeg, 1911, 6.

7   AM, 37th Annual Report of the Christian Women's Union of Winnipeg, 1919, 7.

8   AM, 39th Annual Report of the Christian Women's Union of Winnipeg, 1921, 7.

9   AM, 29th Annual Report of the Christian Women's Union of Winnipeg, 1911, 6.

10   Ibid.

11   AM, 65th Annual Report of the Christian Women's Union of Winnipeg, 1947, 3.

12   AM, Middlechurch Home of Winnipeg, Annual Report 1968, 17.

13   AM, Annual Report of the Christian Women's Union of Winnipeg, 1954, 6.

14   AM, Annual Report, Middlechurch Home of Winnipeg, 1958, 7.

15   Davies, "Renovating the Canadian Old Age Home," 159.

16   AM, 64th Annual Report of the Christian Women's Union of Winnipeg, 1946, 4.

17   AM, 97th Annual Report for the year ending March 31, 1981, 9.

18   Obviously the annual reports provide a very narrow and mediated version of the residents' true feelings about the home. However, in the absence of any known first-person testimonies about life in the home, these reports are used with caution to gain a sense of the residents' feelings about Middlechurch. Bettina Bradbury encountered a similar challenge when using the chronicles kept by nuns in her effort to study the residents of nineteenth-century Catholic institutions. Bradbury, "Elderly Inmates and Caregiving Sisters," 130.

19   AM, 53rd Annual Report of the Christian Women's Union of Winnipeg, 1935, 6.

20   AM, 68th Annual Report of the Christian Women's Union of Winnipeg, 1950, 4.

21   Davies, "Renovating the Canadian Old Age Home," 162; Snell, *The Citizen's Wage*, 46.

22   AM, 32nd Annual Report of the Christian Women's Union of Winnipeg, 1914, 6.

23   Middlechurch Home of Winnipeg Historical Society Book Committee, *Our Heritage*, 44–45.

24 AM, 58th Annual Report of the Christian Women's Union of Winnipeg, 1940, 9.

25 Davies, "Renovating the Canadian Old Age Home," 163–165.

26 AM, 28th Annual Report of the Christian Women's Union of Winnipeg, 1910, 7.

27 AM, 50th Annual Report of the Christian Women's Union of Winnipeg, 1932, 5.

28 AM, 49th Annual Report of the Christian Women's Union of Winnipeg, 1931, 5.

29 AM, 64th Annual Report of the Christian Women's Union of Winnipeg, 1946, 4.

30 AM, 59th Annual Report of the Christian Women's Union of Winnipeg, 1941, 7.

31 AM, 25th Annual Report of the Christian Women's Union of Winnipeg, 1907, 7.

32 AM, 28th Annual Report of the Christian Women's Union of Winnipeg, 1910, 6.

33 AM, 30th Annual Report of the Christian Women's Union of Winnipeg, 1912, 7.

34 AM, Middlechurch Home of Winnipeg Annual Report, 1961, 8; AM, Middlechurch Home of Winnipeg, Annual Report, 1964, 6. This theme is also threaded throughout *Our Heritage: The Middlechurch Home of Winnipeg*.

35 AM, Annual Report of the Christian Women's Union of Winnipeg, 1953, 6.

36 AM, Middlechurch Home of Winnipeg Annual Report, 1959, 11; AM, 90th Annual Report for the Year Ending December 31, 1973, 8; AM, 96th Annual Report for the Year Ending March 31st 1980, 8.

37 AM, Middlechurch Home of Winnipeg Annual Report 1964, 5; AM, 90th Annual Report for the Year Ending December 31, 1973, 8; AM, 96th Annual Report for the Year Ending March 31, 1980, 8.

38 AM, Annual Report of the Christian Women's Union of Winnipeg, 1956, 6; AM, Annual Report, Middlechurch Home of Winnipeg, 1958, 8.

39 Davies notes the presence of a similar trend in British Columbia (Davies, "Renovating the Canadian Old Age Home," 166–173).

40 AM, Middlechurch Home of Winnipeg, Annual Report, 1960, 19; AM, Middlechurch Home of Winnipeg, Annual Report, 1965, 14; Davies, "Renovating the Canadian Old Age Home," 156.

41 AM, 35th Annual Report of the Christian Women's Union of Winnipeg, 1917, 6.

42 AM, 37th Annual Report of the Christian Women's Union of Winnipeg, 1919, 6.

43 AM, 30th Annual Report of the Christian Women's Union of Winnipeg, 1912, 6.

44 AM, 29th Annual Report of the Christian Women's Union of Winnipeg, 1911, 7.

45 AM, 42nd Annual Report of the Christian Women's Union of Winnipeg, 1924, 4.

46 AM, 47th Annual Report of the Christian Women's Union of Winnipeg, 1929, 5.

47 AM, 31st Annual Report of the Christian Women's Union of Winnipeg, 1913, 5; AM, 32nd Annual Report of the Christian Women's Union of Winnipeg, 1914, 7.

48 AM, 33rd Annual Report of the Christian Women's Union of Winnipeg, 1915, 7. The familial nature of these references lends support to the idea that Middlechurch favoured the notion of "home" rather than "institution."

49 The term "inmate" was also used in institutions in Montreal, Ottawa, and rural Ontario in the nineteenth century. See Bradbury, "Elderly Inmates and Caregiving Sisters," 129–155; Cook, "'A Quiet Place...to Die,'" 25–40; and Stewart, "The Elderly Poor in Rural Ontario," 217–233.

50 AM, 31st Annual Report of the Christian Women's Union of Winnipeg, 1913, 4; AM, 50th Annual Report of the Christian Women's Union of Winnipeg, 1932, 5.

51 AM, 45th Annual Report of the Christian Women's Union of Winnipeg, 1927, 7.

52 AM, Annual Report of the Christian Women's Union of Winnipeg, 1952, 5.

53 AM, 43rd Annual Report of the Christian Women's Union of Winnipeg, 1925, 6.

54 AM, 93rd Annual Report for the Year Ending December 31, 1976, 10.

55 Snell, *The Citizen's Wage*, 46.

56 AM, 25th Annual Report of the Christian Women's Union of Winnipeg, 1907, 11.

57 AM, 29th Annual Report of the Christian Women's Union of Winnipeg, 1911, 7.

58   AM, 66th Annual Report of the Christian Women's Union of Winnipeg, 1948, 5.

59   AM, 25th Annual Report of the Christian Women's Union of Winnipeg, 1907, 11.

60   Ibid.

61   AM, Middlechurch Home of Winnipeg, Annual Report, 1964, 6.

62   AM, 94th Annual Report for the Period Ending March 31, 1978, 12; Middlechurch Home of Winnipeg Historical Society Book Committee, *Our Heritage*, 117–127.

63   AM, Middlechurch Home of Winnipeg, Annual Report, 1964, 10.

64   AM, 39th Annual Report of the Christian Women's Union of Winnipeg, 1921, 7.

65   AM, Christian Women's Union of Winnipeg 1883–1957 Presents the 50th Annual Report of the Middlechurch Home, 13.

66   Middlechurch Home of Winnipeg Historical Society Book Committee, *Our Heritage*, 117.

67   Ibid., 46.

68   AM, 98th Annual Report for the Year Ending March 31, 1982, 2.

69   AM, 38th Annual Report of the Christian Women's Union of Winnipeg, 1920, 6.

70   AM, 65th Annual Report of the Christian Women's Union of Winnipeg, 1947, 5.

71   AM, 95th Annual Report for the Period Ending March 31, 1979, 9.

72   AM, Annual Report of the Christian Women's Union of Winnipeg, 1955, 5.

73   AM, Annual Report of the Christian Women's Union of Winnipeg, 1954, 5.

74   AM, 30th Annual Report of the Christian Women's Union of Winnipeg, 1912, 7.

75   AM, 36th Annual Report of the Christian Women's Union of Winnipeg, 1918, 6.

76   AM, 28th Annual Report of the Christian Women's Union of Winnipeg, 1910, 7.

77   AM, 41st Annual Report of the Christian Women's Union of Winnipeg, 1923, 7.

78   AM, Annual Report of the Christian Women's Union of Winnipeg, 1954, 5.
AM, Christian Women's Union of Winnipeg 1883–1957 Presents the Fiftieth Annual Report of the Middlechurch Home, 13.

79   AM, 61st Annual Report of the Christian Women's Union of Winnipeg, 1943, 7.

80   AM, Middlechurch Home of Winnipeg, Annual Report, 1960, 16.

81   AM, Christian Women's Union of Winnipeg 1883–1957 Presents the Fiftieth Annual Report of the Middlechurch Home, 14.

82   Early annual reports suggest that the residents did enjoy some excursions prior to this time. Mention was made of a visit to Hyland Park in 1910 (AM, 28th Annual Report of the Christian Women's Union of Winnipeg, 1910, 7) and to the Exhibition in 1911 and 1913 (AM, 29th Annual Report of the Christian Women's Union of Winnipeg, 1911, 7, and AM, 31st Annual Report of the Christian Women's Union of Winnipeg, 1913, 6).

83   AM, Annual Report of the Christian Women's Union of Winnipeg, 1955, 5; AM, Middlechurch Home of Winnipeg, Annual Report, 1960, 16; AM, Middlechurch Home of Winnipeg, Annual Report, 1961, 9; AM, 89th Annual Report for the Year Ending December 31, 1972, 9; AM, 93rd Annual Report for the Year Ending December 31, 1976, 10; AM, 94th Annual Report for the Period Ending March 31, 1978, 11.

84   Middlechurch Home of Winnipeg Historical Society Book Committee, *Our Heritage*, 85.

85   AM, 57th Annual Report of the Christian Women's Union of Winnipeg, 1939, 11.

86   Davies notes similar sentiments in British Columbia in the mid-twentieth century (Davies, "Renovating the Canadian Old Age Home," 171 and 173).

87   AM, 46th Annual Report of the Christian Women's Union of Winnipeg, 1928, 5.

88   AM, 42nd Annual Report of the Christian Women's Union of Winnipeg, 1924, 5.

89   AM, Annual Report of the Christian Women's Union of Winnipeg, 1952, 7.

90   AM, Annual Report of the Christian Women's Union of Winnipeg, 1955, 5.

91 AM, 89th Annual Report for the Year Ending December 31, 1972, 9.

92 AM, Annual Report of the Christian Women's Union of Winnipeg, 1955, 5.

93 AM, Annual Report of the Christian Women's Union of Winnipeg, 1956, 5.

94 AM, Christian Women's Union of Winnipeg 1883–1957 Presents the 50th Annual Report of the Middlechurch Home, 13.

95 AM, 89th Annual Report for the Year Ending December 31, 1972, 8.

96 AM, Middlechurch Home of Winnipeg, Annual Report, 1965, 5.

97 AM, 43rd Annual Report of the Christian Women's Union of Winnipeg, 1925, 13.

98 AM, 54th Annual Report of the Christian Women's Union of Winnipeg, 1936, 6.

99 AM, 32nd Annual Report of the Christian Women's Union of Winnipeg, 1914, 8; AM, 60th Annual Report of the Christian Women's Union of Winnipeg, 1942, 8.

100 AM, Middlechurch Home of Winnipeg, Annual Report, 1964, 10.

101 AM, Annual Report for the Year Ending December 31, 1970, 8.

102 Barry McPherson, *Aging as a Social Process: An Introduction to Individual and Population Aging*, 2nd ed. (Toronto: Butterworths, 1990), 134.

103 Middlechurch Home of Winnipeg Historical Society Book Committee, *Our Heritage*, 26, 44, and 46.

104 It should be acknowledged that another theory was also articulated at this time (1960–1961). Disengagement theory, which essentially runs counter to activity (substitution) theory, promotes the idea that elderly people should be permitted to withdraw from activity and society. McPherson, *Aging as a Social Process*, 135–137.

105 Middlechurch Home of Winnipeg Historical Society Book Committee, *Our Heritage*, 119.

106 Megan Davies provides positive confirmation that increased activity among institutionalized seniors was promoted in British Columbia during these years. Davies, "Renovating the Canadian Old Age Home," 172.

107 AM, 100th Annual Report for the Year Ending March 31, 1984, 14–15.

108 AM, 35th Annual Report of the Christian Women's Union of Winnipeg, 1917, 6.

The Spirit of Service: Winnipeg's Voluntary War Services During the Second World War

Jody Perrun

Observing the growth in the armed services and general public support for the mobilization of manpower and resources, Mark S. Watson of the *Baltimore Sun* concluded in October 1940 that Canada was more united behind the war effort than it had been in 1914–1918: "One cannot see all these [military] camps, filled with men of English, Scotch, Irish, Welsh and French descent, the factories, and the unexcited civilians of city and farm without being aware of an intense unity.... One is tempted to say that Hitler has seemingly done more than Canadian statesmanship to weld English and French Canada into one united nation."[1]

Watson may have exaggerated, but national unity in wartime was obviously an issue of crucial importance, and it was the overriding concern of Prime Minister Mackenzie King during the Second World War. There is more to the issue than the nation-wide relations between French and English that occupied Watson or King. Despite the fact that the struggle waged on the home front manifested itself in myriad local, everyday activities, much of the written history of Canada's various war efforts focuses on national issues, and relatively little study has been directed at the community level. Two exceptions, Ian Miller's portrait of Toronto during the Great War and Serge Durflinger's of Verdun during the Second World War, emphasize the unity of citizens behind the war effort.[2] The case of Winnipeg seems more complex.

While Toronto was a bastion of English Canada during the First World War and Verdun was shared by English and French during the Second, Winnipeg from 1939 to 1945 was a conglomeration of ethnic origins, a microcosm of an emerging Canadian mosaic.[3] Winnipeg was the second largest city in western Canada (after Vancouver) in 1941 with nearly 222,000 people; if the suburban areas now incorporated in the City of Winnipeg are included, the total was close to 300,000.[4] The foreign-born population of Winnipeg proper made up 35 percent of the whole (77,523) with nearly half that number (34,037) coming from countries other than Great Britain or the United States. If we look at ethnicity, the numbers stand out even more clearly, with nearly 40 percent (84,597) of Winnipeggers claiming an ethnic origin other than British or French.[5] There were large communities of Ukrainians (22,578), Jews

(17,027), Germans (12,170), Poles (11,024), and Scandinavians (9177), with a variety of other ethnic groups living in the city.

Historian Jeff Keshen argues that in spite of the extensive use of propaganda and social pressure to encourage "right-thinking," or the occasions when discrimination, anti-Semitism, or black marketeering defied the message to pull together, Canadians "proved unbounded in the generosity of their contributions of volunteer labour, money, material, and, at least outside of Quebec, willingness to serve militarily.... Such responses provided substance and longevity to the image of the Second World War as a conflict uniting people in a common and noble cause."[6] This image of a "good war" for North Americans has had fairly wide currency, yet the war experience on the home front defies easy characterization. There is some intriguing evidence to contradict the "unity in a noble cause" thesis. The Ukrainian community in Winnipeg is a case in point: while all factions declared their loyalty to Canada, those with communist or nationalist sympathies spent as much effort and rhetoric opposing each other as they did the common Axis enemy.[7] And despite the voluminous propaganda about fighting a war in support of liberal democratic values, the treatment of Canadian-born Japanese relocated from British Columbia's coastal areas following the attacks on Hong Kong and Pearl Harbor devalued the entire concept of civil liberties. Government policy mandated the uprooting of an entire community. Many Japanese-Canadian families came to work on the sugar beet farms of Manitoba, while others were interned in camps throughout Canada.[8] Then there were the ultra-patriots, like Winnipeg lawyer E.K. Williams, later president of the Canadian Bar Association and chief justice of the Court of King's Bench in Manitoba. He condemned any "shirkers" who did not make sufficient sacrifices for the war effort, or did not conserve scarce materials. Williams lashed out at young, fit men who chose not to enlist, media stories and advertising that were not sufficiently focussed on the war effort, politicians too concerned with their own power, and above all, the communist "Quislings... [who] have been disloyal to Canada.... They have no place in this country. We should place the mark of beasts on them and put them where they belong."[9] There were plenty of examples of both unity and division within Winnipeg's various communities, and Williams was not the only citizen whose enthusiasm in supporting the war led to condemnation of other viewpoints.[10]

So to what extent did Winnipeg's diverse groups put their political, social, or ideological differences aside and work together to serve the war effort? Although there are some significant examples of dissent, there is abundant evidence that the majority of Winnipeg residents indeed felt that this was "their" war, and put their shoulders to the wheel to make contributions to the war effort as numerous and varied as their places of origin. Voluntarism was an important way in which they showed their colours, and a survey of the many types of voluntary work undertaken by Winnipeggers reveals a snapshot of a multi-faceted community that, to a great extent, was united in serving the cause of Allied victory.

The war was a catalyst for voluntary service in Winnipeg and across Canada. By 1939 the government and other concerned parties recognized that maintaining servicemen's morale was essential to the creation of an effective military force, and that morale would suffer if the troops lacked facilities for relaxation and pleasant diversions from the hardships of training and combat, or if they were distracted from the task at hand by worries about family problems back home. It was also evident that civilian morale partly depended on opportunities to get involved and connect personally to the war effort. National service organizations like the Red Cross, Young Men's and Young Women's Christian Associations, Knights of Columbus, and the Salvation Army traditionally had been relied upon to fulfill most of these requirements for "auxiliary" or "war services" through voluntary work, and at the war's outbreak the Department of National Defence set up a directorate of Auxiliary Services to provide direction and oversight.[11]

The Red Cross was probably the most active of the national organizations, with a hand in various services for both civilians and armed forces personnel. Red Cross volunteers knitted socks, sweaters, and other field comforts for the troops and shipped a variety of goods overseas for civilian relief. They packed parcels for prisoners of war and ran an enquiry bureau to help the families of prisoners seek information about their loved ones. There was also a blood donor service, and Red Cross blood banks meant the difference between life and death for many wounded soldiers, sailors, and airmen. The YM/YWCA and Salvation Army offered their recreational facilities to men and women in uniform, operated hostels and other leave centres, hostess houses at military camps for men to visit their families and friends, and rooms registries to help service wives find accommodation in crowded cities. The Knights of Columbus, among other contributions, offered a flower order service to make local deliveries for men serving overseas.[12] Other groups also participated in many forms of voluntary war work, most notably the Canadian Legion and the Imperial Order Daughters of the Empire (IODE). The Legion assumed significant responsibilities from September 1939, catering to the troops' requirements for sports and entertainment, educational services, and dependents' welfare.[13] The IODE continued a service it had provided during the Great War, donating reading material to both the Royal Navy and the

Royal Canadian Navy and furnishing libraries for service hospitals. It also undertook the very special task of maintaining the graves of airmen killed in Canada while training under the British Commonwealth Air Training Plan.[14] All of these organizations were active in Winnipeg and local residents contributed to their operations. But the lead role in providing voluntary services in Winnipeg was taken from the war's beginning by local rather than national organizations, and the work they did was not limited by any strict definition of auxiliary services. Rather, it expanded in a wide range of home-grown initiatives. Some of these initiatives were so successful in attracting the support of local residents that Winnipeg shortly became renowned for its level of voluntary war and community services.

The most outstanding success, and the initiative that established Winnipeg as a leader in the mobilization of volunteer services, was the creation of the Central Volunteer Bureau. The outbreak of war in 1939 led a group in Toronto to organize a national survey of women willing to contribute their time for voluntary war service. The Voluntary Registration of Canadian Women would be administered locally, so on 20 September 1939 approximately 1800 women gathered at the University of Manitoba's Broadway campus to approve the creation of a volunteer registry for war or emergency service. The committee that formed to administer the survey included leaders of social welfare organizations like Monica McQueen, executive secretary of Winnipeg's Council of Social Agencies. They were concerned that momentary enthusiasm for war work might endanger consistent, long-term voluntary support for the city's social services. There was at that time little national war work to be done, however, so it was apparent that the most effective use of the registration would be at the local level. To capitalize on the wave of early enthusiasm for the war effort, the committee thus reinvented its mandate to include community service as well as war work.[15]

The relationship between the two types of voluntary work was clear, according to McQueen: "The women were quick to realise the urgency of keeping up community services so that the boys who were going overseas could have the peace of mind that comes from knowing that someone was looking after his family, and that definite thought and planning was under way to help him when the time came to return to civilian life."[16] The dual focus on community and war service made the Winnipeg organization a success, according to *The Survey*, an American journal for social workers, which stated, "Many women who previously had shown no interest in community work came to perceive the relationship of community welfare to total defence and soon were engaged in driving children to clinics, acting as hospital aids

... and doing the various clerical jobs that social agencies ask of volunteers. Busy and useful, they felt themselves part of a whole community effort."[17]

Registration began on 10 October when the Greater Winnipeg Bureau for the Voluntary Registration of Canadian Women—later called the Central Volunteer Bureau (CVB)—opened its office at the corner of Portage Avenue and Hargrave Street. The bureau's radio appeal to women over sixteen years of age stressed patriotic motives:

> Even if you can only give a few days a week of your time, or only a few hours every week, you will be helping your country.... There will be plenty of jobs to do—plenty of war work, don't forget that—but there will be other essential jobs which will require sacrifice and time: unpaid, inglorious jobs which are important if we want to keep Canada a free, democratic country. Any work which keeps Canada running at this time is war work. And it is up to the women of Winnipeg to do it. It is up to us to hold the Home Front.[18]

The registration effort initially generated a list of 7000 volunteers and gathered information on their interests, training, experience, and availability. The immediate task was to organize an efficient file-card system to facilitate the process of matching volunteers with suitable skills to requested placements. It was a huge undertaking in itself, but there was no shortage of assistance. Unemployed stenographers and married women with office experience set up the filing system during the day, while others helped out in the evenings after their shifts at places like Great-West Life or the city libraries. It took seven weeks to get the system up and running. Material assistance was volunteered in addition to "manpower." With no cash on hand at their start-up, the bureau received loans of office space, furniture, and equipment from local businesses, as well as printing and mimeographing services. The CVB made no public appeal for funds; it received initial support from the Junior League, supplemented by the Catholic Women's League, the Professional and Business Women's Club, and other groups.[19] A major sponsor after 1940 was the Patriotic Salvage Corps, which was operated by volunteers supplied from the CVB.

Many of the war and community service agencies in Winnipeg got volunteer help from the CVB, and many of the bureau's members also belonged to these organizations, so there was a lot of inter-agency cooperation. To cite one example, members of the Roman Catholic, Anglican, and United Churches and the ladies' auxiliaries of the Legion, Winnipeg Grenadiers, Fort Garry Horse, and Queen's Own Cameron Highlanders joined other CVB workers in the Red Cross prisoner-of-war parcel-packing plant on Lombard Avenue, about 800 volunteers in all. This plant opened at the end of 1942 and was the largest of five operations across Canada. The Winnipeg parcels were originally intended to be shipped to prisoners in Japan, but since the Japanese would not accept them they went to camps in Europe. By 1944, the plant had produced more than a million parcels, averaging about 24,000 a week.[20] These parcels were a lifeline for prisoners. Two disabled Dieppe veterans attested upon their return from German captivity that without them, "we would have died."[21]

The CVB benefitted from weekly columns devoted to its activities in both daily newspapers, the *Free Press* and the *Tribune*, which kept readers informed and applied subtle pressure to contribute by showing people how much their neighbours were doing for the war effort. The scope of unpaid work done by its members was impressive. In 1940, 8000 volunteers distributed ration books. They provided the "manning" pool for Women's Voluntary Services activities, such as first aid courses and air raid precautions blackout demonstrations. Other tasks included running a car service for the general hospital; teaching art at St. Joseph's Vocational School, dance classes at the Jewish orphanage, and golf for the YWCA; providing clerical assistance for the August 1940 National Registration of manpower; driving babies to the milk depot and Children's Aid workers to visit unmarried mothers.[22] To enumerate the entire range of placements staffed by the CVB would require a very long list. Volunteers helped with community events and services, worked in health and welfare institutions, assumed administrative and clerical positions, provided auxiliary services for the troops in the service centres and hostels in Winnipeg, ran the salvage effort, and assisted federal bodies like the Dependents' Advisory Board and the Department of National War Services.

Winnipeg's CVB was the first in either Canada or the United States to combine voluntary war work with general community service. In 1941 a National Film Board production, *The Call for Volunteers*, held up the "Winnipeg Plan" as a model for volunteer organizations. Winnipeg was also recognized by the American Association for Adult Education in a booklet entitled "Women in Defence." Margaret Konantz, the CVB's president, took requests in the autumn of 1942 from cities like Fort William, Regina, Saskatoon, and Edmonton to offer advice on creating similar organizations. The next year, she made additional trips to Vancouver, Victoria, and Calgary.[23] By 1942, according to the CVB's annual report, there were "literally hundreds and hundreds of volunteer offices" throughout the United States and Canada modelled on the Winnipeg plan.[24]

By 1942 the CVB had added 1500 men to its register and, while men filled an expanding array of volunteer placements, the bureau's core was its female members.

Its officers were virtually all women, and a list of names reads like a Who's Who of Winnipeg's female population. Monica McQueen was the first chairman. Margaret Konantz became president and was later Manitoba's first female member of Parliament. Her mother, Edith Rogers, the first female elected to Manitoba's Legislative Assembly (in 1920), was a member of the CVB's advisory board and had been active in voluntary services during the First World War. Mary Speechly, active in numerous women's organizations and wife of prominent physician Dr. H.M. Speechly, was also on the board. Other leaders included the local feminist, city alderman, and lieutenant-governor's wife, Mrs. Margaret McWilliams, and the wives of *Free Press* editor George Ferguson, Military District No. 10 commanding officer H.J. Riley, and Premier John Bracken.[25]

The Central Volunteer Bureau helped staff a wealth of projects that made distinct contributions to the war effort. One activity that was popular among many voluntary associations was the provision of clothing and relief supplies for shipment overseas. During its first year of operation, the CVB established a refugee clothing bureau for victims of the fighting in Europe, with material assistance from the Red Cross.[26] Then, as people followed news of the Blitz over Britain, the focus shifted there. In 1941 a joint endeavour united the many groups simultaneously collecting and shipping clothing to British victims of German bombing. The new organization, Victory Bundles of Manitoba, combined the efforts of hundreds of groups across the prairies and neighbouring areas of the United States, with fifty in Winnipeg alone.

V-Bundles, as it was often called, centralized the collection and shipment of relief contributions not only for Winnipeg, but for all three Prairie provinces. As with the CVB, space for V-Bundles' workrooms was donated. Dry cleaners, shoemakers, seamstresses, tailors, and hundreds of other volunteers both male and female helped repair and pack donated articles, with "only first-class goods" being shipped. The rule was "not just to give away what you did not want, but to give what you would appreciate most if you had lost everything."[27] The British Women's Voluntary Services was the official distributor of clothing relief supplies from abroad, and the clothing representative for the borough of Bermondsey wrote to Konantz in 1943 to express her appreciation: "We have been through some very tough times in this part of London, but the thrill of being able to clothe people with some good, clean clothes after having lost all they possess in one blow, is beyond describing ... nothing I write can describe the gratitude that has been shown, or the comfort that your clothes have given people."[28] As the war continued, clothing drives were also held on behalf of the Aid to Russia Fund and a Greek Clothing Relief campaign.

While some volunteers worked to furnish clothing supplies for the needy in Europe, others participated in another recycling activity common across the country but especially successful in Winnipeg. Salvage collection became an important activity as stocks of materials necessary for war production became stretched. Paper was in short supply and rags were sought for building materials, clothing, and industrial uses. Scrap metals were collected for the manufacture of weapons and equipment. Cooking fats and bones were needed to make explosives and aircraft glue. And after Japan's advance in the Pacific cut off Allied supplies of natural rubber, the call went out for old tires, hoses, and other rubber products. In February 1941 the Department of National War Services initiated a National Salvage Campaign to increase awareness of the need to conserve scarce materials, to involve average Canadians in the national war effort, and to provide a measure of leadership to local groups across the country that had already started to collect salvage.[29] One of the first had been organized in Winnipeg months before.

The city's overwhelming response to a Saint Boniface Hospital request for donations of used medicine bottles inspired the creation of one of the most successful and widely recognized salvage organizations in North America, the Patriotic Salvage Corps. Margaret Konantz led the initiative to organize collection of salvageable materials in the summer of 1940, well before their importance to the national war effort was generally recognized. The Salvage Corps experienced some growing pains with its first drive in August: volunteers accepted everything that people dropped off at school collection points, only to realize that half the material was unmarketable after they spent a month sorting it. The corps quickly refined its approach with specified categories of acceptable materials it could resell. Methods of collection evolved from school pickups and individual house calls to a scheduled curbside service like recycling companies use today. The new practice of "boulevard" pickups commenced on 1 March 1942 and greatly increased the amount of material received. Fortunately, the organization had grown along with the demand for salvage. By this time the Corps had moved from its original home in the fire station at Gertrude Avenue and Osborne Street to larger premises at 755 Henry Avenue west of Sherbrook Street. It now called on sixty volunteer drivers operating a fleet of twenty trucks. While the Salvage Corps would add some male volunteers, women did the bulk of the work. News reports reflected contemporary concerns over acceptable gender roles even as they celebrated the volunteers' achievements. The women wore white coveralls as their uniform, and one reporter reassured readers that it was "amazing ... how trim and feminine they can look even after a long, hard day out in the snow and slush."[30] Children were also crucial to the operation. They were initially pressed into service to bring their family's recyclables to the schools or go door-to-door in their neighbourhoods. Movie theatres encouraged them by offering free Saturday matinees where the price of admission was a bundle of rags, gramophone records, or tins of cooking fat.[31]

In 1943, a series of systematic drives was planned to collect materials especially needed for the war effort: fats in March, rags in April, rubber in May, ferrous metals in June, non-ferrous metals in July. Public events were held to generate publicity and support for such efforts, similar to Victory Loan spectacles, if on a smaller scale. In the case of the metals drive, a large map of Germany was displayed at Portage and Main, with an Allied bomber above. Enemy cities were figuratively blown off the map as the metals came in. The drive opened with a parade of school children armed with scrap metal "weapons" marching to a ceremony at Portage and Main. In another event connected with a national Red Cross aluminum drive, Winnipeg housewives pelted an effigy of Hitler hung in the Hudson's Bay parking lot with a barrage of donated aluminum pots and pans; other groups held similar "pot Hitler" events, one of which was put on by Polish groups with the cooperation of the Polish consul. Advertising and news articles urged everyone to "Get in the Scrap," and post-office stamps on letters reminded Canadians to "Save metals, rags and waste paper."[32] One classified ad put a humorous spin on the work:

> JOHN R. – COME HOME, ALL IS FOR-
> given – Help me get out that old garden
> hose, your old tires and overshoes for
> the scrap rubber drive Nov. 19, 20, 21. –
> Love, Mary.[33]

A huge number of volunteers contributed their time to the Salvage Corps. By 1943 the total was estimated at over 33,000, including teachers, students, truck drivers, sorters, and salespeople. Their accomplishments were impressive. The corps collected over 94 million pounds of material and operated four retail stores to sell reusable clothing and household goods it collected along with the other salvage. Victory Shop No. 1 handled clothing and knick-knacks, No. 2 sold furniture and other goods, and there was also a general Salvage Shop and a Book Shop. A Treasure Ship project during the 1943 Christmas season collected silver, china, antiques, and other valuables, raising over $11,000 to help finance a hostel for merchant mariners in Halifax. For the next two Christmases, toys collected house-to-house by Girl Guides were repaired and sold in the Victory Shops. There was even a Salvage Corps Doll Shop. The corps ultimately earned almost $400,000, with net profits of over $112,000 donated to various war services.[34]

Winnipeg's salvage drives made a tangible contribution to the war effort at home and overseas. In addition to providing eight mobile kitchens for areas suffering under German bombing raids, they earned money to purchase wireless sets for searchlight crews defending British airspace. At home, the Patriotic Salvage Corps gave indirect aid to the war effort by discouraging waste, recycling necessary materials, and funding war service projects like the Central Volunteer Bureau. Its success prompted an article in the *Philadelphia Inquirer* that noted that Winnipeg's salvage corps was "one of the best known on the continent," largely because "Manitobans collect more than twice as much salvage as does the average Canadian." Ottawa agreed that Winnipeg furnished the "model for Salvage Corps across Canada."[35]

One element of the salvage effort that evolved to serve a much wider purpose was the Block Plan originally instituted to keep Winnipeg housewives aware of pickup schedules and necessary materials. As it was expanded by the Central Volunteer Bureau in 1942, it divided the city into zones with block captains "to provide the quickest, most efficient method of mobilization of Winnipeg women for any worthwhile project of city wide scope." It had routine tasks, such as canvassing for the Women's Division of the Red Cross and for the Community Chest, but it was put to use in other important ways. Block captains helped organize victory gardens, signed up 3000 women for a vegetable canning project, found 4500 blood donors, assisted the Department of Agriculture by conducting a bread survey, and later disseminated information on veterans' benefits. The basis of organization was simple: "A woman a block in every part of the city ... responsible for houses in her particular block," with block captains directed by zone and regional leaders.[36] According to one observer, the Block Plan allowed housewives who could not leave their areas to contribute their services, and it built "community solidarity and citizen participation in a very real and tangible fashion."[37]

As a growing number of people got involved with voluntary work in the community or on behalf of armed forces personnel, the need arose to form a coordinating body to maximize the efficiency of their efforts. There was a great deal of overlap, especially during the war's opening stages. The national auxiliary service organizations were responsible, in theory, for providing services at military camps and bases. As needs escalated with the growing war effort, they gradually expanded their operations to include urban areas. This led to increased costs, competition for the public donations that funded war services, and duplication of programs. Minimizing competition for donations became increasingly important as war charities proliferated, and by the end of 1940 Ottawa mandated joint appeals. Then in 1942, the government decided to fund directly the war services delivered by the national auxiliary service organizations, partly to prevent interference with solicitation for Victory Loan subscriptions. To keep costs down, Ottawa encouraged the national organizations to focus exclusively on services for troops in camps and overseas. The Council of Social Agencies had already taken a lead on organizing Winnipeg's war services in June 1941 when it invited representatives of the auxiliaries and welfare agencies to participate in what became known as the Greater Winnipeg Coordinating Board for War Services. This was at first only an advisory body, but in April 1942 the Department of National War Services delegated to local citizens' committees the administrative responsibility for providing and funding auxiliary services to troops in urban areas.[38]

The Greater Winnipeg Coordinating Board was an inclusive body whose membership was open to any group working to provide war or welfare services in the city. The inaugural meeting on 11 June 1941 was attended by approximately 150 delegates, including the mayor, lieutenant-governor, members of the provincial government, Department of National Defence, regimental or other unit associations and ladies' auxiliaries, the Canadian National Institute for the Blind, Children's Aid Society, Young Men's Hebrew Association, and the Board of Trade, to mention only a small cross-section of groups that took an active part in the Coordinating Board's work. Other members were added as circumstances dictated. For example, because the city became an important transit point for American troops and equipment en route to bases in the northwest or work on the Alaska Highway, the growing number of US personnel in Winnipeg made it logical for the board to add an American voice. A representative for American forces in the city joined the board in January 1944, and another from the American Legion joined later in the spring.[39]

The coordinating board served as a mechanism for its member organizations to rationalize their efforts, and it worked through a number of committees, each responsible for a different area of service. While it would be as ponderous to describe every function of the board as it would be to list the work of every individual voluntary organization, a survey of some representative activities undertaken by its committees indicates the scale of cooperative effort invested by a diverse group of interested parties. Some services had already been consolidated under a single agency or umbrella group, as in the case of the Central Volunteer Bureau, which simply constituted the board's corresponding Voluntary Services Committee. Similarly, the Regional War Services Library Committee became part of the Board's Education Committee. The library committee had been formed in the fall of 1940, comprising a number of local groups already working to supply the demand for reading materials for service personnel at home and overseas. Under this committee, the Canadian Legion's Educational Services division supplied educational and technical books, the Manitoba Library Association provided works of fiction, the IODE offered magazines, and the National Council of Jewish Women looked after newspapers. The committee collected donated reading materials in street bins, at schools, the post office, and Eaton's and Hudson's Bay department stores. It sorted, repaired, and packed books and periodicals for shipment at two central depots. The CVB contributed additional volunteers to help with collecting and sorting, as did the Red Cross and other groups like the Women's Club, the Whirlwind Club, Boy Scouts, Girl Guides, and cadets.[40]

The entertainment committee fulfilled a need that was as important as reading material to the maintenance of servicemen's morale, putting on live shows for the troops in Winnipeg and military bases throughout the province. This undertaking demanded a significant contribution of time and effort from committee members and performers. The committee formed nineteen troupes, each with thirty to forty members. They performed at military and air force bases across the whole of Military District 10, including weekly shows at Shilo that required regular travel from Winnipeg. During nine months in 1944, for example, the committee staged 210 shows both in and outside the city, for audiences totalling more than 179,000 troops. They also entertained service personnel in Winnipeg at the Orpheum Theatre or the military hospitals at Fort Osborne Barracks and Deer Lodge, and made arrangements to bring in visiting troupes such as the Massey-Harris Company's "Combines," the "Army Show," "Meet the Navy," and the RCAF's "Swing-time Revue."[41]

The Train Reception Committee carried a comparable workload. Its eighty members from sixty-four different Winnipeg organizations arranged receptions for troop trains that became famous across the country, in the process coordinating the work of thousands of volunteers. Because Winnipeg had no central station for passenger trains during the war, volunteers had to duplicate their work at both the Canadian National Railway and Canadian Pacific Railway stations. Train Reception volunteers met more than 500 trains and well over 100,000 servicemen and women between 1942 and 1945. Troops passing through were met between the hours of 8 a.m. and 11 p.m., but volunteers remained on call to meet men returning home at any hour. The committee routinely created an "aura of gaiety and expectancy" at the stations, which were adorned with flags and "Welcome Home" banners. Bands played to set a festive mood while "young hostesses, their faces bright with excitement," passed out refreshments, souvenir packages, or magazines. Canadian Legion guides assisted relatives and led the returning men through the station to the reception.

Often the mayor was on hand to deliver an official greeting. The most anticipated moments occurred in "a specially prepared, quiet room set apart from the crowded rotunda," where long-separated family members awaited the moment of reunion.[42] As word spread among servicemen about the amenities furnished at these receptions, Winnipeg gained such a reputation that the Department of National Defence recommended that other cities follow the Train Reception Committee's example.

The reunions at Winnipeg's train stations were not the only activities planned by the board that concerned servicemen's families. Most of the armed forces units raised in the city had regimental associations or ladies' auxiliaries, and these groups were commonly concerned with ensuring the welfare of comrades on active service and their dependents. For some of these groups, fulfilling this role during the Second World War was simply a continuation of the work they had done for families of veterans of the Great War during the 1920s and '30s. For the many armed forces auxiliaries active in the city during the 1940s, the coordinating board's Dependents' Welfare Committee served as a point of liaison with representatives from welfare agencies and with each other. It was also a point of reference for those with questions about resources or problems related to family welfare, such as finances, housing, veterans' civil re-establishment benefits, or medical care. But the committee went beyond a simple problem-centred orientation; it also created a trust fund for dependents of the Winnipeg Grenadiers who fell at Hong Kong and formed a subcommittee to welcome war brides to the city. These women greeted newcomers at the train station, provided introductions to members of their husbands' unit auxiliaries, and hosted a welcoming tea in the spring of 1945 to help them get acquainted. At a national conference of war service agencies in January 1945, the Winnipeg organization for welcoming British wives was singled out "as being the most satisfactory."[43]

Regimental associations and ladies' auxiliaries were unique in their direct connection to the men on active service. The welfare of servicemen's families was perhaps their most pressing concern, since most everyone had a husband or son or brother in the army. The Fort Garry Horse Women's Auxiliary was one such group that did representative work. In December 1939, one of its members conveyed the spirit shared by these organizations: "In these grave days ... the ladies of the Auxiliary, recognizing the many opportunities for service, realize that there are many wives and friends of the Regiment to whom the word 'work' has taken on a new significance. To these we extend a very sincere invitation to join us." The war offered not only "a multitude of opportunities to assist in this great fight for democracy," but also provided the "opportunity for better acquaintance, grounds on which to build a splendid fellowship."[44]

The most common task undertaken by these fellowships was knitting donated wool into field comforts. For this purpose the Hudson's Bay Company donated a "Wool room" that served as the Fort Garry ladies' headquarters. The auxiliary also raised funds to buy Victory Bonds or purchase medical equipment for Deer Lodge Military Hospital, sold cookbooks, and held numerous teas and raffles to raise money for "cigarettes and comforts for the Regiment."[45] The women shared in the Train Reception Committee's work and held summer picnics and Christmas parties for the children of the regiment. Hospitalized veterans or active servicemen were cheered by their visits and by the Christmas presents and "ditty bags" containing toiletries, candy, and books they brought. The auxiliary's social welfare committee donated money and hampers to families in need, as did the regimental association itself, which maintained a benevolent fund for this purpose. Undoubtedly the most difficult yet most essential task was performed by members who visited the families of men killed or wounded on active service. Their commitment was conveyed by another member, Mrs. R.B. Carter, who had the "privilege to write to the many mothers, wives and sisters of [those] Garry Boys who had been killed, were missing or wounded[,] to try to express to them a message of love, sympathy and friendship from us as members of the Auxiliary."[46] Miriam MacEwing, the president of the Women's Auxiliary, further reported that "for all its sadness, it was an unforgettable experience. To meet courage and faith and character in the face of despair, as we did most undoubtedly, is to be immeasurably strengthened. It fills you with determination to face any inevitability the same way—and to go on in this Auxiliary with even greater effort."[47] Cooperation between these unit associations and other voluntary organizations, fostered by the coordinating board, was mutually beneficial. The Red Cross helped by shipping the auxiliary's parcels of food and comforts overseas, where they were stocked for camps and hospitals in the United Kingdom and other war zones. In return, Fort Garry ladies pitched in with work on Red Cross and other groups' projects. By the end of 1944, according to the Women's Auxiliary's secretary, twenty-six members were working at the prisoner-of-war parcel plant and 90 percent had received Red Cross pins for faithful service.[48]

One of the coordinating board's largest undertakings was to furnish a recreation centre for service personnel on leave. The United Services Centre was housed from 1942 to 1945 in the Annex of Eaton's downtown department store, and it offered troops a canteen, dance floor, lounges and reading rooms, a check room for baggage, uniform mending, and a games area with billiards, table tennis, and even slot machines. Visitors could send telegrams, buy cigarettes or a ticket to a hockey game, and arrange accommodations with local hostesses or the United Services Lodge, a hostel operated by the coordinating board. Some of these services were also offered at smaller locations like the Airmen's Club, run by the Winnipeg Women's Air Force Auxiliary for men training in the British Commonwealth Air Training Plan, but the United Services Centre was open to members of all the armed services.[49]

The response by both volunteers and patrons was outstanding. The centre received donations of all the money and equipment needed to begin operation, including fire insurance, appliances for the kitchen, even the renovation work and decoration. Contributors numbered 189 different organizations and individuals from the military, commerce and industry, the arts, service clubs, and individuals. In 1943 alone, the Central Volunteer Bureau helped place over 8000 volunteers at the United Services Centre.[50] The facility required a staff of 150 women per day, and it was no doubt a big job to keep that many volunteers satisfied and all of the positions filled, especially the less glamorous ones, regardless of illnesses, vacations, personal problems, or other considerations. Yet as one Winnipeg resident told her soldier-husband, "Almost every woman I know goes down to the New United Service Centre, and feels for a time the thrill and interest of welcoming and serving service people from all over the world."[51] Visitors gratefully took advantage of the facility. The centre's staff had planned, in 1942, for an average of 500 to 700 visitors per day, or about 21,000 per month. They grossly underestimated its appeal. The first month of operation saw over 55,000 visitors, and the number only increased as the war continued. Staff counted 9000 patrons on New Year's Eve, 1943, and 7603 on VE Day. As Gertrude Laing wrote in 1948, "The United Services Centre remains the biggest single volunteer undertaking not only of the Co-ordinating Board, but of the City of Winnipeg."[52]

The board's role in coordinating work on collaborative projects like the United Services Centre was vital because so many parties were active in providing war services and the enthusiasm of volunteers could sometimes produce minor problems. In the case of patient visiting at Deer Lodge Hospital, for example, the duplication of effort caused by a number of smaller groups working outside the framework of the board's Joint Hospital Visiting Committee apparently caused confusion and some embarrassment for both patients and staff. Small difficulties like these notwithstanding, the coordinating board was proactive in fulfilling needs for different war services as they arose, and the level of success it attained was largely attributable to the perhaps unusual degree of cooperation between the various groups that comprised its membership. In Gertrude Laing's opinion, "the Board enjoyed the confidence of the member parties because it was organized on a very broad base. No one organization exercised more influence than any other, and membership was freely open to all the war service groups in Winnipeg that wished to join."[53]

This was not necessarily the case in all cities. During the war's first two years, disorganization resulted from jurisdictional competition between the Departments of National Defence (DND) and National War Services (DNWS), and overlap due to the expansion of work by the national auxiliary service organizations. There was some evidence by late 1941, according to one DNWS memo, "that voluntary civilian services are disintegrating."[54] The coordinating committee that had been set up in Calgary had already ceased to function and there were serious problems in Edmonton. The chairman of Edmonton's committee, T.H. Thomas-Peter, had written to the minister of national war services, J.T. Thorson, in September 1941 complaining about a lack of cooperation from DND's auxiliary service officers, appointed in each military district to provide liaison between armed forces units and war service groups. Thomas-Peter noted that the Edmonton Council for the Coordination of Auxiliary War Services was prepared to disband unless Ottawa confirmed its authority "to demand cooperation from the auxiliaries and their officers, and . . . to control unauthorized war workers for the sake of lending maximum efficiency to their efforts."[55] Thomas-Peter's attitude may have contributed to the problems in Edmonton. His preoccupation with the council's authority to "demand cooperation" and enforce control stood in direct contrast to the disposition of Winnipeg's coordinating board as described by Laing. Ottawa's solution, as noted above, was to transfer direction of citizens' committees to DNWS and give it the responsibility for providing services in urban areas, thus simplifying the jurisdictional tangle, providing hitherto missing bureaucratic leadership, and ending much of the overlap with the national service organizations.

Other features of the DNWS plan were already in evidence in Winnipeg, such as establishing volunteer registration bureaus, affiliation with local salvage organizations, and liaison with the department's Women's Voluntary Services Division.[56] Winnipeg in fact led the way with a number of war service initiatives. By war's end Ottawa had recommended the "Winnipeg Plan" for both the CVB and troop train receptions and acknowledged the city's organizations for salvage collection and clothing relief as models for others to follow. The block plan, too, influenced plans in other cities for salvage operations and provision of wartime information.[57] In consideration of all their activities, the aspect that truly stands out is the amount of sheer hard work that volunteers put in year after year, and the broad base of women, men, and children who shared in it. The effort they expended was indeed considerable, but it was one indication of the debt they felt they owed to the men who had left home to fight for their country.

There can be no doubt that the level of voluntary service performed by Winnipeg residents was exceptional. But who among the city's various social groups offered their time and effort, and why? Jay White has pointed out in his study of Halifax that "working women and those raising young families were usually unable to devote much time to [voluntary] activities. Well-to-do women gravitated easily to war service since voluntarism and charitable fundraising were common within their social class, and they were more likely to employ domestics at home, allowing them free time to devote to voluntary work."[58] Many leaders of the Central Volunteer Bureau, for example, fit this demographic. But it was not just married, upper-class housewives with little to do who took part in voluntary work; working men and women also got involved. The Great-West Life Company formed a War Service Unit with a variety troupe that performed throughout the province to entertain servicemen, and the unit staffed other volunteer activities organized by the coordinating board. Employees of other Winnipeg companies also got into the act. There were numerous "Business Girls' Groups" formed at the city's banks, insurance houses, grain companies, and railways.[59]

Children were also heavily involved in a range of war service activities. Westminster United Church had a Wolf Cub pack that assisted with "patriotic deliverys [sic] of circulars" and collected salvage and magazines.[60] Girl Guides and Brownies sewed or knitted for V-Bundles, helped at the blood donor clinic, the prisoner-of-war parcel plant, the magazine depot, or at a canteen they ran at the Winnipeg Auditorium for Red Cross workers. Schools participated in a number of projects. For example, Daniel McIntyre Collegiate Institute's grade 11 class raised money to buy wool for Red Cross knitting and held clothing drives, while Fort Rouge School children knitted for the IODE and helped raise money for a Milk for Britain fund. Meanwhile, fourteen-year-old *Free Press* carrier Paul Pelchuk and his thirteen-year-old helper, Allan Geddes, responding to appeals for the Aid to Russia Fund, organized a quiz contest and a schedule of movie nights. They used a projector Allan received for Christmas, borrowed from the Department of Mines and Natural Resources some travel and nature movies to screen in addition to some of their own comedy shorts, sold tickets for three cents each, and gave out candy as quiz prizes. They donated $4.50 to the Red Cross.[61]

If voluntarism was not limited to housewives, was such service performed by various ethnic groups alike? Questions have been raised concerning the degree to which Canada's ethnic communities joined in supporting the war effort. Ninette Kelley and Michael Trebilcock claim in their study of Canadian immigration history that a supposed paucity of contributions from ethnic communities to Victory Loan drives was evidence of a relative lack of support for the war effort.[62] There is no basis for such a conclusion regarding popular participation in Winnipeg's Victory Loan campaigns, community services, or the war effort in general.[63] If there had been any concerted reticence, one could expect that voluntary commitments to war services by minority groups would have been lacking. There is some evidence that early in the war, leaders of voluntary service associations, many of whom indeed came from Winnipeg's old stock British majority, may have been slow to reach ethnic minority residents. In late October 1939, Monica McQueen, chairman of the provincial board administering the Voluntary Registration of Canadian Women survey, noted that "so far the response from the foreign born population has not been very good."[64] This was very early in the game, however, only two weeks after registration commenced in Winnipeg. The provincial board contained Polish, Ukrainian, and French representatives, and it was soon apparent that Winnipeg's ethnic groups were ready to serve.

For example, the CVB's file card system listing the skills of volunteers was cross-indexed "so that if we want a French speaking telegraph operator with car, and free any time, we can find out all about her in two seconds, or if we want a Polish woman who will have two soldiers to dinner any time, we will have her telephone number right away."[65] The CVB itself worked on behalf of those in need, regardless of ethnicity. Early in the war it organized a Finnish Relief Tag Day, and its Refugee Clothing Bureau cooperated with Polish, Finnish, and Jewish relief committees. According to Monica McQueen, it was staffed by "more than 200 volunteers of every race and creed ... working there every week for the victims of Nazi aggression."[66] The chairman of the Greater Winnipeg Coordinating Board for War Services, W.J. Major, also testified to the cross-cultural response of Winnipeg's volunteers: "It is no exaggeration to say that thousands of our citizens, particularly women, are working on the various committees of the Board.... The members of the committees come from all branches of our citizenry—from all nationalities and from all denominations."[67] To cite one final example, Community Chest contributions showed no signs of division based on ethnicity. Mr. F.R. Denne, director of the 1942 Community Chest drive in Winnipeg, described the campaign as "the smoothest running one we have ever had. I have been associated in some way with every drive since the Chest inception in 1922 but there never was one in which this City was so closely united. Everyone regardless of race or creed, were with us." The campaign raised over $340,000, 108 percent of the objective.[68]

Many members of Winnipeg's ethnic communities had solid reasons to back the war effort because their families had immigrated from regions later overrun by the Axis powers. The Polish community was one of the most active. A Polish Defence Committee was set up to collect relief supplies for refugees in the old country, and on 5 October 1940 about 300 volunteers for the Polish National Relief Fund tag day raised over $5000 for the Polish government in exile. Polish Canadians with continuing ties to their ancestral land obviously had a deep interest in Allied victory, given the decimation of Poland by the German invasion that started the war. Thousands of Poles fought alongside Allied troops, many of whom served in the Royal Air Force. A visit to Winnipeg by the Duke of Kent in August 1941 was therefore noteworthy, since the duke was inspector-general of the RAF. A garden reception was held at Government House on 15 August 1941, with over one hundred of Winnipeg's Polish community leaders invited to meet him. They represented groups such as the Polish Gymnastic Association Sokol, the Polish branch of the Canadian Legion, the Polish Veterans' association, the Federation of Polish Societies, the Polish National Defence Committee, and various churches. Hundreds of other Poles turned up unofficially to catch a glimpse of the duke, who was greeted by a group of young people wearing traditional Polish costumes.[69]

Likewise, there could be little doubt where Jewish Winnipeggers' sympathy lay. On 19 August 1941 the *Free Press* reported that a Winnipeg man had lost five brothers and a sister in Nazi-occupied Poland. Mr. J. Silverstein of Boyd Avenue received a letter from his niece that was smuggled out of the Warsaw ghetto, describing how three of the brothers apparently "left for Russia" after being bombed out of their homes, while another went looking for the fifth brother, supposedly in Lublin. None returned. The sister had been killed earlier in the war.[70] When the Dominion government held its conscription plebiscite in the spring of 1942, Winnipeg's Jews were among those calling for a Yes vote "as an important step in the direction of total war."[71]

Even small minority groups like Winnipeg's Chinese were conspicuous in supporting the war effort. At a special meeting of the Chinese National League's headquarters on Pacific Avenue in October 1940, members heard guest speaker Dong Yeu Wai of Victoria declare that "it was the patriotic task of every Chinese Canadian to carry on his duty in wartime." That duty apparently included supporting war service organizations. A few days earlier, the Chinese were specially mentioned in the

Free Press for donations to the Red Cross Drive.[72] Like the Poles, they had a particular interest: although Canada was not yet involved in the Pacific war, the Chinese had already been fighting Japan for nine years. Members of Winnipeg's Chinese community sustained their commitment to the war effort over the long term; in June 1943 the *Tribune* profiled a group of Chinese women who met every Friday at the United Church's Chinese Mission on Logan Avenue. They not only worked for the Red Cross, they also donated sewn and knitted articles to the IODE for shipment to Britain. They were currently holding a tea with proceeds going to the Chinese Refugee Relief Fund.[73]

One minority group of special interest is the French community of Winnipeg and St. Boniface, since the conscription crises of 1942 and 1944 posed a particular threat to French-English unity on a national scale. A detailed examination of the Franco-Manitoban response to the war is beyond the scope of this chapter, but the French Canadians of metropolitan Winnipeg did not display any particular ethnic cohesion in its voting behaviour during the 1930s and 1940s. Residents did not automatically elect French candidates, but voted on the issues of the day.[74] Political scientist Murray S. Donnelly has gone so far as to say that as a distinct community, "Winnipeg ... has never been particularly conscious of the existence of St. Boniface."[75] Winnipeg's most prominent historian, Alan Artibise, ignores the French community as a factor of any significance in his treatment of this period.[76] Since they did not stand out from the general population in their response to the war effort, it is likely that French Canadians were subject to a similar range of opinion as other residents. They, too, bought Victory Bonds, collected salvage, and donated blood. Like other towns across Canada, St. Boniface adopted the Royal Canadian Navy minesweeper that was its namesake and raised money for comforts and supplies to support her crew. One group, the Free French Association, took a strong stand against Vichy France and raised money to support the resistance led by Charles de Gaulle.[77]

There are other indications that it was not just members of Winnipeg's Anglo-Saxon majority that invested their time in voluntary war work. Beyond the very wide range of direct services it provided for armed forces personnel, the Greater Winnipeg Coordinating Board acted officially on behalf of the Department of National War Services in handling applications for war charities fundraising permits. The list of permits issued in 1944 alone gives an indication of the number of groups doing voluntary war work, and of the ethnic community's participation. In 1942–43 there were sixty-one Winnipeg organizations registered as war charities. The list included, among others, the Jewish Women's Organization, Jewish People's Committee,

Lutheran Church Soldiers' Welfare Club, Polish Gymnastic Association Sokol, and the Ukrainian Young Women's Club. Ukrainian women sent comforts and cigarettes to servicemen at home and overseas, visited wounded veterans at Deer Lodge hospital, volunteered for the Red Cross, and raised money to buy two ambulances.[78]

Perhaps the most intriguing question is not who participated in voluntary service, but why they did so. This is, of course, an intangible issue that is difficult to measure. It is likely that some of those who volunteered their services were driven along by social pressure or caught up in a moment's enthusiasm. One woman wrote to a friend, "it seems it will be necessary for me to take in a refugee (having offered to do so in a rash moment when I registered with the V.R.C.W.)"[79] For those with loved ones serving overseas, motives were much more profound, especially as the war dragged on and casualties mounted. The War Service Unit of the Westminster United Church Women's Association met every Wednesday to perform voluntary work such as sewing and knitting for V-Bundles. Members worked at the Red Cross parcel-packing plant, contributed money to the Aid to Russia Fund, bought war savings certificates that they donated to the church, and sent Christmas parcels to men and women overseas.[80] They shared sentiments that bound them together with women in regimental and unit associations across the country: "Sadness and loss are seldom mentioned but they cannot always be ignored. Grief at the death of Mr. George Morrow, beloved friend, gay companion, and of Wallace McKay, both 'lost at sea' from the same transport; anxiety for the safety of Wilson Caldwell, posted 'missing'; deep concern for our men at Hong Kong; love and sympathy for our boys, 'prisoners of war' in France, or Poland, or Germany – these are some of the experiences that unite all in a common sympathy, and spur to further effort."[81] Similar emotions were expressed by the secretary of the Fort Garry Horse Women's Auxiliary in a letter to the regiment's commanding officer in Europe, conveying thanks for efforts to maintain often tenuous lines of communication. "The distance is so great," she wrote, "the years so long[,] and mail so precious, you can readily understand the anxiety of loved ones."[82] Anxieties increased when the fighting intensified overseas during the defence of Hong Kong or the invasions of Sicily and Normandy. As the auxiliary's president recorded, "Courage ran high" on 24 June 1944, the day of their summer picnic at City Park, "as our Regiment was in action in France and it wasn't too easy to rise above concern. At the end of the day we sent a cable to our Commanding Officer, expressing our pride and hope."[83] Many women joined such associations and offered their time as a way to keep their mind off worries about their men overseas, commiserate, and make a material contribution to the welfare of soldiers, sailors, and airmen.

There was also a sense that the home front must prove itself worthy of the sacrifices made by those offering themselves for active service at the battle front. One way to do that was to improve social services to ensure that servicemen's families and those less fortunate did not fall through society's cracks. As the Central Volunteer Bureau's chairman reported in September 1940, "We must keep those social services up in war time because we want our Canadian boys to come back and find that their children have been cared for, their old folks looked after, and we want them to find Winnipeg ready and willing to help them in the difficult years of demobilisation and the return to civilian life."[84] These comments suggest a cognizance of the disaffection among returned soldiers in 1919 and a determination to make sure that few would have cause to ask once more what they had been fighting for.

There is sufficient evidence to conclude that despite whatever centrifugal tensions may have divided Winnipeg's various ethnic, political, or socio-economic groups, there was a substantial degree of consensus in supporting Canada's war effort. This is not to say that the war erased divisions and prejudice, for there were still plenty of examples of both. The president of the Association of Canadian Clubs told a Winnipeg audience that "the intolerance on the part of the Anglo-Saxon toward anyone with a foreign-sounding name has been infinitely more harmful" than the supposedly subversive behaviour of a few members of the ethnic minority.[85] Whatever the degree of acceptance felt by the British-stock majority toward the city's other ethnic communities, those with "foreign-sounding" names did their bit alongside those from the majority. When a group of local Royal Canadian Naval Volunteer Reserve trainees left for the east coast in June 1941, the newspapers estimated that 2000 people turned out to see them off. One of those trainees, Paul Verdeniuk, "had a large group singing him goodbye in Ukrainian."[86] Among the members of the Winnipeg Grenadiers dispatched to Hong Kong in the autumn were 104 Ukrainian-Canadians, 38 of whom were killed in action.[87] And when Canadian soldiers returned to France in 1944, the commander of the Royal Winnipeg Rifles reportedly told the *Winnipeg Tribune* that "I have got a grand, remarkable bunch of boys; I estimate [that] forty percent of this unit is made up of lads of foreign extraction" representing eleven nationalities.[88] Their families thus had much the same hopes invested in the war's outcome as any other residents, and they were just as willing to contribute by volunteering. Winnipeggers of all stripes gave their time and money to the numerous war and community service initiatives mounted in the city: the upper class along with the working class; the Anglo-Saxon majority and the various ethnic minorities; Catholics, Protestants, and Jews; men and children as well as the women who did so much of the organizational work. Groups that may not have associated in peacetime shared in wartime a practical sort of unity, a spirit of service.

Notes

Generous financial support from the Social Sciences and Humanities Research Council of Canada, the Faculty of Graduate Studies and the Departments of History and Economics at the University of Manitoba, and Dr. James Burns has made this research possible. I want to thank the staff at the Archives of Manitoba, the Manitoba Legislative Library, the University of Manitoba Archives, the Fort Garry Horse Regimental Archives, the United Church Archives, and the *Winnipeg Free Press* Archives for their assistance. Special thanks also to Dr. Barry Ferguson for his sound advice and moral support over the last six years.

1   *Winnipeg Tribune*, 5 Oct. 1940.

2   Ian Miller, *Our Glory and Our Grief: Torontonians and the Great War* (Toronto: University of Toronto Press, 2001); Serge Marc Durflinger, *Fighting from Home: The Second World War in Verdun, Quebec* (Vancouver: University of British Columbia Press, 2006).

3   This term was popularized by the Canadian Pacific Railway's immigration promoter in Western Canada, J.M. Gibbon, in his *Canadian Mosaic: The Making of a Northern Nation* (London: Dent, 1939). My thanks to Barry Ferguson for providing this reference.

4   According to the 1941 census, Winnipeg's population was 221,960; the suburbs added 75,779 for a total of 297,739. Alan Artibise, *Winnipeg: An Illustrated History* (Toronto: Lorimer, 1977), Appendix.

5   Winnipeg residents of British origin made up almost 59 percent of the population. Those with French origin (6969) made up 3.1 percent.

6   Jeffrey A. Keshen, *Saints, Sinners, and Soldiers: Canada's Second World War* (Vancouver: University of British Columbia Press, 2004), 40.

7   See, for example, *Winnipeg Free Press*, 16 May 1942.

8   See Ken Adachi, *The Enemy That Never Was: A History of the Japanese Canadians* (Toronto: McClelland and Stewart, 1976); Peter Takaji Nunoda, "A Community in Transition and Conflict: The Japanese Canadians, 1935–1951" (PhD diss., University of Manitoba, 1991); and Louis Dion, "The Resettlement of Japanese Canadians in Manitoba, 1942–1948" (MA thesis, University of Manitoba, 1991).

9   *Winnipeg Tribune*, 16 January 1942, clipping in Archives of Manitoba (hereafter AM), P2631, Chisick collection, general scrapbook January to July 1942.

10   The 1942 conscription plebiscite led to much finger-pointing over the proportion of "No" votes in certain areas of the city. See "Where the 'No' Vote Lay Here," *Winnipeg Free Press*, 29 April 1942, 11, and "Manitoba's 'No' Vote," *Winnipeg Free Press*, 1 May 1942, 13.

11   Library and Archives Canada (hereafter LAC), RG 44, vol. 7, Citizens Committees Conference, Hill to Dir. Auxiliary Services, 10 December 1941, and Memo re: Organization of Citizens Committees, n.d. The terms "war services" and "auxiliary services" usually referred to the voluntary organization of recreational activities for service personnel and welfare services offered to their dependents.

12   Gertrude Laing, *A Community Organizes for War: The Story of the Greater Winnipeg Co-ordinating Board for War Services and Affiliated Organizations, 1939–1946* (Winnipeg: n.p., 1948), 3–6. I am grateful to Serge Durflinger for bringing this source to my attention.

13   AM, MG 10, C67, Royal Canadian Legion, box 33, Alex Cairns and A.H. Yetman, "The History of the Veteran Movement, 1916–1956," v. II, 12–13.

14   AM, P5513, "Minutes of the 44th Annual Meeting IODE 27 May—1 June 1944," 44–45 and 99.
This first service was of some significance owing to the wartime shortage of paper, especially in
Britain, "where the home supply of reading matter has been exhausted"; IODE *Bulletin* 25 (May
1943): 11.

15   AM, P666, Social Planning Council of Winnipeg (hereafter SPC), file 5, VRCW and the origins
of the CVB, 1939; LAC, MG 28, I 10, Canadian Council on Social Development, vol. 259, file 7,
McQueen to Whitton, 27 Jan. 1940; Laing, *Community*, 14–15.

16   LAC, MG 28, I 10, vol. 259, file 7, Monica McQueen, "A Year of Volunteers – Winnipeg's Newest
Agency," n.d., 1.

17   AM, P666, SPC, file 5, VRCW and the origins of the CVB, 1939, clipping from *The Survey*,
published January 1941.

18   AM, P666, SPC, file 5, VRCW and the origins of the CVB, 1939; *Winnipeg Free Press*, 21
September 1939.

19   LAC, MG 28, I 10, vol. 259, file 7, McQueen, "A Year of Volunteers" and memo, "Central Volunteer Bureau," n.d.

20   University of Manitoba Archives (hereafter UMA), MSS 24, *Winnipeg Tribune* collection, file
5486, Prisoners of War, 1941–45; *Winnipeg Tribune*, 25 November 1942.

21   *Chatelaine*, March 1944, 72.

22   Laing, *Community*, 17, 21; AM, P666, SPC, file 5, VRCW and the origins of the CVB, 1939; file 9,
CVB – annual meeting, 1942; and file 7, CVB annual report, 1940.

23   Laing, *Community*, 16–17; AM, P666, SPC, file 10, CVB – annual meeting, 1943.

24   AM, P666, SPC, file 9, CVB – annual meeting, 1942.

25   AM, P666, SPC, file 8, CVB annual meeting, 1941; Laing, *Community*, 55.

26   McQueen, "A Year of Volunteers," 3.

27   Laing, *Community*, 21, and 83–85.

28   UMA, MSS 1, Margaret Konantz papers, Box 2, Folder 1, Incoming Correspondence 1940-1945,
Richardson to Konantz, 7 Jan. 1943.

29   LAC, RG 44, vol. 7, Preliminaries to Salvage Campaign.

30   AM, P196, Patriotic Salvage Corps, scrapbook file 5, "Volunteer Drivers in White Take Pride in
Strenuous Work," news clipping, n.d.

31   Laing, *Community*, 22–28; McQueen, "A Year of Volunteers"; AM, P2631, Chisick collection,
1942 scrapbook; AM, P196, Patriotic Salvage Corps, scrapbook files 3 to 5.

32   *Winnipeg Tribune*, 27 Feb. 1943; Department of National War Services, Office of the Director of
Voluntary and Aux. Services, Bulletin #9, 27 June 1943, copy in AM, P664, SPC, file 10, Cdn War
Service Cttee – various reports, 1940–45; AM, P196, Patriotic Salvage Corps, scrapbook files 4
and 5; *Winnipeg Free Press*, 28 June 1943; UMA, MSS 122, Laurence F. Wilmot collection (hereafter Wilmot collection), box 6, file 7.

33   AM, P196, Patriotic Salvage Corps, scrapbook file 5.

34   Laing, *Community*, 25–28; AM, P196, Patriotic Salvage Corps, scrapbook file 5.

35   AM, P196, Patriotic Salvage Corps, scrapbook files 4 and 5; Laing, *Community*, 28. UMA, MSS 1,
Margaret Konantz papers, box 2, folder 1, clipping from Philadelphia *Inquirer*, Dec. 1943.

36   AM, P666, SPC, file 10, CVB – annual meeting, 1943.

37   Laing, *Community*, 18–19 and 30–31; AM, P642, SPC, file 22, "Annual Report of the Secretary of
the Council of Social Agencies, 9 June 1943," 8.

38   LAC, RG 44, vol. 7, Citizens Committees Conference, Memo re: Organization of Citizens
Committees, n.d.; Pifher to Davis, 10 Nov. 1941; Thorson to Ralston, 18 Nov. and 10 Dec. 1941;
Laing, *Community*, 31–32.

39   AM, P664, SPC, file 3, Greater Winnipeg Coordinating Board for War Services (hereafter GWCBWS) minutes, 11 June 1941; LAC, RG 24, vol. 11457, file NDWG 1270-152, vol. 1, GWCBWS minutes, 11 May 1944; Ken Ford, "War's Brightlights," *Globe and Mail*, 8 Nov. 1943.

40   AM, P666, SPC, file 4, Publications, 1943-45, Second Annual Meeting, GWCBWS, 11 June 1943; LAC, RG 24, vol. 11457, file NDWG 1270-152 vol. 1, GWCBWS minutes, 24 Nov. 1944; Laing, *Community*, 44-51.

41   Laing, *Community*, 38-42; LAC, RG 24, vol. 11457, file NDWG 1270-152 vol. 1, GWCBWS minutes, 11 May and 24 Nov. 1944; AM, P664, SPC, file 4, GWCBWS minutes, 1944.

42   Laing, *Community*, 67-69, 73.

43   LAC, RG 24, vol. 11457, file NDWG 1270-152 vol. 1, "Report of the War Services Conference, Montebello, Quebec, Jan. 22 to 26th, 1945," 6; Laing, *Community*, 79 and 92; AM, P664, SPC, file 4, GWCBWS minutes, 24 Nov. 1944.

44   Fort Garry Horse Regimental Archives and Museum (hereafter FGH), *Blue and Gold* 4, 11 (Dec. 1939): 8.

45   FGH, *Blue and Gold* 5, 12 (Aug. 1940): 5; Regimental Association minutes, 11 Feb. 1943.

46   FGH, Women's Auxiliary, "Casualty Visitor's Report," 3 Jan. 1945.

47   FGH, Women's Auxiliary, "President's Report," 3 Jan. 1945.

48   FGH, Women's Auxiliary, "Balance Sheet, 1945" and "Secretary's Report 1944"; Regimental Association minutes, 24 Oct. 1939.

49   Laing, *Community*, 53-58.

50   AM, P666, SPC, file 10, CVB – annual meeting, 1943, and file 4, Publications, 1943-45, "Second Annual Meeting, Greater Winnipeg Coordinating Board for War Services," 11 June 1943.

51   UMA, Wilmot collection, box 6, file 7, Hope to Laurence Wilmot, 28 Dec. 1943.

52   Laing, *Community*, 59. Laing was the coordinating board's executive secretary.

53   Laing, *Community*, 95; AM, P4651, Family Bureau of Winnipeg, Co-ordinating Board Reports, 26 April 1945; P664, SPC, file 5, GWCBWS minutes, 4 May 1945.

54   LAC, RG 44, vol. 7, file 9, Citizens Committees Conference, "Memorandum Re: Organization of Citizens Committees," n.d. [late 1941?].

55   LAC, RG 44, vol. 7, file 9, Citizens Committees Conference, Thomas-Peter to Thorsen [sic], 16 Sept. 1941.

56   LAC, RG 44, vol. 7, file 9, Citizens Committees Conference, "Memorandum Re: Organization of Citizens Committees." Margaret Konantz, one of the CVB's leaders, was an active member of Women's Voluntary Services. She was selected by DNWS to study WVS activities in Britain in February 1944 and later authored the department's report *Women's Voluntary Services for Civil Defence, Great Britain* (Ottawa: King's Printer, 1944).

57   James M. Whalen, "The Scrap That Made A Difference," *Legion Magazine* (November/December 1998), http://www.legionmagazine.com/features/canadianreflections/ 98-11.asp (accessed 16 January 2007).

58   Jay White, "Conscripted City: Halifax and the Second World War" (PhD diss., McMaster University, 1994), 307.

59   These included the Bank of Montreal, Canadian National Railways, the Canadian Wheat Board, Monarch Life Insurance, the National Grain Company, Searle Grain Company, and the Winnipeg Electric Railway Company; AM, P664, SPC, file 10, Canadian War Service Committee – various reports, 1940-45, "Great-West Life War Service Unit, Annual Reports for the Unit Year May 31, 1942 to May 31, 1943"; Laing, *Community*, 97.

60   United Church Archives, University of Winnipeg (hereafter UCA), "Westminster United Church Annual Report, 1941," 29-30.

61 *Winnipeg Tribune*, 4 Nov. 1944; AM, MG 14, B35, Ralph Maybank papers, box 6, newspaper clippings 1928–43; *Winnipeg Free Press*, 12 March 1942, clipping in AM, P2631, Chisick collection, 1942 scrapbook.

62 Ninette Kelley and Michael Trebilcock, *The Making of the Mosaic: A History of Canadian Immigration Policy* (Toronto: University of Toronto Press, 1998), 273.

63 Subscriptions from general sales and payroll deduction, which offer the best gauge of ordinary Winnipeggers' bond-buying behaviour, increased through each successive Victory Loan drive. The ratio of applications to population also improved to a point where one in every three residents bought a bond by the ninth and final loan in the autumn of 1945. AM, P5005, National War Finance Committee – Manitoba Division, "Analysis of Final Results, Canada's Ninth Victory Loan, October 22nd to November 10th, 1945," 19–19A.

64 AM, P666, SPC, file 5, VRCW and the origins of the CVB, 1939, McQueen to Hyndman, 27 Oct. 1939.

65 McQueen, "A Year of Volunteers," 1.

66 LAC, MG 28, I 10, vol. 259, file 7, McQueen to Whitton, 27 Jan. 1940; McQueen, "A Year of Volunteers," 3.

67 AM, P664, SPC, file 8, correspondence, 1941–45, memo by W.J. Major, chairman GWCBWS, n.d.

68 LAC, MG 28, I 10, vol. 258, file 4, Denne to Davidson, 6 Nov. 1942.

69 AM, P666, SPC, file 5, VRCW and the origins of the CVB, 1939; *Winnipeg Free Press*, 7 Oct. 1940 and 16 Aug. 1941.

70 *Winnipeg Free Press*, Tuesday 19 August 1941.

71 *Winnipeg Free Press*, 7 April 1942, clipping in AM, P2630, Chisick collection, 1942 scrapbook.

72 *Winnipeg Free Press*, 7 and 11 Oct. 1940.

73 Verena Garrioch, "When There's Work To Do, We Do It With A Will," *Winnipeg Tribune*, 12 June 1943.

74 Roger E. Turenne, "The Minority and the Ballot Box: A Study of the Voting Behaviour of the French Canadians of Manitoba, 1888–1967" (MA thesis, University of Manitoba, 1969), 126. The population of the City of St. Boniface was 18,157 in 1941, of which 6922 were of French ethnic origin and 7005 of British origin. See Canada, Dominion Bureau of Statistics, *Eighth Census of Canada* (Ottawa: King's Printer, 1941), 446–447.

75 Murray Donnelly, *Dafoe of the Free Press* (Toronto: Macmillan, 1968), 29.

76 Alan Artibise, *Winnipeg: An Illustrated History* (Toronto: Lorimer, 1977), 109–162.

77 The Naval Museum of Manitoba, "HMCS St. Boniface," http://www.naval-museum.mb.ca/ships/stbonifa.htm (accessed on 24 April 2006); Winnipeg *Free Press*, 14 and 19 Aug. 1941, 11 Oct. 1941.

78 AM, P664, SPC, file 4, GWCBWS minutes, 1944; P666, SPC, file 4, Publications, 1943–45, "Second Annual Meeting," 11 June 1943, and Program, Ukrainian Young Women's Club concert, 25 March 1945; Paul Yuzyk, *The Ukrainians in Manitoba: A Social History* (Toronto: University of Toronto Press, 1953), 193.

79 AM, MG 14 B 44, Howard W. Winkler papers, box 5 file 2, Booth to Winkler, 15 June 1940.

80 UCA, Westminster United Church annual reports, 1941–43.

81 UCA, "Westminster United Church Annual Report, 1941," 16.

82 FGH, Women's Auxiliary, MacKenzie to Wilson, 30 Jan. 1945.

83 FGH, Women's Auxiliary, "President's Report," 3 Jan. 1945.

84 AM, P666, SPC, file 7, CVB annual report, 1940.

85 *Winnipeg Tribune*, 19 June 1941.

86 The Naval Museum of Manitoba, "The Naval History of Manitoba," http://www.naval-museum.mb.ca/history (accessed 26 November 2004).

87 Yuzyk, *Ukrainians in Manitoba*, 193.
88 Quoted in Thomas M. Prymak, *Maple Leaf and Trident: The Ukrainian Canadians during the Second World War* (Toronto: Multicultural History Society of Ontario, 1988), 109.

Drinking Together: The Role of Gender in Changing Manitoba's Liquor Laws in the 1950s

Dale Barbour

Home wrecker or harmless social lubricant? When Manitobans discussed revising their liquor laws in the 1950s their language was alive with gendered implications. Since the nineteenth century, liquor had been tied to masculine space—men joined together to drink, while female drinkers were eyed with suspicion and, in the view of the middle class, members of the working class, male and female, should never meet over alcohol.[1] It was a situation that was enshrined in law in Manitoba in 1928 when public drinking was confined to all-male beer parlors. But by the 1950s the gender line was wearing thin. Men and women were drinking together, pouring drinks under the table in supper clubs or sneaking drinks outside of dance halls, in defiance of both convention and the law. But even as Manitobans discussed where women should be able to drink, they also considered where they couldn't—the all-male beer parlor. Of course, gender does not operate in a vacuum—as much as the beer parlor was masculine, it was also working class. The downtown location of these beer parlors allowed speakers to avoid using the term class in their critiques, even though they meant it just the same.

I am primarily concerned with the city of Winnipeg in the 1950s. I have tapped the *Winnipeg Tribune* archives, specifically the liquor clipping files from 1943 to 1957, and the 1955 *Report of the Manitoba Liquor Enquiry Commission*, headed by former Manitoba premier John Bracken, as primary sources.[2] This study is centred on the commission, but I am less interested in the policy process than I am in the language used by people both for and against more liberal drinking laws, including the language of the report itself.

I will be using Kathy Peiss's concept of homosocial and heterosocial space, as outlined in *Cheap Amusements: Working Women and Leisure in Turn-of-the-Century New York* as a theoretical base for my discussion. Heterosocial refers to the mixing of both genders while homosocial refers to the social mixing of people of one gender and not, it should be noted, to sexual orientation.[3] In *Cheap Amusements*, Peiss traces the transition of leisure spaces in North American industrial cities from being focussed on homosocial activities to those that were heterosocial.[4] She describes late nineteenth-century male public leisure as a homosocial affair—a saloon culture of camaraderie, frivolity, and the trading of rounds of drinks. It was not a place for women and those who did partake risked being labelled prostitutes.[5] Instead of the saloon, women frequented new, alcohol-free, commercial entertainments such as dance halls and movie theatres. Within these spaces, a dating culture emerged in which courting was removed from the scrutiny of parents and taken into the public sphere.[6] But as Carolyn Strange illustrates in *Toronto's Girl Problem: The Perils and Pleasures of the City, 1880–1930*, the rise of women as social actors and their movement into this evolving heterosocial public space weakened patriarchal control over their leisure time and, it was feared, emphasized their sexuality.[7] In response, a discourse was constructed "that linked women's pleasure to immorality and their independence to danger."[8]

Prohibition marked a definitive encounter between the law and drinking culture. Prince Edward Island was the first to initiate it in 1901 and Quebec was the last in 1919.[9] Manitoba enacted prohibition in 1916, but the era was short-lived. Mirroring a trend that took place across the country, Manitoba ended prohibition in 1923 by allowing the sale of liquor in government-run stores and then, in 1928, went further to allow the sale of beer by the glass in the new beer parlors. The end of prohibition did not mean a return to the saloon. Instead, new laws were introduced in the hope that a new kind of drinking place would be established. While the rules varied across the country, there was one matter on which all provinces could agree: women would be permitted to enter beer parlors only in a highly regulated setting, if at all.[10] British Columbia and Ontario created all-male beer parlors that had a separate section for women and their escorts.[11] Men could not enter the women's side on their own and women were not to stray into the men's side. This division of space by gender had the side effect of opening space for gay, lesbian, and transgendered people to slip through regulation that was targeted primarily at preventing "improper" heterosexual activity rather than homosexual contact.[12]

The *Manitoba Liquor Act* of 1928 did include provisions for similar gender segregation in Manitoba's beer parlors.[13] And in 1928 a Winnipeg Beach hotel briefly opened a women's beer parlor. But being unaware of the ins and outs of the new law, the female proprietor failed to obtain a proper licence and the women's beer parlor was promptly closed.[14] No other businesses followed up on the attempt, and Manitoba's beer parlors were constituted as all-male establishments.

By the end of the 1940s, boundaries were crumbling. Mariana Valverde describes the growth of an "enlightened hedonism" after the Second World War and links the new cocktail lounges that emerged in 1947 in Ontario and after 1957 in Manitoba with consumer culture:[15] "Class, sex, and gender had to be simultaneously reorganized in relation to spirits drinking in order to make the cocktail lounge possible. In respect to sex and gender, heterosexuality in the context of public drinking, which in the era of beer parlors had been associated with prostitution, was now revalorized and made central to the new legal category of the cocktail lounge. But this was a new, historically specific form of heterosexuality, namely the postwar heterosexuality associated with middle-class consumerism and early marriage."[16] The bar had been forbidden in beer parlors but its return to the new cocktail lounges did not so much signal the return of the saloon but rather its final burial as a working-class masculine institution. As Valverde notes, "the class and gender meanings of spirits drinking dramatically shifted in the post-World War II period."[17] It was assumed that respectable customers—read middle-class customers—could discipline themselves to a greater extent than beer parlor patrons could.[18]

Mixed-gender drinking was not an issue for the *Winnipeg Tribune* in the 1940s. Articles fretted about the amount of revenue the province was bringing in from liquor sales and whether this was morally acceptable, but the question of whether men and women should drink together hardly entered the public discussion.[19] In some ways the concept slid into Manitoba by stealth when social and ethnic clubs were allowed to serve alcohol in 1928.[20] Winnipeg Centre MLA Stephen Juba noted that the social clubs catered to different classes in the community and created inequity because members could drink in mixed company while the general public lacked the same privilege.[21] Meanwhile, Winnipeg North Liberal MLA Frank Chester argued in 1950 that ethnic clubs in the north end of the city were not being granted the same liquor privileges as other clubs. The Liquor Commission said bluntly that it was because clubs in North Winnipeg were "admitting practically anyone" and "practically became mixed beer parlors."[22] The position of the ethnic and social clubs at the regulatory and legal edge of society provided the early entry points where mixed drinking could emerge.[23] This space grew exponentially when veterans' clubs were allowed liquor licences and the possibility of mixed drinking in 1953.[24]

Whether ethnicity was an entry point for alcohol or simply a scapegoat is debatable. Canadian Temperance Federation general secretary Rev. John Linton linked ethnicity to changes in liquor culture in 1956 when he warned the province to tread carefully when it came to changing liquor laws. Linton argued that the increased number of drinkers could be blamed on the "breakdown of taboos" in two world wars and the "influx of settlers from European countries where patterns of drinking were different."[25] Of course, linking ethnicity to alcohol was nothing new—it had been a focus in the arguments of groups such as the Dominion Alliance in arguing for prohibition at the turn of the century.[26]

Ethnic and social clubs were the legal places where people could drink in mixed company. However, people were ignoring the law and drinking together at dances, supper clubs, and socials. As one woman interviewed by the *Winnipeg Tribune* said: "I'm a member of a club licensed to serve beer to men and women and it's worked out very well there. And I don't like going to supper dances and thinking we've got to finish that bottle that's under the table."[27] Breaking the law by drinking under the table was a given. Even the Women's Christian Temperance Union acknowledged that people were ignoring the law: "The management serves the mixer and the patrons bring their bottles. We are thus rearing a generation of law-breakers."[28] Alcohol was part of heterosocial space by the early 1950s. The only question was whether society at large was prepared to acknowledge it.

The public acceptability of alcohol in heterosocial space would be the central question when the Manitoba Liquor Enquiry Commission was convened in 1954, though gender was only referenced in one of the several questions placed before it. Retired politician John Bracken was picked to head the commission. Premier of Manitoba between 1922 and 1942, Bracken had been in power when the post-prohibition liquor law was drawn up in 1923 and when it was amended in 1928. He was renowned as a "teetotaler" and acknowledged that his party had been in favour of prohibition but, through the laws passed in 1923 and 1928, had solidified the Manitoba government's role as the barkeeper of the province.[29]

The tenor of the Report of the Manitoba Liquor Enquiry Commission—or Bracken report—was set in part one, entitled, "The Basis of the Liquor Problem and Traditional Ways of Dealing With It."[30] Nearly 350 pages of the 751-page Bracken report outline the dangers of alcohol consumption, a situation not lost on reviewers such as Manitoba Co-operative Commonwealth Federation (CCF) leader Lloyd Stinson, who called it a "textbook of temperance."[31] Under the section "The Problem as Interpreted," the report offers a glossary of technical terms. With respect to why there needed to be a "control law" for liquor, the report states: "Because the 'liquor' here referred to means alcoholic beverages, the trade in which for several hundred years has been considered by all countries to require control because of its anti-social effects."[32] The definition for "tension": "Nervous state arising from the inhibitions of modern society, complexities of modern life or the worries of business or other affairs. Said to be one of the chief causes of drinking; and the lessening of which is considered to be the chief benefit, though a temporary one, from drinking." The definition for skid row is also included: "The part of the population which has been completely demoralized by alcoholic consumption; the part of a town frequented by such persons."[33]

These definitions can be read alongside the language of the rest of the report. Liquor consumption, the report notes, can reduce intelligence and in turn impair moral sense: "The moral restraint which prevents anti-social action and even a depraved course of action is no longer active." And what is the impact of this progressive deterioration of one's moral sense? "Improper advances may be made to respectable women, or the drinker may seek questionable sexual outlets which his normal restraints would forbid."[34] Tapping Freudian terms, the report suggests that when alcohol is "sufficiently present in the nervous system, the 'censor' [Freud's term], whose function it is to 'restrain or divert inappropriate sexual impulses,' is off guard." And from there: "The close association between the brothel and the bar has been widely observed."[35] These comments are telling because they speak to why mixed drinking was considered a threat, particularly in beer parlors. The view was not only that every woman who entered alone was a potential prostitute, but that men might lose their moral sense due to alcohol and commit immoral sexual acts with women who were present. Women when mixed with alcohol were a moral threat to men, and men who were drinking could not be trusted in the presence of women.

The Bracken report put its own spin on what it saw happening in the world. It ticked off changes ranging from social dislocations following the Second World War to an increase in leisure time and social events, and to a trend towards the use of alcohol at social events, coupled again with the "tensions of modern life."[36] It noted: "The effects of two world wars on two succeeding generations do not disappear over night: that such consequences have always shaken previous concepts of morality is a matter of history, and on top of this in our case has come a period of economic prosperity unprecedented in our time. The ethical standards of a previous era have thus suffered from the clash of many forces never before witnessed on such a scale in this part of the world."[37] Later the report notes: "society has made remarkable economic gains in recent years and will make more; but social gains have not kept pace with them."[38] There is an ambivalence about modernity within the Bracken report, an ambivalence reflected in the definition of terms such as "tension."

Race enters this exchange primarily through the discussion around Aboriginal people.[39] While the federal government granted Aboriginal people access to alcohol in 1951, it fell to the provinces to make the changes in their own jurisdictions. For

Manitoba, that meant the Aboriginal question was part of the Bracken report and the general liquor laws discussion. Within that discussion, Aboriginal people were defined, and "othered," almost entirely by race. The notion that Aboriginal people did not have the "moral capabilities" to handle alcohol was repeated in a number of *Tribune* articles.[40] In contrast, gender almost never entered the picture. If Aboriginal people had any gender it was inevitably male.[41] Secondly, while women are quoted in the discussion around mixed drinking parlors, Aboriginal people are never quoted directly about whether they feel they should have drinking rights.[42] The closest we come to a quote is second-hand and offered by Anglican Rev. R.T. Milburn who quotes an Aboriginal person on The Pas Indian Reserve as having said: "It's not very dignified for me, as a man, to pay $2 for an 80 cent bottle of wine, drink it in hiding in a hurry and then run back to the reservation." Access to alcohol was portrayed as being critical for defining masculinity, which meant that denying Aboriginal people legal access to alcohol was an infringement on their masculinity.[43] The quote is found in an article headlined, "Probe Chief Seeks Indian Pow-Wow on Fire Water." The play on traditional stereotypes and othering through use of antiquated terms hardly needs pointing out.

The Bracken report outlined the distribution of beer parlors within Winnipeg. Due to licensing restrictions, the vast majority of beer parlors were exactly where they had been in 1928—huddled downtown in the area between the CN and CP railway stations. "The neighborhood beer parlor with its healthy atmosphere of friendly neighborliness has, therefore, not developed," the report noted. It went on to say, "some of the licensed parlors are now in undesirable locations and are of an unpleasant and socially questionable type."[44] The downtown beer parlors were thus cut off from the wealthy areas of the city, a case of spatial segregation by class. The Bracken report did not use the term "skid row" in this instance, but that's probably what it had in mind.[45]

A "committee of five men interested in social problems" visited Winnipeg's beer parlors in the winter of 1954–55 at the behest of the commission. The term "social" problems" suggests what the committee expected to find. Its report constructs a class-based masculine culture in which "laboring class" patrons attended the parlors. The report describes with almost anthropological precision the behaviour of the patrons.[46] Social clubs and veterans clubs, while discussed in the report, did not warrant a visitation.

It was to the working-class beer parlor that the Bracken Commission turned when contemplating the flaws and possibilities of liquor laws. The regulation of alcohol has historically focussed on controlling space—creating "a kind of moral architecture to shape customers' (and owners') behaviour."[47] This concept wasn't lost on the authors of the Bracken report. With respect to Manitoba's drinking establishments, they noted that beer parlor restrictions that forbid food, frivolity, music, entertainment, or games of any sort ensure that only one activity is possible: "All in all it may be said that Manitoba beer parlors are places where men may drink and drink and may do nothing else."[48]

Throughout the discussion in the 1950s, normalized heterosexuality was held up as the model of what mixed drinking could accomplish. When drinking was promoted, it was inevitably something that a husband and his wife did together. It was an argument that assigned women the role of moderating influence. The International Union of United Brewery, Flour, Cereal, Soft Drink and Distillery Workers argued in 1950 that "'Mixed' parlors and sale of beer with meals will do much to make drinking here 'the civilized and pleasurable custom it should be.'"[49] Meanwhile, United College professor R.N. Halstead suggested alcohol needs to be "placed before the public in places where a person can dine and drink in the presence of his wife and friends."[50] Winnipeg alderman H.B. Scott also had lofty expectations of what the introduction of women would do for mixed drinking parlors and cocktail bars: "profanity would disappear" and "drunkenness would decrease."[51] Women were part of the new moral architecture being considered for drinking establishments. In this discussion, we hear echoes of Adele Perry's *On the Edge of Empire: Gender, Race, and the Making of British Columbia, 1849–1871*: "White women's importance lay not as autonomous political subjects but rather in their ability to shape and control white male behaviour, as *objects* that would shape the behaviours and identities of the true *subjects* of colonization, white men."[52] Nearly one hundred years later, the same discourse was alive and well, with women called upon to tame men. Of course, the possibility of women getting drunk was never part of the discussion.

Even when supporters of mixed drinking did argue from a pure "equality" point of view, they centred the argument within the traditional heterosexual home. As an unnamed source quoted in the *Winnipeg Tribune* said in 1953: "Women are now represented in every sphere of government, business and professions and, as homemakers, they are said to control the spending of 80 per cent of the family income. Surely, with that record, it is safe to assume they are mature enough to drink intelligently."[53] The Manitoba Provincial Council of Women and the Manitoba Women's Institute surveyed 2460 women and found that the majority in Winnipeg favoured some form of mixed drinking. The people in favour suggested that the "wife should be able to go in, rather than to sit in the car waiting for her husband." As with most arguments in favour of mixed drinking laws, the discussion was framed around a husband and wife. The notion of a single woman going in to meet a single man was not put forward.[54] Those speaking against mixed drinking used similar language to make their points: "who would look after the children?" It "would tend to break up the home." Or, playing on the fears of dangerous heterosexuality, that it was simply "demoralizing."[55] Similarly, the United Church of Canada quoted the Bracken report in arguing that there is a "close association between the brothel and the bar."[56] The discourse linking prostitution to alcohol would be repeated often by critics of more liberal drinking laws, but with little uptake among the general public.

In the run-up to the release of the Bracken Commission, a survey of people reported that they expected little change. Implicit in their pessimism was the view that the existing laws were antiquated and that more liberal drinking laws represented modernity. The commission's ambivalence about modernity seemed apparent to all. As a "businesswoman" stated: "How can we expect a fair liquor law with a teetotaler like Bracken heading the commission? We'll be stuck with a horse and buggy law forever." Similarly a "housewife" said, "I guess the recommendations will depend on what the temperance people think" and a "salesclerk" added, "No change. Manitoba leaders are too frightened of the old-fashioned thinking that's popular in this province."[57] Even temperance supporters linked access to alcohol with modernity. In an appearance before the commission in 1954, Women's Christian Temperance Union executive member Mrs. W.W. Thompson had to state repeatedly to the commission that the WCTU had only 200 members. They were incredulous, having expected it to represent a larger force. Thompson explained the dwindling numbers of the group: "The old people are dying and the young people—I imagine a good many of them are drinking, so they won't join."[58]

When Bill 14, outlining the new liquor laws, was brought forward in February 1956, the lead for the story was: "A blueprint for future drinking customs in Manitoba—relegating the present drab all-male beer parlors to a minor role—was unveiled by the provincial government Thursday."[59] Similarly, when the report was released in September 1955, the *Winnipeg Tribune* headed off its article by mentioning that "it urged equality of drinking on a sweeping basis for every Manitoban including women and Indians over 21."[60]

After all the discussion on beer parlors, they were the one establishment that was almost ignored by the changing laws. The report called for mixed drinking in restaurants and the new cocktail lounges, but beer parlors were denied that option.

Some male citizens had warned the commission that "to allow mixed drinking in parlors would destroy this last 'stronghold for males only.'"[61] In fact, the addition of a supper-hour closing and increased food and drink options were the only significant changes made to beer parlors. Linking of masculinity to space certainly seemed borne out in Winnipeg by men's comments on supper-hour closures at the beer parlor: "It just isn't self respecting for a man to leave a parlor this early," and "my wife will figure something's wrong when she sees me coming home."[62] But the rationale for keeping women out of beer parlors went beyond nostalgia for lost masculine space: "The Commission, having surveyed the on-premise picture as a whole, felt that, while some of the present beer parlors were attractive, many were not acceptable for women. We decided, therefore, that though women must be recognized as citizens having equal rights with men, the privilege of public drinking should not be extended to them in beer parlors."[63]

To put it more succinctly, women were equal but still in need of protection. We shouldn't be surprised. Women were considered vulnerable to men when alcohol was involved—a critical discourse when beer parlors were being labelled as strictly masculine space. Beer parlors in Winnipeg were marked by class. When the report stated that it did not want women going into beer parlors, what it was really stating was that it did not want women in working-class establishments. However, women would be allowed to drink in new establishments, with the hope that these new spaces would be better, due to the proximity of food and their sex's "moderating influence."[64] The province was still in the business of trying to control space, and this time women were being used as part of the control mechanism.

For its part, the Bracken report offered one other explanation for opening up the liquor privilege in Manitoba: people simply were not obeying the old laws. As Bracken noted: "We cannot hope to hold people to a law they do not believe in. We hope, by producing facts and figures with our report, to make the people of Manitoba say, 'this is a good law, we'll go along with it.'"[65] Rather than legislated moderation, the Bracken report argued for self-control.[66] In practice the law still attempted to control space in all the new establishments and even outline exactly what new foods could be introduced to beer parlors.

On 1 March 1957, following local option votes across the province, new drinking establishments began opening their doors. In Winnipeg, the Royal Alexandra Hotel's dining room could now serve liquor. The *Winnipeg Tribune* focussed its story on a couple, Mr. and Mrs. G.R. Saunders of Winnipeg, as they shared a bottle of wine in this "new and exciting experience." With twenty members of the staff watching, waiter Mauro Martinelli paused until the stroke of twelve and then "tipped the first few drops into a glass, Mr. Saunders tasted it, savored it, and nodded assent."[67] The *Winnipeg Tribune* trumpeted it as a "new era in the history of Manitoba" and a "revolution." It was both and neither. Heterosexuality was triumphant. Drinking spaces were redefined as heterosocial space, but it was the man who gave approval for the wine. For all the new heterosocial space that had been created, gender hierarchies were still in place.

The most interesting parts of the 1950s liquor discussion in Manitoba were happening under the table. Critics tried to restrain the debate with familiar suggestions that alcohol and women bred prostitution. Men, of course, could not be trusted around women because once they were into the sauce they would lose their moral judgement. Even the argument for equal access to alcohol was made in specific gendered terms: that women who could be trusted to raise children and run a household should be able to handle the responsibility of drinking alcohol, or that a man and wife ought to be able to have a drink together. Women in this discussion were always part of something more, whether it be family or marriage. And socialized drinking was always discussed in the context of a married couple sharing a drink. How those couples might have met was a question that was rarely put on the table. City police morality inspector Peter Cafferty offers a glimpse in a report to the Manitoba legislature in 1950 focussed on the abuse of banquet permits: "There are cases where 400 or 500 persons are assembled in a hall, 50 to 75 per cent women and girls, and it's an easy matter to make money on sale of liquor."[68] Clearly, they were not all walking into these banquets as married couples, and not all the women—indeed few, if any—were prostitutes.

The reality was that men and women were meeting over drinks in the 1950s, whether through clubs, banquets, or the smuggled bottle of alcohol that was poured under the table in a supper club. The Bracken report acknowledged this reality when it said a law was only enforceable when it met with approval from the people. By the time the province of Manitoba was drafting its revised liquor laws, alcohol and heterosocial space were already united. But still, what of all the problems associated with alcohol that were spelled out at length in the first half of the Bracken report? Blame the beer parlors. The sins of alcohol were visited upon the working-class beer parlors, just as the saloon had born the brunt of prohibition anger. The beer parlors were irredeemable masculine space. And in the end, that homosocial nature was their undoing, for while clubs and dance halls could be sold as locations for proper heterosexuality, the beer parlor never could. So in the 1950s, as heterosocial space—space for marriage and space, though they were loath to admit it, for dating—grew, the homosocial space of the beer parlor was the odd "man" out.

Notes

1   Joan W. Scott, "Gender: A Useful Category of Historical Analysis," in *The Feminist History Reader*, Sue Morgan, ed. (New York: Routledge, 2006), 133–148.

2   "Bracken Heads Liquor Probe," *Winnipeg Tribune*, 13 April 1954.

3   Kathy Peiss, *Cheap Amusements: Working Women and Leisure in Turn-of-the-Century New York* (Philadelphia: Temple University Press, 1986), 4–5.

4   Ibid., 40.

5   Ibid., 28.

6   Beth Bailey, *From Front Porch to Back Seat* (Baltimore: Johns Hopkins University Press, 1988), 13.

7   Carolyn Strange, *Toronto's Girl Problem: The Perils and Pleasures of the City, 1880–1930* (Toronto: University of Toronto Press, 1995), 3 and 5.

8   Ibid., 10.

9   Craig Heron, *Booze: A Distilled History* (Toronto: Between the Lines, 2003), 180.

10 Robert A. Campbell, *Sit Down and Drink Your Beer: Regulating Vancouver's Beer Parlours, 1925–1954.* (Toronto: University of Toronto Press, 2001), 59, 63, and 75.

11 Heron, *Booze*, 290.

12 Campbell, *Sit Down and Drink Your Beer*, 75–76.

13 Geoffrey Bernard Toews, "The Boons and Banes of Booze: The Liquor Trade in Rural Manitoba, 1929–1939," *Manitoba History* 50 (October 2005): 20–21.

14 Val Werier, "Behind the News: Law Allows Women Beer By the Glass," *Winnipeg Tribune*, 20 September 1952.

15 Mariana Valverde, *Diseases of the Will: Alcohol and the Dilemmas of Freedom* (Cambridge: Cambridge University Press, 1998), 97.

16 Ibid., 158.

17 Ibid., 159.

18 Campbell, *Sit Down and Drink Your Beer*, 108.

19 "Liquor Nets $4 ½ Million In Province," *Winnipeg Tribune*, 28 February 1946; "Manitoba Spending on Liquor Attacked," *Winnipeg Tribune*, 14 February 1949; "Mixed Drinking Question not Topical," *Winnipeg Tribune*, 10 March 1949; and "Province Says No to Cocktail Bars," *Winnipeg Tribune*, 29 March 1949. (Don't mistake the "No" for a policy statement. The story was gleaned from an exchange between governing and opposition parties.)

20 Val Werier, "Mixed Drinking? We've had it for Many Years," *Winnipeg Tribune*, 20 August 1955.

21 *Report of the Manitoba Liquor Enquiry Commission*, 20.

22 "Liquor Probe to Study Hotel Control," *Winnipeg Tribune*, 26 October 1950.

23 Valverde, *Diseases of the Will*, 97.

24 Juba was elected as Winnipeg mayor in 1956, just as the local option votes were giving the thumbs up to mixed drinking in Winnipeg.

25 "Temperance Leader Urges Hold-Off on New Outlets: 'All Canada Eyes Liquor Session,'" *Winnipeg Tribune*, 20 February 1956.

26 Heron, *Booze*, 168.

27 "The Women want Mixed Drinking," *Winnipeg Tribune*, 18 November 1953.

28 "WCTU Approves Selling Cocktails," *Winnipeg Tribune*, 21 October 1954; "Request Changes," *Winnipeg Tribune*, 22 July 1954.

29 "Bracken Heads Liquor Probe," *Winnipeg Tribune*, 13 April 1954.

30   *The Report of the Manitoba Liquor Enquiry Commission*, 5.

31   "Stinson Attacks Liquor 'Remedy,'" *Winnipeg Tribune*, 29 February 1956. Stinson was critical of its recommendations. He was pleased with the temperance elements.

32   *Report of the Manitoba Liquor Enquiry Commission*, 32.

33   Ibid., 36 and 39.

34   Ibid., 40, 45, 47, 48, and 106.

35   Ibid., 49, 55, 73, 216, and 226. "On Guard Manitoba! It All Began in a Glass of Beer," *Winnipeg Tribune*, 19 September 1956.

36   *Report of the Manitoba Liquor Enquiry Commission*, 256.

37   Ibid., 266.

38   Ibid., 349.

39   The report does comment on liquor habits across the world, and some of the comments, particularly around the Irish, play into ethnic stereotypes. See *Report of the Manitoba Liquor Enquiry Commission*, 171, 173, 175, and 178.

40   Gordon Sinclair, "Selkirk Bootleg Outlets Scored," *Winnipeg Tribune*, 16 July 1954. "Local Option Vote Set to Permit Treaty Indians to Drink Liquor," *Winnipeg Tribune*, 16 April 1956.

41   "Inquiry Favors Sale of Liquor to Indians," *Winnipeg Tribune*, 9 November 1951.

42   I reviewed *Winnipeg Tribune* clipping file "Liquor category" between 1943 and 1957 and found no interviews with Aboriginal people.

43   Gordon Sinclair, "Probe Chief Seeks Indian Pow-Wow on Fire Water," *Winnipeg Tribune*, 7 August 1954.

44   *Report of the Manitoba Liquor Enquiry Commission*, 407–408.

45   Campbell, *Sit Down and Drink Your Beer*, 108–109.

46   *Report of the Manitoba Liquor Enquiry Commission*, 413–414.

47   Heron, *Booze*, 281.

48   *Report of the Manitoba Liquor Enquiry Commission*, 282 and 404.

49   Ben Lepkin, "'Mixed' Parlors Urged," *Winnipeg Tribune*, 12 December 1950.

50   "'Saloon Era' Liquor Laws Under Attack," *Winnipeg Tribune*, 20 November 1952.

51   "Ald. Scott Wants Winnipeggers to Have Say on Bars: Let People Set Own Liquor Rules," *Winnipeg Tribune*, 15 July 1954.

52   Adele Perry, *On The Edge of Empire: Gender, Race, and the Making of British Columbia, 1849–1871* (Toronto: University of Toronto Press, 2006), 146. Emphasis in original.

53   "The Women Want Mixed Drinking," *Winnipeg Tribune*, 18 November 1953.

54   "Liquor Outlet Hike Opposed by Women," *Winnipeg Tribune*, 27 October 1954.

55   Ibid.

56   Peter Desbarats, "Wets Start Gentle Drive In Favor of More Outlets," *Winnipeg Tribune*, 17 October 1956. "On Guard Manitoba! It All Began in a Glass of Beer," *Winnipeg Tribune*, 19 September 1956.

57   "Nobody Seems Very Hopeful," *Winnipeg Tribune*, 30 July 1955.

58   "WCTU Approves Selling Cocktails," *Winnipeg Tribune*, 21 October 1954.

59   "'Social Glass' Outlets Urged," *Winnipeg Tribune*, 24 February 1956.

60   "Self-Control Drinking Set for Manitobans," *Winnipeg Tribune*, 3 September 1955.

61   "New Pub Game: Beat the Clock," *Winnipeg Tribune*, 17 July 1956.

62   Ibid.

63   *Report of the Manitoba Liquor Enquiry Commission*, 434.

64   Ibid., 436.

65 George Brimmel, "They Study Laws .... But Drink Probers Won't Enter Pubs," *Winnipeg Tribune*, 24 September 1954.

66 *Report of the Manitoba Liquor Enquiry Commission*, 100.

67 "Glass of Wine Heralds Era," *Winnipeg Tribune*, 1 March 1957.

68 "Morality Chief Charges Banquet Permits Abused," *Winnipeg Tribune*, 25 October 1950.

Winnipeg's Palliser Furniture in the Context of Mennonite Views on Industrial Relations, 1974–1996

Janis Thiessen

The movement of Manitoba's Mennonites from rural to urban centres began in the early twentieth century but accelerated after the Second World War. Three reasons have been suggested for this migration in Manitoba: increased mobility due to improved access to transportation, the immigration of urbanized Russian Mennonites in the post-war years, and the close proximity to Winnipeg of the two Mennonite reserves in Manitoba.[1] The effect on the population of Mennonites in Winnipeg was dramatic: in 1951, 3460 of the city's total population of 356,000 (or 0.97 percent) were Mennonites; in 1971, 17,850 of 540,000 (3.3 percent); and in 1991, 21,900 of 652,000 (3.4 percent).[2] One of the consequences was the emergence of a group of influential Mennonite business leaders in the last half of the twentieth century, of which Palliser Furniture's DeFehr family became one of the most successful. The increased engagement with industrial capitalism that resulted from the post-war urban migration required a renegotiation of Mennonite understandings of labour relations. Over time, Mennonites' outright rejection of unionism on religious grounds was modified, though it attained only ambivalent opposition and never reached full acceptance.[3]

The Mennonite Church and Industrial Relations, 1930s–1960s

In Manitoba, the decade of the 1970s was notable for its labour activism. A union-supported government, the New Democratic Party, under the leadership of Edward Schreyer, was elected to office for the first time in 1969. It revised the *Labour Relations Act* in 1972, granting more favourable terms to workers regarding compulsory union dues check-off, unfair labour practices, and union certification. High inflation, together with wage and price controls, resulted in a record number of strikes in the mid-1970s both in the province and nationally.[4] Among Manitoba Mennonites, employers and employees alike, the strengthened labour movement of the 1970s was a concern.

For decades, Mennonites in North America had rejected involvement in unions, a stance which stemmed in part from their religious objections to communism and socialism. A number of North American Mennonite denominations and organizations issued statements on these issues from the 1930s through the 1960s.[5] Union membership was refused by Mennonites in part because the threat of strike action was considered an exercise of force on the part of labour. Management use of force, through the control of labour conditions and terms of employment and the ability to terminate employees, rarely was critiqued in the same manner.[6]

The Mennonite Church, one of several major denominations within the larger body of Mennonites in North America, passed a resolution against union membership as early as 1937.[7] The resolution made reference to the most often cited scripture passage used by Mennonites to defend their position against organized labour: Christians should not join unions because of the apostle Paul's admonition: "Be ye not unequally yoked together with unbelievers: for what fellowship hath righteousness with unrighteousness? and what communion hath light with darkness? And what concord hath Christ with Belial? or what part hath he that believeth with an infidel? And what agreement hath the temple of God with idols? for ye are the temple of the living God; as God hath said, I will dwell in them, and walk in them; and I will be their God, and they shall be my people."[8]

The resolution concluded that church members could not join a union. In an effort to be balanced, church members who were also employers were informed that they "should by fairness and liberality seek to forestall labor dissatisfaction among their employees." Somewhat unrealistically, the resolution noted that the church itself should, "in anything that savors of class strife," maintain impartiality, "not favoring the unscriptural practices of either capital or labor."

Four years later, a broader statement on industrial relations was approved by the denomination. Class conflict was condemned as a power struggle emanating from "an absence of the Christian principle of love."[9] The statement echoed Mennonite theologian Guy Hershberger's advocacy of passive meekness,[10] declaring that "Biblical nonresistance enjoins submission even to injustice rather than to engage in conflict." As a consequence, Christian employees could not be involved in unions because of the threat of force implied in "the monopolistic closed shop, the boycott, the picket line and the strike." At the same time, Christian employers were not to join manufacturers associations if the group's purpose was to counteract the labour movement through use of "the lockout, the blacklist, detective agencies, espionage, strike-breakers and munitions." Mennonite employees were to be assisted in negotiating their exemption from union membership through the creation of a Committee on Industrial Relations.[11]

A study conference of the Mennonite Church in 1951 acknowledged that members were not adhering consistently to the 1941 statement.[12] Conference participants concluded that they needed to produce educational literature guiding Mennonites on the types of employment contracts that were compatible with their religious beliefs. This inconsistency, they wrote, weakened "the position of the church on the entire question of nonresistance and the recognition we seek to obtain for that position..." By 1954, the Mennonite Church softened its official position. The Committee on Economic and Social Relations (formerly the Committee on Industrial Relations) acknowledged in 1954 that unions "serve a useful purpose for the maintenance of justice and a balance of power in a sub-Christian society." Mennonites were free to "cooperate with the union (as ... with the state) in so far as doing so does not conflict with ... Christian testimony."[13] This brief survey of one denomination's struggles with the principles of the union movement illustrates the context of Mennonite discussion as members of this once-rural community entered cities in the middle decades of the twentieth century. The denomination was slowly adjusting to the idea that the direct relation between individuals and their God might have to be filtered through state and union but this view was far from being unanimous.

As an emphasis on social responsibility took hold among North American Mennonites, opposition to union membership declined, particularly among more educated urban Mennonites of higher socio-economic status. Surveys conducted in the late 1980s found 54 percent of Canadian and American Mennonites did not oppose union membership.[14] Nonetheless, the percentage of North American Mennonites who actually were members of labour unions remained very low (5 percent in 1972, 6 percent in 1989).[15]

Manitoba Mennonites and the Canadian Union Movement in the 1970s

Manitoba's Mennonites experienced the union debate in the 1970s and 1980s. At some Manitoba workplaces, Mennonite workers strongly resisted unions on the basis of religious convictions; a number sought exemption from union membership in the 1970s. Their situation prompted the intervention of Mennonite Central Committee (MCC) Manitoba.[16] MCC Manitoba chair Peter Peters and Peace and Social Concerns Committee members Diedrich Gerbrandt and Harold Jantz met with Russell Paulley, Manitoba's Minister of Labour, on 17 December 1974. They asked him to guarantee workers' rights to reject union membership on grounds of conscience. Section 68(3) of the *Labour Relations Act* allowed employees working under collective agreements to remit their dues to a charity rather than the union, provided that they had religiously based conscientious objections to joining and paying dues to a union.[17] MCC asserted that the Manitoba Labour Board had been "turning down all applications for exemption [under this section]. Among the eight or so cases heard by the board during the past months have been three Mennonites."[18] Paulley responded with a letter in January 1975, observing that the delegation's concern was with the labour board's interpretation of Section 68(3) and not with the legislation itself. He advised them to address their concerns directly to the labour board.[19]

Schreyer's government had amended the legislation from its original formulation. In support of the Rand Formula, the New Democrats had argued that no one should be exempted from paying union dues. When the bill reached the committee stage, however, the objections of the Plymouth Brethren were taken into account. This group "believed that a certain master-servant relationship exists between employers and employees" and declared that they "would in fact sooner quit their jobs than to pay dues to a union, because by paying such dues they felt they were sinning against the Commandments of God."[20] Accordingly, section 68(3) was proposed and passed. The government noted, however, that "the amendment was designed to make allowances for specific religious—i.e., ecclesiastical—beliefs, and not to exempt everyone who is morally opposed to unions."[21]

It was this distinction between ecclesiastical and personal moral beliefs that ultimately proved problematic for Henry Funk, a Mennonite baker who sought exemption under Section 68(3). He was fired from his job at McGavin Toastmaster in Winnipeg for his refusal to join the union as was required by the collective agreement. He applied to the Manitoba Labour Board in 1975, requesting exemption. As a member of the Mennonite Brethren Church, Funk declared he objected to "the violent tactics of unions" and to taking an oath of membership. His application was dismissed because the relevant section was not applicable to his circumstances: Funk had been hired in violation of the collective agreement, which had a clause requiring that new employees be hired only after signing an application to join the union.

Even in the absence of this clause, the chair of the Manitoba Labour Board, Murdoch MacKay, observed that Funk's application would not have been successful. The Mennonite Brethren Church had no official stance against unions at that time, and so Funk's opposition to joining one was founded upon personal rather than religious beliefs, MacKay contended:

> [Mr. Funk] did not testify that his Church ever directly forbade him to join a union. He felt that the tone of the sermons were against unions but there was never any direct reference to them.... [His minister's] testimony was that the Church did not have a rule against joining a Union nor was it treated as a

sin. [The minister] thought most ministers of his Church would suggest that unionism was contrary to their beliefs but would not specifically preach against unions.... The Mennonite Church has some rules, [tenets] or sanctions, the breach of which are clearly contrary to church law. Joining a union falls short of a breach of their churches' [sic] laws and is only detrimental if the conscience of the adherent feels that way.[22]

Though objecting to coercion by the union, Funk was not opposed to the coercion of the courts. He took his case to the Manitoba Court of Appeals, which ruled in his favour in 1976.[23] The question the court had to decide was whether the labour board had adjudicated on the basis of Funk's personal beliefs or those of the Mennonite Brethren Church to which he belonged; if the latter, then the board had overstepped its bounds. The court found that the position of the Mennonite Brethren Church on union membership was irrelevant; since Funk believed that union membership violated his personal religious beliefs, he was exempt under Section 68(3) of the Manitoba *Labour Relations Act*.

Henry Funk described his experience at a meeting of the Canadian Mennonite Health Assembly (CMHA) held 23 to 25 April 1975. The group met in Winnipeg to discuss the role of labour unions in Mennonite-operated hospitals and personal care homes.[24] The assembly raised $700 to fund Funk's appeal, believing his court case "could well set a precedent in our position to organized labor." Two Mennonite nurses discussed their experience with the Manitoba Nurses Association, and a representative of a Mennonite nursing home outlined "his board's position in the event that a union organized his staff."[25] John Redekop, professor of political science at the University of Waterloo, delivered a lecture on labour-management relations from a biblical perspective.[26] The event culminated in a recommendation by those assembled that MCC and the CMHA "should work together to make our [Mennonite] constituency more aware of the labor laws of the areas in which we live, and how we could best respond to them."[27]

The question of union membership accordingly was raised at the annual meeting of MCC Manitoba in Winnipeg on 22 November 1975. The meeting was attended by 327 church delegates and 250 guests.[28] Peace and Social Concerns committee member Harold Jantz requested that Mennonite churches examine the question of whether church members should join unions and suggested that churches offer assistance to conscientious objectors to unions. His presentation "sparked a discussion which indicated that Mennonites have differences of opinion on the degree to which they should become involved in secular structures, such as unions, courts, and political parties."[29]

Jantz advocated the use of the courts (much as Funk had done) and of letters to the appropriate government officials as two methods whereby Mennonites could seek exemption from union membership. Jake Neufeld, Altona postmaster and president of his union local, stated that he had "refused to call the 17 members to a strike" when indoor postal workers struck nationally that summer.[30] June Buhr, a Mennonite employed at the Winkler hospital, explained that Mennonite nurses objected to unions because strikes left patients without care.[31] A Mennonite's allegiance, she said, was to God and Christ, not the union. Further, the Bible taught people "to be content with their wages, and not to 'render evil for evil or to exercise vengeance.'" Not everyone at the meeting agreed with the wholesale criticism of unions. According to a memo recording the discussion, "Comments from the floor also cautioned employers not to take advantage of employees and a suggestion was made that churches should speak to the matter of underpaying employees also." The assembly passed a resolution that MCC Peace and Social Concerns be given a mandate to "be a resource and to represent individuals and groups who request assistance" on the issue of labour relations.[32]

MCC Manitoba responded by organizing three seminars on labour-management relations in Steinbach, Winkler, and Winnipeg on 27, 28, and 29 January 1976. A total of more than 200 people attended, including representatives from Loewen Windows (a Mennonite-owned manufacturer of wood windows in Steinbach, Manitoba), Triple E (a Mennonite-owned manufacturer of recreational vehicles in Winkler, Manitoba), and the Mennonite owner of Kitchen Gallery (a cabinet manufacturer in Winnipeg).[33] The pastor of Steinbach's Grace Mennonite Church explained to the local newspaper that the motivation for the seminar in part was "the unhappiness of the postal strike" of 1975. The question of Mennonite participation in organized labour had been caused by their post-war movement to the cities, he maintained. "While we didn't want to become part of the labor unions because there's something about the power strategy that we didn't like, urbanization has simply demanded involvement."[34] The seminars were advertised in church bulletins throughout Manitoba: "With the present unhappy spirit in relations of labor and management toward one another, many Christians are increasingly asking themselves what their response ought to be. These seminars will attempt to give some answers, from a biblical understanding, of the kind of relationships which acknowledge the Lordship of Christ and bring about reconciliation."[35]

The perspective presented at these important seminars was clearly anti-union. MCC's Harold Jantz declared, "There is no reason why we have to buy the adversary concept."[36] The intention of the organizers was to invite as speakers individuals working in "a business or industry where they do not have a union but rather some alternative means of relating to management."[37] Instead, the speakers were University of Waterloo political science professor John Redekop and Gerald Vandezande of the Christian Labour Association of Canada. Redekop described Canadian labour-management relations in the 1970s as being "in a very sorry state."[38] The responsibility for this situation, he said, lay with workers consumed with materialist desires for whom "quitting time [is] the only highlight of the working day." Professionals, whom Redekop placed in a separate (and superior) category, also suffered from this "lack of purpose." He suggested that workers of all sorts were preoccupied with the false notion that "society owes me a constantly improving living standard."[39] And he criticized Canada's labour movement for its militancy and lack of respect for signed contracts and the law: "While the average taxpayer who strays from the straight and narrow path of the law quickly finds himself subjected to law enforcement, governments at all levels nowadays wait for days and weeks while strikers who are blatantly flouting explicit back-to-work directives deliberate at their own good pace whether or not they will obey the law. Almost invariably governments stand idly by, waiting patiently. This seed of dereliction can bear only bitter fruit."[40]

After proffering this negative assessment of labour, Redekop continued with a critique of both Christian employers and employees. Among Christians, "class antagonism, selfish individualism, unchristian capitalism, sloth, insensitivity, economic blackmail, exploitation, and the propensity to see employees as commodities rather than people are much too common."[41] He declared that Mennonites must accept the biblical command and refuse to be unequally yoked with unbelievers. Redekop thus introduced the Bible in his veiled condemnation of Mennonite members of labour unions.

Despite his apparent attack on the principle of unionization in the workplace, Professor Redekop did not offer uncritical support for management either. Though he encouraged workers to see issues from "management's point of view," he also urged them to participate in unions: "As employees have we tried to influence union policy? Do we attend meetings? Do we speak up and spell out our principles? Do we stand for elective office? Or do we merely draw back and complain?" And he challenged employers to listen to their workers: "Do we honestly try to see issues from the other side of the table? As employers do we indulge in hatred and innuendo provided these are directed against unions? Do we ever seriously look for positive dimensions of unionism?"[42]

Redekop concluded with an outline of a biblical view of labour, asserting that work was part of the order of creation, part of a meaningful life and service to

God. He repeated his reference to 2 Corinthians 6:14–16, observing that a Christian "weighs very carefully the entire matter of being yoked together with materialistic pagans,"[43] thereby implying that Christians could not be union members. And yet he declared that since love rather than nonresistance was a biblical imperative, then both management and labour

> as a last resort, have the right to use power, short of physical violence or psychological destruction, to press their claim for justice as they see it. Management can go so far as to dissolve the enterprise and let some other firm fill the void and under certain circumstances school boards, hospital boards, city councils, and private bosses have the right to lock out slothful employees. Labour can go so far as to strike but employees have no right to prevent others from accepting the employment conditions which they have rejected. In this manner both sides can exercise freedom of choice for themselves but they have no right to force their decisions on others.[44]

For all its qualifications and evasions, Redekop's presentation was decidedly anti-union. The picture he sketched of management rights and employee individualism flew in the face of contemporary labour-capital relations in the province of Manitoba.

Speaker Gerald Vandezande was even more direct in his condemnation of unions. He distributed a list of objections to unions that had been prepared by his organization, the Christian Labour Association of Canada (CLAC). These objections included unions' "acceptance of coercion and force," and such union practices as closed shops, membership oaths, and adversarial relations with management.[45] Also on his list was the CLAC's objection to the Manitoba Labour Board's rulings regarding Section 68(3): "The demand for a formal church rule against union membership, as the Labour Board has demanded, fails to recognize the nature of the church as a voluntary association... [and] fails to recognize as well that the exercise of conscience is precisely the practice of taking a general teaching of the church and applying it to a particular situation." Vandezande clearly had not been satisfied by the reply he had received from Schreyer's representative in 1974. The CLAC document concluded that Christians should not have to become "economic martyrs" by quitting jobs that required them to join a union, though it suggested that they should be willing to do so.[46]

From these illustrations, it is apparent that Vandezande and Redekop held nearly identical views. Both promoted the CLAC, arguing that too many unions "demand allegiance above God" and that the CLAC advocated "reconciliation" rather than adversarialism. In advocating this approach to labour-management relations, they were endorsing a view proposed by members of the Christian Reform religious tradition (Dutch Calvinist), who had founded the CLAC in 1952 as an alternative to the mainstream union movement in Canada. Redekop and Vandezande thus were opposing the "adversarial nature" of Canada's collective bargaining system and rejecting affiliation with the Canadian Labour Congress.[47] As Redekop told the participants in the Steinbach seminar, "some might have to change vocations or [what would be far worse] deny faith and ethics."[48]

By the 1990s, the suspicion regarding organized labour had largely evaporated. The debates of the 1970s were replaced by ambivalent acceptance of unions in general, if not in particular cases, as evidenced by Mennonite church statements. There were few, if any, Mennonite denominations that explicitly prohibited union membership in the 1990s.[49] The confession of faith of the combined Mennonite Church and General Conference Mennonite Church, adopted in 1995, makes no mention of union membership in the article that traditionally would have included it: Article 22, on Peace, Justice, and Nonresistance.[50] The Confession of Faith of the Mennonite Brethren Conference has an Article on work, rest, and the Lord's day. It does not address labour union membership, but states: "As creatures made in the image of God, Christians imitate the Creator by working faithfully as they are able. They are to use their abilities and resources to glorify God and to serve others. Because they bear the name of Christ, all believers are called to work honestly and diligently and to treat others with respect and dignity."[51]

Nonetheless, not all Mennonites had abandoned their concerns regarding organized labour. John Redekop still viewed union membership as a threat to Anabaptist Christian understandings of non-violence, though his stance had mellowed considerably from the position he had espoused at the 1976 MCC Manitoba seminars. The *Canadian Mennonite Encyclopedia* entry on labour unions, which he wrote in 1999, concludes:

> Many [Mennonite] leaders and congregations have not known what advice to give striking teachers, nurses, physicians, factory workers, and, especially in Canada, postal workers and other government employees. The situation becomes even more difficult when Mennonites belonging to the same congregation find themselves involved on opposite sides during a crisis situation or when church members find themselves caught up in illegal strikes or lockouts.... On balance, Mennonites have had major difficulty successfully relating the peace position to their interaction with labor unions. In the years ahead ethical issues dealing with labor unions will be one of the most important practical testing grounds of Christians committed to the way of peace and reconciliation.[52]

While some Mennonites in the 1990s still believed that union membership was problematic, the necessity of living and working in an urban (and at times unionized) environment meant that they were no longer willing to condemn unions out of hand as they had done two decades earlier.

Palliser Furniture: A Case Study in Mennonite Business Leadership

Winnipeg's Palliser Furniture, one of the most successful Mennonite-owned businesses in the province, can be taken as an illustration of the ambivalent views of Mennonites on the subject of unions in labour-management relations.[53] This story begins in 1979, when Dave DeFehr, one of two sons of the company founder and at that time a key figure in the company, ruminated on the responsibilities of a Mennonite in the western world's capitalist system. The story ends, at least for the purposes of this discussion, in a unionizing campaign in 1996. The two aspects of this story—employee share ownership and unionized workforces—illustrate the ambivalence that has marked Mennonite views of the capitalist workplace.

Both employee share ownership and profit sharing at Palliser Furniture were initiated by then co-owner Dave DeFehr, son of the company's founder.[54] In a letter to his father and brothers in 1979, he argued that the family's religious beliefs necessitated the implementation of these programs:

> Some of the reasons for making the above suggestions come from the way I understand the Bible on this matter, some from purely pragmatic considerations and some from a mixture of the two.... Western society has developed an economic system in which great disparities between owners and employees are possible and accepted (??)[55] by society as a whole. Consequently any company which reduces these disparities even marginally is looked upon favourably by its employees. I would suggest however, that our point of reference should not be Western society, but rather the biblical teaching on this matter and secondarily an objective sense of fairness.... As Christians we believe wealth and material possession are ultimately owned by God and are to be used to God's glory.... I think much of what happens in the western economic world is unchristian. On the other hand, because of the great degree of flexibility within our economic system, a Christian business can exist and flourish.[56]

It may have been the labour unrest of 1970s Manitoba that prompted DeFehr's ruminations. The question of how to adhere to Christian principles while participating in urban industrial capitalism was one that many Manitoba Mennonites—employers and employees alike—were confronting at the time.

The Mennonite ownership of Palliser Furniture offered at least a partial answer to this question with their provision of profit sharing and employee share ownership plans in the early 1980s. Profit sharing was introduced in 1981. Twenty percent of profits before taxes were set aside for distribution among employees. The amount an employee received was determined by "his/her level of earnings, the success (or lack of success) of the division in which he/she is employed, years of service with the company, and level of responsibility."[57] Full-time workers were eligible for participation after nine months' employment. Half the bonus was distributed as cash; half was deferred until retirement.[58] Management stressed that profit sharing was "not a substitute for adequate levels of pay or for future increases. The policy of Palliser Furniture is to pay wages and salaries equal to or greater than the industry average and to grant increases in line with changes in the cost of living."[59]

Management gave as reasons for initiation of the profit sharing plan its desire to enable employees to share in the company's success, and its belief that profit sharing would serve as a "catalyst" for greater "cooperation and understanding among employees." And it warned workers that the profit share was "an incentive bonus and not an automatic cheque."[60]

Palliser Furniture began offering non-voting shares to senior employees in 1982. Before making this decision, the DeFehr family and their lawyers debated what form employee share ownership should take: "would it be based on years of service, management level or those persons whom senior management would select as providing an incentive for employees to improve productivity and stay with the company as well as a reward for services rendered?"[61]

The DeFehrs were warned by their legal counsel, W.A. Redekopp, that employees who became shareholders often underwent an attitude change, becoming unwilling to "accept directions, authority and instructions from senior management."[62] Company expansions and acquisitions would become more difficult, Redekopp wrote, because "you are likely to be subject to criticism and at the very least will be required to answer questions in great detail as to why certain decisions were made. Requests will be made to see financial statements and you may be asked to devulge [sic] the salaries of the executives as well as any fringe benefits that are received, whether they are real or imagined by the employees, e.g. travel abroad, etc."

Making shares available to employees would not necessarily increase their loyalty to the company. However, "presumably some good will would be created among those employees who would be permitted to purchase shares. Hopefully this good will could be translated into higher productivity by all of the employees."[63]

The DeFehrs discussed the possibility of setting differences in the initial distribution of shares to compensate for the different degrees of seniority among employees.[64] Offering stock to long-term shop floor employees was viewed as the least likely possibility. Ultimately the decision was made to make non-voting shares available to those "with extra responsibility" after ten years' employment and to all others after fifteen years' employment.[65] Those eligible received an initial gift of shares equal in value to ten weeks' pay. In 1989, the eligibility requirement for all employees, regardless of level of responsibility, was set at ten years of service.[66] Only a small fraction of Palliser employees were shareholders in the late 1980s; it is unknown to what extent employee share ownership continued after that period.[67]

According to an academic study conducted in 1992, there were three types of profit sharing plans then in use in Canada. Some paid the profit share immediately (in cash or shares or both), some were deferred plans, and others were a combination of the two. Nationally, only 18 percent of private companies had profit-sharing plans. Of those companies, 75 percent had cash-based plans. The majority of them were created in the 1980s and allocated profit share according to a fixed percentage ranging from 1 to 33 percent with a median of 10 percent. Only 30 percent of private companies with profit-sharing plans allocated the payout according to employee salary. In the majority of these plans (73 percent), all full-time employees were eligible participants.[68]

Whether employee share ownership and profit-sharing plans are necessary outgrowths of a Mennonite faith that emphasizes mutual aid or conditions for preserving a non-union workforce is a moot point. It is a small minority of Canadian companies that offer either plan; certainly not all that do so are Mennonite-owned. In the early 1990s, only 4 percent of privately held Canadian companies had employees as shareholders. Of these companies, 83 percent issued voting stock to employees.[69] Palliser Furniture's employee share-ownership program is thus in the minority of such plans.

If Palliser's employee share ownership and profit-sharing plans were an intentional response to the 1970s concerns over unionization, by the mid-1990s, it was clear that the response had been insufficient. In the large city of Winnipeg, Mennonites and non-Mennonites worked side-by-side, and their attitudes toward unionization were not necessarily the same. A group of twenty-two workers at Palliser's Logic Division (which manufactured particle board and laminate case goods) sought union representation in 1995. These employees—Canadians of Métis, Aboriginal, Asian, Laotian, and Cambodian backgrounds—did not share the Mennonite ethnic and religious identity of their employers. They spent four or five months exploring their options, contacting the Canadian Autoworkers Union, the Steelworkers, and the United Brotherhood of Carpenters and Joiners of America (UBCJA). They ultimately decided that UBCJA Local 343 would best represent their interests. An organizing drive was launched accordingly during the first three months of 1996.[70]

The motivations for the 1996 drive, according to the union representative, were objections to management paternalism and mandatory chapel attendance. A report in the *Winnipeg Free Press* ascribed the drive to employee disagreement with "the company's faith heritage" as exemplified by the chapels. Palliser's 1970 employee handbook describes these services: "Everyone is expected to participate in this [weekly] Chapel Service. It is for the purpose of making Special Announcements and to give us all some spiritual food. 'Man does not live by bread alone, but by every word that proceedeth out of the mouth of God.' Matt. 4:4. Whenever there is a holiday during the week there will be no Chapel Service. This Chapel Service is inter-denominational and anyone that knows a Pastor that could serve in either German or English may advise Management of same."[71]

The 1993 employee handbook renamed the chapel an "assembly" and noted that the time spent in assembly was paid time. The purpose of the assembly had expanded beyond solely religious concerns, though religion remained a theme. Assemblies now were held to discuss production reports and changes in benefits or policies, to introduce new personnel, to provide information on methods of stress reduction, to address chemical dependencies, as well as to provide direction for spiritual or personal growth.[72]

Wages were another, though lesser, motivation for organizing. A union newsletter distributed at the plant declared, "We believe Palliser Furniture falls below industry standards in terms of wages and working conditions."[73] UBCJA Local 343 claimed to have spoken to all 400 employees at the Logic Division and found that everyone made under ten dollars an hour, whereas the company claimed the average wage was at least eleven dollars.[74] While gain sharing may have been part of the company's wage calculations, the union dismissed this benefit.[75] Gain sharing at Palliser was tied to performance and was "no substitute for a fair wage"; employees could lose their share if they were late or committed some other infraction more than three times in a pay period. A flyer distributed to workers outlined the union objections to gain sharing in detail:

> Rather than giving pay increases to keep up with inflation, [many North American companies] try to offer profit sharing schemes as a substitute.... It may be fair to pay managers with bonuses because they make big money anyway and it's their good or bad decisions which result in profit or loss. It's unfair though to dump the same performance burden on line workers. They have no say in the operation of the Company and they should not have to share the risks brought on by bad decisions or corporate greed. Your hourly wage shouldn't rise or fall

due to things you have no control over.... Are you a member of the "working poor" even though you work for one of the richest and most successful companies in Canadian history? Think about it. The Palliser system of gain sharing is for suckers. You need a good base rate first, then we can talk about a *fair* profit sharing system. A real profit sharing system would be based on a percentage of the profit for the whole Plant shared among all the employees depending on how many hours they worked.[76]

Palliser's profit-sharing plans and other bonus systems were not the only financial issues that prompted the union drive in 1996. Another significant question was the company's description of government-mandated benefits. The union believed that statements made in the 1993 employee handbook about such programs as the Canada Pension Plan and Unemployment Insurance could be interpreted, particularly by the many immigrant workers for whom English was a second language, as claiming these benefits to be exclusive to Palliser rather than universal. The handbook noted that "also included in your total benefit program are those benefits provided in cooperation with governmental agencies: workers' compensation, unemployment, etc. The cost of these programs, paid by PALLISER, is significant."[77]

The Canada Pension Plan was described in the handbook as a "mandatory government pension plan.... For every dollar you contribute to this plan, PALLISER contributes another dollar on your behalf."[78] The handbook's description of Unemployment Insurance was as follows: "The Federal Government of Canada administers the Unemployment Insurance program designed to assist those who are temporarily out of work. Each employee and PALLISER pay for this program through regular contributions. For each dollar you contribute, PALLISER will contribute approximately $1.25."[79]

Worker's Compensation was also detailed in the 1993 employee handbook. "As a Palliser employee, you are covered by a Worker's Compensation program.... The Company pays for the entire cost and provides this coverage at no cost to you beginning with your first day of work."[80] The union's response was to assert in their newsletters: "You should not consider [workers'] compensation, UI [Unemployment Insurance], CPP [Canada Pension Plan], two weeks of paid vacation as part of a benefit package provided by an employer out of generosity, they are required by law";[81] and "Benefits are not benefits if the Company charges you for them. Don't be fooled when the Company lists UIC [Unemployment Insurance Commission], CPP, WCB [Workers' Compensation Board] or mandatory vacations as benefits. Don't be fooled when they list Supplementary Health as a benefit, if you get deducted for it."[82]

Palliser's response, under its new leadership, was to oppose the union tooth and nail. Though this story is difficult to piece together, it seems that the company employed threats of plant closures and inducements of wage sweeteners. Henry Wallman, formerly a painter and then a manager at Palliser, had retired from the company before the 1996 attempt to unionize. His contacts with other employees kept him informed of the situation: "Yes, I was gone then already. But they have tried [to unionize], yes. The boss had told them, that time—this is just what I have heard before—'If you guys elect, let in a union, then the next morning, there will be a lock on the door.' It is still not unionized."[83]

Union documents support Wallman's suggestion that the response of Palliser management was to threaten to close the Winnipeg plant and create an extra shift at their branch plant in North Carolina.[84] The union leafleted the North Carolina plant to warn of these tactics. Two issues of the newsletter distributed to Palliser's Winnipeg workers addressed the concern that production would be transferred to the United States if the union drive was successful:

Will Palliser close down Logic if the union is certified? Palliser is one of the largest and most successful manufacturers in Manitoba. It has received millions of dollars in federal and provincial loans to expand its operations in the past decade.[85] Palliser claims to want to work with its employers. It would not be in keeping with its commitment to a "cooperative working environment" to punish workers for exercising their legal right to unionize.[86]

Companies tell workers that if they won't work for peanuts, the plant will close and move to some other country where the labour is cheap and the workers are desperate so they won't complain. It's a race to the bottom to see who will work for less. The Company will be in for a surprise if they continue to threaten to move "LOGIC" to Troutman, North Carolina. The Carpenters Union is organizing there, too. The new Global Economy doesn't recognize borders and capital has no conscience. International Unions are the only way for workers to protect themselves.[87]

Don't be fooled by the Company's 'Petition'.... You are being asked to sign a petition to keep the Union out. *Feel free to sign this petition.* It is being done to intimidate you and the best way to protect yourself is to sign the petition even if you have already signed a Union card. The Labour Board will not recognize the petition. They will recognize your Union card. Be patient and be careful.[88]

In the end, fewer than 65 percent of employees signed union cards, and so a vote on union certification could not be held.[89] The union claimed a partial victory in that pay raises followed the failed organization attempt.[90] Patrick Martin, former business manager of UBCJA Local 343, asserted that Palliser management became more respectful as well. Prior to the union drive, he did not "think Art and Frank [DeFehr] knew what assholes they had on the assembly line" as supervisors. Future union drives at Palliser may be more successful with the changing composition of the workforce. Henry Wallman notes, "I think they [management] tried always to please so that [workers] were not too anxious to get a union. But those, at that time, were mostly, like I said before, immigrants to Canada from Paraguay, Germany. But now they have younger people, so I don't know, that could change there." Many of these younger people are Southeast Asian Canadians who formerly were employed in the unionized garment factories in Winnipeg.[91] Their history of unionism and non-Mennonite background may make them more receptive to union drives.[92]

Conclusion

The rural to urban shift of Mennonites in postwar Manitoba resulted in their increased involvement in industrial capitalism and the creation of a Mennonite entrepreneurial class. Even though Mennonite churches had long objected to union membership on religious grounds, they were challenged by the militant labour movement of 1970s Manitoba and the 1972 changes to the Manitoba *Labour Relations Act* to search for a new understanding of these issues. The membership of the Canadian Mennonite Health Assembly and Mennonite Central Committee Manitoba requested the assistance of their leadership in addressing these questions. In response, MCC Manitoba organized a series of seminars on labour-management relations in 1976 with the assistance of the Christian Labour Association of Canada. From outright rejection of union membership in the pre-war years, Mennonites moved to a position of greater ambivalence by the 1990s.

This ambivalent position is exemplified by the unsuccessful effort to organize a division of Palliser Furniture in the early 1990s. The Mennonite owners of the company, motivated by their religious understandings of labour relations (and perhaps prompted by labour unrest in the province at the time), introduced profit-sharing and employee share-ownership plans in the early 1980s. These efforts were not enough to forestall an organization attempt in the mid-1990s. The experience at Palliser demonstrates how difficult it is to reconcile Christian principles with the challenges of labour-management relations. Employee share ownership and profit-sharing plans may have been sufficient to convince the majority of the Mennonite workers at Palliser that unionization was unnecessary and unwanted, but this belief was by no means universal within the company's workforce.

The tension between the modern Mennonite emphasis on social responsibility, as exhibited by labour's demands for economic justice, and the traditional Mennonite insistence on avoidance of confrontation was evident in the struggle of Manitoba Mennonites with their response to labour activism in the 1970s. Pacifism often had been dismissed as passivity in the past; now the adherence to the principle of non-violence could be seen as an excuse for accepting economic exploitation. Though North American Mennonites' attitudes toward unions may have undergone change during this period, they continued to avoid becoming members. It was not the Mennonite workers at Palliser who initiated the union drive in 1996. Perhaps Mennonite workers recognized that national unions had limited effectiveness in a global capitalist system, as evidenced by Palliser's threat to transfer production to the United States. With international free trade, Palliser Furniture became a major Canadian participant in the global economy, opening factories in Mexico, Indonesia, and Lithuania in the late 1990s. It remains an open question whether a new international labour movement emerges to counteract the effects on workers of globalization, and to what extent Mennonites will be a part of it.

Notes

1   John Friesen, "Manitoba Mennonites in the Rural-Urban Shift," in *Mennonites in Urban Canada: Proceedings of the Conference on Urbanization of Mennonites in Canada*, ed. Leo Driedger, *Mennonite Life* 23, 4 (October 1968): 152–158.

2   Statistics Canada, "Selected Religions, for Census Metropolitan Areas and Census Agglomerations – 2001 Sample Data: Winnipeg (CMA), Man." 1 April 2003, http://www12.statcan.ca/ english/census01/products/highlight/Religion/Page.cfm?Lang=E&Geo=CMA&View=2a&Code =602&Table=1&StartRec=1&Sort=2&B1=602&B2=1 (accessed 3 October 2003); Demographia, "Canada: 20 Top Census Metropolitan Areas: Population from 1931," 2001, http://www. demographia.com/db-cancma.htm (accessed 2 February 2004); Leo Driedger, "Ethnic Urban Dominance: Demographic, Ecological and Institutional Patterns," *Canadian Journal of Urban Research* 4, 2 (December 1995): 212, Table 1.

3   My thanks to Palliser and the DeFehrs for access to papers and interviews, as well as Local 343 of the United Brotherhood of Carpenters and Joiners and their former business representative, Patrick Martin. I am grateful to Gerald Friesen for his detailed and expert editorial advice on an earlier draft of this article and to Gregory Kealey for supervising the dissertation from which this article stems. My thanks as well to SSHRC, the University of New Brunswick, and the Metropolis Project for funding this research. Some portions of this paper were published in "Communism and Labor Unions: The Changing Prespectives of Mennonites in Canada and the United States," *Direction* 38, 1 (Spring 2009): 17–28, and "Committed to Christ or Conformed to this World? Postwar Mennonite Responses to Labour Activism," *Studies in Religion/Sciences Religieuses* 36, 2 (2007): 317–338.

4   Between 1974 and 1976, there were twenty-three to thirty strikes in Manitoba and 921 to 1173 strikes in Canada. Labour Canada, *Strikes and Lockouts in Canada, 1974–1975,* 1976; James A. McAllister, *The Government of Edward Schreyer: Democratic Socialism in Manitoba* (Kingston and Montreal: McGill-Queen's University Press, 1984), 108; Manitoba Labour and Immigration, "A History of Manitoba Labour and Immigration," http://www.gov.mb.ca/labour/labmgt/history.html (accessed 20 July 2004); D.N. Sprague, *Post-Confederation Canada: The Structure of Canadian History Since 1867* (Scarborough, ON: Prentice-Hall, 1990), 311. There was a record 1218 strikes in Canada in 1974; the highest number of strikers was 1.5 million in 1976. Errol Black and Jim Silver, "Labour in Manitoba: Facing the 1990s," in *Hard Bargains: The Manitoba Labour Movement Confronts the 1990s,* eds. Errol Black and Jim Silver, Manitoba Labour History series (Winnipeg: Manitoba Labour Education Centre, n.d.), 6–7.

5   These groups included the Mennonite Church; the General Conference Mennonite Church; the Lancaster Mennonite Conference; the Brethren in Christ; the Church of God in Christ, Mennonite; the Mennonite Brethren; and Mennonite Central Committee.

6   Roy Vogt, "Mennonite Studies in Economics," *Journal of Mennonite Studies* 10 (1992): 65; T.D. Regehr, *Mennonites in Canada, 1939–1970: A People Transformed* (Toronto: University of Toronto Press, 1996), 158.

7   Mennonite Church, "Resolution on Unionism," 20th session, 24–26 August 1937, Turner, OR, in *Mennonite Statements on Peace and Social Concerns, 1900-1978,* ed. Urbane Peachey (Akron, PA: Mennonite Central Committee U.S. Peace Section, 1980), 105. Several Bible passages were cited in support. Verses such as Isaiah 9:6 and Matthew 26: 61–63 declared that the highest authority for Christians was God—not the union oath of membership. Other verses, such as Matthew 5:38–45 and John 18:36, suggested that Christians should not press demands for justice or seek to establish the kingdom of God on earth. Scriptural references to nonresistance (Romans 12:17–21, 2 Corinthians 10:4, Ephesians 4:31–32, James 5:6) were used to argue that the coercive nature of strikes and the adversarialism of collective bargaining were incompatible with Christian values.

8   2 Corinthians 6:14–16, King James Version. The New Revised Standard Version replaces the agrarian image "unequally yoked" with the less evocative "mismatched." This same passage was used by the bishops of the Lancaster Mennonite Conference in 1941 as the rationale for their opposition to union membership. Mennonite Church Lancaster Conference, "Labor Unions," board of bishops special meeting, 24 September 1941, Ephrata, PA, in Peachey, 107. An earlier meeting of the bishops in 1933 also condemned union membership, but did not quote from 2 Corinthians. Mennonite Church Lancaster Conference, "Labor Unions," board of bishops, 18 October 1933, Lancaster PA, in Peachey, *Mennonite Statements,* 107.

9   Brethren in Christ Church, "Industrial Relations," 71st session, 4–9 June 1941, Milford, IN; Mennonite Church, "Industrial Relations," 22nd session, 26 August 1941, Wellman, IA, in Peachey, *Mennonite Statements,* 102–103 and 105–106.

10   See his "Nonresistance and Industrial Conflict," *Mennonite Quarterly Review* 13, 2 (April 1939): 135–154, and *The Way of the Cross in Human Relations* (Scottdale, PA: Herald Press, 1958).

11   The Committee on Industrial Relations was known after 1951 as the Committee on Economic and Social Relations. In 1965, it was merged with the Peace Problems Committee to become the Committee on Peace and Social Concerns of the Mennonite Church. Mennonite Central Committee formed its own Peace and Social Concerns Committee in 1964. *Canadian Mennonite Encyclopedia Online,* "The Way of Christian Love in Race Relations (Mennonite Church, 1955): a CMEO Source Document," 1999, http://www.mhsc.ca/encyclopedia/contents/W39.html (accessed 20 July 2004).

12   Mennonite Church, "Organized Labor," study conference, 24–27 June 1951, Laurelville Mennonite Camp, PA, in Peachey, *Mennonite Statements,* 106–107.

13 John H. Redekop, Canadian Mennonite Encyclopedia Online, "Labor Unions," 1989, http://www.mhsc.ca/ (accessed 2 July 2004). Other Mennonite groups followed suit. The Church of God in Christ, Mennonite, opposed union membership in 1953. By 1967, the denomination left union membership to the individual as "a matter of conscience." Employment in union shops was permitted if the equivalent of dues could be paid to charity and if Mennonite employees refrained from voting on certain union issues (presumably strike votes). Similarly, the Mennonite Brethren Church decided in 1969 not to forbid union membership. Mennonites were warned, however, that they should not engage in union-related violence or intimidation. The prejudice against unions had not completely disappeared: the original motion had included the phrase "nor should we judge or condemn those who are members of unions." This wording was removed when the motion was amended. Church of God in Christ, Mennonite, "Labor Unions," special delegate conference, 27 September 1953, Galva, KS; "Labor Unions," general conference, 4–8 August 1967, Ste. Anne, MB; and Mennonite Brethren Church, "The Christian and Labor Unions," 51st session, 23–26 August 1969, Vancouver BC, all in Peachey, *Mennonite Statements*, 104–5.

14 A further breakdown of Canadian and American Mennonites who did not oppose union membership included the following: Blue-collar Mennonites 58 percent, business 61 percent, students 51 percent, housewives 40 percent, professionals 65 percent, farmers 37 percent. Leo Driedger, *Mennonites in the Global Village* (Toronto: University of Toronto Press, 2000), 45, Table 2-6.

15 J. Howard Kauffman and Leland Harder, *Anabaptists Four Centuries Later: A Profile of Five Mennonite and Brethren in Christ Denominations* (Scottdale, PA: Herald Press, 1975), 146; J. Howard Kauffman and Leo Driedger, *The Mennonite Mosaic: Identity and Modernization* (Scottdale, PA: Herald Press, 1991), 92 and 207–8.

16 Mennonite Central Committee is the relief, service, and peace agency of the North American Mennonite and Brethren in Christ churches.

17 This section has been replaced by section 76(3), which specifies that the employee must be "a member of a religious group which has as one of its articles of faith the belief that members of the group are precluded from being members of, and financially supporting, any union or professional association" and that the employee "has a personal belief in those articles of faith." Government of Manitoba, "Continuing Consolidation of the Statutes of Manitoba: The Labour Relations Act," 9 June 2004, http://web2.gov.mb.ca/laws/statutes/ccsm/l010e.php (accessed 20 July 2004).

18 MCC Canada press release, 10 January 1975, "MCC Manitoba (1975–80)," Volume 3650, Mennonite Heritage Centre, Winnipeg, MB (hereafter MHC).

19 Letter from A. Russell Paulley, Minister of Labour, to Peter Peters, MCC Manitoba, 27 January 1975, "MCC Manitoba (1975–80)," Volume 3650, MHC. No mention of this meeting, or of the Manitoba Mennonites' concerns in general, is made in the Andrew Russell Paulley papers. Don Hurst, access and privacy officer, Manitoba Labour and Immigration Workplace Safety and Health Division, letter to the author, Winnipeg, MB, 16 June 2005 in response to FIPPA requests #2005.767, 2005.768, and 2005.769.

20 Letter from Egon Frech, special assistant to Premier Edward Schreyer, to Gerald Vandezande, executive director, CJL Foundation, 16 September 1974, "MCC Manitoba (1974–80)," Volume 3636, MHC.

21 Ibid.

22 "Reasons for Decision" re the application by Henry Funk to the Manitoba Labour Board under Section 68(3) of the *Labour Relations Act*, with McGavin Toastmaster Ltd. as employer-respondent and Bakery and Confectionery Workers' International Union Local 389 as bargaining agent and agreement holder, 1975, "MCC Manitoba (1974–80)," Folder 6, Volume 3636, MHC.

23 Manitoba Court of Appeals, *Henry Funk v. Manitoba Labour Board*, 5 January 1976, "MCC Manitoba (1975–80)," Volume 3650, MHC; "Labor board decision overturned," *Steinbach Carillon*, 7 January 1976, 1:1.

24 Letter from H. Klassen, Donwood Manor, to Mennonite Churches of Manitoba, 19 March 1975, "MCC Manitoba (1975–80)," Volume 3650, MHC. The Canadian Mennonite Health Assembly was formed as the Canadian Association of Mennonite Hospitals and Homes in 1966. It changed names in 1973. Centre for Mennonite Brethren Studies, "Canadian Mennonite Health Assembly," 16 August 2003, http://www.mbconf.ca/mbstudies/holdings/other/cmha.en.html (accessed 20 July 2004).

25 While the proceedings do not detail either the nurses' experience or the board's position, it is clear that they were not pro-union.

26 The topic of this speech (and presumably its content) was the same as that of a presentation Redekop later made at a series of seminars on labour-management relations organized by Mennonite Central Committee Manitoba in January 1976.

27 Proceedings from the 1975 Conference of the Canadian Mennonite Health Assembly held at Donwood Manor, Winnipeg MB, 23–25 April 1975, "MCC Manitoba (1975–80)," Volume 3650, MHC.

28 Delegates were those who had been chosen to represent their congregations and had voting rights; guests were interested observers.

29 "Mennonites struggle with union membership issue," *Steinbach Carillon*, 26 November 1975, 2:1.

30 The Canadian Union of Postal Workers, as a result of the 1975 strike, received a 71 percent wage increase and had their workweek reduced to thirty hours. Sprague, *Post-Confederation Canada*, 311.

31 Nine Mennonite nurses at this hospital had refused to join the union and requested assistance from MCC. Memo from Arthur Driedger, executive director of Peace and Social Concerns Committee, MCC Manitoba, to committee members, 13 June 1975, "MCC Manitoba (1975–80)," Volume 3650, MHC.

32 Ibid.

33 Two hundred five people were registered: sixty-one at Steinbach, seventy-two at Winkler, and seventy-two at Winnipeg. Others may have attended without signing their names at the door. "MCC Manitoba (1974–80)," Folder 6, Volume 3636, MHC.

34 "Labor, management, meeting at Steinbach," *Steinbach Carillon*, 21 January 1976, 1:1.

35 Labour-Management Relations Seminar advertisement, "MCC Manitoba (1974–80)," Folder 6, Volume 3636, MHC.

36 "Labor, management, meeting at Steinbach," 1:1.

37 Letter from Arthur Driedger, executive director of Peace and Social Concerns Committee, Mennonite Central Committee Manitoba, to Gerald Vandezande, former head of the Christian Labour Association of Canada, 22 December 1975, "MCC Manitoba (1974–80)," Folder 6, Volume 3636, MHC.

38 John H. Redekop, "Labor-Management Relationships: A Biblical Perspective," 1, "MCC Manitoba (1974–80)," Volume 3636, MHC.

39 Ibid., 2.

40 Ibid., 1. Redekop noted, "There are, of course, also some positive trends but since they are not controversial we will omit listing them. It is the negative ones that cause the problems." Ibid., 2.

41 Ibid., 2–3.

42 Ibid., 3.

43 Ibid., 4.

44 Ibid., 10.

45 "Item 7: What are our concerns?" "MCC Manitoba (1974–80)," Volume 3636, MHC.

46   In addition to the CLAC handout, a number of other documents were made available to the audiences at the seminars. These included copies of the 1974 letter from Egon Frech (special assistant to Manitoba Premier Edward Schreyer) to Gerald Vandezande, of Section 68(3) of the Manitoba *Labour Relations Act* and the similar Section 39(1) of the Ontario *Labour Relations Act*, as well as the 1969 Mennonite Brethren Church statement, "The Christian and Labor Unions," and the "Reasons for Decision" in the case of Henry Funk's application under Section 68(3) to the Manitoba Labour Board. The membership oaths for the International Brotherhood of Electrical Workers, Canadian Union of Public Employees, Canadian Union of Postal Workers and the Bakery and Confectionery Workers' International Union of America were also distributed.

47   Christian Labour Association of Canada, "CLAC Tour," 2004, http://www.clac.ca/Flash_Tour.asp (accessed 20 July 2004).

48   "Labor-seminar speaker: 'Christians may have to pay high price,'" *Steinbach Carillon*, 4 February 1976, 1:1; Redekop, "Labor-Management Relationships," 10–11.

49   The principle of local church autonomy among Mennonites, however, allows individual congregations (to some extent) to make their own decisions on matters of doctrine.

50   Mennonite Church, *Confession of Faith in a Mennonite Perspective* (Scottdale, PA: Herald Press, 1995), Article 22. http://www.mennolink.org/doc/cof/.

51   Canadian Conference of Mennonite Brethren Churches, *Confession of Faith*, 30 March 2004, http://www.mbconf.ca/believe/confession/work.en.html (accessed 5 January 2005).

52   Mennonite Historical Society of Canada, *Canadian Mennonite Encyclopedia Online*, s.v. "Labour Unions," by John H. Redekop, 1999, http://www.mhsc.ca (accessed 5 January 2005).

53   Palliser was founded by Russian Mennonite immigrant Abram Albert (A.A.) DeFehr in 1944. Before the privatization of Manitoba Telecom Systems in 1997, Palliser was the largest private employer in the province, and in 2005 had over 3000 workers.

54   Majority control of Palliser has remained in the hands of the DeFehr family. In 1996, Art DeFehr bought out his siblings, eventually selling back one division of the company (DeFehr Division) to his brother, Frank. Michael J. Knell, "Palliser selling off eight-unit retail chain," *Furniture Today*, 29 April 1996, 46.

55   Notation in original.

56   Letter from Dave DeFehr to A.A., Frank and Art DeFehr, Winnipeg, 4 September 1979.

57   Palliser Furniture employee newsletter, issue 2, 1 (March 1983).

58   Palliser Furniture employee newsletter, issue 10, 6 (March/April 1991): 8.

59   Palliser Furniture employee newsletter, issue 2, 1 (March 1983).

60   The validity of Palliser's claims cannot be determined, as profit sharing statistics are not available.

61   Memo from W.A. Redekopp to A.A., Frank, Art and Dave DeFehr, n.d.

62   Ibid.

63   Ibid.

64   Palliser Furniture, executive committee meeting minutes, 19–20 January 1979.

65   Palliser Furniture employee newsletter, issue 1, 5 (September 1982). Palliser had 125 shareholders in 1989 and 188 shareholders in 1991. Palliser Furniture employee newsletter, issue 8, 2 (July 1989); 10, 7 (May/June 1991): 5.

66   Palliser Furniture employee newsletter, issue 8, 2 (July 1989).

67   According to their employee newsletters, Palliser had eighty-seven shareholders in 1987 and 125 in 1989. Palliser Furniture, employee newsletter, issue 6, 1 (July 1987); 8, 2 (July 1989). I was not granted access to share ownership information at Palliser Furniture. The December 1993 employee handbook does not list share ownership as a benefit. Perhaps share ownership is restricted to those employees of the company who hold managerial positions.

68   Richard J. Long, "The Incidence and Nature of Employee Profit Sharing and Share Ownership in Canada," *Relations Industrielles* 47, 3 (1992): 473, 475 and 477–478.

69   Ibid., 473.

70   Patrick Martin, former business representative for United Brotherhood of Carpenters and Joiners (UBCJA) Local 343, personal communication, Winnipeg, MB, 10 July 1997.

71   Palliser Furniture, *A.A. DeFehr Mfg. Ltd. Employee Policy*, 1 October 1970.

72   Palliser Furniture, *Employee Handbook*, December 1993, 29.

73   UBCJA Local 343 newsletter, 1996, courtesy of UBCJA Local 343.

74   Patrick Martin, personal communication, 10 July 1997.

75   Gain sharing was a variation on profit sharing at Palliser Furniture. Workers who produced more than quota received a bonus; however, the quota was increased accordingly.

76   UBCJA Local 343, *Palliser Union News* 1, 8 (February 1996), courtesy of UBCJA Local 343.

77   Palliser Furniture, *Employee Handbook*, December 1993, 41. In this and the following quotes, the capitalization of "Palliser" is in the original.

78   Ibid., 43.

79   Ibid., 66.

80   Ibid., 69.

81   UBCJA Local 343, *The Palliser Union News* 1, 1 (31 January 1996), courtesy of UBCJA Local 343.

82   UBCJA Local 343, *The Palliser Union News* 1, 5 (February 1996), courtesy of UBCJA Local 343.

83   Henry Wallman, former painter and manager, Palliser Furniture, interview by author, 25 June 1999, Altona, MB, tape recording.

84   UBCJA Local 343, *The Palliser Union News*, n.d., courtesy of UBCJA Local 343.

85   Palliser received assistance from the Industrial Development Bank (IDB) in 1963, requested $150,000 from the Manitoba Development Fund in 1968, received $298,160 from the Department for Regional Economic Expansion (DREE) in 1976, received $688,000 from DREE in 1982 and $1.5 million from Western Economic Diversification in 1988. "North Kildonan firm shows phenomenal growth in 25 years," unnamed newspaper article (1969), courtesy of Palliser Furniture; Palliser Furniture application to the Industrial Development Bank, form 58B (rev. 10/67), 11 June 1968; letter from J.D. Collinson, director-general of DREE, to A.A. DeFehr, 8 September 1976, courtesy of Palliser Furniture; "DeFehr plant staff doubled," *Winnipeg Free Press*, 26 May 1984, 44; Western Economic Diversification Canada, press release, 3 October 1988, courtesy of Palliser Furniture.

86   UBCJA Local 343, *The Palliser Union News* 1, 1 (31 January 1996), courtesy of UBCJA Local 343.

87   UBCJA Local 343, *The Palliser Union News* 1, 6 (February 1996), courtesy of UBCJA Local 343.

88   Ibid.

89   Later that year, the Manitoba *Labour Relations Act* was amended by the Conservative government led by Premier Gary Filmon. Automatic union certification was ended; all applications for certification required a secret ballot vote. Applications where less than 40 percent of workers signed union cards were rejected. An NDP government led by Premier Gary Doer was elected in 1999; in 2000, the *Labour Relations Act* was amended to reverse the changes instituted by the Filmon government. Human Resources and Skills Development Canada, "Labour and Workplace Information, 1996–1997," http://www110.hrdc-drhc.gc.ca/psait_spila/eltc_dllc/1996_1997/index.cfm/doc/english#legislation_2 (accessed 8 March 2005); Manitoba Labour and Immigration, "A History of Manitoba Labour and Immigration," http://www.gov.mb.ca/labour/labmgt/history.html (accessed 20 July 2004).

90   Patrick Martin, personal communication, 10 July 1997.

91   Until the arrival of Southeast Asian refugees in 1979–1980, Palliser's workforce was predominantly Mennonite. Many Canadian Mennonites sponsored southeast Asian refugees through their churches from 1979 through the early 1980s. A history conference on this subject, "Mennonites Meet the Refugee: A 25 Year Retrospective," organized by the Chair in Mennonite Studies at the University of Winnipeg and Mennonite Central Committee Canada, was held in the fall of 2005; several of the conference papers were published in *Journal of Mennonite Studies* 24 (2006).

92   Efforts to organize Palliser Furniture continue. In November 2004, a pamphlet produced by the Manitoba Committee of the Communist Party of Canada, titled "Fight for Workers' Rights at Palliser: It Takes a Struggle to Win," was available at the Winnipeg office of Project Peacemakers. (Project Peacemakers is an affiliate of Project Ploughshares, an ecumenical peace centre founded by Mennonites and the Society of Friends [Quakers] in 1976.) The pamphlet describes "sweating, piece work, intense speed-up, incentives to cover up injury benefits, reductions in incentives and lowering of wages ceilings for piece work," limited vacations, and the elimination of profit sharing in some plants, and advocates the formation of a union at Palliser.

The Early History of the Winnipeg Indian and Métis Friendship Centre, 1951-1968

Leslie Hall

An increasing number of Aboriginal people moved to urban areas in Canada after the Second World War.[1] They shared common experiences and had similar needs that were not being sufficiently addressed by the services existing at the time. The Winnipeg Indian and Métis Friendship Centre (IMFC) opened in 1959 to answer these needs by providing referrals and counselling on employment, housing, and other concerns, in addition to providing a welcoming place where Aboriginal people could socialize and attend cultural and educational events. According to the National Association of Friendship Centres, by 1997 there were 114 similar Friendship Centres open across Canada and 750,000 people using their services.[2] It is often said that the Winnipeg centre was a model for the national movement. This paper examines the process by which the Winnipeg Friendship Centre was developed, how its early model for administration took shape, how the administrative structure incorporated Aboriginal leadership during the first few years of operation, and how the centre developed programs to meet the needs of Aboriginal people in Winnipeg. Drawing upon a number of interviews with participants in its creation, I suggest that the community development design of the Friendship Centre's administration and programming was crucial to its success. The centre functioned well because of the collaboration between Aboriginal and non-Aboriginal IMFC members and because of the strong leadership provided by Aboriginal community members. It was the initiative of the Aboriginal leaders and members of the Centre that created programming designed specifically to meet the needs of newly urban Aboriginal people, to revitalize their trust in their cultural heritage, and to build a stronger urban community.[3]

The 1951 revision of Canada's *Indian Act* reduced the level of federal government control over Aboriginal daily life. Prohibitions on potlatches and powwows were abolished as were the special passes needed to leave the reserve. Although the revised Act appeared more open to cultural pluralism, the principle of assimilation that had guided policy formation prior to 1951 was maintained.[4] The changes in the Act resulted in more geographic freedom for peoples living on reserves than had been permitted by Indian agents in the previous half-century.[5] Meanwhile, work on farms and in lumber or construction crews declined due to technological changes that reduced employment opportunities relied on since the 1880s.[6] Due to the inadequacies of census data on Aboriginal people at this time, exact statistics on population changes are difficult to establish. It is clear, however, that as in the rest of Canada, Aboriginal people increasingly lived in urban centres and had a high birth rate in the post-World War II era.[7] The above factors, combined with the population increase and a lack of employment on reserves, resulted in a young, mobile group of Aboriginal people, many of whom moved to the city seeking jobs, education, and an escape from the residential school legacy.

The move to urban centres made the relative poverty and higher level of social and economic problems experienced by Aboriginal people more visible to the rest of Canada and created a new category for public policy because Aboriginal people in urban centres fell outside existing health, education, and social welfare programming offered by the federal and provincial governments. As a result, Aboriginal migrants to Winnipeg, thought to number about 5000 in the late 1950s, had difficulty accessing services to assist with the transition to their new home. This situation necessitated a governmental re-evaluation of policies relating to Aboriginal peoples.[8]

As a part of the effort to redesign Indian policy during the 1950s and 1960s to address urban Aboriginal populations, governments and community groups initiated research projects intended to pinpoint the nature of the circumstances encountered by Aboriginal people in the city. The federally commissioned *Hawthorn Report* detailed the needs of Aboriginal people, particularly identifying issues related to health care, education, housing, and employment as well as the overrepresentation of Aboriginal people in the court system.[9] It also noted that Aboriginal people had a higher mortality rate, frequently from diseases that had few fatalities in the rest of the population, which was an indicator of poverty. They were arrested more often and for less serious offences than non-Aboriginal people.[10] The conditions Aboriginal people encountered were made worse by a lack of social support and family networks in urban centres.

Much of the research during the time focussed on the "urban Indian problem." The use of that phrase is problematic, however, because it identifies Aboriginal people themselves as the problem. Many of the reports written during the 1950s lumped the *causes* of the problems faced by Aboriginal people in the city in with the *actual problems* themselves. Rhetoric such as this attempts to make Aboriginal individuals the problem that the rest of Canada must "solve." A presentation at the Indian and Métis Conference in 1954 argued that the "problem" stemmed from "cultural traits which strongly contrast with ours."[11] These traits were said to be an "obstacle to securing and holding a job, a room and social participation on par with the other residents of the city."[12] The Manitoba provincial government suggested that the "problem" was experienced by both European-Canadian and Aboriginal people as a consequence of "problems which the white population experiences because of the people of Indian descent, and ... the problems which Indians have because they live amongst the white man."[13] These reports suggested that the "cause" of the problem was the culture clash between the "traditional" culture of First Nations people and the "modern" culture of the city, and therefore Aboriginal individuals would have to change their personalities and cultures to fit into the city's political and social order.

Aboriginal peoples argued strongly that their cultures were not incompatible with urban living or the modern world and that the "problem" was actually a series of circumstances that Aboriginal people faced when attempting to access adequate housing, employment, and social services. These were compounded by systemic discrimination and the lack of clarity in defining federal and provincial jurisdictions, as well as inadequate financing and education created by the reserve and residential school system. Furthermore, they suggested that cultural programming at an urban referral/social centre would assist people in adjusting to urban living by providing a stronger sense of Aboriginal history and values and by offering newcomers a more accessible social network. This was particularly the case for former residential school students who relocated to Winnipeg. Mary Guilbault, one of the Friendship Centre's Aboriginal founders, described residential schools as a major cause of the problems faced by Aboriginal people in the city since the strict regime imposed in the schools left many students initially unprepared for the independence afforded by the city. She also emphasized how young people were often unable to return to their parents after attending residential school and relocated to Winnipeg with insufficient education and no family support.[14] Similarly, Stan McKay Jr., who was associated with the centre as a young man in the 1960s, argued that the total institution of the residential school resulted in problems for Aboriginal people in the individualistic environment of the city: "To come out of that type of institution where you are told when to get up, fed, told where to go and what to do and then sent to bed—where the whole thing is ordered for you—it's very much like being incarcerated. To then come out of that program of incarceration into a city with few skills to survive in any community, much less an urban one which is very individualistic, [is difficult]."[15] Percy Bird, another Aboriginal man who was active at the centre during this period, also argued that the loss of cultural identity caused by residential schools, combined with repeated acts of discrimination, resulted in a diminished sense of pride for many people, which sometimes resulted in substance abuse. Substance abuse left people unable to reliably attend work and created difficulty in obtaining housing.[16]

The programming that was needed in urban centres, according to these people, would address immediate needs, including employment and housing, and also the social and psychological legacy of residential schools and reserve life. It would serve the dual purpose of assisting people to become members of the urban community while also embracing their cultural heritage.

Despite somewhat differing understandings of the needs of Aboriginal people in Winnipeg and differing ideas of the best long-term solution, the federal and provincial governments both provided funding when the Welfare Planning Council resolved in 1958, at an annual Winnipeg Indian and Métis Conference, to open a referral centre. The council used a community-development model that drew upon Aboriginal input, initially from Aboriginal elders who were a part of the Urban Indian Association, and later from other members of the centre, to develop programming that both met the needs of Aboriginal people and supported their heritage without necessitating cultural change or assimilation. Although the federal and provincial governments appear to have preferred short-term grants in the hope that the programs would not need to be sustained, the Welfare Planning Council and the elders involved in creating the centre were able to find ongoing funding to address the continuing needs of the growing Aboriginal population.

Federal government officials, the first of four key factors that affected the Friendship Centre movement, had made it clear in public statements and in correspondence with the provincial government during the late 1950s that they intended to reduce their responsibilities to Aboriginal people who lived off the reserves.[17] J.H. Gordon, director of the federal government's Welfare Services and Indian Affairs, argued at the 1954 Indian and Métis Conference that Aboriginal people living in urban centres were a provincial responsibility and should not be eligible for special programs based on their heritage:

> The department has consistently maintained the position that Indians on leaving their reserves and having established residence in non-Indian communities should be eligible for the same range of benefits from the province or community as Canadian citizens of other ethnic origins. The suggestion is sometimes made that the same welfare and other special services provided by the Indian Affairs branch on reserves should be extended to Indians off their reserves. This, I think, would be a tragic mistake. Rather we must make sure that Indians have

free and ready access to the welfare resources of the community to meet their needs which are basically the same as those of other persons.[18]

Under the umbrella of the Department of Citizenship and Immigration, the federal government introduced a variety of programs designed to improve services off-reserve and to collect information on the current and future needs of Aboriginal people. These programs included attempts to transfer some federal programs to the provinces, initiation of Aboriginal advisory boards, and funding of research on the administration of justice in relation to Aboriginal people. The federal government also sent representatives to the annual Indian and Métis Conferences in Winnipeg in the 1950s. Eventually, when faced with the proposal for a Friendship Centre in 1958, Ottawa decided to grant limited, short-term funding to the project.[19]

The Manitoba provincial government, a second factor in the centre's development, maintained that it could not provide social services for Aboriginal people in Winnipeg because it had "neither the constitutional authority nor the financial resources required,"[20] but it had to reconsider its position during the 1950s. The provincial position, expressed to the Joint Parliamentary Committee considering the services available to urban Aboriginal people, echoed the federal position on culture change: "We must realise, however, that their culture will have to change before it allows them to integrate fully with other Canadians ... we would be doing great harm to the Indians if we prevented their culture from changing to adjust to contemporary living. The end product of the changes that should take place will still be an Indian culture, but a 20th century Indian culture conceived for modern times and practical for modern problems."[21] Despite its paternalistic outlook, the provincial government was willing to embark on an important policy initiative: the introduction of community-development programming.

The provincial interest in "community development" as a policy strategy contributed to one crucial additional support in the creation and design of the Friendship Centre and, ultimately, to its sustainability by shifting the control of the centre into the hands of the members. Community development as a movement is a "philosophy with a value system based upon the right of individuals and groups to choose their own goals and decide the method which should be utilised to reach them."[22] The chosen program is then carried out through the initiative and hard work of the local people with technical advice from community-development officers.[23] Jean Lagasse, a Manitoban who has been described as "one of the 'fathers' of community development in Canada," was commissioned by the Manitoba government to study the relatively new approach to determine whether it might assist Aboriginal people.[24] Lagasse was also a member of the Welfare Planning Council and was later appointed director of community development for the Province of Manitoba.[25] He became an enthusiastic advocate of community development because it depended on local people's actions to "improve their own economic and social conditions, and thereby become effective working groups in programs of local and regional significance."[26] Lagasse's community-development solution included involving people from the community to help "improve their own economic and social conditions, and thereby become effective working groups in programs of local and regional significance."[27] Supporting community development as a policy allowed the province to channel some grant money into programming for Aboriginal people without overtly accepting responsibility for the problems encountered by Aboriginal people in urban centres.

A third political participant, the citizens who attended the Indian and Métis Conferences hosted by the city's Welfare Planning Council during the 1950s, had mixed views on the subject of Indian policy. The council was expected to develop a "balanced and co-operative approach to community needs and resources through its membership," which included local and national social welfare agencies, government departments, and non-profit organizations, and was supported by both voluntary and tax funding.[28] It was a "co-ordinating, fact-finding body, a planning centre for welfare needs, services and projects ... [and] serves its members whenever they ask for help, information or advice ... or whenever a welfare problem confronts the community."[29] It established an Indian and Métis Committee to investigate the needs of Aboriginal residents of Winnipeg in the early 1950s. It also sponsored annual Indian and Métis Conferences in Winnipeg, beginning in 1954, to research and discuss the needs of Aboriginal people in the city.[30]

The Indian and Métis Conferences were initially structured similar to academic conferences, with a heavy emphasis on academic research papers and presentations by government officials. A few Aboriginal representatives, such as Chief George Barker, president of the Manitoba Indian Brotherhood, also attended.[31] However, the majority of reports on the conferences that survive in archival records, newspapers, and interviews suggest that Aboriginal people were not included on the agenda and were not central in the deliberations. Joyce Meyer of the *Winnipeg Tribune* quoted an "Indian representative" at the 1959 Indian and Métis Conference as saying: "I think the Welfare Council is doing its best—and in good faith. They are always ready to listen ... but maybe next year they should leave a few gaps in the agenda in case Indians have something to say. This year there were no gaps at all."[32] Rev. John Pilling and Bernice Pilling, in a 2004 interview, expressed their excitement at being included in those first Indian and Métis Conferences, but also their distress at the absence of Aboriginal voices in the years between 1956 and 1961. They described these conferences as a forum for sharing and inspiring research, albeit with alarmingly limited Aboriginal input.[33]

The people involved in the Indian and Métis Conferences between 1954 and 1958 consisted mostly of non-Aboriginal people interested in community work, such as Jean Lagasse, Beatrice Brigden, Lloyd Lenton, Rev. Edward Scott, and W.L. Morton. Lagasse was involved as the community development officer for the provincial government. Brigden was a well-known community volunteer and an advocate for women's rights and for Aboriginal people. Lenton was involved in various volunteer efforts in Winnipeg and was well respected by the people at the Friendship Centre.[34] Rev. Scott was an Anglican minister in Winnipeg who was deeply concerned about Aboriginal issues.[35] W.L. Morton, a historian and professor at the University of Manitoba, chaired the conference committee. The personalities and experiences of the individuals on the planning committee shaped the character and administrative focus of the Friendship Centre during the early years. It appears that these individuals, all European-Canadian, were willing to adopt a philosophy of community development that contributed to the success of the partnership.[36] The Indian and Métis Committee of the Welfare Council had individual subcommittees to research topics such as recreation, employment, housing, education, and counselling.[37] In 1957 the Leisure Sub-Committee of the Indian and Métis Committee decided to recommend that the next Indian and Métis Conference establish a central agency where an Aboriginal person could be "led to help himself."[38]

The fourth and final group involved in the founding of the Friendship Centre embraced Aboriginal activists who had formed the Urban Indian Association to discuss the needs of Aboriginal people in the city and to develop appropriate responses. This group worked independently of the aforementioned groups until 1958 when its members attended the Indian and Métis Conference and agreed to a partnership that would result in the Indian and Métis Friendship Centre. The group included Mary and Ernie Guilbault, Marion Meadmore, Jimmy Elk, and others. All were Aboriginal residents of Winnipeg who were concerned with the problems faced by young Aboriginal people as they moved into the city.[39]

Members of this group were known for their community work and their experience with non-profit organizations. Meadmore, who grew up on the Peepeekisis Reserve in Saskatchewan, was a founding member of the Urban Indian Association and went on to become the first female Aboriginal lawyer in Canada.[40] Mary and Ernie Guilbault both attended residential schools and moved to Winnipeg after they graduated. During the early years of the Friendship Centre, and while raising five children with her husband, Mary Guilbault completed a Master's of Social Work at the University of Manitoba. These individuals recognized the value of community organizing. They met regularly in each other's homes to research and design plans to address the needs of the Aboriginal population. Mary Guilbault and Meadmore spearheaded various independent research efforts to assess the needs of urban Aboriginal people as well as to consider what people in other cities were doing to address these needs. According to Guilbault they wanted to provide a meeting place and to assist people in obtaining housing, employment, and health care.[41] In a 2004 interview Guilbault elaborated: "Social agencies of the period ... did not deal specifically with the so-called 'Native Problem.' Native people living in and migrating to the City had no support organisations to which they could go for guidance and assistance, economically or socially. The only support urban Natives had was each other. People like myself and others assisted some Native families in dealing with the welfare system but there was nothing of a major or organised nature."[42]

In an effort to research possible programming solutions, members of the Urban Indian Association travelled to Regina, Banff, Edmonton, and other cities, attended several of Winnipeg's Indian and Métis Conferences, and corresponded with government officials. Guilbault describes the activities of the association as follows: "Anything we did at that particular time we did on a voluntary basis and luckily enough any study that was done by the Urban Indian Association was done on a voluntary basis and they—the lawyers that we got advice from—never charged us for anything.... we had a very unusual kind of people who were very willing—and compatible with our cause. There never appeared to be a threat to anyone; there was always that common understanding and respect at all times."[43] The association began to raise money to fund a referral centre that would enable its members to expand the informal programs they were already offering out of their homes. Money was raised through dances held in local halls because the group had difficulty accessing community or government funding.[44]

The interests of the federal and provincial governments intersected with the activities of the Welfare Planning Council and the Urban Indian Association at the fourth annual Indian and Métis Conference in 1958. At this meeting the groups resolved to open a referral agency to provide guidance on matters of employment, housing, education, health, and other community services for Aboriginal people moving to

Winnipeg.[45] Guilbault remembers that, after the Indian and Métis Conference, the Urban Indian Association was concerned that Welfare Council officials would take control of the Friendship Centre and shape it in their own image without Aboriginal influence.[46] Her concerns stemmed both from a historic unwillingness on the part of government bodies to listen to Aboriginal people when designing policy, and also from the lack of Aboriginal influence during the conference's early years.

After a year of planning by a provisional board of directors selected by the Winnipeg Welfare Council and by an Indian Advisory Council selected by the board of directors, the IMFC opened in the spring of 1959. The centre moved into a small rented space in an office building on Donald Street, in the heart of inner-city Winnipeg, where many of the centre's members lived. It included an office, lounge, recreation room, kitchenette, and craft room. It was open during the weekdays, Sunday afternoons, and three evenings a week for recreation.[47] The IMFC became a member organization of the Welfare Planning Council, and many of the people involved in the IMFC continued their association with the Welfare Planning Council through the annual Indian and Métis Conferences. Initial funding for the centre was provided in the form of three grants, the first from the Winnipeg Foundation for $3500, the second and third from the Province of Manitoba and the federal Citizenship Branch for $4000 per year for a two-year trial period. After the successful two-year trial period, the IMFC continued to be funded by assorted limited-term grants from the federal, provincial, and municipal governments, and various community agencies. The three primary goals of the centre were to help Aboriginal newcomers adjust to urban life, to inform the larger community about the problems of Aboriginal people in the city in order to help resolve them, and to work with community groups, churches, and the government to provide improved access to health and welfare services.[48] Despite receiving funds from the federal and provincial governments, which generally supported an assimilationist policy, Guilbault says: "it was always known that the Friendship Centre would be used as a stepping stone into society for everything—that [the centre] would be a learning place ... we never intended to have the Friendship Centre be used as a place of assimilation."[49]

A planning committee was established by the Welfare Planning Council to set up the administration of the Friendship Centre. This committee included Lloyd Lenton, Canon Edward W. Scott, Ian Harvey, Rev. Ruest, Mary and Ernie Guilbault, Marion Meadmore, and Dorothy Betz—four European Canadians and four Aboriginal representatives. The committee determined that the centre would be run by two equal, but different, governing bodies, the board of directors and the Indian Advisory Council.

A third, subsidiary group of thirty people who represented various "community organisations which have an interest in the welfare of Indian and Métis in the city,"[50] formed a group called the Advisory Committee which provided additional advice to the board during the first year of operation.

The role of the board of directors was to administer public funds, determine policy, hire staff, appoint committees, and generally supervise the administrative affairs of the centre. The board of directors' minutes and proceedings contained many discussions on how to include Aboriginal people in the administration of the Friendship Centre. One memo stated: "it is our belief that people of Indian origin should come to compose a large portion of Board membership and the time may well come in the foreseeable future when either the majority or all of the board members might well be from this group."[51] At a meeting on 9 March 1958 during planning for the centre, the question was posed "how can Indian people be drawn into the planning? Should there be a Council of Indians? What part would they play?"[52] It was resolved to find Aboriginal people to participate in the planning process and in the administration of the IMFC, which resulted in the creation of the Indian Advisory Council.

The board of directors initially consisted of sixteen non-Aboriginal community members and four representatives from the Indian Advisory Council. The Welfare Council felt that ideally board members would "represent a cross section of the community (business, labour, professional service groups, church, Indian and Métis people),"[53] and made an effort to have Aboriginal people assume positions on the board each year when positions became available.[54] The board and the executive director appear to have listened to the suggestions of the Indian Advisory Council and to have encouraged Aboriginal people to assume positions of authority on the board of directors and on the staff.

The Indian Advisory Council, initially one of the main sources of Aboriginal influence at the Friendship Centre, met apart from the board meetings, had fundraising responsibilities, and designed and implemented programming at the centre. The board of directors and the executive director relied on the Indian Advisory Council to identify needs and suggest appropriate programs. The board believed that the "success of the Centre is due in part at least, to the fact that many Indian people feel a responsibility for planning and carrying out projects and programme at the centre and we suggest that only when the Indian people themselves are involved in a responsible way, can a service for Indians be effective."[55] Joan Adams, the first executive director, expressed concern that the council's relationship to the board of directors, and its role as an administrative overseer for the centre, be carefully defined so that people would not regard it as a club but as an administrative council.[56] The council was responsible for making recommendations to the board of directors on programming and staffing, and for raising funds to supplement government grants. It consisted of twelve Friendship Centre members elected by the other centre members. The constitution stated that the council was intended

1. To involve people of Indian origin in helping to plan activities and programs relating to the centre, such programs include activities of a social, recreational, educational and welfare nature.
2. To act in an advisory capacity to both the staff and Board of the Centre.
3. To provide one means of leadership development among people of Indian origin.
4. To draw up and enforce regulations concerning behaviours at the centre.
5. To raise funds, as deemed advisable, to be used at the discretion of the council.
6. To provide speakers to speak on the work of the centre and matters relating to people of Indian origin for church and community groups.
7. To seek to pass on to the community at large a true picture of people of Indian origin.[57]

Four members of the Indian Advisory Council sat at the board of directors meetings to present policies and participate in discussions. The advisory council was intended to encourage the development of leadership skills for Aboriginal people. It also raised funds, provided speakers, advised the staff and board, created and enforced behaviour regulations at the centre, and acted in the role of public relations.

What is unclear is the extent to which the board of directors' intentions to allow Aboriginal people to take over the board, evidenced in board minutes and correspondence, were made clear to Aboriginal members of the centre. It is possible that, although the board minutes are unmistakeable on this point, the intention may not have been made clear to all the Aboriginal people at the Friendship Centre. When Flora Zaharia joined the Friendship Centre in 1962, she was asked to join the Indian Advisory Council. She expressed frustration in an oral history interview in 2004 that Aboriginal people had a group that met separately from the board of directors and said that she had been, and was still, upset by this expression of inequality. Zaharia said that she voiced her concerns to the council after observing several of its meetings. She advocated increased Aboriginal participation in the official aspects of the centre and encouraged other council members to take action in securing positions on the board.[58] Mary Guilbault did not share Zaharia's view. She recalled during an interview in 2004 that the advisory council was a necessary part of the centre during the first few years because it allowed Aboriginal people to control the programming and day-to-day aspects of the centre that were important for meeting the needs of the population, while the board of directors negotiated funding and other necessary administrative arrangements.[59]

Whether or not all Aboriginal members of the Friendship Centre were aware of the board's apparent willingness to encourage the shift to an all-Aboriginal board and staff, there is a strong indication in the extant records that Aboriginal people used the opportunities made available at the centre to their advantage. Moreover, the board's minutes, the only textual record available from the time period, suggest that the centre was run as a cooperative venture between Aboriginal and non-Aboriginal people. By 1962, seven of the eighteen board members were Aboriginal representatives from the Indian Advisory Council, and by 1968 the board of directors was entirely Aboriginal.[60] By 1963 the centre staff was entirely Aboriginal. Thus, even though the centre was officially run by a group of predominantly non-Aboriginal people on the board from 1958 to 1963, it seems to have been co-managed in practice by Aboriginal leaders who served as advisors and day-to-day administrators.

It is important to note that, while the people at the centre identified with different Aboriginal language and culture groups, the centre was intended to be a meeting place for all Aboriginal people including Status, non-Status, and Métis, because they experienced similar challenges of marginalization and discrimination regardless of legal status. Therefore, the centre did not differentiate between Aboriginal groups when developing programming. Referral counsellors took into consideration "Status" for individuals only if it could be used to gain access to needed programs or services outside the centre. Within the centre, the issue of Status/non-Status and First Nations/Métis had little impact on the programs and on funding received from community groups such as the Winnipeg Foundation and the Community Chest. Funding in the early years was generally intended to be inclusive of all Aboriginal people because there were few precedents at that time for more targeted activities in Winnipeg. Although many different First Nation and Métis cultural groups used the centre, the people interviewed for this study all suggested that in the city there was a shared Aboriginal identity based on commonalities of experience in contrast to the dominant culture. Programs such as the Pow-Wow Club and other cultural events created a social and cultural space at the centre while simultaneously assisting people to obtain the educational and other skills needed to work among the non-Aboriginal majority in the city.

Verna McKay, a former United Church worker and volunteer at the centre, described the design of the programming at the Friendship Centre as an attempt "to respond to needs that arose in the community."[61] Once a need was identified, the centre developed a program to address it and applied for various funding grants. The programs at the centre fell into several main categories including referral and counselling, housing, court worker support, and cultural and social activities. The referral aspect of the Friendship Centre was initially very important: counsellors referred people to the appropriate offices of the Department of Indian Affairs, Community Development Services, Council for Native Employment, Special Schools Division, Neighbourhood Services, and other social service agencies depending on the specific needs of the individual.

The first year of the Friendship Centre focussed primarily on educational and recreational programming. According to the first-anniversary pamphlet, these programs helped "Indians and Métis to a full realization of their many capabilities and their ambitions in a city environment" and "encouraged young people to broaden their outlook and interests in the community by joining other youth groups, and cultural activities in the City of Winnipeg."[62] Mary Guilbault described the early years at the Friendship Centre as "a place of awakening" due to the programming and the opportunities for advancement for the Aboriginal members of the IMFC.[63]

Access to housing was one of the most pressing needs. Young girls especially appeared to have trouble obtaining housing, partly because they often struggled to find employment. The lack of housing could lead to vagrancy charges for young people who stayed in public places while they looked for work.[64] Dorothy Betz, the first female Aboriginal court worker at the centre, recalled in an interview that many of the court cases she became involved in related to vagrancy and disruption of the peace charges caused by a lack of housing and also by the absence of meeting places where Aboriginal people could get together for entertainment.[65] Frustrated by the lack of access to housing caused by the cycle of poverty and by difficulties in finding jobs for the migrants, Betz actually set up temporary housing for young people in her own home. She went to an army barracks that was refurbishing the soldiers' quarters and received half a dozen bunk beds which she set up in her basement. Betz then approached the jail on Portage Avenue to request that the young women picked up on vagrancy charges be released into her custody. When the girls were released they were able to stay with her while they looked for work and other housing. Betz and Verna McKay both described the difficulties in securing employment for Aboriginal people with no fixed address because employers felt that without a permanent address the people would be unreliable.[66] Access to a place to stay could help break the cycle of poverty and make the young Aboriginal migrants more attractive to potential employers.

In 1962 the centre appointed its first court worker using a grant from the provincial government and the Winnipeg Foundation.[67] According to the board of directors, Aboriginal people often had "little understanding of the legal procedures in which they were involved and the results of such short term sentences were seldom creative but very often, in fact, damaging both to the persons concerned and also to the general attitude of Indian people to law enforcement agencies."[68] The court workers provided guidance and translation as necessary and were the liaisons between the Aboriginal clients, attorneys, police, and judges. They advised the defendant of the courses of action available to them, sometimes acted as legal representatives on simple court matters, or assisted in locating legal aid. They worked with people who had been referred to them by City Welfare, Indian Affairs, Children's Aid, hospitals, and through word of mouth.

When Dorothy Betz, a young Aboriginal woman, took on the position of court worker, she insisted on spending months researching and observing in the court system in order to understand the proceedings. She said that once her position as court worker became known Aboriginal people would seek her out on their own behalf, and other people within the community would make recommendations and draw cases to her attention.[69] Betz would also act as legal counsel for some Aboriginal people on simple charges. In other cases she would suggest to the judge that she be allowed to supervise community service for defendants instead of their going to jail.[70]

The Friendship Centre's cultural and social programming was the main vehicle for developing leadership and a sense of community among Winnipeg's Aboriginal residents. The centre provided a safe place off the streets for young people to gather and make friends. Dorothy Betz argued that Aboriginal people living in Winnipeg "didn't have a place of our own—all we had was Main Street but we weren't too ecstatic about it."[71] Main Street was located in the heart of the northern part of Winnipeg, where many Aboriginal people lived. Because of its close proximity to lower income housing, it was often a gathering place for young Aboriginal people new to Winnipeg. Verna McKay described the centre's social programs as "such a good place for so many people in those early years, and that's what a Friendship Centre is, it's a place where people can find themselves support for who they mean to be. And they could do that with friends who care and who they could trust."[72] The Friendship Centre was a casual meeting place where people played cards and socialized and also a formal gathering place for groups such as Alcoholics Anonymous, the sewing club, the youth group "Club 376," and other programs.

In the first few years, the Friendship Centre's programming increased significantly. Between 1962 and 1965 home visits and referrals increased from 150 to 486, hospital visits increased from 300 to 734, social activities increased from 150 to 275, and a hugely successful court worker program (from 200 cases in 1962 to 823 in 1965) was established.[73] The people interviewed, both non-Aboriginal and Aboriginal, expressed significant excitement and enthusiasm over the early years of the centre's existence. Phrases such as "those were good years," and "it was a place of awakening" were repeated often, although transcriptions fail to convey the visible excitement still displayed in interviews even fifty years after the centre first opened.

The Indian and Métis Friendship Centre was established after four years of research by the Indian and Métis Committee of the Welfare Council of Winnipeg and funded by both the federal and provincial governments in an attempt to address the needs of the new urban Aboriginal population. It was a trailblazer for urban Aboriginal organizations. Its particular strength lay in the cooperation between the many concerned groups and committed individuals, both Aboriginal and non-Aboriginal. The community development design of the Friendship Centre's administration and programming was crucial to its success. The centre went beyond the pragmatic concerns of housing and employment and helped create social networks that contributed to individual self-worth. The combination of an Indian Advisory Council and a board of directors during the early formative years of the centre was a unique way to use the strengths of both the non-Aboriginal and Aboriginal members of the centre. Despite encountering some reluctance from the federal and provincial governments to fund the program, and the government emphasis on assimilation, the European-Canadian and Aboriginal leaders at the Friendship Centre managed to design sustainable programs to address the needs of the Aboriginal people in Winnipeg. The community development aspect of the creation of the centre, particularly the willingness of non-Aboriginal board members to listen to the Indian Advisory Council, resulted in the development of a successful institution. Its Aboriginal leadership was a product both of the initiative of the Aboriginal members and of the leadership training and encouragement provided by the board of directors. In 1960 when the Indian and Métis Conference conducted a review of the centre, its success was attributed to "the fact that many Indian people feel a responsibility for planning and carrying out projects and programmes at the centre and we suggest that only when Indian people themselves are involved in a responsible way can a service for Indians be effective."[74]

Notes

1   One of the more difficult aspects of writing Aboriginal history is the profoundly political nature of terms used in the relevant literature. For the purposes of this article, "Aboriginal" will be used for the different First Nations and Métis populations within Manitoba, unless quoting directly from a source that uses a different term, or when referring to a proper noun. This is in keeping with current academic practice and the labels currently used by the IMFC, which according to a personal communication with Billy-Jo De la Ronde, executive director, IMFC, on 6 March 2003, uses "Indian" and "Métis" when referring to individuals, and uses "Aboriginal" when referring to the members of the Friendship Centre as a whole.

2   National Association of Friendship Centres, Canada, http://www.nafc-aboriginal.com (accessed 5 March 2007).

3   For this paper I have used a combination of written primary sources and oral history interviews with elders from the IMFC. The Archives of Manitoba (AM) hold the IMFC records from 1954 to 1982, including board of directors meeting minutes, pamphlets, letters and other publications, and case files for referrals. Other collections consulted at the Archives of Manitoba included the Social Planning Council (formerly the Welfare Planning Council) records and the Beatrice Brigden files. The sources from AM were supplemented by the Legislative Library scrapbooks of newspaper clippings for the pertinent years. The people interviewed for this paper were found by looking for people's names in the IMFC records, recommendations from archivists and professors, and recommendations from the current staff at the Friendship Centre.

I would like to extend my sincere appreciation to individuals who participated in the interviews for this paper. Mary Guilbault, an Aboriginal elder at the centre, was recommended by the current executive director of the IMFC as well as by other community members. Guilbault was a founding member of the Urban Indian Association as well as the IMFC. She was an active participant in the set-up of the centre and appears many times in the records. Verna McKay, a former United Church worker and volunteer at the centre, also worked with Aboriginal women's organizations in later years. Percy Bird, also an elder at the centre, was on the board of directors, and on the board of other Aboriginal organizations in Winnipeg during the 1960s and 1970s. Dorothy Betz was the first female court worker at the IMFC, and also served on the board of directors. Grant Froman was employed by the Children's Aid Society of Winnipeg as a child welfare worker. Though the position was not directly affiliated with the centre, his office was located there in order to make his clients feel comfortable when they came to seek his guidance. In actual practice, however, Froman spent the majority of his time out on site visits and not at the IMFC. Stan McKay, Jr., Verna McKay's step-son and current Native Circle Conference coordinator, was a youth member of the centre while attending the nearby University of Winnipeg after completing his tenure at residential school. Dorothy Betz, also an elder at the centre, was a member of the Indian Advisory Council and board of directors and was asked to take a position as court worker in 1965. Flora Zaharia, an elder originally from the Blood Reserve in Alberta, was a member of the board of directors, and expressed keen interest in increasing the involvement of Aboriginal people at the IMFC. Rev. Mr. and Mrs. Pilling, now retired, are non-Aboriginal citizens who were interested in Aboriginal concerns and attended the Indian and Métis Conferences. They also volunteered at the centre during the early years. All those interviewed currently reside in Manitoba, except the Pillings, who live in Calgary.

4   Rick J Ponting, Roger Gibbins, and Andrew J. Siggner, *Out of Irrelevance: A Socio-Political Introduction to Indian Affairs in Canada* (Toronto: Butterworths, 1980), 13 and 18.

5   Ponting, Gibbins, and Siggner, *Out of Irrelevance,* 13 and 18.

6   Helen Buckley, *From Wooden Ploughs to Welfare: Why Indian Policy Failed in the Prairie Reserves* (Montreal: McGill-Queen's University Press, 1993), 69.

7   James Frideres, *Aboriginal Peoples in Canada: Contemporary Conflicts*, 5th ed. (Toronto: Prentice Hall, 2001), 238–9.

8   Raymond Breton, Gail Grant, and David L. Anderson, *The Dynamics of Government Programs for Urban Indians in the Prairie Provinces* (Montreal: Institute for Research on Public Policy, 1984).

9   Harry B. Hawthorn, ed. *A survey of the contemporary Indians of Canada: a report on economic, political, educational needs and policies*, Vol. 1 (Ottawa: Indian Affairs Branch, 1966).

10   Menno Boldt, "Intellectual Orientations and Nationalism Among Leaders in an Internal Colony: A Theoretical and Comparative Perspective," *The British Journal of Sociology* 33, 4 (December 1982): 489; see also Edward W. Scott (Chairman of the Board of Directors of the Indian and Métis Friendship Centre), "Memorandum Concerning Possible Court Worker to work in the City of Winnipeg Police Courts with People of Indian Origin," Winnipeg, MB, 1962(?), AM, Indian and Métis Friendship Centre, P735, Folder 1.

11   Welfare Council of Greater Winnipeg, "Indian and Métis 4th Annual Conference Proceedings" (Winnipeg, MB, 23–25 January 1958), AM, Indian and Métis Friendship Centre, P734, Folder 1.

12   Ibid.

13   Joint Parliamentary Committee – Appendix "JI," 1960, no. 8, 769, quoted in Jennifer E. Rogalsky, "'Good Canadians in every sense': The Citizenship Council of Manitoba, 1948–1975" (MA thesis, University of Manitoba, 2000), 94.

14   Mary Guilbault, interview with Leslie Hall, Winnipeg, MB, 31 March 2004.

15   Stan McKay Jr., interview with Leslie Hall, Winnipeg, MB, 29 March 2004.

16   Percy Bird, interview with Leslie Hall, Winnipeg, MB, 9 March 2004. See also J.W. Berry, "Aboriginal Cultural Identity," *The Canadian Journal of Native Studies* 19, 1 (1999): 25.

17   Harvey Bostrom, "Government Policies and Programs Relating to People of Indian Ancestry in Manitoba," in *The Dynamics of Government Programs for Urban Indians in the Prairie Provinces*, eds. Raymond and Gail Grant Breton (Montreal: The Institute for Research on Public Policy, 1984), 186.

18   J.H. Gordon, "[illegible] of Indians in Non-Indian Communities," presented at the Welfare Council of Greater Winnipeg, "Indian and Métis 4th Annual Conference Proceedings" (Winnipeg, MB, 23–25 January 1958), 10–11, AM, Indian and Métis Friendship Centre, P734, Folder 1.

19   "Thumbnail Sketch of the History and Development of the Indian and Métis Friendship Centre, Winnipeg Manitoba," 1 September 1964, AM, Indian and Métis Friendship Centre, P2386, Folder 6.

20   David Lloyd Anderson, ed., *The Dynamics of Government Programs for Urban Indians in the Prairie Provinces* (Montreal: Institute for Research on Public Policy, 1984), xxx.

21   Joint Parliamentary Committee, Appendix "JI," 1960, no 8, 771, quoted in Rogalsky, "'Good Canadians in Every Sense,'" 5.

22   J. Lagasse, "Community Development in Manitoba," *Human Organisation* 20, 4 (Winter 1961–2): 235.

23   Lagasse, "Community Development in Manitoba," 234.

24   Jim Lotz, *Understanding Canada: Regional and Community Development in a New Nation.* (Toronto: NC Press, 1977), 40; F. Robert Langin and Geneva Ensign, "Ways of Working in a Community: Reflections of a Former Community Development Worker," *Canadian Journal of Native Studies* 8, 1 (1998): 131.

25   Lotz, *Understanding Canada*, 40.

26   Jean Lagasse, "A Community Development Program for Manitoba" (Winnipeg, MB: Community Development Services, Dept. of Welfare, unpublished manuscript, 1962), 1.

27   Ibid.

28 Welfare Council of Greater Winnipeg, "Constitution," Winnipeg, MB, November 1954, AM, Social Planning Council of Winnipeg, P659, Folder 5.

29 Welfare Council of Greater Winnipeg, "Indian and Métis Conference 6th Annual Proceedings," Winnipeg, MB, 21–24 February 1960, AM, Indian and Métis Friendship Centre, P734, Folder 1. Also in AM, Social Planning Council of Winnipeg, P659, Folder 2.

30 Welfare Council of Greater Winnipeg, Indian and Métis Committee, "Minutes," Winnipeg, MB, 16 December 1954, AM, Social Planning Council, P725, Folder 6.

31 Welfare Council of Greater Winnipeg, "Indian and Métis Committee Minutes," Winnipeg, MB, 1954, AM, Social Planning Council, P725, Folder 6; George Barker's memoir, *Forty Years A Chief* (Winnipeg: Peguis Publishers, 1979), does not mention the conferences.

32 Meyer, "Their Conference, But Couldn't Talk," *Winnipeg Tribune*, 2 March 1959.

33 John and Bernice Pilling, interview with Leslie Hall, Winnipeg, MB, 15 May 2004.

34 Interviews with Dorothy Betz, Percy Bird, and Mary Guilbault.

35 Solange de Santis, "Services Mark Life of Former Primate," *Anglican Journal*, September 2004, http://www.anglicanjournal.com (accessed 11 October 2004).

36 Welfare Council of Greater Winnipeg, Indian and Métis Committee, "Leisure-time and Recreation Sub-committee. Minutes," Winnipeg, MB, 4 December 1957, AM, Social Planning Council, P647, Folder 10.

37 Welfare Council of Greater Winnipeg, Indian and Métis Committee, "Minutes," Winnipeg, MB, 16 December 1954, AM, Social Planning Council, P725, Folder 6.

38 Welfare Council of Greater Winnipeg, Indian and Métis Committee, "Leisure-time and Recreation Sub-committee. Minutes," Winnipeg, MB, 4 December 1957, AM, Social Planning Council, P647, Folder 10.

39 Mary Guilbault, interview with Leslie Hall, Winnipeg, MB, 12 March 2004.

40 Assembly of First Nations Official Web site, http://www.afn.ca (accessed 12 October 2004).

41 Mary Guilbault, interview with Leslie Hall, Winnipeg, MB, 12 March 2004.

42 Ibid.

43 Mary Guilbault, interview with Leslie Hall, Winnipeg, MB, 31 March 2004.

44 Ibid.

45 Vera Fast, "Provincial Archives of Manitoba: Indian and Métis Friendship Centre Finding Aid," AM, and Indian and Métis Friendship Centre of Winnipeg, *40th Anniversary Souvenir Album 1958–1998* (Winnipeg: Indian and Metis Friendship Centre of Winnipeg, 1998), 1.

46 Mary Guilbault, interview with Leslie Hall, Winnipeg, MB, 12 March 2004.

47 "Indian and Métis Friendship Centre 1st Anniversary," 1960?, AM, P734, Folder 1.

48 Indian and Métis Friendship Centre of Winnipeg, *40th Anniversary*, 1.

49 Mary Guilbault, interview with Leslie Hall, Winnipeg, MB, 2 April 2004.

50 Welfare Council of Greater Winnipeg, "Indian and Métis Conference 6th Annual Proceedings," Winnipeg, MB, 21–24 February 1960, AM, Indian and Métis Friendship Centre, P734, Folder 1 (also in AM, Social Planning Council of Winnipeg, P659, Folder 2). "Report on Development of the Indian and Métis Friendship Centre April 15th - June 30th, 1959," AM, MG14 C19.

51 "Report of the Indian and Métis Friendship Centre for the Period of January 1st, 1959 to December 31st, 1959," AM, MG14 C19.

52 Referral Service for People of Indian Origin, Provisional Board of Management, "Meeting Agenda" (9 March 1958), AM, Beatrice Brigden Papers, MG14 C19.

53 Edward W. Scott (Chairman of the Board of Directors of the Indian Métis Friendship Centre), "Memo to the Board Members of the Indian and Métis Friendship Centre," Winnipeg, MB, 29 May 1959, AM, Beatrice Brigden Files, MG14 C19.

54 "Proposed Constitution for Centre Council," n.d., AM, Beatrice Brigden Papers, MG14 C19.

55 "Report of the Indian and Métis Friendship Centre for the Period of January 1st, 1959 to December 31st, 1959," AM, MG14 C19.

56 Indian and Métis Friendship Centre, "Board of Directors, Meeting Minutes," Winnipeg, MB, 19 May 1959, AM, MG14 C19.

57 "Proposed Constitution for Centre Council," AM, Beatrice Brigden Papers, MG14 C19.

58 Flora Zaharia, interview with Leslie Hall, Winnipeg, MB, 3 April 2004.

59 Mary Guilbault, interview with Leslie Hall, Winnipeg, MB, 2 April 2004.

60 "Indian and Métis Friendship Centre Submission to the Community Chest April 1962," AM, P2384, File 15, and Indian and Métis Friendship Centre, *40th Anniversary.*

61 Verna McKay, interview with Leslie Hall, Winnipeg, MB, 30 March 2004.

62 Indian and Métis Friendship Centre, "1st Anniversary Brochure" (1960?), AM, Indian and Métis Friendship Centre, P734, Folder 1.

63 Mary Guilbault, interview with Leslie Hall, Winnipeg, MB, 10 May 2004.

64 Evelyn Peters, "Developing Federal Policy for First Nations People in Urban Areas: 1945–1975," *Canadian Journal of Native Studies* 21, 1 (2001): 73.

65 Dorothy Betz, interview with Leslie Hall, Winnipeg, MB, 30 March 2004.

66 Dorothy Betz, interview with Leslie Hall, Winnipeg, MB, 30 March and 1 April 2004, and Verna McKay, interview with Leslie Hall, Winnipeg, MB, 30 March 2004.

67 Indian and Métis Friendship Centre, "Annual Report 1962," AM, Beatrice Brigden Papers, MG14 C19.

68 Edward Scott (Chairman of the Board of Directors of the Indian and Métis Friendship Centre), "Memorandum Concerning Possible Court Worker to work in the City of Winnipeg Police Courts with People of Indian Origin," Winnipeg, MB, 1962?, AM, Indian and Métis Friendship Centre, P735, Folder 1.

69 Dorothy Betz, interview with Leslie Hall, Winnipeg, MB, 30 March 2004.

70 Dorothy Betz, interview with Leslie Hall, Winnipeg, MB, 1 April 2004.

71 Dorothy Betz, interview with Leslie Hall, Winnipeg, MB, 30 March 2004.

72 Verna McKay, interview with Leslie Hall, Winnipeg, MB, 30 March 2004.

73 "Educate Indian Early: Director," *Winnipeg Tribune*, 9 February 1966.

74 Mrs. Elmer (Dorothy) Betz and Mrs. Ernest (Mary) Guilbault, "Letter to The Parliamentary Committee on Indian Affairs," Winnipeg, MB, 19 January 1960, AM, Beatrice Brigden Papers, MG14 C19.

Prairie Metropolis: A Personal View

Ed Rea

In terms of a European presence Winnipeg is much younger than are communities in central and eastern Canada. But we Europeans are newcomers, perhaps even interlopers, in this land. The junction of what we have named the Red and Assiniboine rivers has been the site of habitations for many centuries. It has been the jumping-off point for travellers to the west and the north: First Nations, Métis, fur traders, farmers, settlers, businessmen, all have passed through in their turn. Most of them paused here only briefly, though a sufficient number have stayed to try their fortune that Winnipeg's population is now well over 600,000. But making one's way in Winnipeg has often been a chancy enterprise. There has always been the sense that our fate would be determined elsewhere, that we were part of someone else's plan.

The first great intrusive reality was the Hudson's Bay Company, HBC, translated locally as Here Before Christ. Armed with its Royal Charter of 1670, the company held economic, administrative, and political power from the Red River to the Rockies and beyond. Here, at Red River or Fort Garry, as the community was alternately known, its officers dominated social and cultural life as well. And thus began the thread that links all our history—a history of dissent, a seldom-gratified attempt to be the masters of our own condition. There were small victories. Free traders (as they were rather euphemistically known) like Andrew McDermot and his son-in-law A.G.B. Bannatyne, and others, defied the company's monopoly until in the 1840s the trade was declared free. From that point on, with its economic control undone, the company's will to govern went into decline. The pressing question became who or what would replace it.

There was, of course, the expansionist United States—Minnesota became a state in 1858—and there had been for years a trade link with St. Paul that could easily become a political tie as well. Indeed there was a small group here who would have preferred such an eventuality. And then there was Canada. Since at least the 1850s, Ontario, as it became, had cast covetous eyes on the Northwest. Led by George Brown's *Globe*, the Toronto business community had sought to establish economic hegemony over a vast western hinterland. Such a future, in truth, was Ontario's great anticipated gain from Confederation. So began a delicate negotiation among the British government seeking to off-load responsibility, the HBC trying to salvage what it could from its collapsing authority, and Canada, on behalf of Ontario, determined to acquire the West as cheaply as possible. No one had bothered to consult the people of Red River.

By 1869, when a deal was struck to buy out the charter of the HBC, Red River had been slowly maturing for over fifty years. French and English, Catholic and Protestant, First Peoples and Métis, despite differences of race and religion, had developed a relatively harmonious society. Tolerance was a result of isolation and lack of alternatives. It would be pressure and ambition from outside that would force change. All the inhabitants of Red River were apprehensive as to their future, in which they apparently were to have no say. The most numerous, cohesive, and determined among them, the Métis, led by Louis Riel, refused to be delivered into the hands of the threatening migration from Ontario. And so began what was misnamed in Ontario as the Riel Rebellion. The details may be left aside, but it must be asserted that there was no rebellion. The legitimate authority in the region, the British Crown, was never challenged, only the pretensions of Canada.

At bottom, the unpleasantness at Red River was about the security of land holdings, the social arrangements at the settlement, and the community's resolve to have some say in their disposition. So the resistance of the Métis forced a negotiated compromise: the creation of Manitoba with Winnipeg as its capital. Determined dissent had won at least half a loaf. But as Riel well knew and the Aboriginal population was learning to its dismay, the tide of immigrants could not be held back. By the mid-1870s Manitoba had been remade in the image of Ontario and Winnipeg was dominated by a new commercial elite whose deity was progress.

Winnipeg was incorporated and began its civic life in 1874. The first mayor was Francis Evans Cornish, who had been mayor of London, Ontario, before moving west. Such was the enthusiasm for the democratic process that 562 votes were cast by the 382 eligible electors. The vote was restricted to adult, white males who owned property in the city. The twelve aldermen, all local businessmen, set about providing Winnipeg with services: sewer and water, fire equipment, sidewalks, and a general hospital, built on land donated by Andrew Bannatyne. In the early days, many of the local elite took their responsibilities seriously. They were, after all, building a home and a future. But the key to Winnipeg's economic development was the much anticipated transcontinental railway. Without it we would remain a stagnant backwater. With it, we would be the entrepôt to the growing West, the nexus of the national transportation system with all the economic benefits that would follow.

When the Canadian Pacific Railway (CPR) indicated that they would cross the Red River further north at Selkirk, there was civic despair. It made sense, the route was shorter, the riverbanks were more stable, and the danger of flooding was less. But railways are about politics as much as anything else, and Winnipeg's leaders set about to change the mind of the CPR. The price was substantial: $300,000 for a bridge across the Red, thirty acres of land for shops, a further cash subsidy of $250,000, and a promise of no taxes forever on their property. At this the CPR indicated that perhaps they could come through Winnipeg after all. We could not live without the railway; we would learn that it would be difficult to live with it as well. But in the short term it meant a tremendous boom period for Winnipeg and the entire West.

Despite the veneer of civility in the first generation, Winnipeg for its first fifty years was still very much a frontier town. There was customarily a very large population of unattached males, many of them transient. As in most other frontier towns, this meant brothels and booze. The largest brothel in the city was located just opposite the front door of Manitoba College, the local bastion of Presbyterianism. This scandalous situation prompted the expected demand for its removal. It was a story repeated in almost all western cities in North America. In Winnipeg, the prostitutes were dispersed to the periphery, the city would expand to include them, and they would be on the move again. Just after the turn of the twentieth century, they were given unofficial approval by city council and the police, who had been under pressure to get the women off the street and out of sight and thus remedy this deplorable condition. A red-light district was created in Point Douglas near the rail yards, which ultimately grew to fifty-three houses. Free from police harassment, sex workers arrived from all across the West. The madams were routinely hauled into court and made to pay quarterly fines for violation of the liquor laws. It was rather like a licence to continue their trade.

Some years ago, I attempted to sort this out by going through the tax rolls to see who actually owned these houses. I could not trace them. The real estate transactions and the taxes were handled by a phantom company, which did not appear in the contemporary list of real estate companies and was operated, allegedly, by a cousin of the police chief. In 1910 another wave of reform swept the city, and the mayor was challenged on the issue of condoning prostitution. In reply, he charged his opponent with defaming the fair name of Winnipeg, and he won the election! Shortly after, the women were dispersed again. Winnipeg was no more successful than other western cities in dealing with this persistent question.

An even greater problem was alcohol. We are prone to make fun of the difficulties and to cluck about the antiquated laws of the past. But booze in Winnipeg for most of the city's formative years was a terrible scourge. It was everywhere and it was cheap. The drinking age, if and when it was enforced, was sixteen years. Beer was sold by the pail. Whisky was a nickel a glass. And the innumerable saloons, all male of course, were concentrated downtown and in the working-class neighbourhoods. In fact, they were the social clubs of the working class. But far too many of the men drank to excess, and were often encouraged to do so. The liquor industry was a very powerful force, and licensing was an integral part of the political patronage system. Polite society turned a blind eye and blamed the lot of the working poor on their propensity to drink too much and sniffed their disapproval.

Without meaning to mitigate the evil, it must be pointed out that to some extent the game was loaded against the working class. For example, in the early years of the twentieth century, working people in Winnipeg laboured ten-hour days, six days a week. They were paid the last day of the month by cheque. Employers would not forego interest by keeping cash around or incur bank charges by paying more frequently. Banks were open from 10 a.m. to 3 p.m. five days a week for the convenience of themselves and the business community. So where was the working man to take his monthly cheque? To his friendly saloon keeper. These worthies abetted, if they did not invent, the custom of buying a round of drinks after cashing your cheque. The worst evils of the liquor trade were finally swept away by prohibition during the Great War. When the sale of alcohol resumed in the 1920s, it was under the stern control of the provincial government, whose righteousness was sustained by the profits that resulted.

My point about the structure of social conditions can be noted in other aspects of Winnipeg's life. We built wonderful green spaces. But for whom? Assiniboine (an urban treasure), Kildonan, and St. Vital parks were all acquired and developed before the Great War. They were all situated a long way from those areas where working people lived. But city council, pressured by the local ministerial association, would not permit the street cars to run on Sunday, the only day workers had any leisure. Likewise, under the guise of defending the *Lord's Day Act*, the province refused to allow the trains to run to Winnipeg Beach on Sunday, so ordinary folk could not interrupt the summer idyll of their betters. Why the apparent callousness and insensitivity? What explains this unwillingness to ameliorate the conditions and expand the opportunities of the less fortunate? Although it may have appeared so, it was not simply mean-spiritedness. One possible explanation lies in the notion of insecurity.

The first generation who formed the social, economic, and political elite of Winnipeg was remarkably homogeneous. They were British and Protestant, and so was their vision of the future of Winnipeg and western Canada. They tended also to be self-made businessmen, free of the restraints of local tradition and social obligation, and separated by class from their employees. If there was one word to characterize them, it was boosterism. As the gateway to the West, Winnipeg's future seemed unlimited. The civic hyperbole was ubiquitous. The most frequent and, I suppose, most fervent comparison was with Chicago. Winnipeg would be to our Prairie West what Chicago was to the American Midwest. But how secure was their control? How justified their confidence and optimism? The test of any society's social and cultural maturity is its ability to absorb immigrants, especially those of different backgrounds. This becomes even more problematic for an elite group whose roots are so shallow, whose position of dominance so recently established.

Between 1895 and the outbreak of the Great War, one of the great population movements in human history took place. Tens of millions of people left central, eastern, and southern Europe, seeking a better life in North America, Australia, or South America. The Canadian government actively sought the peasantry of Europe to bring the Prairie West into production. There were even giddy projections claiming that western Canada would be the home of one hundred million people. Between 1901 and 1921, three million of these foreigners, as they were dubbed, chose Canada, many of them heading for the much-advertised free land of the Prairies. Almost all of these passed through Winnipeg, and thousands of them, for a variety of reasons, simply stayed here.

They arrived with little money, some clothes, a treasured icon or two. They possessed few skills, had little formal education, and faced a frightening and potentially hostile world. They sought the comfort of the familiar, and so began the development of the ethnic neighbourhoods of working-class Winnipeg, and the myth of the North End portrayed in brilliant novels later on by John Marlyn, Adele Wiseman, and others. But the impact of the immigrants was sudden and profound. In 1901, Winnipeg's population was 42,000. By the end of the Great War, it was over 200,000.

And they were so very different, these Slavs and Jews and Scandinavians. It was not simply the externals: the languages and religions, the babushkas and prayer shawls, perogies and garlic. The confrontation was more than just culture clash. Whether they were conscious of it or not, Winnipeg's elite were very much in the British tradition of possessive individualism and the Protestant ethic. But these newcomers, these foreigners, were from a peasant background. The rhythms of their lives were natural: birth, growth, death, like the rhythms of the seasons. How could people so alien, so different in so many ways, ever be absorbed? Such was the apprehension of the host society that no one considered the newcomers might contribute something of value—beyond their broad backs—to the new West. To neutralize this presumed cultural threat to the British, Protestant vision of the future held by the local elite, the immigrants must be made to conform.

So all the social institutions of the day were bent to the task: the Sunday schools of the Protestant churches, the YMCA, Frontier College, and especially the public school system. The schools were to inculcate the values of imperial patriotism and competitive individualism. The school materials of the day were full of such urging, enjoining children to make something of themselves. The design was to produce "good Canadians" as defined by the Department of Education, which of course reflected elite values. One of Winnipeg's leading citizens and Canada's bestselling novelist, the Rev. Charles W. Gordon, whose pen name was Ralph Connor, put the issue succinctly in a novel entitled appropriately *The Foreigner*. His protagonist, a Presbyterian minister like himself, said "my main line is the kiddies ... make them good Christians and good Canadians, which is the same thing." By Christian he meant Protestant, by Canadian he meant British. Meanwhile Winnipeg's most popular newspaper, the *Free Press*, thundered against the balkanization of the Canadian West. The adult generation of these newcomers was considered irredeemable, and not surprisingly, one result was generational conflict within the ethnic communities as the children sought acceptance through conformity, while their elders clung to the old ways. Cultural emasculation was a painful transition.

Governing ourselves has been a continuing challenge. Winnipeg began with a traditional mayor and council arrangement. Not surprisingly, it was dominated by the business community and became something of a complacent and closed elite, whose competence increasingly came under scrutiny. During the early years of the twentieth century, the so-called Progressive era, we shared the passion for efficiency and believed it could be applied to local politics. Following the example of other cities, mostly American, we installed an elected Board of Control in 1908. The controllers were to act as an inner policy group, head up the major departments and, most surely, keep a restraining hand on council. It did not serve well and in 1918 was abandoned by the voters just as enthusiastically as they had endorsed it.

But there were other, equally painful, changes going on as well. In 1912 there began a short but quite severe economic recession and two years later the Panama Canal opened, thwarting Winnipeg's dream to become the dominant metropolitan centre of the West through its control of transportation. The much cheaper sea route to the West Coast blighted that hope. The Great War wrought many changes. What had been largely an agricultural country was now a growing industrial power. In Winnipeg there also came women's suffrage (Manitoba led the nation in this democratic reform), prohibition, and an increasingly militant labour movement.

The end of the war did not leave us content. Like many other places, we battled the great flu epidemic and buried our dead. Winnipeg's economy, like the nation's, fell into a brief but sharp recession. There was a very active labour movement here, and Winnipeg was described as "the most strike prone city in Canada." The workers' leaders were very much in the tradition of class-conscious and militant British labour and had little patience with the business unionism of central Canada dominated by the American Federation of Labor. A strike of the street railway workers in 1906 revealed the hostile environment. They wanted union recognition and better wages. There was significant public support as people chose to walk in sympathy to show their dislike of the private street-railway company. For its part, the company brought in strikebreakers who were little better than thugs. The strike was broken. There was no union recognition and the workers received a one cent per hour raise. The next year the Winnipeg police force was increased from 55 to 250 to ensure the protection of property rights.

To a very real extent, the General Strike of 1919 grew out of the attempt by Winnipeg and western labour to throw off the more conservative policies of the craft unions of central Canada. But by opting for industrial unionism and its primary weapon, the general strike, Winnipeg's labour leaders were in uncharted waters. A general strike is not simply a bigger and better strike, as they seemed to imagine at the outset. It not only holds a community to ransom, it is also an attempt to shift economic power from capital to labour. In North American society, that is a revolutionary notion. So there are only two possible outcomes: the workers take over or the strike must be broken. The principle can not be compromised. The political, judicial, and military powers of the nation were ranged against the strikers. Locally, a Citizens Committee of 1000, organized, financed, and directed by the business community, were determined to defeat what they were pleased to label a Bolshevik conspiracy. So it behooved them to associate the strike leadership with alien ideas and alien forces, despite the fact that every one of the strike leaders was British or Anglo-Canadian. Ethnic relations in the city were poisoned for decades to come, and mutual resentment abated only slowly.

With their attempt to exercise economic power in tatters, the labour movement shifted their attention to control of city council. Political action might accomplish some gains for working people. But that meant challenging the very "citizens" group that had opposed the strike and contributed to its failure. Thus, one important aftermath of the General Strike was the creation of two political forces, one official under the banner of labour and the other unofficial, known by a variety of names over the years but commonly called the Citizens' League. From 1920 until at least the 1980s, the two groups contended for control of council. On only one occasion did labour manage to secure as many seats as the citizens, and the casting vote of the mayor continually frustrated them. Otherwise, the league dominated city council and used its power to limit services and restrict welfare costs. The league devoted itself to keeping taxes down, the budget in balance, and convincing the Winnipeg electorate that they were not a political party. They based their appeal to the voters of the city on the slogan, "Keep Party Politics out of Winnipeg!" Despite the hypocrisy, they were remarkably successful.

Blatant prejudice was succeeded by more subtle forms of discrimination. Employment opportunities were tied to ethnicity. The medical school and to a lesser degree the law faculty had ethnic quotas in place until the 1940s. The Depression of the 1930s exacerbated these tensions. Endemic unemployment and the demand for relief fell heavily on the city as its revenues fell when people could no longer pay their taxes. There were constant and conflicting pressures on city council to maintain the credit of the city and to provide relief to the people. Winnipeg even had to endure Canada's initial doctors' strike, however brief. But there was an end to it. Yet it was a terrible irony that the misery of the Depression here, as elsewhere, was relieved by the misery of war.

Winnipeggers tried to maintain a semblance of public life by relying on themselves during those difficult years. There was a quite remarkable burst of creative activity: amateur theatre, dance, and especially music flourished. Trial courts, particularly criminal, always had a large and attentive audience. Public libraries were never as well patronized. The stigma of being on relief was relieved to some extent by a willingness to work together to create new social institutions like the community clubs that provided diversions for all ages.

The Second World War, with its almost insatiable demand for labour, was another turning point for Winnipeg. For the first time, the majority of the people were able to achieve a general degree of competence. Money was a magic solvent. In addition, the traumatic impact of foreign immigration had been survived. The host society had successfully neutralized the presumed threat. The long boom that followed the war solidified the gains. A symbolic moment came in 1970, when Manitoba marked its centennial. Folklorama, a festival celebrating the rich ethnic diversity of Winnipeg, was held for the first time and has reappeared annually ever since as a highlight of the summer season. Ten years earlier it is doubtful if it would have succeeded. One of the benefits has been the revival of ethnic consciousness among the third and fourth generations. It is no longer a handicap to be one of "the others." For old Winnipeggers, it was quite astounding that, in the 1973 provincial election, the leaders of the three major parties included a German Catholic and two Jews. It is precisely this social mix that gives Winnipeg its distinct character.

Even so, national economic policy still holds us in thrall. Politicians respond to pressure, and Ontario and Quebec have the votes. From transportation policy to specific crises such as the F-18 contract that went to Montreal, rather than to the (superior) bid from a local firm, and the departure of the NHL hockey team, the Jets, we are periodically reminded of our hinterland status. These are not just economic disappointments but blows to our self-esteem. But there is a wonderful resiliency about this city. We will not be the Chicago of the North. Our hinterland has been reduced to northern Manitoba and northwestern Ontario. We will likely continue to be a branch plant junior partner of Toronto.

Despite the environmental handicaps, Winnipeg is a good place to live. The social mix is endlessly stimulating. The cultural life (with symphony, ballet, opera, and theatre) is richer than one might expect in a city this size. Popular culture—sports, festivals, music, and community events—seems to thrive. And we will continue to assert our place in this often distracted country of ours.

Selected Sources in the History of Winnipeg Published Since 1990

Arnason, David, and Mhari Mackintosh, eds. *The Imagined City: A Literary History of Winnipeg.* Winnipeg: Turnstone Press, 2005.

Beattie, Norman. "The Cab Trade in Winnipeg, 1871–1910." *Urban History Review* 27, 1 (1998): 36–52.

Bercuson, David J., Kurt Korneski, James Naylor, and Tom Mitchell. "History Television and the General Strike: Three Views." *Labour* 45 (2000): 255–257 and 259–270.

Blanchard, Jim. *Winnipeg 1912.* Winnipeg: University of Manitoba Press, 2005.

Bocquel, Bernard. *Au Pays de CKSB: 50 Ans de Radio Française au Manitoba.* Saint-Boniface: Les Editions du Blé, 1996.

Bumsted, J.M. *St. John's College: Faith and Education in Western Canada.* Winnipeg: University of Manitoba Press, 2006.

_____. *The University of Manitoba: An Illustrated History.* Winnipeg: University of Manitoba Press, 2001.

_____. *The Winnipeg General Strike of 1919: An Illustrated History.* Winnipeg: Watson and Dwyer, 1994.

Burley, David G. "Frontier of Opportunity: The Social Organization of Self-Employment in Winnipeg, 1881–1901." *Social History/Histoire Sociale* 31, 61 (1998): 35–69.

Carbone, Stanislao. *Italians in Winnipeg: An Illustrated History.* Winnipeg: University of Manitoba Press, 1998.

Dafoe, Christopher. *Winnipeg: Heart of the Continent.* Winnipeg: Great Plains Publications, 1998.

Dupuis, Michael. "William R. Plewman, the *Toronto Daily Star*, and the Reporting of the Winnipeg General Strike." *Labour* 57 (2006): 167–181.

Eyford, Ryan. "From Prairie Goolies to Canadian Cyclones: The Transformation of the 1920 Winnipeg Falcons." *Sport History Review* 37, 1 (2006): 5–18.

Fraser, Larry. *Crossroads Capers: Stories of a Railroad Town, its People, Times and Places.* Summerland: Valley Publishing, 1998.

Gourluck, Russ. *Going Downtown: a History of Winnipeg's Portage Avenue.* Winnipeg: Great Plains Publications, 2006.

Gourluck, Russ. *A Store Like no Other: Eaton's of Winnipeg.* Winnipeg: Great Plains Publications, 2004.

Henderson, Stuart. "'While there is still time…' J. Murray Gibbon and the Spectacle of Difference in three CPR Folk Festivals, 1928–1931." *Journal of Canadian Studies* 39, 1 (2005): 139–174.

Huck, Barbara, ed. *Crossroads of the Continent: A History of the Forks of the Red and Assiniboine Rivers.* Winnipeg: Heartland Associates, 2003.

Jones, Esyllt. *Influenza 1918: Disease, Death and Struggle in Winnipeg.* Toronto: University of Toronto Press, 2007.

_____. "Politicizing the Labouring Body: Working Families, Death, and Burial in Winnipeg's Influenza Epidemic, 1918–1919." *Labour* 3, 3 (2006): 57–75.

Keshavjee, Serena. *Winnipeg Modern: Architecture, 1945–1975.* Winnipeg: University of Manitoba Press, 2006.

Kinnear, Mary. *Margaret McWilliams: An Interwar Feminist.* Kingston: McGill-Queen's University Press, 1991.

Klassen, Henry C. "McCaine Electric: An Electrical Contracting Business in Winnipeg, 1918-1995." *Prairie Forum* 23, 2 (1998): 225-246.

Korneski, Kurt. "Britishness, Canadianness, Class, and Race: Winnipeg and the British World, 1880s–1910s." *Journal of Canadian Studies* 41, 2 (2007): 161-184.

Lehr, John C., and John H. Sherwood. "The Two Wheeled Workhorse: The Bicycle as Personal and Commercial Transport in Winnipeg." *Urban History Review* 28, 1 (1999): 3-13.

Levine, Allan, ed. *Your Worship*. Toronto: James Lorimer, 1989.

Lindsay, Debra. *The Clothes Off Our Back: A History of ACTWU 490*. Winnipeg: ACTWU, 1995.

Martin, Michael David. "The Landscapes of Winnipeg's Wildwood Park." *Urban History Review* 30, 1 (2001): 22-39.

Mitchell, Tom. "'Repressive Measures': A.J. Andrews, the Committee of 1000 and the Campaign against Radicalism after the Winnipeg General Strike." *Left History* 3, 2-4, 1 (1995-96): 133-167.

Mott, Morris, and John Allardyce. "Curling Capital: How Winnipeg Became the Roaring Game's Leading City, 1876-1903." *Canadian Journal of History of Sport* 19, 1 (1988): 1-14.

Silver, Jim. *Thin Ice: Money, Politics and the Demise of an NHL Franchise*. Halifax: Fernwood Publishing, 1996.

_____. *The Failure of Civic Reform Movements in Winnipeg Civic Elections, 1971-1992*. Winnipeg: University of Winnipeg, Institute of Urban Studies, 1995.

Silver, Jim, Joan Hay, and Peter Gorzen. "Aboriginal Involvement in Community Development: The Case of Winnipeg's Spence Neighbourhood." *Canadian Journal of Native Studies* 25, 1 (2005): 239-288.

Smith, Doug. *The Winnipeg Labour Council, 1894-1994: A Century of Labour Education, Organization and Agitation*. Winnipeg: Manitoba Labour Education Centre, 1994.

_____. *Joe Zuken: Citizen and Socialist*. Toronto: James Lorimer, 1990.

Stokes, Lawrence D. "Fact or Fiction? German Writer A.E. Johann, a Winnipeg Communist, and the Depression in the Canadian West, 1931-1932." *Labour* 57 (2006): 131-142.

Stunden Bower, Shannon. "The Great Transformation? Wetlands and Land Use in Manitoba during the Late Nineteenth Century." *Journal of the Canadian Historical Association* 15 (2004): 29-47.

Walz, Gene. *Cartoon Charlie: The Life and Art of Animation Pioneer Charles Thorson*. Winnipeg: Great Plains Publications, 1998.

Werner, Hans. *Imagined Homes: Soviet German Immigrants in Two Cities*. Winnipeg: University of Manitoba Press, 2007.

Yee, Paul. *Chinatown: An Illustrated History of the Chinese Communities of Victoria, Vancouver, Calgary, Winnipeg, Toronto, Ottawa, Montreal and Halifax*. Toronto: James Lorimer, 2005.

Theses and Dissertations

Bugailiskis, Giles. "Quiet Dignity: Aspects of Building Schools in the Winnipeg School Division Number 1: 1871-1928." MA thesis, University of Winnipeg, 1991.

Covernton, Gillian. "A system of morality veiled in allegory": The Private Rituals and Public Performances of Freemasons in Winnipeg, 1864-1900." MA thesis, University of Manitoba, 2005.

Fields, Sari. "Financial Fetters: Mothers, Lone Parents, and Welfare Reform, Winnipeg in the 1960s." MA thesis, University of Manitoba, 2002.

Hall, Leslie Elizabeth Macdonald. "'A place of awakening': The Formation of the Winnipeg Indian and Metis Friendship Centre, 1957-1964." MA thesis, University of Manitoba, 2005.

Hummelt, Bob. "Trouble on the Home Front: Perspectives on Working Mothers in Winnipeg 1939-1945." MA thesis, University of Manitoba, 2001.

Jones, Esyllt Wynne. "'Searching for the Springs of Health': Women and Working Families in Winnipeg's 1918-1919 Influenza Epidemic." PhD diss., University of Manitoba, 2003.

Korneski, Kurt. "Liberalism in Winnipeg, 1890s–1920s: Charles W. Gordon, John W. Dafoe, Minnie J.B. Campbell, and Francis M. Beynon." PhD diss., Memorial University of Newfoundland, 2004.

Kozminski, Megan. "Patrolling Winnipeg 'according to order': A Social History of Policing in a Prairie City, 1874–1900." MA thesis, University of Manitoba, 2004.

LeGras, Claude A. "The Shaping of a New Order in the West: The Influence of Winnipeg's Agricultural and Industrial Exhibitions, 1870–1915." MA thesis, University of Manitoba, 2007.

Macfarlane, Christine. "'Unfortunate Women of my Class': Prostitution in Winnipeg, 1870–1920." MA thesis, University of Manitoba, 2002.

McKay, Marion Lynne Clark. "Saints and Sanitarians: the Role of Women's Voluntary Agencies in the Development of Winnipeg's Public Health System, 1882–1945." PhD diss., University of Manitoba, 2005.

Payment, Shirley. "The Big Project: James M. Shaver at All Peoples' Mission, Winnipeg, 1921–1941." MA thesis, University of Manitoba, 2000.

Quinonez, Guillermo Emilio. "A Study of Medical Specialization: the History of the Department of Pathology at the Winnipeg General Hospital (1883–1957)." MA thesis, University of Manitoba, 2007.

Stunden Bower, Shannon. "Wet Prairie: An Environmental History of Wetlands, Flooding and Drainage in Agricultural Manitoba, 1810–1980." PhD diss., University of British Columbia, 2006.

Thiessen, Janis. "Friesens Corporation: Printers in Mennonite Manitoba, 1951–1995." MA thesis, University of Manitoba, 1997.

Werner, Hans P. "Integration in Two Cities: A Comparative History of Protestant Ethnic German Immigrants in Winnipeg, Canada and Bielefeld, Germany, 1947–1989." PhD diss., University of Manitoba, 2002.

Woloschuk, Tanya. "'Preserving the 'moral formation of the child': The Regulation of Catholic Girls in Winnipeg, 1908–1948." MA thesis, University of Manitoba, 2005.

Articles from *Manitoba History*

Hartman, James B. "The Churches of Early Winnipeg." *Manitoba History* 45 (2003): 20–33.

Hinther, Rhonda. "The Oldest Profession in Winnipeg: The Culture of Prostitution in the Point Douglas Segregated District, 1909–1912." *Manitoba History* 41 (2001): 2–13.

Kraft, Scott. "Writing Immigrant Winnipeg: A Literary Map of the City through the First World War." *Manitoba History* 52 (2006): 18–30.

Nerbas, Don. "Wealth and Privilege: An Analysis of Winnipeg's Early Business Elite." *Manitoba History* 48 (2004): 42–64.

McCullough, A.B. "Winnipeg Ranchers: Gordon, Ironside, and Fares." *Manitoba History* 41 (2001): 18–25.

Methot, Melanie. "Reverend Frederic B. Duval: Winnipeg's Fearless Foe of Social Vices." *Manitoba History* 44 (2002–03): 32–41.

Passfield, Robert W. "'Duff's Ditch': The Origins, Construction, and Impact of the Red River Floodway." *Manitoba History* 42 (2001–02): 2–13.

Selwood, John, John C. Lehr, and Mary Cavett. "'The Most Lovely and Picturesque City in All of Canada': The Origins of Winnipeg's Public Park System." *Manitoba History* 31 (1996): 21–29.

Stunden Bower, Shannon. "'Practical Results': The Riel Statue Controversy at the Manitoba Legislative Building." *Manitoba History* 42 (2001–02): 30–38.

Trachtenberg, Henry. "Ethnic Politics on the Urban Frontier: 'Fighting Joe' Martin and the Jews of Winnipeg, 1893–96." *Manitoba History* 35 (1998): 2–14.

Zeilig, Martin. "Emma Goldman in Winnipeg." *Manitoba History* 25 (1993): 23–27.

Contributors

Dale Barbour grew up on a Centennial Farm in Balmoral, Manitoba, before going on to work for newspapers in Dauphin and Portage la Prairie, Manitoba, and Rosetown, Saskatchewan. He became an editor with the University of Manitoba in 2001 and was irresistibly drawn into the academic world, earning his bachelor and master's degrees. Suitably smitten, he's now off to the University of Toronto to earn a PhD in history.

Crista Lue Bradley is an archivist at the University of Regina. She holds an MA in History-Archival Studies from the University of Manitoba where her research focussed on specialized archival public programming for older Canadians. Crista has served on various committees for both national and provincial archival associations and co-curated the Saskatchewan Council for Archives and Archivists' virtual exhibit of archival materials designed specifically for older Canadians.

Angela E. Davis was born in Hansworth, Middlesex, England, and trained as a nurse before immigrating to Canada in 1951. She started painting while raising her family. She graduated from the University of Winnipeg in 1977, received an MA there in 1979, and was awarded a PhD in history from the University of Manitoba in 1987. Davis wrote and taught extensively on Canadian art history. Her publications include *Art and Work: A Social History of Labour in the Canadian Graphic Art Industry to the 1940s*. She died in 1994.

Gerald Friesen supervised the research of many of the contributors to this volume. He teaches history at the University of Manitoba and has written a number of books on Canadian history, including *The Canadian Prairies: A History*.

Leslie Hall completed her MA in western Canadian history at the University of Manitoba. Currently, she works as a community programmer at the Galt Museum and Archives in Lethbridge, Alberta.

Esyllt W. Jones lives and teaches history in Winnipeg. She is the author of the award-winning *Influenza 1918: Death, Disease and Struggle in Winnipeg*.

Kurt Korneski graduated with a BA from Northern Illinois University. He received his PhD from Memorial University of Newfoundland in 2004. He worked as a post-doctoral fellow at the University of Manitoba from 2004 to 2006 and is now assistant professor in the Department of History at Memorial University of Newfoundland.

Megan Kozminski completed her thesis research at the Winnipeg Police Museum. She graduated with an MA (History) from the University of Manitoba in 2004. After working for a historical research firm for several years, she co-founded a Winnipeg-based custom publications company. Megan currently serves as publisher and marketing director for a series of lifestyle publications. She plans to publish her original research on law and order in the prairies in a work of historical fiction.

Marion McKay is a senior instructor and associate dean of undergraduate programs in the Faculty of Nursing at the University of Manitoba. In addition to graduate work in community health nursing, she earned an MA and PhD in history at the University of Manitoba. Her research explored the role that female social reformers played in the establishment of public health nursing programs in Manitoba and the subsequent integration of these programs into the publicly funded health care system.

Tamara Miller holds a PhD from the University of Manitoba and works for Finance Canada providing analysis and advice on a range of policy issues. She has also contributed an article on Margaret Scott to Sharon-Ann Cook, Lorna R. McLean, and Kate O'Rourke's edited collection *Framing our Past: Canadian Women's History in the Twentieth Century* (2001).

Jody Perrun is a native Winnipegger and holds a PhD in history from the University of Manitoba. His current specialization is the history of the Second World War, and his doctoral dissertation was a study of the Winnipeg home front from 1939 to 1945. His MA thesis (Carleton, 1999) focussed on First Canadian Army's operations during the Battle of Normandy. He has worked as a historical consultant for documentary films on the Second World War and for the Juno Beach Centre in Courseulles, Normandy. He also assisted with the research for the recent two-volume official operational history of the Royal Canadian Navy in the Second World War, *No Higher Purpose* and *A Blue Water Navy*. He currently teaches for the Division of Continuing Studies, Royal Military College of Canada.

J. Edgar Rea was born in Kingston, Ontario. After serving as a navigator with the RCAF from 1953 to 1959, he obtained his BA (1961) and MA (1963) from the University of Manitoba, followed by a PhD from Queen's University (1971). In his forty-year teaching career in the Department of History at the Universty of Manitoba he was known as a dynamic lecturer who developed popular courses on the history of Manitoba and Winnipeg. His numerous publications include a history of the Winnipeg General Strike as well as a prize-winning biography of Manitoba Senator T.A. Crerar. Professor Rea died in 2003.

Janis Thiessen received her MA from the University of Manitoba and her PhD (2006) from the University of New Brunswick. She has been a teacher at Westgate Mennonite Collegiate in Winnipeg since 1995, the secretary-treasurer of the Canadian Oral History Association since 2005, and a sessional lecturer at the University of Winnipeg since 2007. She is currently a SSHRC Postdoctoral Fellow at the University of Winnipeg (2009–2011).

Cassandra Woloschuk received her BA (Hons.) from the University of Windsor in 2003 and her MA from the University of Manitoba and University of Winnipeg in 2005. She is currently a doctoral candidate in the Department of History at the University of Guelph. Her dissertation examines children's leukemia treatments in post-war Canada.

Index